THE REDEMPTION & RESTORATION OF MAN
IN THE THOUGHT OF RICHARD BAXTER

THE REDEMPTION &
RESTORATION OF MAN
IN THE THOUGHT OF
RICHARD BAXTER

A Study in Puritan Theology

J. I. Packer

(Thesis presented for the degree of D.Phil. in the University of Oxford, Trinity term, 1954.)

REGENT COLLEGE PUBLISHING
Vancouver, British Columbia

The Redemption & Restoration of Man
in the Thought of Richard Baxter
Copyright © 1954, 2003 by J. I. Packer

Published 2003 by Regent College Publishing
5800 University Boulevard, Vancouver, B.C. Canada V6T 2E4
www.regentpublishing.com

The views expressed in works published by
Regent College Publishing
are those of the author and may not necessarily
represent the official position of Regent College.

The paper used in this publication meets the minimum
requirements of the American National Standard for Information
Sciences—Permanence of Paper for Printed Library Materials,
ANSI Z39.48-1984.

National Library of Canada Cataloguing in Publication Data

Packer, J. I. (James Innell)
The redemption and restoration of man
in the thought of Richard Baxter

Includes bibliographical references and index.
ISBN 1-55361-020-2 (Canada)
ISBN 1-57383-174-3 (United States)

1. Baxter, Richard, 1615-1691—Contributions in the doctrine of
salvation. 2. Salvation—History of doctrines—17th century. I. Title.
BX5207.B3P32 2003   234'.092   C00-910417-8

NOTE FROM THE AUTHOR:
The present text of this work is almost exactly as submitted to Oxford University for a doctoral degree in 1954. It is hoped to publish an update on Baxter in due course. Meantime, the writer stands by everything that the present text affirms. Special thanks are due to pastor Robert Johnson and editor Rob Clements for all their work on the manuscript, and to Geoffrey F. Nuttall, happily still with us, my superb supervisor of long ago.

.

Contents

(For synopses of argument, see the beginning of each chapter.)

Introduction

The following study of Richard Baxter's teaching on the doctrine of man's salvation will, it is hoped, fill a gap in Baxter studies. "His opinions have been a battle-ground for critics ever since he left the world,"[1] just as they were in his own lifetime. In 1699, eight years after his death, Thomas Edwards, Esq., published *Baxterianism Barefac'd*, in which he sought to "crucify Baxter between the Quakers and Roman Catholics, exhibiting the doctrines of these two parties … in parallel columns, and Baxter between them,"[2] trying to prove Baxter's theology identical by turns with each. Orme (1830) was cautious and tentative: "He was inimical to all the existing systems of doctrine … then contended for, or ever before known in the world … He opposed Calvinism; he opposed Arminianism … Baxter was probably such an Arminian as Richard Watson; and as much a Calvinist as the late Dr. Edward Williams."[3] "There is certainly truth in this (i.e. Orme's dictum); and yet not much," commented the author of the Essay prefixed to the 1838 reprint of the *Practical Works*; "it is as impossible to identify Baxter with any formal creed, as with any known sect."[4] J. Hunt (1870) considered his theology "moderate Arminianism."[5] On the other hand, Alexander Gordon wrote: "Baxter's Calvinism differed from that of the Westminster divines, simply by the purity

---

1. J. Stoughton, *History of Religion* (ed. 4, 1901), IV:381.
2. Baxter, *Practical Works*, 23 vols., 1830, I:480 (*Life* by W. Orme). Citations from *Works* in the present book are taken from the Orme's edition, if the work of Baxter being quoted is included there.
3. *op. cit.*, 482, 484.
4. Identified by T. W. Jenkyn (Essay before 1846 reprint of *Making Light of Christ…* etc., xlviii) as "Mr. Philip of Maberly": *Practical Works*, 4 vols., 1838, I:xxxvii.
5. *Religious Thought in England*, 1870, I:265.

of its adhesion to the original type, unaffected by the anti-Arminian reaction."[6] A. R. Ladell thinks that "as he grew older he shed considerably the Calvinism that is evident in...*The Saints' Everlasting Rest*."[7] Powicke quotes a summary of Amyraldus' hypothetical universalism and asserts: "On the whole, no better statement could be desired of Baxter's corresponding position."[8] Dr. I. Morgan is content to echo this judgment.[9] The existence of such divergent views shows that a fuller investigation than any yet attempted will not be out of place. Moreover, some widely held opinions about Baxter's theology need to be called in question. It is said to be "vague."[10] It is supposed to be inconsistent. "It would be easy to array, in appearance, Baxter against Baxter; and very difficult to reconcile him with himself," writes Mr. Philip.[11] The *Aphorisms of Justification* are, according to Orme, "neither always consistent with truth nor with one another."[12] Baxter's books are supposed to be full of "refined and intangible distinctions."[13] Powicke describes Baxter as "dreadfully entangled in explanatory theories which explain nothing."[14] I question the justice of these strictures. I have found in Baxter nothing but the dazzling precision of a man who knows exactly what he thinks and how to say it. I suspect that the impression of obscurity which Baxter's books have given to his critics is due to their failure to grasp the key which unlocks his system: his so-called "political method," which none of them mentions. When the grounds and nature of this "method" are understood, the appearance of arbitrariness and confusion vanishes, and everything falls into place. This, I hope, will become clear in what follows.

The arrangement of this study has been dictated by its aim and subject-matter. Part I consists of four studies designed to fix Baxter's place in Puritanism and his connection with Puritan theological development. This was desirable, partly because scholars have not always agreed on the point and partly because, as we shall see, Baxter's theology must be understood and explained as the product of a particular age and situation. Only an English Puritan of the mid-seventeenth century could have brought it to birth. In Parts II-IV, Baxter's view of man, of Christ's redeeming work and of the new life which the Holy Spirit creates, are successively expounded. We shall pay attention to the sources and evolution of Baxter's thought in such detail as is

6. *Heads of English Unitarian History*, 1895, 98.
7. *Richard Baxter*, 1925, 132
8. F. J. Powicke, *A Life of the Reverend Richard Baxter* (hereafter, *Life*), 1924, 237f.
9. *The Nonconformity of Richard Baxter*, 1946, 77 f.
10. *Practical Works*, 1838, xlii.
11. *op. cit.*, xlv.
12. *Works*, I:447.
13. 443.
14. *Life*, 278.

necessary for appreciating the finished product. Each of these parts consists of chapters of 'Doctrine' followed by a chapter of 'Use', indicating how the doctrine impinges on life and practice. This classical Puritan expository method has been adopted because the scope of our study demanded consideration of the means of grace and Christian life and experience at some point, and it seemed fittest to give them the place which they occupied in Baxter's own mind: that is, to expound them as practical corollaries of theoretical principles. It should be noted, however, that the chapters of 'Use' are, comparatively, far sketchier than the rest. Baxter wrote far more on the 'uses' of doctrines than on the doctrines themselves, but the proportions of this study forbade any correspondingly extended treatment of the practical side of his teaching. At the end of the exposition, an attempt is made at a critical and constructive evaluation of this most Puritan and catholic theologian.

I have wherever possible allowed Baxter to speak for himself. When he wrote so much, and so much of it so well, on all the topics to be covered, any other course seemed foolish. No reports could match the vividness and force of his own plain, terse, pithy prose. I have relied chiefly on printed sources; examination of the MS treatises preserved at Dr. Williams' Library led me to endorse Orme's verdict: "among the printed works of Baxter sufficient is to be found already on all the subjects of which they treat."[15] For clarity's sake, seventeenth-century spelling has sometimes been modernized, though not in book titles. And enough of the Latin has been translated to enable non-Latinists to follow the argument, though not more.

Abbreviations
C.R.   = *Calamy Revised*, ed. A. G. Matthews, 1934.
C.T.   = Baxter, *Catholick Theologie*, 1675.
C.T.S. = Calvin Translation Society.
D.N.B. = *Dictionary of National Biography*.
E.T.   = English translation.
J.E.H. = *Journal of Ecclesiastical History*.
J.R.   = Baxter, *A Treatise of Justifying Righteousness*, 1676.
                    (N.B. The third pagination is cited as "Mr.
                    Cartwright … considered," the fifth as "The
                    Substance of Mr. Cartwright … considered.")
M.T.   = Baxter, *Methodus Theologiae Christianae*, 1681.
P.S.   = Parker Society edition.
R.B.   = *Reliquiae Baxterianae*, ed. M. Sylvester, 1696.
R.D.   = H. Heppe, *Reformed Dogmatics*, 1950.

15. *Works*, I:765

Part I

THE THEOLOGIAN

"His whole life he accounted a warfare, in which Christ was his Captain, his arms, prayers and tears. The Cross his banner, and his word *Vincit qui patitur*."

"He was ἀνὴρ τετραγωνός, immoveable in all times, so that they who in the midst of many opinions have lost the view of true religion, may return to him and there find it."

—John Geree,
The Character of an old English Puritane, or Non-conformist, p. 6.

Chapter 1

Puritanism as Baxter Saw It

SYNOPSIS

1.   Introduction:
           Puritan origins
           Aim of chapter: to demonstrate Baxter's
                           understanding of the Puritan
                           and sympathies within it.

2.   Baxter's use of terms: Puritan
                            Nonconformist
                            Disciplinarian.

3.   Baxter's principles for interpreting Puritan history:
       "Cain and Abel malignity";
       "Over-doing is undoing".

4.   a. Disciplinarian history to 1640.
       b. Conditions in Baxter's youth.
       c. Disciplinarian history to 1660; the Associations.

5.   Baxter's attitude to religion of
           an Antinomian type;
           a Quaker type.

6.   Conclusion: Baxter endorsed Puritan piety and Disciplinarian ideals.

Chapter 1

Puritanism as Baxter Saw It

"... this incredible Age ..." —Baxter, 1665

The reformers set themselves to overhaul the faith, worship, organization and life of the Church in the light of "God's Word written." In Europe, the Calvinist churches arrogated to themselves the title "Reformed," claiming that the Lutherans had abandoned the work of Reformation when only half done. In England, the name "Puritan" was given to that party within the established Church which sought a thoroughness of reformation comparable to that of the "best Reformed churches."[1] The Elizabethan settlement of 1559 appeared a makeshift; but, at first by accident[2] and then, as soon as she had established herself, by Elizabeth's design, it was left unaltered. The Puritans remained a dissatisfied minority within the Church, vocal in protest from time to time concerning the imposition of ceremonies, the structure of the hierarchy, the state of the ministry and the inroads of Arminianism. By 1625, the Puritan attitude on the first two of these issues had modified somewhat, and the party's former aggressive unanimity had gone; but Puritanism had meanwhile acquired an illustrious pastoral tradition and a distinctive devotional theology and broadened into a predominantly religious movement inspired by a small group of gifted clerics, whose influence and ideals spread far beyond the limits of the church reform party. This was the Puritanism Baxter knew as a boy at Eaton-Constantine.

---

1. According to Fuller (*Church History of Britain*, 1837 ed., II:474) "the odious name of PURITANS" was first applied to ceremonial recusants in 1564; Heylin (*History of the Reformation*, 1849 ed., II:421) says 1565.

2. In 1563 a comprehensive program of ritual reform was carried in the lower house of Convocation by 45 against 35 of those present, but defeated by one vote when proxies were counted (58-59).

This chapter is designed to show how Baxter understood the tradition which he endorsed, and to indicate his relation to the principal strands which went to make up, or unraveled themselves from, the Puritan movement as a whole. Since we wish to introduce the man no less than the movement, we shall let him speak for himself as far as possible. In any case Baxter was both an acute observer and a competent historian[3] and his account has considerable historical interest of its own.

First, it is necessary to say something about Baxter's use of words. "Puritan" he employs in the sense in which he met it in 1627 when it was popularly employed[4] as a term of contempt to express "vulgar hatred of serious godliness in conformists and nonconformists."[5] He knew that its meaning had originally been more technical:

> the same name in a Bishops mouth signified a Nonconformist, and in an ignorant Drunkard or Swearers mouth, a godly obedient Christian. But the People being the greater number, became among themselves the Masters of the sense.[6]

Baxter keeps to the popular usage. He is fond of referring to "what is said by the old *Conformists*, how the word *Puritan* was used with the utmost malice by *Papists* and *Drunkards*, and ungodly *Persons* against those who were firm *Protestants*, and would not Drink and Whore as they did."[7] The usage persisted: "how oft hear we curses and revilings against conforming puritans, or as some call them, Church Whigs," he wrote in a book that appeared in 1689.[8] He notes in passing that "in *Spalatensis's* time, when he was decrying *Calvinism*, he devised the name of *Doctrinal Puritans*, which comprehended all that were against Arminianism," and that "divers bishops have affirmed that the Jesuits were the masters of this nickname here in England, and the promoters of it,"[9] but never employs the word in this way himself.

---

3. In a preface to his *Church History*, 1680, entitled *What History is Credible, and what not*, Baxter lays down his principles of historical judgment. He demands that sources be quoted, and instances as exemplary in this respect Rushworth, Fuller, Camden, Usher and Fox. *Ira* and *studium* invalidate testimony; "I will believe none of these revilers, further than they give me cogent proof." In this class he puts Heylin, and (*Third Defence of the Cause of Peace*, 1681, 87) Bancroft and Sir Thomas Aston.

4. *Works*, XV:cccclxxv.

5. *Works*, XV:cccclxxvii.

6. *R.B.*, I:32.

7. *Third Defence of the Cause of Peace*, 1681, 52. Baxter quotes specimen passages from Bishop Downame, Robert Abbot and Robert Bolton in *Works*, XVII:73f. (*Vain Religion of the Formal Hypocrite*, 1660).

8. *Works*, XV:544 (*Cain and Abel Malignity*, written in 1685-6).

9. *R.B.*, I:32; *Works*, XVII:74. See Note A, 18.

Ministers and laymen who desired reform in church worship or government prior to 1640 and those ejected in 1662 he denotes by the negative description "nonconformist" or "nonconformable."[10] Sometimes he indicates their programme by calling them "disciplinarians."[11]

The principle by which he interpreted Puritan history was explicitly theological. The movement, he tells us, began with a dispute among the godly, but ultimately resolved itself into the unending struggle between godliness and ungodliness, Cain and Abel, Christ and Satan. In order to explain "the notable Division" whereby in the Civil War "the *generality* of the People through the Land ... who were then called *Puritans, Precisians, Religious Persons* ... adhered to the Parliament" while "the Gentry that were not so precise and strict" and "the Rabble" sided with the King, Baxter enunciates the following general principle:

> There is a universal and radicated Enmity between the *Carnal* and the Spiritual, the *Serpent's* and the *Woman's* seed, the *fleshly Mind*, and the spiritual Law of God ... in *England*, as well as in other Countries ... So that everywhere serious godly People ... were spoken against and derided by the Names of Precisians, Zealot, Over-strict, the holy Brethren, and other Terms of Scorn.[12]

"These things being supposed," Baxter opens the story with the troubles at Frankfort, where "One part of them were for Diocesans ... The other were for *Calvin's* Discipline and way of Worship; for the setting up of a Parochial Discipline instead of a Diocesan." The Elizabeth Settlement favored the former.

---

10. It should be noted that the ejections of 1662 followed a refusal, not to conform, but to subscribe. "I know not three Men in the three Counties about me, that would not have then [i.e. in 1662] conformed, if that would have kept them in their livings" (*Third Defence*, p. 30). Most who were nonconformist in opinion [i.e. who desired reformation] in the years before 1640 conformed in fact, and Baxter's use of "conformist" and "nonconformist" with reference to these years is occasionally equivocal. In any case, after 1662, "Conforming is quite another thing than before the Wars" (*R.B.*, II:430), and some "who were for the old Conformity; for Bishops, Common Prayer Book, Ceremonies, and the old Subscription" (ibid., 387) became nonconformists and were ejected.

11. e.g. *R.B.*, I:32. On Episcopal lips, the negative classification "nonconformist" was extended after the Restoration to cover all dissenters. "Many sects go under the name of Nonconformists from whom we differ incomparably more than we do from the *Conformists*; as the Quakers, Seekers, Behmenists and some others" (*Defense of the Principles of Love* (1671), first pagination, 70; cf. *R.B.*, II:387). But Baxter never uses the word with such latitude.

12. *R.B.*, I:31. This principle is axiomatic in Baxter's reading of all Church history. In the epistle prefixed to *Cain and Abel Malignity*, Baxter again reviews the story of Puritanism in light of it. "There is a double history needful to the full understanding of this book" (described as a "reprehensive lamentation of English malignity," *Works*, XVII: ccclxxv) ... 1. The history of Adam's fall, and the great depravation of human nature thence arising ... 2. The history of the advantages that malignity hath got in England ... " (XVII:ccclxxviii). The story is told most fully, as far as 1655, in *Works*, XIV:141 ff. (*Reformed Pastor*).

This lamentable Breach was never healed: The discountenanced Party were fervent Preachers, of holy Lives, and so were many of the Bishops also in those days! But when *Jewel, Pilkington, Grindal*, and such like were dead, many succeeded them whom the People took to be other kind of Men. And the silenced Disciplinarians (as then they were called) did by their Writings, their secret Conference and Preaching, and their Godly Lives, work much upon such as were religiously addicted.

The bishops demanded subscription to "Episcopacy, Liturgy, Ceremonies, and all" in order to safeguard their position, and thereby "kept and cast out very many worthy Men"; "the ignorant Rabble" supposed that the Bishops were opposed to strict piety as well as nonconformity, "and they cried up the Bishops … And thus the Interest of the Diocesans and of the Prophane and Ignorant sort of people were unhappily twisted together in England." However, in the battle between godliness and profanity, not a few conformists (including bishops[13]) were, as Baxter gladly recognized, on the nonconformists' side.

In reviewing the course of controversy on narrower issues, Baxter invoked a further principle taught, in his view, by church history, that "over-doing is undoing."[14] Excess in any direction beyond the Scripture standard is devilish wisdom. In this case, he held, both parties had over-done. "The advantages that malignity hath got in England" included, besides Episcopal misdemeanours, "the presbyterians' provocations by over-opposing episcopacy" and "the parliament's casting out (with a multitude of flagitious ministers) some doctors, for being against them, for the king";[16] zeal had swallowed up charity on both sides, and, as a result, by 1689:

> our divisions are grown to a fixed factious enmity; and malice and worldly interest will hear no motions or petitions for peace; and yet madly plead all for love and peace, while they implacably fight against them, and accuse those as enemies of peace, who beg peace of them and cannot obtain it.[17]

---

13 ."… what learned, Holy, Incomparable men, abundance of the old Conformists were"— including, in a long list, Bishops Jewel, Grindal, Potter, Davenant and Hall (*Defence of the Principles of Love*, first pagination, 57).

14. Cf. the passages quoted in G.F. Nuttall, *Richard Baxter* and *Philip Doddridge*, 24, notes 18 and 19. For an example of Baxter's use of this principle, cf. *Works*, IX:193f., in which the fourth-century insistence on Nicene orthodoxy "concerning some unsearchable mysteries about the Trinity" as a test of communion and condition of salvation is attributed to Satan, "seemingly now a Christian of the most judicious and forward sort," "drawing us from our Christian simplicity." "But what got he by this one game?...He necessitated some living judge for the determining of fundamentals… He got a standing verdict against the perfection and sufficiency of Scripture … Did not this one act found the seat of Rome? . . . Oh what the devil hath got by over-doing!"

16. *Works*, XVII:ccccclxxviii.

17. *Works*, XVII:ccccclxxvii.

The Disciplinarians, in Baxter's view, had merely preserved the ideals of the Edwardian reformers:

> it is usually said that England had more respect to the principles of *Augustine* in Doctrine, and of *Melancthon* and *Bucer* in the points of Reformation, than of *Calvin, Luther*, or any other: And as to *Cranmer, Ridley, Cox* and the other Reforming Bishops, I verily believe it. I know no Divines whose judgment I more consent to than *Bucers* and *Melancthons*: O that all our Clergy would read and weigh what *Bucer* saith copiously and vehemently for Parish-discipline, and pure Communion ... and what he saith of Pastoral Government, Ordination and Order, and of imposing such Ceremonies as ours ...[18]

He describes their policy as follows, claiming first-hand knowledge;[19]

> 1. Their great Concern was to set up Parish Discipline, under Superior Synods. 2. Being themselves almost all in publick Churches, at least *per vices*,[20] and being still in hope of publick reformation, they were greatly against the Brownists violence,[21] that would break those hopes. 3. They held that Christs law was their Rule, which commanded this Discipline, which no Magistrate could dispense with.[22]

At the time of the ejections which followed Bancroft's exposure of the Classis movement and the passing of the 1604 Canons, "a great part of them kept in by the connivance of some peacable Bishops, and by the mediation of

18. *Apology for the Nonconformists Ministry* ("written in 1668, and 1669, for the most of it"—title page; published in 1681), epistle "To the Bishops." The work of Bucer to which Baxter refers is his *De Regno Christi* (*Scripta Anglicana*, 1577, 260 f.) written at Cambridge "to amplify and to round off the suggestions for the Reformation ... in all his other writings," (C. Hopf, *Martin Bucer and the English Reformation*, 1946, 99).

19. "When I knew the minds of many aged Nonconformists about forty years ago as my familiar friends, who were all of the same mind in this as I am, what history can I be more assured of ..." (*Second True Defence*, 1681, 37).

20. Baxter refers to the practice of those suspended or ejected: "many of them did as some do now, get into publick Pulpits for a day and away, where they were not known" (*op. cit.*, 34).

21. "The Chief Nonconformists were against that called *Brownism* or Separatism, and wrote more against it than the Conformists did. I still profess my self to be of their judgment in this" (*op. cit.*, 29). In his view, Separatism (which he considers schismatic) was simply an over-doing reaction. "*Separatists* have almost always risen from the ignorance, ungodliness, and shameful disabilities, idle negligence, pride, covetousness, or cruelty of the Clergy. This is true, as the experience of all ages telleth us" (*Apology for the Nonconformists Ministry*, 1681, 226). This was so in the case of the lay nonconformists at Dudley, against whom in 1639 "I daily disputed ... for I found their Censoriousness and Inclination towards Separation ... to be a Threatening Evil... their Sufferings from the Bishops were the great Impediments of my Success..." (*R.B.*, I:14).

22. *Second True Defence*, 37; cf. the description of them in *True History of Councils*, 1682, 92: "Presbyterian Nonconformists, who earnestly pleaded for Parish-Discipline ... (as *Bucer* also did)."

some Lords and Gentlemen … And when one Bishop silenced them, the next often gave them liberty … and when they were silenced, they went off into another Diocese, where they rubbed out a year or more, and then to another; And so were still in some hope of publick liberty."[23] During these years, the Presbyterian programme for remodelling the hierarchy dropped out of sight. The old Presbyterians were dead, and few succeeded them. "About as many Nonconformists as Counties were left;[24] and those few most stuck at Subscriptions and Ceremonies, which were the hindrance of their Ministry; and but few of them studied or understood the Presbyterian or Independent Disciplinary Causes."[25] Episcopacy as such was no longer seriously objected to. As a result of the advocacy of "those that wrote for the old Conformity,"[26] the vestments and ceremonies were now generally accepted; although, Baxter adds:

> I must profess … that before the unhappy Wars, I knew not one Conformable Divine, to my best remembrance, who was of a religious blameless life, and seemed seriously to believe, and seek the life to come … who did not conform only upon Mr. *Sprint's* argument of Necessity, and had not rather be excused; and would profess, that they did it … merely that they might not be kept from Preaching.[27]

Baxter's reminiscences of his own boyhood are of peculiar interest, as giving a first-hand account of the state of religion in the first quarter of the seventeenth century in what we may assume was a typical country district of England.

> From the age of six till ten, I had four Schoolmasters, Curates of the place[28] successively, that read Common-prayer; two never Preached, the other two

23. *Second True Defence*, 33 f. Baxter gives a list of ministers who thus "kept in."
24. Baxter is referring to the period of his youth: "Before the Parliament 1640, there were not so many Nonconformable Ministers in *England* (Presbyterians, Independents and Anabaptists altogether) as there were Counties in the Kingdom" (*Third Defence*, 59).
25. *True History of Councils*, 92; cf. 90: "Till Mr. Ball wrote for the Liturgy and against Can and Allen & c., and Mr. Burton published his *Protestation Protested*, I never thought what Presbytery or Independency were, nor ever spake with a man that seemed to know it. And that was in 1641."
26. *Third Defence*, 54. Baxter instances John Sprint, *Cassander Anglicanus*, 1618, an apology for his own action in conforming as an alternative to deprivation when his congregation, resenting his "fidelity in opposing their disordered life" ("To the Reader"), had indicted him for nonconformity at a Quarter Sessions; Thomas Paybody, *A just apologie for the gesture of kneeling in the act of receiving the Lords supper* ("which fully satisfied me for Conformity in that," R.B., I:13); and John Burges, *The lawfulness of kneeling … also somewhat of the crosse in baptism*, 1631, which Baxter found less convincing (*R.B.*, I:14).
27. *Second True Defence*, 90. Baxter claims that this was the practice of such Elizabethan Puritans as Humphrey, John Reynolds, Perkins, and Chaderton (*op. cit.*, 39)—the first three "more Nonconformists than I and those of my judgment" (*Apology for the Nonconformists Ministry*, 70).
28. High-Ercall.

seldom; but the two more learned drank themselves into beggary and lefts us. I then came to live at the habitation of my ancestors. There I fonnd (*sic*) one *Sir William Rogers* about four score, Parson of two places twenty miles distant, that never Preached (they told me) in all his life ... After him a pretended Minister, Grandchild to the Parson, took the whole Cure, but never preached once. The Son of the old Parson was there sometime a Minister, that is a Reader, and a famous debauched Stage-player. At this time a Son of the next Neighbour turned Minister, and exceeded them so far that he undertook to Preach, and had a Benefice a great way off, whence after many years scandal he fled upon the discovery that one of the forementioned had forged his Orders. The next Curate ... and my Schoolmaster, was another Neighbours Son, which being set to be a Lawyers Clerk drunk himself into such necessity that he was fain to turn Curate ... He never preached in my time there but once, which was the terriblest Sermon that ever I heard, to hear a man drunk in the Pulpit (or else he had not ventured to Preach) to talk a deal of stark nonsense upon so terrible a Text as *Mat.* 25. *Come ye blessed and go ye cursed.*[29]

As for the laity,

In the place where I first lived, and the Country about, the People were of two sorts; The generality seemed to mind nothing seriously but the body and the world. They went to Church and would answer the Parson in Responds, and thence go to Dinner, and thence to play. They never prayed in their families, but some of them going to bed, would say over the Creed and the Lord's Prayer, and some of them the Hail Mary ... The other sort were such as had their Conscience awaked to some regard of God and their Everlasting State; ... and would much enquire what was Duty, and what was Sin, and how to please God, and to make sure of Salvation; and made this their Business and Interest ... They read the Scripture, and such Books as *The Practice of Piety*,[30] and Dent's *Plain Man's Path Way*[31] and Dod *On the Commandments.*[32]

They used to pray in their families, and alone ... they feared all known sin ... These were, where I lived, about the number of two or three Families in twenty;

29. *Second True Defence*, 58 f. The same story is summarily told in *R.B.* I:1 f., and in more detail with names given and additional information about churches in the surrounding area, in *Third Defence*, 39 f.

30. *The Practice of Piety*, by Lewis Bayly, Bishop of Bangor, 3rd edition 1613, 40th edition 1635.

31. *The Plain-Man's Path-way to Heaven*, by Arthur Dent, preacher of the Word of God at South-Shoobery in Essex; 1st edition 1601, 21st 1631; "about forty years ago," wrote Baxter in 1672, "I had one, said to be of the thirtieth impression" (*Works*, XIX:296). (These were the two books which formed Mrs. Bunyan's dowry.)

32. *A Plaine and Familiar Exposition of the Ten Commandments with a . . . Catechism*, by John Dod and Robert Cleaver; 1st edition 1604, 19th 1635.

and these by the rest were called Puritans ... Yet not one of many of them scrupled Conformity to Bishops Liturgy or Ceremonies.[33]

They attended their parish church: "Before 1638 ... scarce more than one Non-Conformist ... held any Church-Communion but Parochial, in each County."[34] If they visited another church, "it was godly Conformable Ministers that they went from home to hear."[35] Sometimes they would "meet after Sermon on the Lord's Day to repeat the Conforming Ministers Sermon, and sing a Psalm, and Pray"; whereupon the canons of 1604 were invoked against them[36] and some of them were "prosecuted by Apparitors, Officials, Archdeacons, Commissaries, Chancellors, and other Episcopal Instruments."[37]

If we may judge from Baxter's account, there was more anti-episcopal feeling and nonconformist opinion among "the younger hotter sort" of laymen, who had to endure such treatment, than among the clergy in the years before 1640.

> There were but two Nonconformists in all those Countrys [i.e. counties] then. One was one Mr. *Atkins*, my neighbour,[38] who would never talk either for it or against it, but almost always talk so seriously of *Heaven*, and a *Holy Life*, that you could scarce get him to talk much of anything else. The other was that most excellent Disputant *John Ball*,[39] [who, when approached by some young nonconformists] perceiving their humour to be set towards faction and Ceremonious disputes, did so School them, and rebuke their factious humour, that they would never come at him more.[40]

The Et Cetera Oath, however, "stirred up the differing Parties (who before were all one Party, even *quiet Conformists*),"[41] and disputes about Church government began again in earnest. The Westminster Assembly was principally

---

33. *True History of Councils*, 90f. Baxter's was such a family, cf. *R.B.*, I:2. f.

34. *Second True Defence*, 233.

35. *True History of Councils*, 91.

36. cf. Canon LXXIII.

37. *True History of Councils*, 92. Otherwise, there was no discipline at all. "In all my life I never lived in the parish where one person was publicly admonished, or brought to public penitence, or excommunicated, though there were never so many obstinate drunkards, whoremongers or vilest offenders. Only I have known now and then one for getting a bastard that went to the bishop's court and paid their fees; and I heard of two or three in all the country, in all my life, that stood in a white sheet an hour in the church; but the ancient discipline of the church was unknown" (*Works*, XIV:145; written in 1655).

38. At Tipton, he "kept in to the last, even the Lord *Dudley* favouring him" (*Second True Defense*, 34). Baxter was his neighbour at Dudley, 1638-9.

39. "Mr. Mainwaring kept in Mr. Ball at Whitmore" (*op. cit.*, 33).

40. op. cit. 57f.

41. *R.B.*, I:16.

composed of men who had conformed, on Sprint's principles;[42] it represented the best, theologically and pastorally, in Puritanism as it then was.[43] In its debates, three views on church government emerged: Presbyterian, Erastian[44] and Independent.[45] Among the generality of clergy of the Puritan type, of whom most (not all[46]) had supported Parliament in the war—"though not in meddling with Arms, yet in Judgment, and in flying to their Garrisons"[47]— there were two main views on church order, "some of them being most for Church-Government by Synods of Parochial Pastors and assisting Elders, and most for a Reconciliation of the several divided Parties."[48] The latter, "meer Catholicks; men of no Faction … owning that which was good in all … and upon a concord in so much,[49] laying out themselves for the great Ends of their Ministry, the Peoples Edification,"[50] formed the bulk of the Worcestershire Association which Baxter organized,[51] and, we may suppose, of those modelled on it.[52] They would have been happy under a Presbyterian settlement

42. *Defence of the Principles of Love*, second pagination, 13; cf. *R.B.*, I:33.

43. "The Divines there Congregate were Men of Eminent Learning and Godliness, and Ministerial Abilities and Fidelity … as far as I am able to judge by the information of all History of that kind … the Christian World, since the days of the Apostles, had never a Synod of more excellent Divines" (*R.B.* I:73).

44. Exponents of this view in the Assembly were John Lightfoot and Thomas Coleman. A third member, Edward Reynolds, came later to hold it. "May not those be *honest Conformists* who go on Bishop *Reynolds* and Dr. *Stillingfleets* grounds, that no form of Church-Government is of Divine Institution," Baxter wrote in 1681 (*Third Defence*, 49). Reynolds, who became Bishop of Norwich in 1660, died in 1676.

45. The five leading Independents were Thomas Goodwin, Philip Nye, Jeremiah Burroughs, William Bridge and Sydrach Simpson. Joseph Caryl, John Philips, William Carter, Peter Sterry, Anthony Burgess and William Greenhill supported them.

46. Cf. *R.B.*, III:150. (The letter to Dr. Thomas Good there reproduced is also printed in *Second True Defence*, 142 f.)

47. *R.B.*, I:33; cf. the list of chaplains in the Parliament's army, I:42, and the refugees at Coventry, I:44.

48. "Historical Preface" to *Second True Defence*. The former (Presbyterian) party was strong only in and around London (Thomas Hall of King's Norton was the only Presbyterian Baxter knew in Worcestershire); the latter included "the greatest numbers of the Godly Ministers and People throughout *England*. For though Presbytery generally took in Scotland, yet it was but a stranger here" (*R.B.*, II:146).

49. Baxter (characteristically) means a concord in and for *practice*: "so much of the Church Order and Discipline, as the Episcopal, Presbyterian and Independent are agreed in, as belonging to the Pastors of each particular Church." (*R.B.*, I:148). Of lay elders, Baxter wrote ("Agreement," Art. XVII) "Whilst we agree in Practice, we may leave men's several principles … to their own judgments …" (Printed in *The Reformed Pastor*, ed. J. T. Wilkinson, 2nd ed., 1950, 179).

50. *R.B.*, I:97.

51. For details of membership, see G. F. Nuttall in *J.E.H.*, I:197 f. For an account of the affinities of members and of those who refused to join, see *R. B.*, II:148 f.

52. Cumberland and Westmorland ministers independently "agreed on Articles to the same purpose and of the same Sense" before they learned of Baxter's undertaking (*R.B.*, II:162 f.). For some details about later associations formed on the Worcestershire model, cf. Powicke *Life*, 267 f.

rather than none ("we in this country," Baxter records, "did seek for authority from the Parliament many years ago for the establishing of the Presbyterian government," but without success[53]); but a "primitive Episcopacy," as described in Archbishop Usher's *Reduction of Episcopacy to the Form of Synodical Government*, would have pleased them best. These, Baxter claimed, were in fact in the majority, though unrepresented in the Assembly.

The Worcestershire Association was formed for the peaceful promotion of the Disciplinarian and classical ideal: "that ... the Church may be more Reformed and the Discipline of Christ be more faithfully and successfully exercised."[54] If they could not have discipline by establishment, they would have it on a basis of voluntary association. Its members were prepared for the time being to sink their disagreements about Church government in the interests of united pastoral activity. Important though the first might be, the second mattered more still, and therefore was given pride of place. "Let the *two printed Agreements* of the *Worcestershire Ministers*, one for *Discipline* and one for *Catechising* and personal instruction, with my *Reformed Pastor*,[55] be a *standing witness* to *Posterity*, what the Countries Ministers work was, against all *factious Calumny*,"[56] Baxter wrote in 1681; and his most comforting memory of the Commonwealth period, otherwise, to his mind, disfigured by sectarianism and Cromwell, was that:

> In all the Counties which I was acquainted with, there were many young Orthodox faithful Preachers, that gave themselves wholly to do good, for one that was ten Years before . . . Never did I see, before or since, so much Love and Concord among Ministers, and all Religious People, nor read of any Age that had so much for thirteen hundred Years.[57]

This was something which unhappily came to an end with the Restoration and ejections.

---

53. *R.B.*, II:167.

54. Preface to "The profession of the Associated Churches": *The Reformed Pastor*, ut sup., 184; cf. the "Explication" in *Christian Concord*, 106: "if Episcopacy, Presbytery, or Independency, etc., be indeed the way of God, there is no way in the world so likely to set it up as the meeting and loving Association of the Pastors, where all things may be gently and amicably debated."

55. *Christian Concord: or the Agreement of the Associated Pastors and Churches of Worcestershire. With Rich. Baxter's Explication...and his Exhortation to Unity*, 1653; *The Agreement of divers Ministers . . . for catechising or personal instructing all in their several parishes that will consent thereunto*, 1656; and *Gildas Salvianus; The Reformed Pastor . . . With an open Confession of our too open Sins . . .* 1656; composed for a fast day following the subscription of the second Agreement by members of the Association.

56. *Third Defence*, 34.

57. *True History of Councils*, 186.

It remains to indicate Baxter's attitude towards the various types of religion which appeared in Nonconformist circles. While endorsing the tradition of "serious godliness" which went back to the Elizabethan Puritans, he rejected the sectarian "enthusiasms" which blossomed during the Commonwealth. The radicals may for the moment be distinguished as those who appealed to Scripture but propounded a new exegesis of it, "new light" revealed for the last days, and those who appealed directly to the Spirit who had been in the authors of Scripture and was now, so they claimed, in them. Of the first type was Antinomianism, which Baxter attacked unmercifully, as we shall see, on the ground that it made against holiness and bred self-deception. "The Books of *Dr. Crisp, Paul Hobson, Saltmarsh, Cradock*, and abundance such like"[58] were those which from the first he set himself to oppose. Of the second type were "five Sects . . . whose Doctrines were almost the same . . . 1. The *Vanists:* 2. The *Seekers:* 3. The *Ranters:* 4. The *Quakers:* 5. The *Behmenists*."[59] He describes the two last, with Fifth Monarchy Men and "some *Anabaptists*" as "Proper Fanaticks, looking too much to Revelations within, instead of the Holy Scripture."[60] In his dealings with the Quakers at Kidderminster, he failed to recognize in their "Grumblestool Rhetorick"[61] the voice of the Spirit. He held Antinomianism and Quakerism like Separatism to be reactionary movements pure and simple:

> I have seldom observed any Extreme in Hereticks or Schismaticks, which was not notably caused by the Clergys contrary extreme. *Antinomianism* rose among us from our obscure Preaching of Evangelical Grace, and insisting too much on Tears and terrors... The *Quakers* arose from the pride and vanity of Religious people, from which they fled into the Sordid extreme...[62]

We may summarize Baxter's affinities within Puritanism as follows:

1. Baxter identified himself with Puritanism in the popular sense, i.e. with a thoroughgoing Calvinistic piety. He shared the strong pastoral concern which distinguished clerical Puritan leaders. He felt himself entitled to claim spiritual kinship with the Edwardian Reformers and many later conformists. He repudiated the religious novelties of Commonwealth times as dangerous delusions.

---

58. *R.B.*, I:111.
59. *R.B.*, I:74.
60. *R.B.*, II:387.
61. *The Quakers Catechism*, 1655, 25.
62. *Apology for the Nonconformists Ministry*, 226. Despite their "extreme Austerity" (*R.B.*, I:77), Baxter considered spiritual pride the Quakers' great sin, as evidenced by their claims to perfection, their vilifying "the most holy and eminent Servants of God . . . as if heaven was made for them alone"—they "damn all the Church ... for 1600 years"—and their "proud, scornful, railing language" ("Answer to a young unsettled Friend," prefixed to *The Quakers Catechism*).

2. Baxter identified himself with Puritanism in the narrower and technical sense, i.e. with a conscientious nonconformity and, after 1662, non-subscription[63] and with a programme whose permanent element was a demand for competent preaching and discipline in every parish. As he showed after 1662, he would, like his predecessors in this tradition, continue his own ministry illegally if the needs of the church demanded it. Within this body of opinion, whose protagonists were all Puritan in the popular sense, Baxter divorced himself from the Independents and became the leader of the group which after 1662 was popularly (though inaccurately) dubbed Presbyterian.[64] He agreed with the older Nonconformists in rejecting separating principles as schismatic.

Note A: "DOCTRINAL PURITANS"

The passage to which Baxter refers (see p. 18, n. 9) is in M. Antonius de Dominis, Archbishop of Spalato, *The Cause of his Return, out of England,* published at Rome in 1625, and reads as follows (p. 31).

> In England (if we speak of Religion) are many sects: there are Puritans, or rigid Calvinists: there are more moderate which call themselves only Protestants, and Reformed ... The heresies of the Puritans are notorious, to wit, that there is no free will, God to be the Author of sin, God merely because so it pleaseth him to damn many: Christ not to have died for all, to have undergone the punishment of hell, that infants baptized be damñed, &c ..."

So, on p. 33, he refers to "Geneva the mother of Puritans" and mentions the French, Flemish and Italian Calvinists churches in London: "by them Puritanism is especially maintained, and set forward in England." Baxter seems correct in treating this as the earliest appearance in print of "Puritan" used in the sense of "high Calvinist." It antedates the better-known passage (which Baxter probably had read; cf. his reference to the writings by and against Mountagu in *Catholick Theologie,* II. 2), in Carleton's *Examination ... 1625,* p. 121, where Carleton comments on Mountagu's jibe, "Just your *Puritan* Doctrine for *final Perseverance* (*Appello Caesarem,* p. 18) as follows:

> This is the first time that ever I heard of a Puritan doctrine in points dogmatical ... A Puritan doctrine is a strange thing, because it hath been confessed on

---

63. Baxter subscribed at his ordination in 1638 without having studied the issues involved ("so precipitant and rash was I"). He later regretted it. (*R.B.,* I:13, *Penitent Confession,* 1691, 9).

64. The derisive use of the word began in the Parliamentary Army: "hot-headed Sectaries" cried down "all Presbyterians but especially the Ministers [i.e. the Army chaplains]; whom they call *Priests* and *Priestbyters,* and *Dryvines,* and the Dissembly-men, and such like" (*R.B.,* I:5). The term "puritan" had undergone a similar degradation half a century before.

both sides, that *Protestants* and *Puritans* have held the *same doctrines* without variance ... according to the Harmony of the several *Confessions* of these Churches ... What is your end in this, but to make divisions ... that place may be given to the *Pelagian* and *Arminian* doctrines: And then all that are against these must be called *Puritan doctrines.*

The only other reference to this usage which I have found in Baxter's works is a note in *The Vain Religion of the Formal Hypocrite:*[65] "Of Archbishop Laud's tract of doctrinal puritanism ... see Pryne, in his Tryal, p. 156. Divers bishops have affirmed that the Jesuits were the masters of this nickname here in England, and the promoters of it." The passage in Prynne, *Compleate History of the Tryall and Condemnation of William Laud* (1646), is a quotation from Laud's diary for Dec. 23rd, 1624: "the same day I delivered my L. Duke of *Bucking* (sic) a little tract ABOUT DOCTRINAL PURITANISM, in some ten Heads" (Prynne's capitals). This also antedates Carleton's remark.

This evidence is of interest, as illustrating the width of Baxter's acquaintance with the church history of his age.

---

65. *Works,* XVII:74.

Chapter 2

Puritan Theology

SYNOPSIS

1.   Introduction: scope limited to "Puritan" theology in Baxter's sense of
       the adjective.

2.   Growth of the Puritan theological corpus.

3.   "Practical and experimental" emphasis in the Puritans' Calvinism:
       appearing in their definitions of theology.

4.   Factors responsible for this development:
       a natural flowering of Calvinism
       the pastoral situation
       influence of Augustine
       effect of the Renaissance.

5.   Puritan psychology.

6.   Puritan method of Biblical exegesis.
       expository preaching.

7.   Puritan concern about method in systematic theology due to the
       influence of Ramist logic.

8.   Puritan catechisms.

9.   Conclusion: Puritan theology as Baxter's background and heritage.

Chapter 2

Puritan Theology

"It hath been one of the glories of the *Protestant Religion*, that it revived the Doctrine of *Saving Conversion*, And of the *new creature* brought forth thereby … But in a more eminent manner, God hath cast the honor hereof upon the Ministers and Preachers of this Nation, who are renowned abroad for their more accurate search into and discoveries hereof …"

—Thomas Goodwin, Philip Nye
Preface to Thomas Hooker, *The Application of Redemption*

"Systematic theology provided the Puritans with completely satisfying symbols; it dramatised the needs of the soul exactly as does some great poem or work of art."
—Perry Miller, *The New England Mind*, p. 6.

Henceforth, our concern is with "Puritans" as distinct from "nonconformists," and the word "Puritan" will be used in Baxter's sense. In this chapter, we shall give some account of the distinctively "Puritan" theology which Baxter learned in his youth and taught in his manhood.

This theology is expounded in the scores of practical treatises which Puritan pastors brought out at the end of the sixteenth and during the seventeenth centuries. Most of these works were sermons in the pulpit before they became sermons in print. In the production of "sound moral treatises … there had been an unfortunate but perhaps inevitable time-lag after the opening phases of the Reformation,"[1] and, as literacy spread, the Jesuits took advantage of the poverty of the Church of England in this respect to publish devotional books of their own stamp.[2] This effectively provoked the Puritans to try and produce

---

1. Thomas Wood, *English Casuistical Divinity during the Seventeenth Century*, 1952, 37f.
2. "The papists cast in our teeth that we have nothing set out for the certain and daily direc-

something better. During the last years of Elizabeth's reign, William Perkins, of Christ's College, Cambridge,[3] brought out a series of small, simply written devotional books which won great popularity and encouraged others to follow his example.[4] By 1649 there were "excellent books in such plenty, that we know not which to read."[5] Some were systematic guides to Christian practice; most were homiletical expositions of particular texts or passages. Puritan preachers seem to have "introduced the custom of reading sermons,"[6] and it became a common practice for friends and relatives of eminent expositors to publish their manuscripts posthumously. Indeed, notes of sermons, taken down by members of the congregation, passed from hand to hand and sometimes surprised the preacher by later appearing in print—an objectionable practice which testifies clearly enough to the commercial value of the material.[7] Thus "a whole literature"[8] grew.

The doctrine taught in these books was Calvinistic. All good comes from

---

tion of a Christian, when yet they have published, they say, many treatises of that argument" (Richard Rogers, *Seven Treatises...in the which...true Christians may learne how to lead a godly and comfortable life every day*, 1603, "Preface"). The best known of the Jesuit books was Robert Persons' [Parsons'] *First Booke of Christian Exercise, Appertayning to Resolution*, 1582, which Rogers goes on to castigate by name; Edmund Bunny, a Calvinistic churchman of Puritan sympathies, produced an amended edition of it in 1584.

3. *D.N.B.*, s.v.

4. This literature is surveyed in some detail by W. Haller, *Rise of Puritanism*, 1938, chaps. I-IV and 406 ff.

5. Baxter, *Works*, XXII:459 (*Saints' Rest*); and cf. *Church History*, 1680, Preface: "I remember Mr. *Cressey* once wrote to me, that *he turned from the Protestant Religion to the Roman, because there was among us no spiritual Books of Devotion for Soul Elevations, and affectionate Contemplation*. And I told him it was Gods just Judgment on him, that he lived so strange to his Neighbours, because they were called *Puritans*, and to their Writings, which Shops and Libraries abound with." This letter from Hugh Paulinus Cressy (*D.N.B.*, s.v.) is in D. W. L. Mss. 59. III. ff. 266-299, dated June 1st, 1666, and Baxter's reply covers ff. 230-265; the part of his here referred to is on ff. 244b-245a.

6. G.F. Nuttall, *The Holy Spirit in Puritan Faith and Experience*, 2nd ed., 1947, 81. Perkins had endorsed "the received custom for preachers to speak *by heart*," advising them to memorize the skeleton, "nothing carefull for the words," and strongly opposed reading in the pulpit (*The Arte of Prophesying*, in *Workes*, 1609, II:670). But his successors practiced it increasingly. Baxter, fluent as he was, could be accused by Quakers of lacking the Spirit, because "you read your sermons out of a Paper" (*One Sheet against the Quakers*, 1657, 13). He replied that he did so from "regard to the work, and the good of the hearers," and testified in 1671: "I never learned a Sermon without book in my life" (*Defence of the Principles of Love*, second pagination, 22).

7. Perkins only published his *Exposition of the Lord's Prayer* because a pirated edition of these sermons came out, "Faulty both in the matter and manner of writing" (*Workes*, I:325). John Preston, second Master of Emmanuel, appointed Richard Sibbes, John Davenport, Thomas Goodwin and John Ball his literary executors because he feared that otherwise notes and transcripts of his sermons "would be pressed into publike view by one or other, who might perhaps be less careful" (Goodwin and Ball, "To the Reader," in Preston, *Sermons Preached before His Majestie*, 1631).

8. Cf. the estimate of Calvin expressed by Robert Bolton (*D.N.B.*, s.v.), "a man that often

God and all evil from man; fallen man can do nothing but sin; God's will is supreme, and His purpose is to save the elect for the glory of His grace and to punish the reprobate for the glory of His justice. These are Puritan axioms. But Puritan Calvinism is decidedly second-generation. By the close of the sixteenth century, Calvinism in England was no longer debated, but accepted. English theologians were virtually unanimous in asserting it. The doctrines of God's sovereignty, perfect atonement and justification *sola fide*, for which Calvin had had to fight, were a legacy which the Puritans could take for granted. Thus they were free, in a way that their predecessors were not, to give their full and undivided attention to the drama which must be played out on the stage Calvinism had set: the drama of the fate of Mansoul. Here their most elaborate and original work was done. Faith and repentance, regeneration and sanctification, pilgrimage and conflict, were the characteristic and recurrent themes of Puritan theology. Its interest and *rationale* is admirably stated in the following extract:

> Among those things that religion offers to our study, God and our own hearts are the chief. God is the first and last and whole of our happiness; the beginning, progress and completement of it is from him and in him…but our heart is the stage and centre upon which this felicity, as to the application of it, is transacted: upon this little spot of earth doth God and Satan draw up their several armies; here doth each of them show their power and wisdom…each of them challenge an interest in it; it is attacked on the one side and defended on the other. So that here are skirmishes, battles and stratagems managed. That man, then, that will not concern himself…how the matter goes in his own heart, what ground is got or lost, what forts are taken or defended, what mines are sprung, what ambuscados laid, or how the battle proceeds, must needs lie under the just imputation of the greatest folly.[9]

This is to say that to the Puritan theologian the one thing necessary above all else was a thorough acquaintance, intellectual and experimental, with the work of the Holy Spirit in the believer, what was and is commonly referred to in Reformed teaching as the application of redemption. "Puritan thought was almost entirely occupied with loving study of the work of the Holy Spirit, and found its highest expression in dogmatico-practical expositions of the several

---

published his judgment for conformity to prelacy and ceremonies" (Baxter, *Works*, XVII:74) and whom, with Sibbes (another conformist) Stoughton selects as typical "representatives of Puritan teaching" under Charles I (*History of Religion in England*, 4th ed., 1901, I:51): "The more learned and holy any Divine is, the more heartily he subscribes to *Paulus Thurias*, his true censure of his *Institution* … Besides the holy Writ, / No book is like to it." (*Instructions for a Right Comforting of Afflicted Consciences*, 1631, 252).

9. Richard Gilpin, *Daemonologia Sacra*, 1677, reprint of 1867, 3f.

aspects of it."[10] With this interest dominant, the Puritan approach to theology could not be other than "practical and experimental." Christian truth was not merely to be believed, but to be obeyed. Eternal life meant knowing God, not merely knowing about Him. The heart must be purified. Faith must work, and faith must love. Theology was a practical science; Christian activity and Christian experience were the proper fruits of studying it. These convictions were reflected in Puritan definitions of theology. William Ames' is typical:

> Divinity is the doctrine of living to God... Divinity is practical, and not a speculative discipline ... it may not be unfitly called θεωρία or θεουργία, as well as θεολογία, that is a living to God, or a working to God, as well as a speaking of God.[11]

Such an emphasis and interest within Calvinism is of itself natural enough. It is there at the fountain-head. "One of the features of the *Institutes*," Dr. Dakin observes, "is its strong practical bias ... the knowledge of God intended is such knowledge as may form the basis of true piety ... that of St. John's gospel— knowledge leading to eternal life."[12] "The fundamental interest of Calvin as a theologian," wrote Dr. Warfield, "lay ... in the region broadly designated soteriological ... within this broad field, his interest was most intense in the application to the sinful soul of the salvation wrought out by Christ—in a word, what is technically known as the *ordo salutis*."[13] The *Institutio* expresses, justifies and teaches Augustinian religion; that was its aim; and there is in fact little in Puritan practical theology which is not already adumbrated in its pages. But it remains true that the English Puritans outstripped all their Continental Reformed contemporaries in this field. Their unique specialization was a response to the pastoral situation which faced them. On the one hand, the diffusion of a garbled caricature of Calvinism had produced a crop of "afflicted consciences," haunted by the fear of being found graceless and reprobate. (These, it should be noted, formed a class distinct from the "melancholy," whose morbid state of mind the Puritans recognized as having a physical origin and not, therefore, normally susceptible of spiritual treatment.) Godly persons thus tormented needed to be shown within themselves evidence of their election, such "gracious" attitudes and feelings as proved their effectual

---

10. B. B. Warfield, "Introductory Note" to A. Kuyper, *The Work of the Holy Spirit*, 1900, xxviii.

11. *Marrow of Sacred Divinity*, E. T. 1642, 1 and 3; cf. Dudley Fenner, *Sacra Theologia ad unicae et verae methodi leges descripta*, 1585, I:i, 1: "Theologia est scientia veritatis quae est de Deo, ad recte beateque vivendum;" Perkins, *A Golden Chaine; or, The Description of Theologie*, I (*Workes*, I:11): "*Theologie*, is the science of living blessedly for ever."

12. A. Dakin, *Calvinism*, 1941, 14 f.

13. *Calvin as a Theologian and Calvinism To-day*, 1952 reprint, 8.

calling. Only so could their minds be set at rest. Or they might prove to be seeking a Saviour whom they had not yet found. If so, they must be safely guided to Christ. The experience of dealing with a constant stream of these cases convinced the Puritan pastors that all Christian people should be taught the art of self-examination, and thus enabled, as far as possible, to discern and prescribe for their own needs. On the other hand, the majority of men lived carelessly, but presented themselves regularly at church and had no doubts at all of their own eventual felicity. These needed to be disillusioned, shown their sin and led to repentance and faith.

Clearly, in order to perform these tasks, the Puritan minister needed a thorough grounding in what today would be called pastoral psychology. The "spirituall Phisition," whose task it is to diagnose and treat sick souls, must not be content with guesswork and nostrums, after the manner of "blind Empyrikes." He requires a sound theoretical basis, some "certaine rule of art, and well grounded practise." He must understand and be able to recognize health, "the psychological pattern ... which all the saints were supposed to have exemplified,"[14] and to discern deviations from it. He must be able to find out in such cases "what secret causes breed the hidden distemper of the soul."[15] The Puritans took Scripture as the text-book for their study of these topics, and their own hearts as the commentary on it. The Bible was ransacked for its teaching on the states of mind and quality of experience which distinguished sickness from health, life from death, the regenerate from the unregenerate. This exegetical interest was not foreign to Reformation theology, but had never been pursued so intensively as now. A small group of able men in and around Cambridge led the way in this study.[16] The need for a Reformed moral theology was now acutely felt. "While the Reformed theologians were immersed in controversy, the Roman casuistical divinity was freely drawn upon for the guidance of souls within the Reformed Churches themselves. For the time being it was either the Roman product or none."[17] This seemed to the Puritans an intolerable situation, and they set themselves to remedy it. To supply this

---

14. W. Haller, *op. cit.*, 90.

15. Henry Holland, "To the Reader," in Richard Greenham, *Works* (1601 ed.). Holland there voices the felt need of a Reformed moral theology ("the diet and cure of souls afflicted is a very great mystery, wherein but few have travailed") and describes Greenham as "a man in his life time of great hope, and could have given best rules for this unknown faculty."

16. Richard Greenham, Richard Rogers, Perkins, Laurence Chaderton, John Dod and Arthur Hildersham may be singled out for mention among Elizabethans, and Paul Bayne, Richard Sibbes, John Preston, John Rogers, John Cotton and Thomas Hooker among their successors during the first quarter of the seventeenth century. All are the subject of articles in *D.N.B.*

17. Wood, *op. cit.*, 38; cf. the passages quoted from Ames, Jeremy Taylor and Baxter, pp. 39-41, which show that English pastors continued to find Roman casuistry indispensable until the Restoration.

deficiency, Perkins "began well" with his unfinished *Whole Sum of the Cases of Conscience*,[18] and William Ames, his disciple,[19] "exceeded all, though briefly,"[20] in his *De Conscientia*. Baxter's own *Christian Directory*, written in 1664-5 and published in 1673, was to prove "a lasting monument to Puritan endeavour in this field."[21] In a large sense, most Puritan practical writings may be called casuistical, dealing as they did with "our English cases concerning the state of sanctification."[22] In the mass, they constituted the "Sum of Practical Divinity in the *English* method"[23] which became the envy of Continental Reformed theologians.

The growth of this body of practical divinity was conditioned by two important influences. First must be noted the study of Augustine and Bernard. Of John Owen's *Pneumatologia*, the quintessence of Puritan thought concerning the Holy Spirit, Dr. Nuttall writes "There is theology, but, in a way which has hardly been known since Augustine, it is a *theologia pectoris*."[24] The resemblance is not accidental. The Puritans studied and absorbed both the matter of Augustine's theology and the spirit of his piety.[25] Their only quarrel is with his terminology: "*Austin* ... took Justification for what we call Sanctification, or Conversion."[26] The substance of his doctrine of grace they accepted without reserve. Their margins, like the pages of the *Institutio* itself, bear witness to intensive and extensive study of the Bishop of Hippo and his great mediaeval successor. The effect of such study was, inevitably, to center their interest round "justification" in Augustine's sense, the Spirit's work in the heart.[27]

The second conditioning factor was the Renaissance perspective. This combined with Augustine and the *Institutio* to focus the Puritan student's

---

18. *Workes*, II:1 f. Dr. Wood justly observes, "The quite extraordinary contribution made by Perkins in this and other treatises...has not yet received the recognition it deserves" (*op. cit.*, 34).

19. Ames heard Perkins' unfinished course of sermons on the cases of conscience (it was interrupted by the preacher's death), and testifies: "Yet left he behind him many affected with that study; who by their godly Sermons (through Gods assistance) made it to run, increase and be glorified throughout England. My heart hath ever since been ... set upon that study" ("To the Reader" in *Conscience with the ... Cases thereof*, 1643, E. T. of *De Conscientia*, 1630).

20. Baxter, *Works*, II:viii (*Christian Directory*, "Advertisement").

21. Wood, *op. cit.*, 36.

22. Baxter, *loc. cit.*

23. *R.B.*, I:122.

24. G. F. Nuttall, *The Holy Spirit*, 7.

25. It is noteworthy, for instance, that bk. III, chap. vi of Owen's treatise (*Works*, ed. W. Goold, 1850, III:337 f.) is entitled "The Manner of Conversion Explained in the Instance of Augustine," and is an exposition of the experience of "that eminent champion of the truth" (366) as typical and normal.

26. Baxter, "Preface" to W. Allen, *A Discourse of the Two Covenants*, 1673.

27. Baxter's opinion of Augustine is interesting and characteristic: he is "the best rational Divine" (*Third Defence of the Cause of Peace*, 1681, 15); but "I am more taken with his Confessions, than with his grammatical and scholastic treatises" (*Works*, XV:16).

attention on the absorbing question: what is man, and what may he become? The spirit of the age expressed itself in a ceaseless striving after self-consciousness. The seventeenth was "the century which has Hamlet as its prototype and exemplar."[28] It was as children of the secular Renaissance, as well as of the religious Reformation, that the Puritans sought "by intense introspection"[29] to know themselves. Everyman was learning to take his individuality seriously, and the preacher and his congregation found it both congenial and edifying to trace out the progress of his salvation. The Biblical themes of pilgrimage and conflict caught the imagination. The heroic and ultimately triumphant warfare which the Christian wages against the hosts of darkness, the world, the flesh and the devil, became a conception to conjure with. The popularity of Puritan preaching and biography after 1590 bear witness to this new interest in spiritual experience. The vivid imaginative prose in which the unfolding drama of Christian life was described reflects a new awareness, not merely of the evocative power of language, but of the high romance of the theme, and justifies Haller's references to "the Puritan epic of the fall and redemption of man" and "the Puritan saga."[30] Both the matter and the style of Puritan practical theology, as preached and printed, are imbued with the new individualistic outlook, the dramatic conception of life, to which the Renaissance gave birth.

We may here refer to the conceptual apparatus which the Puritans used to anatomize the soul. Their psychology was "a heritage from the Middle Ages ... an eclectic product, to which many writers had contributed[31]—Plato, Aristotle, Stoics, Neoplatonists. Aquinas had compiled it for the purpose of metaphysical analysis. The Puritans used it for psychological dissection. Variations of detail appear in different authors, but the outlines remain constant. The human personality is made up of three components: the *understanding* or reason, a faculty which uses material conveyed by the five exterior senses and the three interior senses (memory, imagination, and *sensus communis*) to discover truth and discern the possibilities of action; the *will*, a faculty which apprehends objects of thought as good, desires them and initiates action designed to secure them; and the *affections*, consisting of the "sensitive appetite" (the sum of desires stimulated and satisfied through the senses) and the affections proper (the whole gamut of emotional dispositions and reactions—love, joy, hope, fear, etc.). The entire man, the Puritans taught, ought to live to God, which means that the reason should be occupied apprehending Him, the affections delighting in Him, the will cleaving to Him and doing His pleasure.

28. G. F. Nuttall, *The Holy Spirit, loc. cit.*
29. W. Haller, *op. cit.*, 91.
30. *op. cit.*, 34, 157, etc.
31. Perry Miller, *The New England Mind*, 1939, 244. For the subject of this paragraph, see chap. IX, "The Nature of Man."

Man was made to love God with all his heart, mind and strength. But the Fall gave rise to a very different state of affairs. How a Puritan theologian, working with this psychology, thought of the chaotic effects of the Fall and the restorative work of God's Spirit we shall see later.

The Puritan preachers were agreed on exegetical and expository method. Their principles in this matter were given their first detailed statement by Perkins in *The Arte of Prophesying or, A Treatise Concerning The Sacred and Onely True Manner and Method of Preaching.*[32] Taking it for granted that Biblical doctrine is God's word and is neither incoherent nor inconsistent with itself, Perkins instructs the student as follows:

> Proceed to the reading of the Scriptures in this order: U sing a grammatical, rhetorical and logical analysis, and the help of the rest of the arts: read first the Epistle of *Paul* to the Romans; after that, the Gospel of *John* (as being indeed the keys of the new Testament) and then the other books of the new Testament will be the more easy when they are read. When all this is done, learn first the dogmatical books of the old Testament, especially the Psalms: then the Prophetical, especially *Isaiah*: Lastly, the historical, but chiefly *Genesis* ... [33]

Two things demand notice here: the direction to read the New Testament in light of Romans,[34] and the description of the Psalms as a "dogmatical" book. The Puritans went to the Psalms in order to supplement the New Testament account of the experiences of the elect soul, convicted, chastened, comforted and restored, and of the believer's proper behavior in each circumstance.

Having interpreted Scripture as a whole, the New Testament by Romans and the Old by the New, the student could safely proceed to the exposition of particular texts. In the pulpit, his task was this:

1. To read the text distinctly out of the Canonical Scriptures.
2. To give the sense and understanding of it being read, by the Scripture itself.
3. To collect a few and profitable points of doctrine out of the natural sense.
4. To apply (if he have the gift) the doctrine rightly collected, to the life and manners of men in a simple and plain speech.[35]

---

32. *Workes*, II:643 f: originally published in Latin, 1592.

33. *op. cit.*, 650 f.

34. This was nothing new: cf. Tyndale's Preface to Romans (*Doctrinal Treatises*, P.S., 1848, 484) in which he translates Luther's verdict on the epistle: "a bright light ... sufficient to give light unto all the Scripture;" and Calvin, *Argumentum in Epistolam Pauli ad Romanos*: "ergo jam ad argumentum ipsum transire satius fuerit; ... quod, si quis veram eius intelligentiam sit assequutus, ad reconditissimos quosque Scripturae thesauros adeundos habeat apertas fores." [Now it would be more satisfying to move to the argument itslef ... because anyone who secures a true understanding of it has an open door for getting to all the most deeply hidden treasures of Scripture.]

"Doctrines," explicit or implicit in the text, might consist of general propositions about God's self-revelation, or man's duty, or Christian experience. Once stated, they should be "confirmed" out of other passages of Scripture before "uses" were introduced. In the Westminster *Directory for the Publick Worship of God*,[36] where the same expository method is commended "as being found by experience to be very much blessed of God, and very helpful to the people's understandings and memories," the "uses" mentioned as desirable are these: "instruction or information in the knowledge of some truth ... ; confutation of false doctrines ... ; exhorting to duties ... ; dehortation, reprehension and publick admonition (which require special wisdom) ... ; applying comfort ... ; notes of trial ... whereby the hearers may examine themselves." Perkins' pupils and successors used this method almost exclusively. It soon replaced the discursive homily which we find in such Puritan pioneers as Greenham, Henry Smith, Richard Rogers and John Downame. Baxter claimed dominical sanction for it. When the Quakers objected to the formal extraction of "Doctrines, Reasons, Uses, Motives" out of a text, he answered them as follows:

> Know you not that Christ himself took a Text, Luk 4, and applied it? Know you not that it was then the common practice of the Church to reade, expound and apply the Scriptures, as Era did? Know you not that there is Doctrine, Reason and Use in all the Sermons and Epistles of the Apostles?[37]

The concern about "methode" which is apparent in this expository scheme derives from Ramist logic, which left its mark deep on Puritan thought. In the 1570's, "the system was established at Cambridge, and identified with Puritanism, principally through the work of the great commentators,"[38] among whom Prof. Miller notes Sir William Temple, George Downame, Alexander Richardson, Anthony Wotton and Ames himself. To this list of its advocates at Cambridge we may add Laurence Chaderton, first Master of Emmanuel and Puritan lecturer at St. Clement's for over fifty years.[39] Chaderton "read logic

---

35. Perkins, *op. cit.*, 673.

36. 1645; s.v. "Of the Preaching of the Word."

37. *The Quakers Catechism*, 23.

38. P. Miller, *op. cit.*, 499. For a survey of the Ramist system cf. chap. V, "The Instrument of Reason."

39. Chaderton seems to have been the first great Puritan preacher in Cambridge. "Before his time," his biographer tells us, "preaching had been a rarity in the University;" but his plain, straightforward exposition, free from the conventional classical tags and airing of erudition and animated by "a wonderful zeal for winning souls," created an audience and set a standard for his successors (W. Dillingham, *Life of Chaderton*, tr. E. S. Shuckburgh, 12). Thomas Goodwin records the statement of a contemporary who testified: "when he heard Mr. Chatterton (*sic*) preach the gospel his apprehension was as if the sun, namely Jesus Christ, shined upon a dunghill ..." (*Works*, 1861, II:lvi).

also in the public schools, and, lecturing on the *Ars Logica* of Peter Ramus, roused a great interest in that study throughout the University, which was afterwards so splendidly maintained by Downham (Downame)."[40] Perkins, Chaderton's younger contemporary, whose influence in the University seems to have been even greater,[41] was a Ramist too. Ramist logic suited the needs of preachers admirably, for it was avowedly designed to facilitate discourse and communication. "Dialectica est ars bene disserendi, eodemque sensu logica dicta est," was its basic postulate.[42] "The crowning achievement of the system was its doctrine of method[43]—i.e. of the way to organize ideas so as to make their content and their truth clear and memorable. Faulty juxtaposition and misconceived relations, it was pointed out, hinder the memory and obscure the truth by misleading the mind; a true method was the key to any and every branch of knowledge. The method itself was one of systematic dichotomy. It proceeded on the assumption that "the content of every science falls of itself into dichotomies"[44]—a dogma which, Ramists held, was amply validated by results. Ramus had developed the method in the first instance in order to overhaul and sort out the allegedly unmethodical jumble of categories which was Aristotle's legacy to logicians, and he had no doubt that it was a method which could be applied with as much success to the study of things as to the study of words. His method thus became a heuristic principle. It was taken as affording a clue to the structure of the universe, and was treated as "a sort of universal organology of all arts and sciences"[45]—including theology, "of all Arts, the supreme, most noble, and the masterpiece."[46] The problem for the theologian, as for any other student, was simply, Ramists held, to find the right point from which to start dichotomizing. It was essentially a problem of arrangement. Accordingly, we find that the principal concern of Puritan systematic theologians (notably Fenner, Perkins and Ames) is to find the correct method of subdividing a more or less fixed and accepted body of material, the

---

40. Dillingham, *op. cit.*, 5.

41. In 1613, Cambridge was "filled with the discourse of the power of Mr. Perkins' ministry" (Goodwin, *Works*, II:lviii), though Perkins died in 1602. Perkins "continued to be studied throughout the 17th century as a authority but little inferior to Hooker and Calvin" (J. B. Mullinger, in *D.N.B.*, s.v.).

42. P. Ramus, *Dialecticae* (1543), f.l. [Dialectic is the art of discussing well, and with that same meaning is called logic.]

43. P. Miller, *op. cit.*, 138.

44. *op. cit.*, 127.

45. Ames, *Marrow*, 3.

46. *op. cit.*, "A Briefe Premonition": "Some . . . will condemn the care of Method, and Logical form as curious and troublesome. But to them a sounder judgment is to be wished, because they remove the art of understanding, judgment and memory from those things, which do almost only deserve to be understood, known, and committed to memory."

precise outlines of which were expected to grow clearer as the analysis proceeded.

The conviction that instruction in theology, as in anything else, must be systematic and methodical found expression not only in the pulpit and in theological text-books, but in the production and use of catechetical literature. Puritan ministers laid great stress on the practice of catechizing. "The Puritan insistence on religious education found constant expression in the preparation of catechisms ... It seems probable that most learned and conscientious ministers prepared catechisms for the use of their congregations." The author continues by listing fifteen ministers connected with Elizabethan Puritanism who brought out catechisms between 1580 and 1593.[47] B. B. Warfield refers to "the amazing fecundity in catechetical manuals of the British churches" in the first half of the seventeenth century, and describes the Westminster Assembly as "eminently an assembly of catechists, trained and practiced in the art, of whom twelve (at least) had published catechisms prior to 1640."[48] Puritan catechisms were designed to impart "the sum of saving knowledge," and were fuller than the Catechism in the Book of Common Prayer; they normally dealt with God the Creator, the Scripture revelation, the Fall, the work of Christ as prophet, priest and king, the work of the Holy Spirit in the believer, the law and the doctrine of justification by faith, and the sacraments as seals and tokens of God's promises, in approximately that order.

In succeeding chapters we shall study Richard Baxter against this background. We shall find him a thorough Puritan from first to last. We shall see that he subscribed to the distinctive tenets of Calvinism, though differing with his fellows as to the correct way to state them. We shall find him employing the "practical and experimental" approach to theology, praising the Puritan masters of it and following in their steps. We shall discover that his psychology and philosophy, his exegesis and his preaching, are characteristically Puritan too. It will be shown that he shared to the full the Ramist concern for method, and that his alleged heterodoxy was entirely the result of adopting a method which, he held, fitted the facts better than any in current use. If Puritan theology is second-generation Calvinism, Baxter's theology is second-generation Puritanism. Baxter valued his heritage, but not blindly. He attempted what seemed to him a needed re-statement of received truth. From this all his troubles arose.

---

47. *Cartwrightiana*, ed. A. Peel and L. H. Carlson, 1951, 157.

48. B. B. Warfield, *The Westminster Assembly and its Work*, 64 and 69; cf. Baxter, *Works*, XIV:289, a remark dating from 1655: "How many scores, if not hundreds, of Catechisms are written in England!"

Chapter 3

The Puritan

SYNOPSIS

1.   Aim of chapter: to demonstrate Baxter's acceptance of Puritan ideals.

2.   A Puritan conversion: through Puritan books and friends. A typical experience.

3.   A Puritan convert:
   Baxter's diary
   practical studies
   ordination.

4.   A Puritan ministry: Baxter at Kidderminster:
   preaching
   catechizing
   family religion and Sunday observance
   discipline
   training and supplying preachers (lay preaching discouraged).

5.   A Puritan writer: Baxter's compendium of Puritan practical theology; his books widely read and translated.

6.   Baxter's advice to theological students.

7.   Conclusion: Baxter endorses the Puritan tradition at all points.

Chapter 3

The Puritan

"*Pseudo-Tilenus* and his Brother … say, I am *Purus Putus Puritanus*, and one *qui totum Puritanismus totus spirat*. Alas I am not so good and happy …"
—Baxter, 1680

In Chapter 1, we showed Baxter's place within the Puritan movement as a whole. In Chapter 2, we reviewed some of the characteristic features of Puritan theology and religion. Our present task is to demonstrate that all his life Baxter accepted and endorsed these views. We shall thus pave the way for the establishment of our main contention, that the whole of his originality in theological matters consisted in his method of stating and defending the Puritan tradition.

All the religious instruction which Baxter received in his youth came from Puritan sources. From the clergy of the immediate neighborhood, as we have seen, he learned and could learn little; and his confirmation was a farce.[1] But his father had been converted "by the bare reading of the Scriptures in private, without either Preaching, or Godly Company, or any other Books," and was a model Puritan paterfamilias. "When I was very young, his serious Speeches of God and the Life to come, possessed me with a fear of sinning!"[2] and this was

---

1. "In the bishops' days, some few … were confirmed; in the country where I lived, about one of ten or twenty; … how it was done, I can tell you … When I was a schoolboy, about fifteen years of age, the bishop coming into the country, many went in to him to be confirmed. We that were boys, ran out to see the bishop among the rest, not knowing any thing of the meaning of the business. When we came thither, we met about thirty or forty in all, of our own stature and temper, that had come for to be *bishopped*, as it was then called. The bishop examined us not … but in a church-yard, in haste, we were set in a rank, and he passed hastily over us, laying his hands on our head, and saying a few words, which neither I nor any that I spoke to understood; so hastily were they uttered, and a very short prayer recited, and there was an end" (*Works*, XIV:481). "We ran thither from School, without the Minister's knowledge, or one word from our Master, to tell us what Confirmation was" (*Second True Defence*, 1681, 101).
2. *R.B.*, I:2.

"the first good that ever I felt on my soul."[3] At fifteen, he read "an old torn Book ... called *Bunny's Resolution*" which his father had borrowed from "a poor Day-Labourer in the Town," and thereby "it pleased God to awaken my Soul, and show me the folly of Sinning, and the misery of the Wicked, and the unexpressible Weight of things Eternal, and the necessity of resolving on a Holy Life."[4] "And about that time it pleased God that a poor Pedlar came to the Door that had Ballads and some good Books: And my Father bought of him Dr. *Sibb's Bruised Reed*,"[5] from which Baxter learned of "the *Love of God* to me, and ... the mystery of Redemption ... After this we had a Servant that had a little piece of Mr. *Perkins's* Works (of *Repentance*, and the right *Art of Living and Dying well*, and the *Government of the Tongue*)[6] ... And thus (without any means but Books) was God pleased to resolve me for himself."[7] Baxter acquired a taste for Perkins. "I remember in the beginning how savoury to my reading was Mr. *Perkins'* short Treatise of the *Right Knowledge of Christ Crucified*, and his Exposition of the Creed; because they taught me how to live by Faith on Christ."[8]

Until he left home[9] "neither my Father nor I had any Acquaintance or Familiarity with any that had Understanding in Matters of Religion, nor ever heard any pray *ex tempore*."[10] Then, at Ludlow Castle, "it pleased God ... to give me one intimate Companion ... a daily Watchman over my Soul! We walk'd together, we read together, we prayed together ... he would be always stirring me up to Zeal and Diligence ... He was unwearied in reading all serious

---

3. *Works*, IX:229.

4. *R.B.*, I:3. For the book, cf. p. 33, note 2, supra. Baxter gives a remarkable testimony to its influence, *Against Revolt to a Foreign Jurisdiction*, 1691, 540: at a "Private Meeting" in Shrewsbury, when he was 21 (cf. p. 41 f., *inf.*), two ministers, "Mr. *Fowler*, Mr. Michael *Old* ...and *my self*" confessed that "the first lively motion that awakened their Souls to a serious resolved care of their Salvation, was the reading of *Bunnys* Book of Resolution;" and Baxter had "since heard of the same success with others." The passage is printed in full in F. J. Powicke, *Under the Cross*, 265 f.

5. *The bruised reede and smoaking flax*, 1630; Baxter probably read the second edition (1631).

6. *Two Treatises*: I. *Of the Nature and Practice of Repentance*; II. *Of the Combate of the Flesh and Spirit*, 1595, 1597; *A Treatise How to Live, and that Well; in all Estates and Times*, 1601, and *A Salve for a Sicke Man. Or, A Treatise Containing . . . . the Right Manner of Dying Well* (two separate treatises), 1595; *A Direction for the Government of the Tongue, according to Gods Word*, 1593, 1595.

7. *R.B.*, I:3 f.

8. *R.B.*, I:5. There is a similar testimony to *A Declaration of the True Manner of knowing Christ Crucified*, 1597, in *Universal Redemption*, 1694 (see App. I), p. 176, where this tract is called "the choicest piece I think that ever he wrote ... which I have cause to thank God that ever I saw."

9. In late 1631 or early 1632, "when I was ready for the University ... where were my vehement desires," Baxter was instead persuaded to go to Ludlow Castle and study under Richard Wickstead, "Chaplain to the Council there." Wickstead proved a disappointment: "He never read to me, nor used any savoury Discourse of Godliness" such as the boy had known at home (*R.B.*, I:4).

10. *loc. cit.* His father used "a form out of the end of the Common Prayer Book" (p.3); Baxter used "the *Confession* in the *Common-Prayer Book*, and some time one of Mr. *Bradford's Prayers* ... and sometime a Prayer out of another Prayer-Book which we had" (p. 4).

Practical books of Divinity; especially *Perkins, Bolton,* Dr. *Preston, Elton,* Dr. *Taylor, Whately, Harris,* & etc.[11] He was the first that ever I heard pray Ex tempore (out of the Pulpit) and that taught me so to pray."[12] When, shortly after he left Ludlow, his friend fell from grace,[13] Baxter, who had always been conscious of having "more knowledge than he, but a colder heart," began to fear the worst. "I was in many years doubt of my Sincerity, and thought I had no Spiritual Life at all ... I called my self the *most hard hearted Sinner,* that could *feel* nothing of all that I knew and talked of; ... all my Groans were for more *Contrition,* and a *broken Heart,* and I prayed most for *Tears* and *Tenderness.* And thus I complained for many years to God and Man ..."[14] A truly regenerate person, he supposed, would be far more deeply "affected" than he by the thought of his sin and of Christ's dying love. "This doubt lay heavy many a year on my own soul, when yet I would have given all that I had to be rid of sin, but I could not weep a tear for it."[15] Again, "I could not distinctly trace the Workings of the Spirit upon my heart in that method which Mr. *Bolton,* Mr. *Hooker,* Mr. *Rogers,* and other Divines describe! nor knew the Time of my Conversion[16] ... But I understood at last that God breaketh not all mens hearts alike;"[17] and that "it is not possible that one of very many should be able to give any true account of the *just Time* when Special Grace began."[18] Again, for a time "I was so foolish" as to make a tranquil life a ground for doubt. "It is about seventeen years since I was troubled ... thinking I was no son, because I was not afflicted," he wrote in 1653, "and I think I have had few days without pain for this sixteen

---

11. For Thomas Taylor, William Whateley, Robert Harris, cf. *D.N.B.* s.vv. Edward Elton, rector of St. Mary Magdalene, Bermondsey, from 1605 to his death, in 1624, was best known for his *Exposition of . . . . Colossians* (1615; 3rd ed. 1637).

12. *R.B.,* I:4.

13. He took to drink, and abandoned Puritan religion, maintaining that "such as *Bolton* were too severe, and enough to make men mad: And the last I heard of him was, that he was grown a Fudler, and Railer at strict men ... " (*R.B.,* I:4).

14. *R.B.,* I:5.

15. *Works,* IX:232 (*Right Method* ... 1653).

16. The works referred to are probably R. Bolton: *Instructions for a Right Comforting Afflicted Consciences,* 1631; T. Hooker, *The Souls Preparation for Christ. Or, a Treatise of Contrition. Wherein is discovered how God breaks the heart, and wounds the soul in the conversion of a sinner to himself,* 1632; J. Rogers, *The Doctrine of Faith,* 1627. In all three, stress is laid on the necessity for a thorough, "affectionate" repentance by the sinner. Hooker describes "contrition" as follows (p.2): "when a sinner by the sight of sin, and vileness of it, and punishment due to it, is made sensible of sin, and is made to hate it, and hath his heart separated from the same." See ch. VIII, infra.

17. *R.B.,* I:7.

18. *op. cit.* p.6; cf. *Works,* IX:222 (1653, as above): "According to that experience which I have had of the state of Christians, I am forced to judge that most of the children of the godly that ever are renewed, are renewed in their childhood ... and that among forty Christians there is not one that can certainly name the month in which his soul began to be sincere; and among a thousand Christians, I think not one can name the hour. The sermon which awakened them, they may name, but not the hour when they first arrived at a saving sincerity."

years since together, nor but few hours, if any one, for this six or seven years. And thus my scruple is removed."[19] "Peace and Comfort" finally came through

> 1. The reading of many Consolatory Books.
> 2.... . When I heard many make the very same Complaints that I did, who were People of whom I had the best esteem, for the uprightness and holiness of their Lives, it much abated my fears and troubles ...
> 3. And it much increased my peace when God's Providence called me to the comforting of many others that had the same Complaints: While I answered their Doubts, I answered my own ...[20]

Then, too, "God was pleased much to comfort and settle me by the acquaintance of some Reverend peaceable Divines:" Francis Garbett, vicar of Wroxeter since 1609, George Baxter, rector of Little Wenlock since 1608 ("very holy men and peaceable, who laboured faithfully with little success till they were above fourscore years of Age apiece"[21]), and Samuel Smith, a prolific Puritan author, of Cressage, "one of my most familiar friends."[22] Moreover, "at about 20 years of Age (i.e., 1635-6) I became acquainted with Mr. *Simmonds*, Mr. *Cradock* and other very zealous godly Nonconformists in Shrewsbury, and the adjoining parts, whose fervent Prayer and savoury Conference and holy Lives did profit me much."[23] So Baxter found peace.

This Odyssey is the record of a typical Puritan conversion. First, a new

19. *Works*, IX:259 f. The "sixteen years" must date from the beginning of the period "from the age of 21 till near 23" when "my Weakness was so great, that I expected not to live above a year" (*R.B.*, I:12). Baxter was 21 on Nov. 12, 1636.

20. *R.B.*, I:9. Before his ordination, he records, "God blessed my private Conference to the Conversion of some" (p. 84).

21. *R.B.*, I:9.

22. *loc. cit.* When Baxter first studied the case for Nonconformity (?1636-7), Garbett and Smith "did send me *Downham, Sprint*, Dr. *Burges*, and others of the strongest that had wrote against the Nonconformists" (p. 13). They and George Baxter belonged to the group "called then conformable Puritans" ("History ..." prefixed to Baxter's *Treatise of Episcopacy*).

23. *R.B.*, I:13. Baxter mentions his association with Richard Symonds and Walter Cradock (*D.N.B.*, s.vv.) in "Reasons ... why Dr. John Owen's Twelve Arguments change not Richard Baxter's Judgment" in *Catholic Communion Defended*, 1684, p. 28: "Mr. *W. Cradocke* ... was a most zealous man for practical godliness, with whom I conversed in my Youth, when in Mr. Rich. Simond's School in Shrewsbury, he was concealed from the Bishops pursuit, by the name of Mr. *Williams*. But how gross an Antinomian he turned after he had learned Separation, his Printed Sermons tell us ..." He is mentioned in *R.B.*, I:111 as one of the Antinomians whom Baxter's "ungrateful Controversial writings" had silenced. In 1650, we find Baxter heartily recommending his *Gospel-Libertie*, 1648 (*Plain Scripture Proof*, pp. 7, 134); but in his *Right Method*, 1653, while attacking the Antinomian view that no sin should make a believer question his sincerity, he wrote sadly: "Such like passages I lately read in some printed sermons of one of my ancient acquaintance, who would never have come to that pass ... if his judgment and humility had been as great as his zeal" (*Works*, IX:124). Baxter is referring to *Divine Drops Distilled*, 1650, or *Gospel-Holinesse*, 1651.

religious concern was awakened; this led to the experience of a fluctuating, struggling faith, shaken by periodic failure and swayed by the winds of doubt; and this, in its turn, gradually gave way to a settled and joyful assurance. The story could be paralleled again and again from Puritan autobiography and hagiology. *Grace Abounding* does not stand alone. The passage from doubt to assurance was often a long and painful process. In Baxter's case, it took five or six years; in Bunyan's, probably four; and Thomas Goodwin, though he could name the day of his conversion[24] and was wrought on "even as our own divines in Great Britain do set out in their discourse of the manner of conversion in the effect of it,"[25] spent seven anxious years seeking "the signs of grace in me," "examining the inherent work in me wrought by the Spirit," before he gained assurance of his salvation.

The young convert continued along the path which the Puritan preachers had marked out. He kept a diary: "I used to keep a daily Catalogue of my daily Mercies and Sins."[26] He "improved" his chronic ill-health, which "made me vile and loathsome to my self, and made Pride one of the hatefullest sins in the world to me! It made the World seem to me as a Carcase ... It set me upon that Method of my Studies, which since I have found the benefit of ... *Divinity* ... always had the first and chiefest place! And it caused me to study Practical *Divinity* first, in the most *Practical Books*, in a *Practical Order*, doing all purposely for the informing and reforming of my own Soul ... By which means my *Affection* was carried on with my judgment ..."[27] In 1638, "being conscious of a thirsty desire of Mens Conversion and Salvation, and of some competent persuading Faculty of Expression, which fervent Affections might help to actuate,"[28] he was ordained. After spending some months teaching "in the new

24. Immediately after a sermon "on Monday the 2nd of October 1620, in the afternoon" (*Works*, ed. J. C. Miller, 1861, II:liv).

25. *op. cit.*, p. lxi. For this "manner of conversion," see chap. VIII *inf.*

26. *R.B.*, I:21. For the Puritan diary, see W. Haller, *op cit.*, pp. 38, 96 f. A notable example (by Richard Rogers, author of the *Seven Treatises*, cf. p. 34, note 2) is printed in *Two Elizabethan Puritan Diaries*, ed. M. M. Knappen, 1933. The first English diarist of this kind seems to have been John Bradford, who wrote "an ephemeris or a journal ... of daily practices of repentance" ("Sampson to the Christian Reader" prefixed to the 1574 reprint of Bradford's *Sermon of Repentance*. *Works* (P.S.), 1848, I:35). Baxter saw in later years that one could easily "over-do" in transcribing the minutiae of spiritual autobiography. In his funeral sermon for Mrs. Elizabeth Baker (*A Treatise of Death*, 1660), having described her elaborate diary with approval, he wisely observed: "To those Christians that have full leisure, this course is good; but I urge it not upon all. Those that ... cannot spare so much [time] ... must ... record only the extraordinary, observable and more remarkable and memorable passages of their lives, lest they lose time from works of greater moment" (*Works*, XVII:601 f.). This was his own mature practice.

27. *R.B.*, I:5 f. "I repent not of this unusual method" (*Works*, XVIII:76). In these early years, he read "the most of all our English practical divines."

28. *R.B.*, I:12.

school at *Dudley*,"[29] he move to Bridgnorth, where "I was in the fervour of my Affections, and never any where preached with more vehement desires of Mens Conversion."[30]

In Baxter's Kidderminster ministry[31] appears the full flowering of the Puritan pastoral ideal. Preaching from texts which he "opened" by the method of doctrine, reason and use, he preached "with greatest importunity" "the great Fundamental principles of Christianity ... the knowledge of God our Creator, Redeemer and Sanctifier, and Love and Obedience to God, and Unity with the Church Catholick, and Hope of Life Eternal."[32] In 1653 he began to catechize the parish by rota.[33] "We spend Monday and Tuesday from morning to almost night in the work," he reported in 1656,[34] "taking about fifteen or sixteen families in a week, that we may go through the parish, which hath above eight hundred families in a year,"[35] "my Assistant ... going through the Parish[36] and the Town coming to me." When the families arrived, "I first heard them recite the Words

29. p. 13. Here "private Christians ... godly honest people" tried to convert him to Nonconformity; and it was either here or with his Shrewsbury friends that he fasted and prayed "before the Parliament began ... in secret" for "a faithful Ministry; and exercise of Discipline in the Church." (Bridgnorth was "privileged from all Episcopal Jurisdiction," p. 15, and secrecy there would have been pointless.) Baxter continues (*Works*, XIV:291): "Oh the earnest prayers that I have heard in secret days heretofore, for a painful Ministry and for Discipline! ... As if they had even wrestled for salvation itself!"

30. *R.B.*, I:15.

31. April, 1641 - July, 1642; Summer, 1647 - April, 1660. Baxter came as Lecturer only and never regarded himself as more, though the Trustees had him made vicar without his knowledge in 1647 (Powicke, *Life*, 81 f.).

32. *R.B.*, I:93. "I came and Preached there twice every Lords-day, and a Thursday-lecture every fortnight, besides Funeral-Sermons, &c., for about a year and a half" (*Apology for the Nonconformists Ministry*, 70). John Cross of Kinver, "the chief means of the good which was done in *Kidderminster* before my coming thither" (*R.B.*, I:24), preached each alternate Thursday. "I preached ... after the war but once (i.e., on Sunday), and once every Thursday, besides occasional sermons" (83). Thursday was doubtless chosen for the Lecture because it was market-day (*Apology*, 71). His assistant (first Richard Sergeant, then Humphrey Waldern, Thomas Baldwin and finally Joseph Read: *C.R.*, S.vv., the first two as Serjeant and Waldron) preached the second Sunday sermon.

33. The *terminus post quem* is the formation of the Worcestershire Association in 1653. Its constitution would certainly have contained some reference to catechizing had Baxter by then proved its value. A request for advice about catechizing (Mss. 59.v.50f) from Abraham Pinchbecke, whom Baxter had urged to this task, is dated Nov. 11, 1653; by this date, it seems, Baxter was a practiced catechist, and known as such. The *Reformed Pastor*, originally conceived as a sermon for a fast day kept by the Associated Ministers on Dec. 4, 1655 after they had subscribed the Agreement for Catechizing, reveals its author as a family catechist of wide experience.

34. *Works*, XIV:xxi (*Reformed Pastor*).

35. The statement in *R.B.*, I:83 (1685) must refer to a later period: "all the Afternoons on Mondays and Tuesdays I spent in this ... And my Assistant spent the Morning of the same days." Baxter probably found it too tiring to deal with "one family at eight o'clock, the next at nine" and so on all day, as he was doing in 1655 (*Works, loc. cit.*).

36. *R.B.*, I:83. The Parish included "beside a great Borough about 20 villages" and was "near 20 miles about" (*Apology*, 75; *R.B.*, I:88). Most of the "ignorant and ungodly persons" were found

of the Catechism,[37] and then examined them about the *Sense*, and lastly urged them with all possible engaging Reason and Vehemency, to answerable Affection and Practice."[38] During this hour's interview, "I spent myself as much as in a Sermon at least."[39] The devotion in which this Reformed evangelist trained his converts was as characteristically Puritan as his own. Stress was laid on family religion,[40] Sunday observance,[41] and the reading of the Bible and of Puritan devotional books.[42]

Moreover, Baxter put into practice the scheme for Church discipline which was the platform of the Worcestershire Association. The plan was of necessity operated on a voluntary basis, and members of the congregation were free to refuse to "live under discipline;" though Baxter withheld the sacraments from them if they did. On the first Wednesday of each month, offenders who had defied private admonition were summoned before a body consisting of Baxter, "three Godly Justices of Peace" who had agreed to cooperate, "four ancient Godly men that performed the office of Deacons" and "above twenty of the Seniors of the Laity," the latter being present merely as witnesses, and there they were publicly admonished and urged to amendment. If they remained unmoved, they were called next day before the monthly meeting of the

---

"in those parts of the Parish which were furthest from the Town" (85). Within this area was "a chapelry, catechized by another assistant" (*Works, loc. cit.*)—Mitton. The rest of the area was catechized by Sergeant, although, Baxter notes, "a considerable part of *Kidderminster* parish, called *Ridnal* (=Wribbenhall), being at *Bewdley Bridge* end, and 2 miles from *Kidderminster* (and some Villages more) usually were Mr. *Tombes* his hearers at *Bewdley*, and I never blamed them. After this (i.e., from 1650) they were Hearers and Communicants to his Successor Mr. *Oasland*, and he took the Pastoral care of them" (*Second True Defence*, 71). The parish is described by Powicke, *Life*, 43.

37. The Westminster Shorter Catechism: cf. *Agreement* ... 1656, art. V, p. 6: "We shall desire all our parishioners to learn the ancient Creed, with our Expository profession ... containing in it the ten Commandments and the Lords Prayer, and the Assemblies shorter Catechism ... or if any pretend Scruples ... they shall use any Orthodox Catechism which themselves will choose ..."

38. *R.B.*, I:83.

39. *Apology*, 72.

40. cf. *Christian Directory*, II ("Christian Economics"). ii-iv (*Works*, IV). "You are like to see no general reformation till you procure family reformation," he had written in 1655 (XIV:99). When Baxter left, "Abundance ... were able to pray very *laudably* with their families" (*R.B.*, I:85).

41. "On the Lord's Days there was no disorder to be seen in the Streets, but you might hear an hundred Families singing Psalms and repeating Sermons as you passed through the Streets ... when I came thither first, there was about one Family in a street that worshipped God ... and when I came away there were some streets where there was not past one Family that did not so ..." (*loc. cit.*).

42. "See that they have some profitable, moving book (besides the Bible) in each family ... such as Mr. Whateley's *New Birth*, and Dod on the Commandments ... and engage them to read it on nights when they have leisure, and especially on the Lord's day" (*Works*, XIV:99: *Reformed Pastor*). Baxter utilized "the Writings which I wrote" for this purpose: "Some small books I gave each family one of ... And every Family that was poor, and had not a Bible, I gave a Bible to" (*R.B.*, I:89).

Associated ministers; and continued obstinacy led to their ejection from the congregation.[43] Although "for very fear of Discipline, all the Parish kept off except about Six hundred" out of sixteen hundred eligible,[44] and, in the case of the five or so "cast out," "one for slandering and all the rest for drunkennes," "their Enmity was much encreased,"[45] Baxter's final judgment on the experiment was favorable:

> We knew it to be an Ordinance of Christ, and greatly conducing to the Honour of the Church; which is not ... a Sty of Swine, but must be cleaner than the Societies of Infidels and Heathens: And I bless God that I ever made trial of Discipline; for my Expectations were not frustrate, though the ejected Sinners were hardened: The Churches Good must be first regarded.

Nothing could be more representative of the "disciplinarian" outlook. This Reformed High Churchmanship was always the context of the Puritan concern for the welfare of the individual.

While at Kidderminster, Baxter gave active expression to his characteristically Puritan concern for the training of a godly ministry. This, to him, was as essential as discipline for God's glory in his Church. The Reformed pastor's task, as evangelist, pastor and ruler, required "over-topping Ministerial abilities,"[46] which, Baxter considered, could not normally be developed outside a University.[47] Accordingly, one of the "good works" which he urged on the rich and led the way in himself was the financing of poor undergraduates. "There went about Eleven or Twelve out of Kidderminster Parish and School to the *University* and *Ministry* in my time."[48] Lay preaching he consistently discouraged, as being improper in principle and unedifying in practice. He records with satisfaction that one of the effects of his Thursday night meetings, at which the morning's lecture was repeated and "cases of consciences" ventilated, was that "by encouraging them here in the fit exercise of their parts, in Repetition, Prayer, and asking Questions, I kept them from inclining to the

43. The details are given in *Treatise of Episcopacy*, II:185 f., and *R.B.*, II:150 (printed in Powicke, *Life*, 114).

44. *R.B.*, I:91.

45. p. 91 f. Details of some of these cases are given by Powicke, *Life*, 109 f. One of those ejected assaulted Baxter "on the Fair-day ... as I went to Church (? to lecture?) ... with a purpose to have killed me."

46. *R.B.*, I:93.

47. "Want of that measure of Learning and Experience, which so great and high Work required" had made the non-graduate Baxter diffident about the propriety of his ordination (12).

48. Powicke, *Life*, 154 f., gives details about four of them, including Joseph Read, later Baxter's assistant.

49. *R.B.*, I:88; cf. *Apology*, 76: "I still found that to let them do what belonged to them as private men, was the means to keep them from that which belonged only to Ministers ... to drive them hard on their proper duty in their families, was the best way to convince them, that they had neither ability nor leisure for more ..."

disorderly exercise of them, as the Sectaries do."[49] Meanwhile, to supplement the ministrations of "Poor weak Preachers, that had no great Skill in Divinity, nor Zeal for Godliness" the Londoners' lecture was set up, three able members of the Association being appointed itinerants for the area.[50] In addition, on the first Thursday of each month "the Neighbour-ministers met at the lecture, and afterwards ... in an honest neighbour's private house[51] ... our usual work was a Disputation on some useful point in Divinity, to exercise and edifie the younger sort."[52]

Moreover, while at Kidderminster Baxter became at once the most prolific and the most successful of Puritan practical writers. He had at first been reluctant to appear in print—"I oft resisted the requests of my reverend brethren, and some superiors, who might else have commanded much more at my hands," he wrote in 1649[53]—but the *Saints' Everlasting Rest* (1650) put him at once in the front rank of devotional authors. He began to receive letters "from learned and judicious divines, importuning me to print more, having understood my intentions to desist."[54] Accordingly, he published in 1653 *The Right Method for a Settled Peace of Conscience*, which further enhanced his reputation. Then, in the following year, he met Archbishop Usher, "who much approving my ... *Directions* for *Peace of Conscience*, was importunate with me to write *Directions* suited to the various states of Christians, and also against particular Sins."[55] Baxter at first refused, but returned to the project three years later. In the Preface to *A Call to the Unconverted to Turn and Live . . . . From the living God*, dated Dec. 10, 1657, he outlined his program as follows:

> Having of late intended to write a "Family Directory," I began to apprehend how congruously the forementioned work should lead the way; and the several conditions of men's souls be spoken to, before we come to the several relations.

50. *R.B.*, I:95. For the institution of this "moveable lecture on the Lord's Day," see the Epistle "To all the Rest of the Ministers of the Gospel in this County" appended to the *Reformed Pastor* (*Works*, XIV:398 f.).

51. Powicke, who asserts that Baxter somehow entertained them in his own two small rooms, (*Life*, 47, note 1) must have overlooked this passage. He confuses these monthly meetings with the gatherings on the other Thursdays, described in the next note.

52. *Apology*, 74. "About 20" were usually present. Baxter was "almost constant Moderator ... (usually) I prepared a written Determination." Baxter enjoyed some clerical fellowship each Thursday; cf. *R.B.*, I:84: "every *Thursday* ... I had the Company of divers godly Ministers at my House after the Lecture, with whom I spent that Afternoon in the truest Recreation, till my Neighbours came to meet for their Exercise of Repetition and Prayer." These Thursday afternoons seem to have been Baxter's nearest approach to a holiday.

53. *Works*, XXI:1.

54. İX:xv.

55. *R.B.*, I:114.

Hereupon I resolved, by God's assistance, to proceed in the order following. First, to speak to the impenitent, unconverted sinners ... And with these, I thought, a wakening persuasive was a more necessary means ... My next work must be for those that have some purposes to turn ... to direct them for a thorough and true conversion ... The third part must be directions for the younger and weaker sort of Christians ... The fourth part, directions for lapsed and backsliding Christians, for their safe recovery. Besides these, there is intended some short persuasions and directions against some special errors of the time, and against some common, killing sins. As for directions to troubled, doubting consciences, that is done already[56] ... And then the last part is intended more especially for families as such, directing the several relations in their duties.[57]

Accordingly, he followed the *Call* (his "wakening persuasive") with *Directions and Persuasions to a Sound Conversion* (1658); *Directions for Weak, Distempered Christians* (1668);[58] *A Treatise of Self-Denial* (1660), against "flesh-pleasing;" *Catholic Unity* (1659), against carnal religious divisions; *The Crucifying of the World by the Cross of Christ* (1658), against worldliness—in Baxter's view three "common killing sins;"[59] and, last, the massive *Christian Directory* (1673), a companion volume to the *Methodus Theologiae* ("one compleat Body of *Theology*, The *Latin* one the theory, and the English one the Practical part").[60] "For the families and persons that cannot have and use so large a volume," an enlarged edition of *The Life of Faith* came out in 1670;[61] and *The Poor Man's Family Book*, a smaller and more popular treatment of the Christian life, designed to replace *The Plain Man's Path-way*, was published in 1674. In these and in his other practical writings, Baxter brought Puritan hortatory prose to its highest point of development; on the strength of them, Doddridge styled him the English Demosthenes.[62] By 1665, his books were

---

56. i.e., *The Right Method*.

57. *Works*, VII:cccxxx f.

58. Sermons preached in the weekly lecture in 1658. "This I intended for the third part ... but was hindered from bringing it to the purposed perfection." He eventually published this "imperfect piece" after the unauthorized appearance of a garbled version of his last sermon at Blackfriars (on the same text, Col. 2:6-7) in order "to cashier that farewell sermon" ("Preface:" *Works*, VIII:cclvi f.) The Preface is dated 1665, but Baxter could not get a license to print it till 1668 (*R.B.*, I:123).

59. A further separate treatise against "pride of life" was projected (*Works*, XI:273: *Self-Denial*) but never apparently written. There is however a detailed treatment of this topic in *Christian Directory*, I:iv, 5.

60. *R.B.*, III:190. Jeannette Tawney's description of the *Directory* alone as "a Puritan *Summa Theologica* and *Summa Moralis* in one" (*Chapters from a Christian Directory*, 1925, Introduction, ix) is misleading.

61. *Works*, II:9 (*Christian Directory*, "Advertisement"). The original *Life of Faith* (4to, 70 pp.) was a sermon preached before Charles II in 1660.

62. Doddridge, *Works*, V:431.

being read as far afield as Poland, Hungary and Switzerland.[63] In the last year of his life, he could write of them as follows: "About Twelve ... are translated into the German tongue; and the Lutherans say They have done good.[64] Some are translated into French[65] ... Multitudes say, they have been the means of their Conversion, and more of their Information, Confirmation and Consolation."[66] The author of the "Preface" to the collected edition of Baxter's *Practical Works*, published in 1707, affirms: "there is no Language in which there are more Valuable Treatises of Practical Divinity to be met with, than in ours; And perhaps ... there are no writings of this Kind ... that have been more esteem'd abroad, or more bless'd at home ... than the Practical Works of this author."[67]

Baxter never renounced his heritage. To the end of his life he saw it as his calling to spread and defend the doctrinal, religious and ecclesiastical views which the Puritan fathers had taught him. He adhered to the judgment expressed in the first book he wrote, that "our English divines are ... the most sound of any in the world."[68] His doctrine, he insisted, was theirs. "See whether all the divines that have been very practical and successful in the work of God

63. Baxter, *Works*, VIII:cclviii.

64. G. Waterhouse (*Literary Relations of England and Germany in the Seventeenth Century*, 1934, 108 f.) gives the following titles: *Der Quacker Catechismus*, 1663; *Von der Verlangnung Unser Selbst*, 1665; *Die Wahre Bekehrung*, 1673; *Nun oder Niemahls*, 1678; *Der Heiligen Ewige Ruhe*, 1684; *Christliches Hauss-Buch* (*The Poor Man's Family Book*) and *Ein Heilige oder Ein Vieh*, 1685; and, after Baxter's death, *Ausgesonderte Schrifften* (including *Right Method*, *Life of Faith*, *The Vain Religion of the Formal Hypocrite*, *The Fool's Prosperity* and *The Redemption of Time*, an essay prefixed to the 1673 reprint, which Baxter sponsored, of William Whateley's tract of that name), and *Theologische Politick*. The translator of the latter refers to earlier versions by himself of the *Treatise of Conversion*, *The Unreasonableness of Infidelity*, and *The Crucifying of the World by the Cross of Christ*, but Waterhouse found no trace of them. Baxter's statement about the Lutherans probably rests on two surviving letters. The first comes from a pastor, Antony Brunsen, a friend of Spener, who wrote from Potsdam on Oct. 27, 1687 (Mss.59.I. f.113-114) to enclose a copy of his own German translation of *The Poor Man's Family Book* and to express his appreciation of it. The second, dated July 2, 1688 (59.VI. f. 56-57) is from Peter Christopher Martin, a student, of Dresden. He attributes his own conversion to *Nun oder Niemahls*, and proclaims himself a great admirer of Baxter's writings. He supplements Waterhouse's list by mentioning German versions of *The One Thing Necessary*, *The Life of Faith*, "praeparationem ευθαναεἰαυ" (?*Dying Thoughts*), "de Conversatione cum Deo" (?*The Divine Life*, of which part II is entitled "Walking with God," and Part III "The Christian's Converse with God"), and "quod imprimis ponerem, Manuale pauperum (*The Poor Man's Family Book*) bis in nostram linguam translatum. Cuius insignis utilitas ... Spenero nostro ... valde probatur."

65. Baxter mentions a French translation of his *Call to the Unconverted*, R.B., I:115. (John Eliot, he there records, also translated it into Red Indian, and Baxter mentions a Dutch edition of it, "my *family booke* and others" in a letter to Samuel Hutchins dated Dec. 16, 1680 (Mss.59. VI f.4).

66. *Penitent Confession*, "Preface."

67. *Practical Works* (1707), I:iii.

68. *Works*, XXII:489 (*Saint's Rest*).

... be not all of the same judgment as I ..."[69] His loyalty to Puritan ideals appears most clearly in the advice which he gives to theological students in the *Christian Directory*. "The poorest or smallest library that is tolerable," he tells them, consists of a Bible, Concordance, commentary, "some English catechisms," Ames' *Marrow, De Conscientia* and *Bellarminus Enervatus*, "some of the soundest English books which open the doctrine of grace" and "as many affectionate practical English writers as you can get, especially ..."—and he lists over sixty.[70] He urges them to study according to the "practical method" which a kindly providence had led him to adopt:

> Begin with a conjunction of English catechisms, and the confession of all the churches, and the practical holy writings of our English divines ...never separate them asunder. These practical books do commonly themselves contain the principles, and do press them in so warm a working manner as is likest to bring them to the heart: and till they are there, they are not received according to their use, but kept as it were in the porch ... Think not that you well understand Divinity, till, 1. You know it as methodized and jointed in a due scheme, ... 2. Till it be wrought into your very hearts, and digested into a holy nature ...[71]

For their subsequent guidance in the ministry, they could turn to the record of Baxter's "comfortable Successes" in his Puritan ministry at Kidderminster, which he wrote "for their sakes that would have the Means of other Mens Experiments, in managing ignorant and sinful Parishes."[72]

Enough evidence has now been brought to show that, not merely as churchman, but as pastor, writer and Christian, Baxter was a Puritan to his finger-tips. He was a traditionalist by temperament, and a defender of the "old paths" of Puritanism by conviction. It seems paradoxical that those of his views which were branded Arminian, Papist and Socinian should have been put forward for no other reason than to vindicate these "old paths"; but this, as we shall see, was the case.

---

69. IX:96 (*Right Method*).

70. V. 587 f. J. H. Alstedius' four-volume *Encyclopaedia* completes the list of indispensable books. The catena of "practical writers" includes works by Prelatical writers (Hammond's *Practical Catechism*, 1644, Pearson on the Creed, Andrewes on the Commandments and ?R. Allestree's *The Whole Duty of Man*), and some Christian biography (Samuel Clark's "Lives " and "Martyrology," and *The Life and Death of Joseph Alleine*, published by Baxter himself in 1672).

71. *Works*, V:582.

72. *R.B.*, I:86.

Chapter 4

The Man and His Mind

SYNOPSIS

1. Aim of chapter: general study of Baxter as a thinker. His practical motive.

2. The basis of Puritan thought: knowledge a hierarchical unity. Augustinian foundation of this scheme. "Ordo" the clue to meaning in the created order.

3. Baxter's assumption of the unity of knowledge: organization of secular studies under theology.
    Corollaries: a. Need to reform University curriculum.
    b. Need to distinguish priorities in study: practical relevance the criterion: physics and history the Christian's priorities: controversy creates further priorities for ministers.

4. Baxter's epistemology: knowledge a mental impression gained via sense. Trustworthiness of sense axiomatic.
    Difficulty of forming true concepts from sense data:
    many perceptions needed to form one concept;
    many inadequate concepts needed to comprehend one thing;
    many concepts needed to abstract one universal;
    many pitfalls inherent in education:
    concepts, taught by words, need revision by things:
    this is a moral and intellectual feat:
    words are inadequate for conveyance of truth.
    Baxter's experience: revision of concepts revolutionized his thought.
    Effects of revision on his: philosophical theology controversial activity and theological reputation.

5. Baxter's reformation of the sciences: physics (bodies and spirits) metaphysics and logic.
    Fruitlessness of his efforts: his assumptions outworn.

6. Catechetical and theological method:
    the first designed to make truths objects of "fides divina";
    the second designed to reveal the mutual relations of these truths.
    Catechetical method: designed to teach the essentials of Christianity

(baptismal covenant and three summaries);
Theological method: difficult to discover and master:
    must fit all Biblical facts;
    presupposes secular studies.
        Baxter's programme for theological education.

7.   Baxter's theological method:
        its scope—creation and redemption;
        its principle of arrangement—trichotomy;
        its key-concept—*regnum Dei.*
    A Scriptural method:
        Methodus Theologiae a characteristic work.

8.   "Affectionate, practical" character of theological knowledge.
    Corollaries:
        a. Heresy a practical matter;
        b. Doctrines that made against practice must be false;
        c. Papist practice proved that Catholics knew God.

9.   Baxter's doctrine of reason:
        Reason an instrument for discerning truth by evidence:
            Christian truth must be demonstrable: Baxter thought
                he could prove it.
    Baxter's conquest of temptations to skepticism.
    Demand for demonstration criticized as Socinian.
        Position of critics:
            the elect through the Spirit perceive the Bible to be the
                Word of God;
            Biblical statements, as such, are the objects of faith.
        Baxter's objections:
            a. Faith possible apart from the Bible.
            b. Canon of Scripture not self-evident.
            c. Nature of Spirit's testimony obscured.
    True method of presenting Christianity:
        false method followed by critics (Owen).

10.   Degrees of certainty within Christian truth:
        agreement not to be expected or required on non-essentials.
    Baxter criticized for omitting perseverance from the Worcestershire
        Profession.

11.   The split within Puritanism: rationalists (Cambridge Platonists);
                                  dogmatists (John Owen).
    Baxter's comprehensive synthesis.

Chapter 4

The Man and His Mind

"A Christian is a sanctified philosopher" —Baxter.

"His thoughts had a peculiar edge" —Calamy, *Own Life*, I:221.

"I have long thought it one of the most principal concerns in Method, to follow the conduct of Nature in suiting our Form to the Matter, and not our Matter to the Form, as the Schools are wont" —Theophilus Gale, "A Summary ..." before W. Strong, *A Discourse of the Two Covenants,* 1678.

"I warned you that Theology is practical ... Theology is, in a sense, experimental knowledge" —C. S. Lewis.

For a just estimate of any constructive thinker, one must know three things: the contemporary climate of thought within which his work was done, his own characteristic cast of mind, and the motives which led him to study and, within his chosen field, to attach significance to, one thing rather than another. The three might be distinguished as intellectual environment, heredity and interest. In Baxter's case, the third has already become clear. His interest and standpoint as a thinker and theologian was determined by the fact that he was a Puritan Christian and a Puritan minister, whose life's work, as he saw it, was to teach and vindicate Puritan ideals, personal, pastoral and ecclesiastical. (We shall later see reason to add, political and philosophical also.) His concern was always practical. Knowledge is for use, and its relative value depends on the degree of its usefulness. "Knowing is not the end of knowing ... Every truth of God is his candle which he sets up for you to work by; it is as food that is for life and action. You lose all the knowledge that ends in knowing ... Every degree of knowledge is for a further degree of holiness ..."[1] The second part of his

1. *Works*, III:241 f.

treatise on I Cor. 8:2-3, *Knowledge and Love Compared* (1689), is an exposition and application of four "doctrines," of which the first three are these:

> Doct. I. Knowledge is a means to a higher end, according to which it is to be estimated.
> Doct. II. The end of knowledge is to make us lovers of God, and so to be known with love by him.
> Doct. III. Therefore knowledge is to be valued, sought and used, as it tendeth to this holy, blessed end."[2]

To seek knowledge for its own sake is a sinful waste of time; to spread unprofitable knowledge, equally so. "If this narrative be useless to the readers, it must needs by the sin of the publisher," is the opening reflection of the last chapter in Baxter's tribute to his wife's memory, and the chapter consists of nineteen "Uses proposed to the Reader from this History, as the Reasons why I wrote it."[3] (Dare we suspect Baxter of rationalizing at this point?) Certainly, his only conscious motive in teaching and writing was to promote Christian faith and life; in his own pregnant phrase, to "do good." It was because this desire was so strong in him that he wrote so much; and it was this desire that determined his special interests. When we address ourselves to Baxter's presentation of "the sum of saving knowledge," the doctrines of man, sin, and salvation, we approach what were to him the most vital topics on which he ever expressed his mind. Our inquiry will thus take us to the heart of his thought, the focal area on which all his other studies and interests were made to converge. This chapter is devoted to an examination of the first and second of the three topics mentioned above. We shall study Baxter's intellectual heritage, the thought-climate of his day, by which he was inevitably conditioned and circumscribed, and his own intellectual character, in virtue of which he came to stand apart from his fellows as an original thinker. To spend time gaining insight into these things is necessary if we are to find the key to Baxter's theology, which has eluded critics for so long. This will appear as we proceed.

Fundamental to all Puritan thought was the seventeenth-century version of the Mediaeval doctrine that all knowledge is a unity and all sciences, physical and moral, form a hierarchy, at the head of which theology stands. The new ideas of Renaissance and Reformation had been assimilated within the framework of this dogmatic world-view and had, indeed, rejuvenated it completely. Faith in reason's ability to discover truth, which had been languishing at the time of the Reformation, had been bolstered up by Ramist logic; classical, literary and historical interests had received a fillip at the Renaissance; the Reformation had given Protestants a new sense of

---

2. XV:185 f.
3. *Breviate of the Life of Margaret*, ed. J. T. Wilkinson, 1928, 150 f.

responsibility for the use of their talents; and the total result was the emergence of a comprehensive Calvinistic culture and the awakening of an omnivorous enthusiasm for the study of everything under the sun. There was, however, a fundamental difference between the Thomist and the Calvinist faith in this hierarchical synthesis of knowledge. The Reformation had brought back into theology an emphasis, foreign to Scholasticism, on the noetic effects of the Fall. The corruption of man's reason was not held to affect the truth of the claim that all knowledge was one; but it meant that none but the regenerate could apprehend that unity, or, indeed, know anything aright. Only they could decipher the "book of Nature" and read in it the Creator's testimony to Himself. Piety was as essential to success in the other sciences as in theology; for fallen man, born blind, cannot see the Creator in His works until he has first met Him as Redeemer through His word. Grace elevates and perfects fallen reason, not merely by supplying information, but primarily by renovating the instrument: grace frees the reason from bondage to a vicious will which refuses to receive knowledge of God, and so enables it for the first time to do its proper work of finding God in things.

The acceptance of the dogma of reason's corruption effectively "'reformed" the Thomist exposition of the synthesis, by shifting the doctrine on to an explicitly Augustinian basis. It was now asserted, not as a conclusion, but as a premise; not as demonstrable by metaphysical argument, but as a starting-point for metaphysics and every other study. The grounds on which it was maintained were no longer philosophical, but religious. It had become a theological principle for interpreting secular fact. The Puritan received it because the Bible told him that God was revealed in all his works; and, as an Augustinian, he believed it in order that he might understand it. Consequently, when the metaphysical physics on which Aquinas had rested it gave way to seventeenth-century experimental science, the doctrine of the hierarchy of knowledge remained unaffected. To the Puritan, the new scientific method was simply a fresh and fruitful way of interrogating Nature about its witness to God. The quasi-mechanical conception of the created order to which it gave rise was no embarrassment to him; he knew that behind all process in Nature was the great First Cause, the Creator, who "ordereth [events] to fall out according to the nature of second causes" and "in his ordinary providence maketh use of means" but "yet is free to work without, above and against them, at his pleasure."[4] He could allow that Nature was a machine without denying that Nature had a meaning; for his God was in the machine, making it do His will. He sought to trace God's meaning in things by setting his reason to work arranging the evidence of his senses according to Ramist principles. Where his

---

4. Westminster Confession, V:ii-iii.

reason found *ordo* (i.e., a satisfying dichotomy), there he believed himself to have found beauty, truth and meaning, and to have gained a fragment of certain knowledge. *Ordo* was creation's witness to its God.

Baxter took this doctrine for granted, and drew out its implications more fully, perhaps, than any man of his day. He echoed the Puritan insistence that knowledge was a unity, corresponding to the unity of fact. One God, above all, through all and in all, gave unity and purpose to the created order in such a way that nothing is fully understood until seen in its true relation to God and to the rest of things. That, Baxter explained, is one of the reasons why in this world we have no perfect knowledge of anything:

> We parcel Arts and Sciences into fragments, according to the straightness of our capacities, and are not so pansophical as *uno intuitu* to see the whole; and therefore we have not the perfect knowledge of any part. As the Creation is one entire frame, and no part perfectly known to any, but the comprehensive wisdom that knoweth all; and as the holy Scripture is an entire frame of holy Doctrine ... so also the works of disposing Providence are perfectly harmonious, and make up an admirable System, which our non-age hindereth us from understanding.[5]

That natural science and world history join hands with Biblical theology to bear one harmonious testimony to God was Baxter's faith, though the sight of it, as he freely acknowledged, was for the moment hid from his eyes. In the world to come, however, "we shall see that Nature and Grace, Scripture and Creatures, Physics and Morals, and all the works of God for man, do constitute one most perfect frame, which we shall admire for ever." Here we believe, and in the light of faith dimly discern fragments of the one great design; there, we shall see the whole. Meanwhile, we must devote ourselves to the elucidation of the pattern as best we can. This meant for Baxter that all secular studies must be pursued within the framework which theology provides. All fact originates and terminates in God; all knowledge of fact, therefore, must begin and end with God, the first and final Cause of all things. "God is the first and the last in our ethics and politics, as well as in our physics ..."[6] The acquisition of knowledge is a two-fold activity: the discovery of isolated truths, followed by the "methodizing" of them. Acquaintance with individual facts only becomes "science" when the second stage is reached ("he knoweth no science rightly that hath not anatomized it, and carrieth a true scheme or method of it in his

---

5. *Holy Commonwealth*, 1659, 493 f.

6. *Works*, XVII:350; cf. XIV:220: "our physics and metaphysics must be reduced to theology."

7. III:244; cf. XV:174: "you have but a half, fallacious knowledge, till you know the true place, and order, and respects [i.e., relations] of the things . . . and till you can draw up a true scheme of the things which you know: it is dreams that are incoherent."

head")[7] and it is here that a theological perspective is a *sine qua non*:

> When you study only to know what is true,[8] you must begin at the *primum cognoscibile* and so rise *in ordine cognoscendi*; but when you would come to see things in their proper order, by a more perfect, satisfying knowledge, you must draw up a synthetical scheme, *juxta ordinem essendi*, where God must be the first and last.[9]

It is true theological orientation which turns classified observations into 'sciences': the criterion of 'science' is the meaning found in the facts, rather than the method used to discover them. The study of the created order, for instance, without regard for its meaning leads, not to 'science,' but to the grossest form of ignorance; it is

> to gaze on the glass and not see the image in it; or to gaze on the image, and never consider whose it is: or to read the book of the creation, and mark nothing but the words and letters, and never mind the sense and meaning. A philosopher, and yet an atheist or ungodly, is a monster; one that most readeth the book of Nature and least understandeth or feeleth the meaning of it.[10]

It is the same with all sciences, natural and moral alike. They must be theological if they are to be true.

From this basic position, Baxter drew some interesting conclusions. In the *Reformed Pastor*, he argued that the University curriculum should be revised in the light of it; some instruction in theology should come first, in order to equip students with true principles for the study of the other sciences. The fact that undergraduates "set themselves to physics, and metaphysics, and mathematics, before they set themselves to theology" is "a grand error in the Christian academies": as a result, "instead of reading philosophy like divines, they read divinity like philosophers," and thus the disorderly curriculum, besides breeding error, "pestereth the church with unsanctified teachers."[11] The ideal course was that which Providence had prescribed for Baxter's own studies. Moreover, it follows that, inasmuch as "all right natural knowledge doth tend to the increase of theological knowledge,"[12] all is grist that comes to the theologian's mill. He should aim to know as much as he can ("I despise none

---

8. i.e., what exists: "ens et verum convertuntur" to Baxter, as to the Scholastics.
9. V:578.
10. XXI:45 f.
11. XIV:219 f. Baxter subjoins an appeal to "all pious tutors" to "read God to their pupils in all."
12. p. 220.
13. XV:16.

of their learning. All truth is useful ..."[13]). But since no man can know everything, and not everything is equally important, he must learn to put first things first. It is, as we should expect, utility that determines priorities in study. "Inter discenda magnum est discrimen; quoad usum et necessitatem. Ideoque sapientiae pars minima non est, res maximas & maxime necessarias prima & maxima diligentia studendas eligere ..."[14] As men, our studies must be directed "ad sanctitatem & salutem nostram promovendum":

> Value truth for goodness ... and estimate all truths and knowledge by their usefulness to higher ends. That is good as a means, which doth good ... As a pound of gold more enricheth than many loads of dirt; so a little knowledge of great and necessary matters, maketh one wiser than a great deal of pedantic, toyish learning ... He that must needs be ignorant of many things should omit those which he can best spare ... One thing is necessary, and all others but as they are necessary to that one: mortify the lust of useless knowledge.[15]

For every Christian capable of them, the priorities, next to theology itself, are physics (which for Baxter included psychology and all natural sciences) and history; for they, more than any, reveal God to the eye of faith.

> The book of the creatures is not to show us more of God than Scripture doth; but by representing him to us in more sensible appearance, to make our knowledge of him the more intense and operative ... Nature must be read as one of God's books, which is purposely written for the revelation of himself ... It is a most high and noble part of holiness to search after, admire and love the great Creator in all his works ...[16]

Just as God is reflected in His creation, so "the image of God ... is engraven on the seal of Providential Disposals,"[17] and therefore:

> History is a very profitable study, if it be used for the right ends, and be rightly chosen. It is a very great help to understand the Scriptures, and to know the former and present state of the church; and to see the wonderful works of Providence, that otherwise would be lost to us.[18]

---

14. *M.T.*, I.iv.141, p. 152. ["There is a great difference between things to learn with regard to their usefulness and the need for them. So it is not the least part of wisdom to choose for primary and hardest study the matters of most necessity."]

15. XV:177 f.

16. XIV:220 f.

17. XIII:15.

18. XI:213.

"Reading the book of creatures" was a Mediaeval discipline which the Puritans revived; reading the book of history was a Renaissance interest which the Puritans directed into religious channels. Baxter stressed their importance over and over again, thereby revealing where some of his roots were.

Such a curriculum might seem comprehensive enough for anyone; but for the theologian in his public capacity, as teacher and guardian of the Church's faith, it is far from sufficient. He dare not shirk the task of contending for truth, and therefore his knowledge must be extended as far as error requires. The active presence of heresy is of itself a call to so much study as is necessary to refute it; "and here," Baxter wrote grimly, "cometh in the calamity of divines:" for:

> If he (the devil) raise up Socinians ... we must read their books, that we may be able to confute them; so must we when he raiseth up Libertines, Familists, Seekers, Quakers, and such other sects. If he stir up controversies in the church, about government, worship, ceremonies ... we must read so much as to understand all that we may defend the truth against them. If Papists will lay the stress of all their controversies on Church History, and the words of ancients; we must read and understand all, or they will triumph. If schoolmen will build their theology on Aristotle ... if we cannot deal with them at their own weapons, they will triumph. If cavillers will dispute only in mood and figure, we must be able there to overtop them ... If the plica, pox, scurvy, or other new diseases do arise, the physician must know them all, if he will cure them ... A divine should know all things that are to be known ... [19]

Such a program might well daunt the bravest. This passage, published in 1689, clearly reflects Baxter's own unique career as a Puritan controversialist; yet it does not state a view that was peculiar to himself. It is no more than an exposition, with contemporary illustrations, of the Reformed and Puritan ideal of a "learned ministry" and its function. Once again, Baxter voices the characteristic Puritan position in its most highly and consistently developed form.

We now pass from Baxter's opinions concerning the unity and utility of the various sciences to a closer study of the particular hierarchical scheme by which he himself sought to weld them together. It is desirable to introduce his "method" by some discussion of his approach to the problems of knowledge in general.

To Baxter and the Puritans, the nature of knowledge was not a matter for dispute. Knowledge, they held, was the impress made by objects upon the substance of the soul. It was the mind's conformity to things. Objects, mediated via the sense, external or internal, impressed themselves on the mind as a seal

19. XV:18.

on wax. The trustworthiness of the senses as a medium of perception was insisted on, as the presupposition of all knowledge and as a damaging argument against transubstantiation.[20] To the Puritan, it was axiomatic that "faith teaches nothing contrary to sense and reason."[21] The later Scholasticism had interposed a *species sensibilis* between objects and the mind as the medium of their apprehension, but Baxter, with Puritan philosophers generally, rejected the doctrine in favor of a simple realism.[22] Assuming that knowledge involved the correspondence of mind to object, any doctrine of an intermediate *species* made it immediately uncertain how far we could be said to know anything. But the Puritans had no doubt that they knew objects directly. The resurgent Platonism of the Renaissance had swept away the cobwebs of Nominalist doubt long before. Ramist logic, with its claim that from the evidence of the senses one could penetrate the whole inner structure and rationality of things, was built upon the assumption that objects were directly known, and this assumption formed part of the Puritans' intellectual inheritance. Baxter's constitutional skepticism inclined him to brood on the limitations of human knowledge in a way that set him apart from his fellows, but he never questioned the trustworthiness of his senses.

What made the acquisition of knowledge so laborious a process, he held, was the extreme difficulty of constructing accurate concepts from the data which the senses afforded. To be under the necessity of apprehending truth by this means, instead of by immediate intellectual intuition, was one of the humbling marks of creaturely status in this world. The difficulty, though not insuperable, was great, and it was here that mistakes were commonly made. In the first place, many distinct acts of sense-perception are needed for an adequate acquaintance with a single object, and faulty or incomplete observation at once leads men astray. Again, the human mind must be acknowledged incapable of embracing the Creator, or any one of His works, by a single act of comprehension. They must be known, in so far as they can be known, by a series of concepts, each of which is, in the strict sense, "inadequate," i.e. not commensurate to its object. "Usually there must go many partial conceptions to one thing or object really indivisible ... inadequate conceptions make up a

---

20. cf. XV:36 f.: "he that denieth the certainty of sense, imagination, and intellective perception of things sensed as such, doth make it impossible to have any certainty ... about those same objects, but by miracle. And therefore the Papists ... when they say, that there is no bread or wine in the sacrament, do make their pretended contrary faith impossible ... there is no faith but on supposition of sense and understanding."

21. John Preston, *The Cuppe of Blessing*, 1633, 13.

22. cf. *M.T.* I.vii.20, p. 187: "de modo intellegendi per *species* plura dicuntur a Philosophis, diversitate, contentione & tamen praesumptione quidem nimia; sed aequali obscuritate & quae meo intellectui nunquam satisfactionem ... praebuerunt."

great part of our learning and knowledge."[23] Furthermore, our apprehension of universals is the result of abstraction from particulars as we conceive them, and can therefore be no nearer the truth than the "inadequate conceptions" from which they are derived. They may, indeed, be even further from it: "Our universal notions are the result of our own comparing things with things. And we are so woefully defective in such comparings, that our universal notions must needs be very defective."[24] And the situation, Baxter held, was made worse by "the faults of our common learning,"[25] which infected the mind with a great deal of error that must later be unlearned ("so that students must at first see through false spectacles ... and receive abundance of false conceptions, as the way to wisdom; and shadows and rubbish must furnish their minds under the name of truth"[26]). In *Knowledge and Love Compared* (I:iii), he sets down at length, with more than usual sarcasm, his considered diagnosis of the trouble, which, he held, was not peculiar to seventeenth-century England, but common to all education everywhere. A review of the passage will advance our own inquiry.

There are two sorts of knowledge, Baxter tells us: "real," or "ontological," and "organical." The object of the first (with which we have so far been exclusively concerned) is things. The object of the second is words and ideas. Logic, grammar and linguistic studies are entirely "organical," and subserve the "real" sciences. Every "real" science has its "organical" part, i.e. its axioms, definitions, key-concepts and so on. Now, the stumbling-block in the educationalist's way is the necessity of introducing the majority of things, especially abstract ideas, through words. Children are taught the meaning of a new word by verbal definition. Hereby a concept is formed in the mind and attached to the word as its "meaning." The word can then be used, to connote (i.e., "mean") the concept and to denote such entities as instantiate it. Thus a vocabulary is built up. To learn words before things, and things through words, in the manner described is necessary, for until we can use words we cannot learn to think and reflect, and only by thought and reflection can we learn to form concepts for ourselves. The alternative would be perpetual ignorance. But it is a process fraught with danger for the pupil. In the first place, he naturally tends to mistake all this "organical" knowledge (of words, and of the meanings which others give them and the way in which others use them) for "real" knowledge; "so that by the time they are grown to be masters of a considerable stock of words, grammatical, logical, metaphysical, &c. and can set these

23. XV:23. For two such "inadequate conceptions," of man's soul and God himself, see below, chap. V.
24. XV:23.
25. p. 21.
26. p. 24.

together in propositions and syllogisms, and have learned *memoriter* the theorems and axioms, and some distinctions which are in common use and reputation, they are ready to pass for Masters of the Arts ... like one that sets up his trade as soon as he hath gotten a shop full of tools."[27] Whereas the truth is, that "words to matter are but as the dish to the meat, and all this while they are but preparing for wisdom and true learning ... and that unless they will equalize a parrot and a philosopher, they must know how little they have attained, and must after learn *things*."[28] "Real" knowledge does not begin until they learn to criticize their "organical" concepts in the light of their own apprehension of the facts. This is the hardest task of all:

> Oh! what labour is it, to ... unlearn all the errors that we have learned! so that it is much of the happiest progress of extraordinary successful studies, to find out our old mistakes, and set our conceptions in better order one by one: perhaps in one year we find out and reform some two or three.[29]

Few have the ability ("the common dullards will fall into the ditch when they leave their crutches ... the half-witted men, that think themselves acute and wise, fall into the same calamity"[30]), and fewer still possess the moral and intellectual integrity that is required for such a task. The majority prefer to treat their first ideas as the last word and to defend them to the last ditch. Of such, Baxter had already written, in his first published book: "for Philosophy and Divinity, they have little more than the Carriers horse when he has a Library on his back."[31] To rush to the defense of this kind of knowledge, instead of reforming it, was to Baxter intellectual irresponsibility, if not actual dishonesty. Pride, the refusal to admit ignorance or error, and mental laziness usually lay at the root of such action. Thus ignorance became inveterate, and error was perpetuated. If the concepts first learned were accurate, less harm would be done; but, Baxter held, in his own day they were not accurate. All the systems of logic, physics and metaphysics taught in schools and universities contained glaring errors.[32] And even were this not so, the ambiguity of words, "the instruments of the communication of thoughts,"[33] would ensure that the most impeccable instruction bred mistakes in the pupils' minds. "A man can think

27. XV:22.
28. *loc. cit.*
29. p. 24.
30. p. 29 f.
31. *Aphorisms of Justification*, 1649, "To the Reader."
32. cf. XV:31: "the systems of arts and sciences grow more and more corrupted, our logics are too full of unapt notions, our metaphysics are a mere confused mixture of pneumatology (a part of physics) and logic," 47: "a very great, if not the far greatest, part of ... physics, is uncertain (or certainly false) as it is delivered to us in any methodist that I have yet seen."
33. XV:22.

more aptly and comprehensively than he can speak. And hence it cometh to pass, that words ... are become like pictures of hieroglyphics, almost of arbitrary signification and use, as the speaker pleaseth."[34] There are as many different shades of meaning attached to particular words, as there are men to attach them; and, since the words in which the most careful definitions are agreed upon must themselves be left undefined, it is likely to remain so.

> So that when tutors read the same book to their scholars ... it is not the same conception always that they thus communicate. And when all is done, *recipitur ad modum recipientis*. It is two to one but the learner receiveth notions with a conception somewhat different from them all. And when he thinks he hath learned what was taught him, and is of his teacher's mind, he is mistaken, and hath received another apprehension.[35]

The only road to an increase of knowledge and a greater measure of agreement is for everyone to learn to adjust his concepts to the facts, rather than to the opinions of others. Facts are the touchstone for ideas. Truth must be discerned by the light of its own "naked evidence": "as Richard Hooker saith in his Ecclesiastical Polity, 'Let men say what they will, men can truly believe no further than they see evidence.' It is a natural impossibility; for evidence is nothing but the perceptibility of truth ..."[36] And until truth becomes evident, judgment should be suspended. "Stop ... till you have evidence; follow no party ... in the dark,"[37] is Baxter's constant advice. Learn how little you really know; avoid the dogmatism of ignorance. Do not go beyond evidence, either in pretending to know what is out of your reach or in holding truths not equally evident with an equal degree of confidence. These were the rules, Baxter claimed, by which he had overhauled his own "juvenile conceptions"; and 'Baxterianism' was the result.

Behind this astonishingly acute and "modern" insight into the limitations of language and of its users lay Baxter's own bitter experience. As a boy at Donnington Free School, top of his form, possessed of a voracious appetite for reading and unusual powers of assimilation, his one ambition had been "literate Fame." When Providence denied him a University education and turned his attention to religion, he soon plunged into the labyrinths of philosophical and polemical theology. At an early age he was enjoying the analytical refinements

---

34 p. 23.

35. *loc. cit.* The Latin tag is one of Baxter's favorite phrases.

36. p. 46. The passage from Hooker is quoted again, *R.B.*, I:128, *et al.* Baxter here defines "evidence" in the common scholastic sense, as the quality of an object which makes it perceptible, rather than as the external grounds of inference about it. When Baxter deviates from this usage, he makes it plain; e.g., XXII:493, note k: "I use the word 'evidence' all along in the vulgar sense as the same with 'signs,' and not in the proper sense as the schools do."

37. XV:82.

of the Schoolmen: "In my youth I was quickly past my Fundamentals, and was running up into a multitude of Controversies, and greatly delighted with metaphysical and scholastic Writings."[38] He had always treated good books as oracles. We saw how anxious he once grew because he had not been converted according to the 'method' laid down by the authorities, Bolton, Hooker and Rogers. Now, conscious of the defects in his own education, he showed a similar exaggerated respect for the pronouncements of those who possessed the learning he lacked. "At first I took more upon my Author's Credit, than now I can do ... At first the *stile* of Authors took as much with me as the Argument ..."[39] Obscurity he took for profundity: "what Books I understood not by reason of the strangeness of the Terms or Matter, I the more *admired*."[40] In the first flush of conscious ability, he ran to extremes, for extremes appealed to him: "at first I was greatly inclined to go with the *highest* in Controversies, on one side or other."[41] All this time, as he later recognized, he was bending himself to the study of words rather than things, the systems and opinions or others rather than the facts themselves. The very ease with which he took things in, and the delight he found in doing so, prevented his digesting what he swallowed. As a result, the young intellectual grew biased and one-sided. But in his early thirties he came to see his mistake and set himself to rectify it as best he could. The results were far-reaching. He came to condemn much of the philosophical theology that had previously been his delight as presumptuous prying into things unrevealed and out of man's reach:

> I was wont to say, I could get more out of *Aquinas, Scotus, Durandus,* and such like in a day, than out of many Ancient Fathers, and later Treatises, in a month ... Those leaves of *Bradwardine* and *Twiss* ... which I was wont to reade with longing and delight, I confess I look on now with fear; and many Learned Schoolmen ... I read, as I hear men swear or take God's name lightly in their common talk ... as I hear children discoursing of State matters, or Theology; or as if I heard two disputing in their sleep.[42]

---

38. *R.B.*, I:126 (1665). Baxter always valued the schoolmen, who, despite many mistakes, "have often done well in fitting words to things, and making the key meet for the lock" (XV:29). On the whole, "nullos meliores inveni Philosophos quam Scholasticos" (*M.T.*, "Praefatio"). The following characteristic statement, published at the end of his life, expresses his mature judgment of them: "I much value the method and sobriety of Aquinas, the subtlety of Scotus and Ockam ... the excellent acuteness of many of their followers ... but how loth should I be to take such sauce for my food, and such recreations for my business! The jingling of too much and too false philosophy among them, often drowns the noise of Aaron's bells. I feel myself much better in Herbert's Temple; or in a heavenly treatise of faith and love ..."

39. *R.B.*, I:129-30.

40. p. 129.

41. p. 130.

42. *Apology,* "Answer to ... Kendall," 1654, 8 f.

When he turned back to the controversies in which he had dabbled before, it was with a wholly different standpoint and with wholly different results:

> I was my self some years confident that *Arminianism* was ... an Enemy to the Soundness and Safety of the Church. But when I had set my self thoroughly and impartially to study it, I found that which so amazed me, that I durst scarce believe what I could not deny; even that from the beginning of the quarrel between *Augustine* and *Pelugius* (sic), all the Voluminous Contentions of the *Thomists* or *Dominicans*, and the *Jesuits*, and *Franciscans*, and between *Lutherans*, and *Zuinglians* (herein) and the *Synodists* and *Arminians*, have been mostly about either *unsearchable* things, which *neither side understood*, or about *ambiguous words*, which one Party taketh in one sense, and another in another; or about the meer *methodizing* and *ordering* of the *notions* which both sides are *agreed in* ... And that when the matter is distinctly opened, it is found that multitudes that write, rail and plot against one another, are really *of one Opinion De rebus*, and *did not know it*.[43]

He returned to the theological battlefield to reconcile the contending parties. He had recoiled from the extremes to which he saw that pride had led him, and had lost his love for controversy. His one desire now was to make peace by showing "dogmatical word-warriors" the truth. He brought to his task a finely chiseled theological vocabulary, the fruit of prolonged study of the facts. And in consequence he spent the last forty years of his life being misrepresented and misunderstood. Both sides repudiated him. The unfamiliarity of his mode of statement was taken as proof of its untruth. His thought was so clear that contemporaries, blinded by its dazzling lucidity, found it hopelessly obscure. The scrupulous care with which he distinguished the meanings of words and degrees of evidence and certainty was construed as a perverse display of pedantic eccentricity; and his Socratic candor in dealing with stupidity and muddle "acted on smaller minds as a maddening irritant."[44] A touch of acid in his later reflections on the weakness of words as stepping-stones to knowledge is understandable.

The epistemology which underlay Baxter's thinking is now clear. That creation, though never more than partly known, embodies a rational design and "meaning" which right reason can discern was to him axiomatic. True

---

43. *An End of Doctrinal Controversies*, 1691, 17 f.; cf. *R.B.*, I:134: "I am more and more sensible that most Controversies have more need of *right Stating* than of *Debating*; and if my Skill be increased in any thing it is in that, in *narrowing* Controversies by Explication, and separating the *real* from the *verbal*."

44. J. M. Lloyd-Thomas, Introductory Essay before *Autobiography of Richard Baxter* (Everyman ed., 1931), xix.

concepts reflected the structure of its parts and *ordo* in the mind reflected their mutual relations. The context of his skepticism concerning the knowability of details was the enormous optimism of this basic Puritan assumption. Adjusting thought and terms to things might be difficult—Baxter felt the difficulty more than most—but it was not impossible. Indeed, Baxter thought he had made more than a little progress in it. His confidence is reflected in the sweeping generalizations in which he gives students advice.[45] The bounds of physics and metaphysics, he told them, must be redefined according to the real nature of their subject-matter. Physics must become a theological discipline made up of two parts, "somatology" and "pneumatology," the study of bodies and of spirits, the two kinds of created substance.

> Unite all Οντολογίαν [ontology], or knowledge of real entities, into one science … study not the doctrine of bodies alone, as separated from spirits; for it is but an imaginary separation, and a delusion to men's minds.[46]

The primary notions of a *body* (a passive corporeal substance) and of a *spirit* (an active incorporeal substance) are furnished, Baxter held, by the data of self-consciousness. Men know what their bodies are; and "men that will but observe the *Operations* of their Souls, may competently know what a Soul or Spirit is."[47] That the whole universe was composed of bodies and spirits Baxter had no doubt. As for metaphysics, it was no science in its own right at all; "part of it belongeth to logic, (the organical part,) and the rest is theology, pneumatology, and the highest parts of ontology, or real science."[48] Logic needed revision, too, if it was to fit the facts. Baxter's own logic was as eclectic and individual as the rest of his thought. It was an Aristotelianism modified and augmented in the light of the Ramist critique. His writings reveal him to have been master both of the traditional Aristotelian syllogism and of the disjunctive mode of reasoning that was distinctive of Ramism. "The wit of Aristotle," he held, "was wonderful for subtlety and solidity; his method (oft) accurate";[49] however, Ramus' criticism was valid: "doubtless, as Aristotle's predicaments are not fitted to the kinds of beings, so many of his distributions and orders … are arbitrary."[50] Baxter had toyed with the idea of writing a text-

---

45. See *Christian Directory*, I:vi.6.vi, "Directions for young Students …" III, q. 173, "What particular directions … should be observed by young students," and *Knowledge and Love Compared*, I:xxi, "Directions for the cure of pretended knowledge …" (III:238 f., V:575 f., XV:173 f.).

46. V:577 f.; cf. XV:25: "to treat of bodies without treating of the spirits that animate or actuate them, is a lame, deluding, unedifying thing."

47. *The Certainty of the Worlds of Spirits*, 1691, Preface.

48. V:578.

49. V:579.

50. XV:48.

book of logic himself.[51] His writings indicate what he would have contributed had he done so: he would have reduced the traditional four causes to three,[52] revised the list of categories and, characteristically, added a new one, *order*.[53] He would also have put forward the doctrine of method which we shall consider below.

It was, however, Baxter's misfortune to be a traditionalist living through an age of transition, when physics, logic and epistemology were in the melting-pot. The old learning was outworn, and "novelists" were casting about for something better. What was coming to the birth did not, however, appear till the end of Baxter's life. Meanwhile, Baxter was spending himself in a gallant but unsuccessful attempt to rejuvenate a dying culture. Thus, for instance, he clung to the physics of the Renaissance. That movement, with its new interest in human nature, had given a fillip to speculation about the activity of spirits, since body and spirit were the only terms then available for discussing the relation of body and mind.[54] Baxter believed the Renaissance doctrine of spirits, and poured scorn on "Sadducees" who denied their existence and thereby, he held, turned thought into physical function and freedom into automatism. "The Epicureans or Democratists," he wrote, in the course of a summary review of the various philosophical schools to date, "were still and justly the contempt of all the sober sects; and our late Somatists that follow them ... many that call themselves Cartesians, yea, Cartesius himself ... and Hobbes, do give much more to mere matter and motion, than is truly due, and know or say so much too little of spirits ... which are the true principles of motion, that they differ as much from true philosophers, as a carcass or a clock from a living man.[55] So Baxter judged; but by the end of the seventeenth century "it was only when you were interpreting any phenomenon ... in terms of the motion of atoms ... that you were giving an account of how things ... really happened."[56] Democritus' atomic theory had returned to stay. Moreover, "pneumatology" was grounded on the Aristotelian assumption of the natural inertia of bodies. It was a theory of motion. And within three years of Baxter's full-dress exposition of it, in *Methodus Theologiae*, it had been entirely antiquated by the publication of Newton's *De Motu* (1684), followed in 1687 by the *Principia*. The birth of the mathematical theory of forces meant the death of all Scholastic and Renaissance speculations about spirits. Mediaeval physics was henceforth,

---

51. cf. *M.T.*, I:iv:145: "Praedicamentorum & notionum Logicarum ineptitudo & confusio vulgaris, animum iam diu ad accuratius aliquid tentandum stimulavit, sed fraenante temporis penuria, & mordaces ingratorum censurae deterrent."
52. Efficient, constitutive and final. He argues the case for this reduction in *M.T.*, I:i: 13 f., 4 f.
53. cf. XV:27, "We doubt not but ORDER should be a most observable predicament ..."
54. H. M. Gardiner and others, *Feeling and Emotion*, 1937, 122 f., 132f.
55. V:579.
56. B. Willey, *The Seventeenth Century Background*, 1934, 7.

not merely out of fashion, but out of date.

Furthermore, the Ramist view of knowledge as classification was abandoned after the Restoration. For explanation in terms of *ordo*, the Royal Society and John Locke substituted explanation in terms of origin. Whereas "to the Renaissance mind satisfactory explanation consisted of giving satisfying names,"[57] to the post-Restoration mind it consisted in discovering causes. Baxter's conception of the goal, and hence the nature, of man's search for knowledge was thus completely outmoded. By the end of his life, a wholly new intellectual and religious outlook had replaced the old. The "age of reason" had dawned. Puritan piety had been dismissed as "enthusiastic," and abandoned in favor of a cold religion of common sense. Men's minds were smaller, their interests narrower, their mental vitality less than had been the case with the great Puritan polymaths. Consequently, the Puritan synthesis broke up. Natural science was reduced from the quest for God in His works to a prosaic study of the laws of change. Theology shrank into a jejune apologetic, and the ideal of uniting all knowledge under its aegis was not so much discredited as forgotten. Nobody had either the interest or the energy to attempt to rebuild the synthesis on the basis of the new physics. By 1724, the thought-climate in England had so changed that one of Baxter's warmest and most able admirers, Philip Doddridge, found the *Methodus Theologiae* "unintelligible."[58]

Against this background, we are now to see how Baxter taught and "methodized" the "body of divinity." And first we must see the relation between these two activities. The aim of the former was to make evident the objects of faith; of the latter, to exhibit their connection in a unified scheme. Christian truth must first be discovered, part by part, before it could be "methodized" as a whole. Catechetical instruction was one thing, and systematic theology was another. The first was designed to lead the pupil to the point at which he perceives the "sum of saving knowledge" in "its own proper evidence"; that is, to be God's truth. What he had hitherto accepted on the authority of the Church or his teacher he now recognizes as God's word, and accepts as such. This transition from "fides humana" to "fides divina," the intellectual aspect of saving faith, was the goal of catechetical teaching. Baxter here was applying in a wider context a principle on which Protestant controversialists had insisted in the Roman controversy, namely, that the "ratio formalis" of faith is acceptance on the testimony of God. Reformed theologians, he tells us,

> distinguish between *human Faith* and *Divine*. (And I hope *God and Man* may be distinguished.) They say that it must be a *Divine Faith* (that is, *The*

---

57. Perry Miller, *op. cit.*, 169.
58. G. F. Nuttall, *Richard Baxter and Philip Doddridge: A Study in a Tradition*, 1951, 18.

Belief of Gods word for the Infallible Veracity of God) that must save us, and
not the belief of man alone: But that a *human Faith* is needful in *Subserviency*
to a *Divine*. God hath appointed *human Teachers* to the Flocks, and ... he will
never *learn*, that will *believe* nothing on his Teachers Credit ... And that which
Man is to teach us, is to see the *Evidence of Gods own Word*, that we may
believe it for *that Evidence*, as our *Teachers themselves* must do.[59]

Systematic theology, on the other hand, followed a "Methodus Synthetica" and
sought to exhibit all the objects of "fides divina" in their true mutual relations.
We must now consider each separately.

The Christian religion, Baxter held, has its essential part, its integral parts
and its accidental parts. The essential part is the baptismal covenant, the
response of faith to God's promise in the covenant of grace. "The briefest
summary of the Christian religion ... is the sacramental covenant of grace;
wherein the penitent believer, renouncing the flesh, the world and the devil,
doth solemnly give himself up to God, the Father, Son and Holy Spirit ... This
covenant is first entered by the sacrament of baptism, and after renewed ... in
the sacrament of the body and blood of Christ."[60] A man who thus covenants
may reject the rest of what the Church and Bible teach, "yet he may and will be
saved, if he sincerely receive but this much."[61] The meaning and obligations of
this covenant are expounded in three summaries: "the first, called the Creed,
containing the matter of the Christian belief; the second, called the Lord's Prayer,
containing the matter of Christian desire and hope; the third, called the law, or
decalogue, containing the sum of moral duties."[62] The Apostles' Creed "is but
the exposition of the three articles of the Baptismal Covenant: 'I believe in
God, the Father, Son and Holy Ghost.'"[63] The Lord's prayer is "a perfect
summary"[64] of what a Christian may and must desire. The Decalogue contains
the principles of Christian morality.[65] These together constitute "the kernel of
the Scripture ... that for which the rest of the Scripture is given us, even to
afford us sufficient help to understand and consent to the covenant of grace;
that our belief, our desires and our practice may be conformed to these

59. *The Protestant Religion Truly Stated and Justified*, 1692, 7.
60. XXI:167.
61. XV:73.
62. XXI:165.
63. XV:68.
64. IV:290 (*Christian Directory*, I:xxiii.2. q.2. The chapter contains a tabular analysis, entitled "A Brief Explication of the Method of the Lord's Prayer.")
65. All the Puritans agreed that " the moral law is summarily comprehended in the ten
commandments" (*Westminster Shorter Catechism*, 41). The Decalogue contained the Law of Nature, promulgated to the Jews and re-promulgated by Christ with new sanctions: "instead of deliv-
erance of the Jews from Egypt, he has made our redemption from sin and Satan, which was thereby
typified, to be the fundamental motive," and moved the seventh-day Sabbath to the first day of the
week to mark the change (XXI:165).

summaries."[66] The Bible has been given to the Church to enable it to understand the summaries; but they themselves were given by Christ to the Apostles,[67] taught by them to every convert, used each Lord's Day in worship and so handed down substantially unchanged throughout the Church's history. Hence their authenticity and truth are more certain and apparent than that of any other part of Christianity.

> They are in the Scripture, and so have all the evidence of tradition which the Scriptures have: and they were, besides that, delivered to the memories of all Christians ... being in every Christian's mind and memory, (they) were faster held than the rest of the Scriptures ... it was far easier to preserve the purity of these summaries, than of the whole body of the Scriptures ...[68]

Over and above the witness of Scripture, the witness of Church history would be sufficient to prove them Dominical. Catechisms, therefore, should be expositions of the covenant and the summaries, the most certain and essential parts of Christianity, and should introduce only so much Biblical doctrine as is necessary to this end. Non-essentials should be ruthlessly omitted. Such catechisms would be safe guides to the further study of Scripture and would lay a sound foundation in the mind for the later task of "methodizing" theology. Their aim should be simply to show what "meer Christianity" is, and that it is true, and thus to lead the pupil into the knowledge of God through Christian practice. Baxter wrote *The Catechising of Families* (1683) on these principles, and appended the three summaries and a paraphrase of the baptismal covenant to his *Poor Man's Family Book* (1674), under the title "The Shortest Catechism."

A child, Baxter held, could learn the rudiments of Christianity, but a true synthetic view of theology was beyond the reach of all but the ablest. There were several reasons for this. In the first place, successful "methodizing" presupposed a thorough acquaintance with the material to be methodized. This must be quarried from Scripture; and painstaking, prayerful exegesis is required for its elucidation. All the facts must be taken into account, and they are not all easily discovered: "in all sciences, and in theology itself ... the great, essential and chief integral parts are few, and easily discerned; but two grand impediments hinder us from a certain knowledge of the rest: one is the great number of particles ... the other is the littleness of the thing, which maketh it undiscernible to any but accurate and studious minds."[69] And the temptation

---

66. XV:69.
67. The baptismal covenant and outline of the Trinitarian Creed, Matt. 28:19; the Lord's Prayer, Matt. 6:9-13; the Law, Matt. 5-7.
68. XV:71.
69. XV:50 f.

to suppress facts in the interests of "method" is strong. "Be especially careful," Baxter urges students, "that you ... throw not away every truth, which you cannot presently place rightly in the frame ... for a further insight into true method ... may reconcile you to that which now offendeth you. What God hath joined together, be sure that you never put asunder; though yet you cannot find their proper places ... False method rejecteth many a truth."[70] Again, Scripture presupposes a great deal for its proper understanding; logic, languages, history, philosophy and psychology, and some knowledge of the general principles of morals and politics.[71] Without these, theological accuracy is out of man's reach.[72] The knowledge which these studies yield is taken for granted by the Biblical writers, as the foundation on which their teaching is rested. Accordingly, when in the *Christian Directory* Baxter comes to set out for the benefit of ordination candidates an "order of their studies ... such as respecteth their whole lives,"[73] a threefold propaedeutic is laid down to fit them for their theological studies. First, they must be trained in a lively piety. "Not that any exact body or method of divinity is to be learnt so early;" what they need to know at this stage is "their daily duty ... danger ... temptations and impediments, and how to escape." Next, "till about eighteen, nineteen or twenty," they should occupy themselves "in the improvement of their memories, rather than in studies that require much judgment"—they should learn languages, logic, history and mathematics. After this, they may advance to physics, politics and other philosophical subjects; and only then will they be ready for theology, for only then will they have sufficient of the "natural" knowledge which Scripture presupposes.

The problem of theological "method," to Baxter's mind, was twofold: what to include, and how to arrange it. His considered decision on the first point was that an account of the whole created order, including man, must precede

---

70. III:248 f.

71. Baxter had most to say about psychology ("that part *Physics* which treateth of the soul," *R.B.*, I:6) and politics, for these, he held, were most commonly overlooked by theologians. For the first: "The knowledge of man's soul is a part so necessary, so near, so useful, that it should take up both the first and largest room in all your physics ... labour therefore to be accurate in this" (V:578). For the second: "It is a preposterous course, and the way of ignorance and error, for a divine to study God's laws ... before [he] know[s] in general what a law or government is, as nature notifieth it to us." To prepare himself for the writing of *M.T.*, "omnes fere quos obtinere potui scriptores *de Anima* perlegi;" "inter scripta humana ... maxime profeci, 1. Quae *operationes animae humanae* clarissime explicant. 2. Et quae *Politicam* seu *Rationes Regiminis* optime tradunt" (M.T., Praefatio). [I read through just about all the writers I could get on the soul; among human writings I profited most from (1) those that explain the workings of the human soul most clearly, and (2) those that best present politics, or the principles of government.]

72. *Works*, XIV:220: "There is somewhat of natural knowledge ... prerequisite, and somewhat of art, before a man can receive theology."

73. V:575.

the exposition of what God and man have done within that order. "Intellexi ... moralitatem esse Rerum modalitatem & ordinem, ideoque Theologiae Physicam, fidei naturam ... praesupponi," Baxter explains.[74] What exists must be known before we can say how it exists; *quid* is a prior question to *quomodo*. Accordingly, the whole first part of the *Methodus Theologiae* (380 folio pages, more than a third of the work) is devoted to an elaborate account of God's nature, man's nature and the rest of living things as well. "I knew how Uncouth it would seem to put so much of these Doctrines (sc., the natural sciences) into a Body of Divinity: But the three first Chapters of *Genesis* assured me, That it was the Scripture-Method."[75] To the problem of arrangement, his answer was systematic trichotomy. Though he never doubted that the Ramists were doing the right thing in seeking knowledge by means of order and arrangement, he was sure that the principle of dichotomy was a key that would not fit the lock when applied to the study of things[76] "Diu credidi omnem legitimam divisionem esse bimembrem; ad Dichotomian maxime propendebam: et adhuc de mere Logicis ... ita judico," he wrote in the Preface to the *Methodus*; "quando vero a re subjecta sumenda est methodus plerumque Trichotomiam praeferendam sentio." "I had been Twenty Six Years convinced that Dichotomizing will not do it," he wrote in 1670; "but that the Divine Trinity

---

74. *M.T.*, Praefatio.

75. *R.B.*, III:70 (1670); cf. the following remark, dating from 1665: "The beginning of Genesis, the books of Job and the Psalms, may acquaint us that our physics are not so little akin to theology as some suppose" (XIV:221). In *M.T.*, Praefatio, he tells us, a propos of this part of his work: "Tres amici, Theologi eximii, haec scripta perlegerunt, taliaque (sc. tot physica) approbarunt: Quartus autem ... quando Οντολογίαν ... legisset, non solum ea ... approbavit, sed ut se Physicis plura adderem, saepe & serio me incitavit." ["Three friends, fine theologians, read these pages, and approved of so much physics; and a fourth, when he had read it, not only approved that, but often seriously urged me to add more to the physics."] This fourth, was Sir Matthew Hale, Lord Chief Justice of England, a close friend and amateur theologian of some skill and wisdom. Baxter refers to the fourth chapter of the book with its huge chart ("Aut fallor enim, aut Theologiae, Pneumatologiae, Somatologiae elementa vere & methodice explicat")—one of the most curious products of physics of the Mediaeval type.

76. Among "our exactest Dichotomizers," whose works gave so little "Satisfaction to my Reason," Baxter lists Dudley Fenner and Ames; G. Sohnius, *Methodus Theologiae*, 1588. L. Treleatius, *Scholastica et methodica Locorum communium sacrae Theologiae Institutio*, 1604, J. Wollebius, *Compendium Theologiae Christianae, Accurata Methodo ... adornata*, Basel, 1626; London, 1647. Other "methodists" whose schemes Baxter had studied were M. F. Wendelinus, *Christianae Theologiae libri duo, methodice dispositi ...*, 1634; A. Polanus, *Syntagma Theologiae Christianae*, 1609; Stephanus Szegedinus (referred to as "Tzegedine"), *Theologiae Sincerae Loci Communes ... perpetuis Tabulis explicati et Scholasticorum dogmatis illustrati*, 1593; and Nicholas Gibbon, *Theology real, and truly scientificall ...*, c.1662 (*R.B.*, III:70). For Baxter's opinion of Gibbon, "our present Busie-boaster," cf. II:205. The privately printed pamphlet which Baxter there states that Gibbon showed him in 1654 was doubtless *The Scheme or Diagramme Adjusted for Future Use ... At present Printed for private Hand*, of which there is a presentation copy in the Bodleian with a Latin address dated 1653. Powicke thinks that in putting Gibbon down as a Socinian Papist Baxter does him an injustice; *Life*, 127 f. Cf. *D.N.B.*, s.v.

in Unity, hath expressed it self in the whole Frame of Nature and Morality."[77]
The idea of trichotomizing, he tells us, was suggested to him by the study of
Campanella's "Principles of Nature,"[78] but the application of it was entirely his
own. Once he set himself to work it out, the results were so striking as to put
him out of doubt that he was on the right track. He found trichotomies
everywhere:

> In anima humana triplex facultas est, Vegetativa, Sensitiva & Rationalis: In
> rationali est facultas Activa Vitalis, Intellectiva & Volitiva: In brutorum anima
> sensitiva est, facultas vitaliter motiva, perceptiva & volitiva. In igne est Virtus
> Motiva, Illuminativa, Calefactiva (& in Sole Eminenter:) ... Et omnis haec
> Trinitas in Unitate (seu Uno) invenitur.

Nor was it in the created order alone that "vestigia Trinitatis" were to be found.
They appeared "per totam doctrinam S. Scripturae, & in Dei imagine in fidelibus
sanctificatis,[79] & in officiis Christianis,[80] & in tota Oeconomia Evangelii
inveniantur."[81]

A further distinctive feature of Baxter's method was the constitutive concept
in which he found the *differentia* that marked off the sphere of theology from
that of other sciences. The first scheme in his *Methodus* (headed "Methodus
Generalis") begins by stating it:

<pre>
                    (Doctrina)
THEOLOGIA est (   ) affectiva-practica de REGNO DEI
                    (Scientia)
super hominibus:
</pre>

> Regni huius triplex est *Status, viz.* 1. Naturae. 2. Gratiae. 3. Gloriae.[82]

---

77. *R.B.*, III:70.

78. i.e. *Prodromus philosophiae instaurandae; ... dissertationes de natura rerum secundum
vera principia*, 1617. In M.T., Praefatio, Baxter also mentions "Metaphysices eius," i.e. *Universae
philosophiae seu metaphysicarum partes tres*, 1638. He also there mentions a work by Francis Glisson,
professor of medicine at Cambridge, as feeling after the same truth: *Tractatus de naturae substantia energetica, seu de vita naturae, eiusque tribus facultatibus, perceptiva, appetitiva et motiva*, 1672.
To this book, however, Baxter owed nothing, for by 1672 the analytical part of *M.T.* had been
completed. "All the schemes, and half the elucidations" were written during the winter, 1669-70.

79. i.e. life, light and love.

80. i.e. in the three spheres of delegated authority; church, state and family.

81. *M.T.*, Praefatio. ["Traces of the Trinity are found through all the teaching of Holy Scripture, and in the image of God in sanctified believers, and in the Christian spheres of service and in
the entire administration of the gospel."]

82. *op. cit.*, I:i, 1. ["THEOLOGY is the affective-practical doctrine/science concerning the
REIGN (KINGDOM) OF GOD over mankind.]

The subject-matter of theology was *regnum Dei*, God's government of his creatures, the archetypal monarchy. This conception, Baxter claimed, had been adumbrated, together with the method of trichotomy, in "Catecheses nostrae communiores, quae primo Baptismum, deinde symbolum fidei, Precationem Dominicam, & Decalogum cum Christi elucidationibus, & Legibus specialibus, & Sacramentum Communionis probe explicant; & quae Methodo Politico Regni Dei Institutionem, Constitutionem & Administrationem ... bene exponunt";[83] and it had been explicitly broached by George Lawson, whose "*Theopolitica* ... reduced Theology to a Method more Political and righter in the main, than any that I had seen before him."[84] Baxter expounded God's kingship as grounded on trinities of Divine attributes and relations to man. It is revealed in three successive forms, as a kingdom of nature, of grace and of glory. The covenants of works and of grace are the laws of the kingdom in its first two forms, and within each dispensation three distinct subjects arise for consideration: "constitutio efficiens," God's legislation; "constitutio effecta," the resultant state of affairs; and "administratio," which last subdivides again into three, "regimen antecedens," "actiones subditorum," and "regimen consequens." Within the framework afforded by these distinctions, Baxter proceeded to set out in tripartite analysis the whole history of God's dealings with man from the creation to the coming end of the world, the whole content of man's duty and, to conclude, a detailed dissection of the threefold summary of Christian virtue, faith, hope and love. He arranged each chapter in the manner typical of Ramist educational works, as a diagrammatic scheme with explanatory comment. The work as a whole is an extraordinary display of methodizing ingenuity, the more so since Baxter reached the views there expounded long before he sat down to trichotomize them. There is nothing in the *Methodus* which was not more or less clearly presented in earlier writings. The reason why the "method" seems fanciful to the modern mind is that we no longer share the Renaissance view of explanation as arrangement and have lost the Platonist's confidence that patterns in the mind can be blueprints of the universe. Baxter, however, knew no such doubts. Moreover, he believed that his method as well as his subject-matter had come straight from the Bible:

> Scripture is not void of so much logic and philosophy as is suited to this design. In a well-fleshed body the distinction and compagination of the parts are hid, which in an ugly skeleton are discerned. So the Scripture is a body of essentials, integrals and accidentals of religion, and every unstudied fellow cannot anatomize it; but it hath its real and excellent method, for all that it is

---

83. *M.T.*, Praefatio.

84. "But," Baxter adds, "he had not hit on the true Method" (*R.B.*, *loc. cit.*). He consistently dichotomized. For Lawson, cf. *D.N.B.*, s.v.

hid to the unskilful. There is a method of Scripture Theology, which is the most accurate that ever the world knew ... I doubt not but I have shown, that the method of theology contained in the Holy Scriptures; is more accurate than any logical author doth prescribe.[85]

Such was his confidence. "Richard Baxter produced a system of theology in a Latin quarto (1681); whatever else this *tour de force* may be, it is not Baxter," observed Alexander Gordon.[86] But Gordon is here, for once, astray both in his facts and in his judgment. The volume is a nine-hundred-page folio, and is as characteristic of Baxter as anything he wrote. Here we see his amazing mind at full stretch: encyclopedic in its range, incisive and clear-cut to the last degree, organizing masses of material with consummate ease, never losing sight of the whole amid the multitude of its parts, always aware of the furthest implications of each tenet, insatiable in his thirst for truth and for the "satisfying" order which to him was beauty. Even in this most scholastic of his books he remains the Puritan, and the *Methodus* ends with practice: "*Meditationes Practicae in Phil. 3.20*," followed by answers to seventeen questions thence arising on the way to lead a heavenly life. Thinking was life to him, and his thinking was never more magisterial than here. It is sad to reflect that so much brilliance was wasted. The book was out of date before Baxter wrote it. By the time it appeared, "methodizing" as an epistemological technique had been outmoded for almost a generation. Hence it was stillborn. Baxter had to print the work, which he regarded as his *chef d'oeuvre*, at his own expense, for no publisher would risk money on it; few read it, and its influence was negligible.

From what has been said, it might be inferred that the study of revealed truth is "notional" and "organical" in the extreme, a matter simply of extracting and arranging the concepts and propositions which the Bible yields. And Baxter's account of the part which reason must play in Biblical study might serve to strengthen this impression:

We must use our best Reason ... to know which are the true Canonical Scriptures, to discern true *Copies*, and *Readings* where the copies differ, to expound the Text, to Translate it truly, to discover the *Order* of sacred Verities that are dispersed through all the Scriptures, to gather them into Catechisms, and *Professions* of Faith, discerning things more necessary from the less needful ... To gather just and certain Inferences from Scripture Assertions: To apply general Rules to particular Cases, in matters of Doctrine, Worship, Discipline, and ordinary Practice, prudently to discern those Duties which are but generally commanded in the Scripture, and left to be discerned by us, in

---

85. *Works*, XV:147.
86. *Addresses Biographical and Historical*, 1922, 213.

particular, according to the determining Accidents, Circumstances and Occurrences.[87]

But theological study was more than an academic discipline. Baxter was not merely the most brilliant of Puritan rationalists. He was more than a rationalist. He never forgot that man, the knowing subject, is more than mind, and that knowledge, is accordingly more than notions. Therefore, as we saw above, he defined theological study as "scientia affectiva-practica." All his Puritan predecessors had agreed with Scotus against Aquinas, that theology was "scientia practica" rather than "scientia theoretica." Baxter himself never tired of making the point.[88] And though he was the first Puritan to describe it as "affectiva" (perhaps here following Gerson, who may also have inspired his constant insistence that "light and heat" must be conjoined if we are to know God), he was doing no more than making explicit what the "affectionate practical English writers" had assumed. Knowledge results from the object's impression on the rational soul. The nature of that impression depends on the nature of the object. In the case of God, the impression effected by contact is the transformation of the whole man: the enlightening of the mind, the rectifying of the will, and the redirection of desire. Where God is known truly, there he is loved and served. Where, however, the will and affections remain unmoved, there may be correct notions in the mind, but they have not yet become "real" knowledge. Man knows God with the heart, not with the head only, "by an affective, practical knowledge," Baxter wrote on John 17:3; "there is no text of Scripture of which the rule is more clearly true and necessary ... that words of knowledge do imply affection. It is the closure of the whole soul with God, which is here called the knowledge of God."[89] The most accurate theological system, therefore, is but a means to "real" knowledge. Accordingly, Baxter never tired of reminding his readers that "*Heaven-work* and *Heart-work,* are the chiefest parts of Christian duty"; "true religion ... consisteth in heaven-work and heart-work, in the love of God and man ..."[90] Brainwork is no more than the preparation for it.

---

87. *The Judgment of Nonconformists of the interest of Reason in matters of Religion*, 1676, 12 f.; an English translation of *M.T.*, I:i, q. 3, 16 f., published "to prove against the Catholics, and incidentally against Anglicans who borrowed Catholic thinking, that the Puritans were one with orthodox Protestants in rejecting fideism" (P. Miller, *op. cit.*, 71), and subscribed by the Presbyterian leaders, Thomas Manton, Bates, Baxter, Thomas Case, Matthew Sylvester, Edward Lawrence, Samuel Fairclough, Joseph Read, John Turner, Benjamin Agas, James Bedford, Matthew Pemberton; and in some copies by Gabriel Sangar, Henry Hurst and Roger Morrice in addition (cf. *C.R.*, s.vv.).

88. cf. XXIII:309: "Practice is the end of all sound doctrine, and all right faith doth end in duty;" XIV:181: "Theology is a practical science;" XIV:221: "practical divinity (and there is no other);" XXI:384: "a doctrine for head, heart, and life"; etc.

89. XIII:11; cf. 183: "nor is it clear and solid knowledge, if it do not somewhat affect the heart, and engage and actuate the life, according to the nature and use of the thing known."

90. *Cure of Church Divisions* (1670) 209, 408, *et al.* The phrase is one of Baxter's favorites.

Here, again, Baxter is making a characteristic Puritan point; and here, again, he drew out its implications with a clear-sightedness and consistency that marks him out from his Puritan contemporaries. If it is true that "Holyness is of the Essence of Christianity,"[91] that fruits in the life are the test and proof of the reality of knowledge of God, then for Baxter three conclusions followed. In the first place, heresy was a practical rather than a theoretical matter. "Profaneness is a hodge-podge and gallimaufry of all the heresies of the world in one. Many other heretics do err but in speculation, and only the brain is infected ... But the heresies of the profane ungodly people are practical, and have mastered the will: the poison is working in the heart and vital parts ... Ungodliness is the greatest heresy in all the world."[92] In the second place, any doctrinal scheme which did not demand and promote holiness was of necessity Satanic. By this criterion, Baxter judged Antinomian theology to be inspired by the father of lies, and fought it tooth and nail all his life. The fact that its exponents were in fact holy men did not move him. It might be so; "but its no thanks to your irreligious Doctrine."[93] He brushed aside their appeal to the Reformers[94] and their claim to exalt Christ. The only relevant fact, to him, was the failure of their doctrine to prescribe and produce a transformation of life. That single fact meant that it could not possibly be of God. And Baxter was prepared to cross swords with anyone, however orthodox otherwise, from John Owen downwards, for giving the slightest countenance to Antinomian tenets. In the third place, if Christian practice proves "real" knowledge of God in Christ, then undoubtedly some Papists had it. He appealed to their devotional books, to one of which, as we saw, he owed his own conversion.[95] And that meant that his youthful views, the standard Puritan views, on the Roman controversy had to be revised. In 1665 he wrote:

> My Censures of the Papists do much differ from what they were at first ... At first I thought Mr. *Perkins* well proved that a Papist cannot go beyond a reprobate; but now I doubt not that God hath many sanctified Ones among

91. *Confession*, "To the Reader."
92. XVI:403 f.; cf. XVII:517: "Ungodliness is all heresy transcendently in the lump, and that in practice ... Heretics only in speculation may be saved, but practical heretics cannot."
93. Epistle before "A Defence of Christ, and Free Grace" in *Scripture Gospel Defended*.
94. Antinomian writers commonly appealed to Luther, and with some plausibility in Baxter's opinion; cf. *Apology for the Nonconformists Ministry*, 131: "*Luther* on the *Galatians* is so acceptable to the *Antinomians*, that I conceive divers passages have need of as candid an ἐπιείκεία [moderation, fair-mindedness, forbearance] as the Doctrine of *Scotus*, and many *Papists* on that point" (sc., justification). Samuel Rutherford devoted a large part of his *Survey of the Spirituall Antichrist* to an elaborate vindication of Luther from the charge of Antinomianism.
95. cf. *Against Revolt to a Foreign Jurisdiction*, 1691, 539: "If an esteemed Minister should Preach part of *The Interior Christian* ... and not tell his hearers *whose it was*, I doubt not but many

them, who have received the Doctrine of Christianity so practically, that their contradictory Errors prevail not against them, to hinder their Love of God, and their Salvation; but that their errors are like a conquerable Dose of Poison which Nature doth overcome.[96]

And he commended their missionary work; next to John Eliot, he wrote in 1658, "I have very Honourable and Grateful thoughts of the Labours of the *Jesuits* and *Friars* for the *Japenians, Brasilians, Chineses* and other Infidel Nations ... and I could wish that the world had a thousand Jesuits for every one, on condition they were employed in no other work."[97] Such honest Christian charity as these passages reflect seems unique in Puritanism.

One further example of Baxter's penetration in drawing out what lay implicit in the assumptions of Puritan culture must here be mentioned: his doctrine of reason, or, rather, of *evidence*. For Baxter's whole interest was in truth, and his only purpose in raising the question, how he knew, was to answer the question, how much he knew. He was not a Romantic, concerned merely to know his own mind and express it; he was a Renaissance man and a Puritan Christian, concerned to know the facts and live by them. Reason, he held, was an instrument for the discovery of truth, and to this end must be trained to work as efficiently as possible. None of its powers, logical or imaginative, analytical or synthetic, may be left to lie fallow; all must be harnessed in the pursuit of truth. Reason was prostituted if its powers were used for any other purpose than this. (Here, we may note in passing, is the ground of Baxter's attack on fiction.) And Baxter's demand for rational demonstration was not dictated by pride in his own reasonableness, but by a humble deference to truth; for it was by rational demonstration alone, he held, that the human mind could know truth for what it is. As we saw, he maintained, with Hooker, the scholastic doctrine that belief, as distinct from a mere uncritical echoing of authority, was, precisely, assent upon evidence. The test of knowledge, therefore, is that the mind has apprehended and can point to the evidence of truth. The human mind is such that without evidence belief, and therefore knowledge, cannot exist. Ideas lodging in the mind for some other reason than because their truth has been demonstrated are not knowledge, and will be discarded as soon as their presence is questioned. The basis for Christian faith, therefore, must be convincing evidence that Christianity is true. Without it, belief would be impossible. Christianity must be *demonstrable*. Baxter claimed that he could

---

godly people, would cry it up for a most excellent Sermon." (This work was a translation, published at Antwerp in 1684, of the 12th edition of *Le Chrestien Interieur . . . par un solitaire* (Jean de Bernieres Louvigny; 1st. ed. 1663). Cf. Mss. 59. III, f. 244b: "Taulerus is a plaine Puritane."

    96. *R.B.*, I:131.

    97. *The Grotian Religion Discovered*, 8.

perform this demonstration: "I will undertake to prove the truth of Christianity."[98]

His confidence in thus challenging the unbeliever had an experimental basis. In the early days of his ministry, he had found himself tempted "to question the certain Truth of the Sacred Scriptures; and also the Life to Come, and the Immortality of the Soul ... by pretence of sober reason ... And here I found my own Miscarriage ... in that I had so long neglected the well settling of my Foundations ... I was fain ... seriously to Examine the Reasons of Christianity, and to give a hearing to all that could be said against it, that so my Faith might indeed be my own."[99] Honest as ever, he had to know the truth. And he emerged stronger than before. He found it possible to prove that "*Godliness* is a Duty so undeniably required in the Law of Nature, and so discernable by Reason itself, that nothing but unreasonableness can contradict it"; and that the evidence of the truth of Scripture was overwhelming, and the objections to it thin and fallacious: "I perceived that whatever the tempter had to say ... was grounded upon the Advantages which he took from my Ignorance, and my Distance from the Times and Places of the Matter of the Sacred History, and such like things which every Novice meeteth with in almost all other Sciences at the first, and which wise well-studied Men can see through." This experience convinced him that rational demonstration, the display of Christian evidences, was a vital part of evangelism and catechetical instruction, for hesitation and reluctance to obey the gospel could often be traced back to self-conscious doubts as to whether it was true. "From this assault I was forced to take notice, that it is our *Belief of the Truth of the Word of God, and the Life to come*, which is the Spring that sets all Grace on work, and with which it rises or falls ... And that there is more of this secret Unbelief at the Root than most of us are aware of; and that our love of the World, our boldness with Sin, our neglect of Duty are caused hence."

Henceforward, Baxter used apologetics as an offensive weapon for conviction, conversion and edification, in a manner unique and, indeed, suspect among his fellow-Puritans.[100] In the "Preface" added to the second part of his

---

98. XI:xiii.

99. *R.B.*, I:21 f.

100. Baxter's earliest apologetic writing is Part II of his *Saints' Rest*, a proof that the Bible is the infallible Word of God. In the Preface, added to the second edition and dated April 2, 1651 (not 1652, as *Works*, ed. Orme, XXII:239, and the 1838 reprint, III:84, following the misprint in *Practical Works*, 1707, III:77), he answers those who objected to this as a digression from the book's main theme: "My business was ... to help Christians to enjoy the solid comforts which their religion doth afford; the greatest hindrance whereof, in my observation, is a weak or unsound belief of the truth of it ... I am sure I digressed not from the way that led to my intended end" (XXII:216). His later judgment of this performance, however, was that he "said not half that which the subject did require" (*R.B.*, I:13, 1665). In 1655 he brought out *The Unreasonableness of Infidel-*

Saints' Rest in the second edition, Baxter states that, like the liberal Anglicans, Chillingworth and Hammond,[101] he had been accused of Socinianism because "I seek to satisfy reason so much of the Scripture's authority ... And how could all the wits of the world do more to advance Socinianism that these men do, by making men believe that only the Socinians have reason for their religion? ... And what more can be done for the disgrace and ruin of Christianity, than to make the world believe that we have no reason for it?"[102] The Calvinists who condemned rational inquiry into Christian evidences as flirting with rationalistic heresy seemed to Baxter both wrong-headed and impious. If their attitude meant anything, it indicated a latent skepticism far worse than that of the Socinians, a confirmed doubt as to the adequacy of the reasons which God had given for belief of the gospel. Such skepticism, Baxter held, could not but open the door to unbelief on the one hand and "enthusiastic" claims to special private revelations on the other; it made God the patron of unreasonableness and made disbelief the only position consistent with intellectual self-respect ("an infant, or a madman, would make the best Christian, if reason were at such odds with faith as they imagine").[103] If, on the other hand, their attitude meant nothing, but was simply a blind, "over-done" recoil from one extreme of error to its opposite, it showed a sad disrespect for truth. To spurn rational proof revealed a contempt for reason which directly dishonored God, part of Whose image man's reason is, for it represented faith, in reality an act of the highest, clearest reason, as an unfounded and unthinking credulity.

Baxter knew that this was not what Owen and his friends intended, but, he insisted, it was what they were actually doing. Their position was as follows: Since faith, in its intellectual aspect, is an assent on Divine testimony, the acceptance of the Bible as God's Word must be faith's foundation, for only in

---

ity ("a supplement to the foresaid discourse," XX:iii), and in 1667 *The Reasons of the Christian Religion,* a full demonstration whose power has been generally recognized ("a monument of convincing Apologetic," Powicke, *The Reverend Richard Baxter Under the Cross,* 1662-1691 (1927), 65; "very powerful," J. M. Lloyd-Thomas, *op. cit.,* xxiii, adducing Dr. Johnson's verdict on it: "the best collection of the evidences of the Christian system"). This was later supplemented by *More Reasons for the Christian Religion, and No Reason Against it* (1672), *Of the Immortality of Man's Soul* (1682), and *The Certainty of the Worlds of Spirits* (1691). The whole argument is summarized in the 1670 *Life of Faith,* Part II, and the proof of a future life and the truth of Scripture in *A Saint or a Brute,* II:iii.

101. Baxter commended and defended Chillingworth (XXII:238); Hammond was one of the "Rational Persons" whose approval of his *Right Method* he greatly valued, *R.B.,* I:109. He recommended Hammond's tract *Of the Reasonableness of Christian Religion* (1650), in the second edition of the *Saints' Rest* (XXII:251, note p), and often praised the other Anglican apologists for Christianity, Jackson, whose exposition of the Creed appears in all his lists of apologetic textbooks, and Stillingfleet's *Origines Sacrae* 1662 ("a very ... worthy labour," XXI:387).

102. XXII:221 f.

103. XXII:251, note p.

the Bible is Divine testimony found. The Bible evidences itself, *propria luce*, as God's Word to the minds of all whom God's Spirit enlightens. This, they held, was the whole truth on the subject.[104] That the Spirit's enlightenment was needed before a man could come to faith, and that argument would be useless without it, Baxter agreed; that the Bible was the authoritative Word of God, he also agreed; but the rest of their account seemed to him to be full of mistakes.

In the first place, the Word of God which is the object of saving faith is, as we have seen, the gospel embodied in the baptismal covenant and the three summaries, which can be proved to have been handed down unchanged within the living Church, and can be known and savingly believed by one who has never heard of Scripture. In the second place, Scripture is so far from being self-evidently such that Church tradition must be invoked to define its limits. The canon is accepted on the basis of historical investigations carried out by the Jewish community before Christ (the Old Testament) and early Christian Church (the New Testament). There is no other way by which it can be known.

> I would have the contrary-minded tell me how they know, without human testimony and tradition, that these are the same books which the prophets and apostles wrote ... Where is the man that ever knew the canon from the apocryphal before it was told him ... ? ... I could never boast of any such testimony, or light of the Spirit, nor reason neither, which without human testimony would have made me believe that the Book of Canticles is canonical, and the Book of Wisdom apocryphal.[105]

And in the third place, the Spirit witnesses to the inspiration of the Church's Bible, not by some mysterious inner impression, but by enabling man to think straight, and so to apprehend the conclusive nature of the objective evidence, internal and external, for the truth of the Bible's contents. This was the "testimonium Spiritus Sancti." Baxter forcibly states his position as follows:

104. Baxter had crossed swords with Owen on this issue in 1654, when they served together on the Fundamentals Committee. Owen had argued, "That no Man could know God to salvation by any other means" than the Scripture; and "I told him, that this was neither a Fundamental nor a Truth" (*R.B.*, II:199). In his later references to the advocates of this position, he seems always to have Owen in mind, for he refers to them as "over-wise," "over-doing," conceited and disingenuous—adjectives which expressed his opinion of Owen as a man and a theologian. Owen expounded the position summarized above in *The Reason of Faith* (*Works*, ed. Goold, IV:1-115). William Cunningham, in all else a Calvinist of the Owen type, admits that in stressing the importance of the external evidence for Christian truth Baxter "rose more above the ordinary current views of his age than Owen or any of his other great Puritan contemporaries" (*Theological Lectures*, 1878, 226).

105. XXII:226. By "tradition," he is careful to explain that he means the "universal, rational, infallible tradition" of history, and not "Romish authoritative tradition" (236).

There is evidence of truth in Scripture, and there are sound reasons for the Christian faith, before the Holy Ghost persuaded men to believe them. The Holy Ghost is not sent to cure the Scripture of obscurity ... but to cure men's eyes of blindness ... not ... to make our religion reasonable, but to make sinners reasonable ... for the believing it ... nor doth he cause us to believe by enthusiasm, or without reason, but he works on man as man, and causeth him to believe but what is credible; and his causing us to believe is by showing us the credibility of the thing ..."[106]

Such were the principles of the true "Methodus Probativa" by which Christianity could be made evident, the method of wise catechists and evangelists.[107] Owen's doctrine, Baxter was sure,

hath greatly hindered the faith of the unskilful ... it came from a preposterous care of the honour of the Scriptures ... hence it comes to pass, that every seeming contradiction or inconsistency in any book of Scripture, in chronology or any other respect, is thought ... to make the whole cause of Christianity as difficult, as that particular text is ... so that if the tempter draw any man to doubt of the standing still of the sun in the time of Joshua, of the life of Jonah in the belly of the whale, or any other such passage ... he must equally doubt of all his religion.[108]

Baxter himself had no doubts about the truth of the Bible; he defended its inerrancy on more than one occasion. But such belief, he insisted, was a *consequence* of a man's Christianity, not a *condition* of it. "The true order of settling your faith, is not first to require a proof that all the Scriptures is the Word of God; but first to prove the marrow of them, which is properly called the Christian religion, and then to proceed to strengthen your particular belief of all the rest."[109] Owen's was a false method, the way to skepticism, for it put the cart before the horse. Its advocates "begin in the middle,"[110] demanding the acceptance of a conclusion as a first principle. But it is not self-evident as such, and cannot be made so. Such a demand, therefore, makes the demonstration of Christianity impossible. But Baxter, a more consistent Puritan at this point than Owen, had no doubt that, beginning from what was indubitable (the evidence of his senses), he could prove Christianity true to anyone who would attend to his reasoning.

Christianity, then, was demonstrable. But not all its parts were equally well attested; and as the evidence for them varied, so did the degree of cer-

---

106. XX:xxxi f.
107. See chap. VII, *inf.*, for a sketch of the proof.
108. XII:95.
109. *loc. cit.*
110. p. 97.

tainty with which they might be held. Principles and premises were more certain than corollaries and conclusions, and immediate perceptions than mediate inferences. The "natural religion" on which Christianity was built was inferred from the indubitable fact of self-consciousness, and was thus more certain than its revealed superstructure; and within that superstructure there was a further hierarchy of certainties. Thus,

> My certainty of the Deity is greater than my certainty of the Christian Faith: My certainty of the Christian Faith in its Essentials, is greater than my certainty of the Perfection and Infallibility of all the Holy Scriptures: My certainty of that is greater than my certainty of the meaning of many particular Texts, and so of the truth of many particular Doctrines, or of the Canonicalness of some certain books.[111]

This was not to imply that Baxter was himself doubtful about any part of traditional Protestant and Puritan theology. His point was, rather, that no derived certainty can be greater, and must in fact be less, than the primary certainties from which it is inferred; and, therefore, that unanimity may not be expected or required of Christians on those topics where the truth is comparatively less certain, because less evident. The essentials, the baptismal covenant and the summaries, are the most certain parts of Christianity, and the denial of them is "intolerable" within the Church. But disagreement on non-essentials, which are less certain than the fundamentals on which they depend, may and must be tolerated. It is, indeed, normal and inevitable; for, though the whole of Christian doctrine can be demonstrated to a sufficiently acute mind, "subjective certainty is as various as men's intellects, where no two are of a size,"[112] and not every truth is demonstrable to everybody. "Recipitur ad modum recipientis."

Here, again, Baxter came into collision with the "over-orthodox," who held that their first principle, the inspiration of the Bible, required them to profess everything which it taught with an equal degree of confidence, and construed Baxter's descending scale of certainty, not as an account of things as they are *quoad nos*, but as infidelity in the bud. We may mention one of the consequent clashes. It occurred in 1653, when, in his *Right Method*, Baxter wrote of the perseverance of believers: "I dare not say, that *I am Certain of this* ... It is my opinion, but I dare not put it into my Creed ..."[113] This was interpreted by the "over-orthodox" as virtual denial. It caused such a furor that Baxter added an

---

111. *R.B.*, I:128.

112. XV:172.

113. *The Right Method For a settled Peace of Conscience, and Spiritual Comfort*, 1653, 165 f. The alternative which he thought possible was Augustine's view that only a proportion of believers, those who were also elect, persevered.

explanatory page in the next edition and in the third omitted the passage altogether, and wrote a pamphlet, *Richard Baxter's Account of his Present Thoughts ... about the Perseverance of the Saints* (1657) to answer his critics. He there indicates the true bearing of his remark. He was not uncertain about perseverance himself; he had no wish to undermine the certainty of others; but he would not make a non-essential doctrine which most Fathers, Augustine, the Arminians and nearly all Roman and Lutheran theologians had denied, a test of church communion, and had, therefore, left it out of the creed which he was composing at the time: namely, the Worcestershire Association's Profession of Faith, which he wrote to be "a test of our people's capacity of Church-communion." Although "I am confident there is not one of the subscribers that doth question the Doctrine," he "purposely avoided the determining of the controversy";[114] non-essentials must not be introduced into a creed. Those who held all truths to be equally certain, and whose creeds in consequence "swelled as big almost as Aquinas summes [summas],"[115] seemed to Baxter willfully blind to the facts of the case.

The last paragraphs reflect a fact of the first importance for understanding Baxter's place in Puritanism: before he began to write, Puritanism had begun to split. As we saw, it was the fusion of Renaissance intellectualism with Reformation religion that had revived the Mediaeval synthesis and created Puritan culture. But to grasp in its proportions and sustain in its wholeness such a vast synoptic outlook as was involved in the Puritan ideal of uniting all knowledge under God was a task for intellectual giants, and few were equal to it. Hence the world-view cast by Puritan theologians and philosophers cracked almost before it was out of the mould. One group clung to the Platonic rationalism which they had learned from the humanists, stressing the dignity, power and office of human reason, magnifying God's self-revelation in the created order and in conscience, refusing to go beyond plain evidence of truth, distrustful of the dogmatism of slapdash exegesis and presumptuous speculation, tolerant of differences on non-essentials within the broad confines of Christian profession and practice. These were the Cambridge Platonists and their successors. They held fast to reason and natural religion, but drifted away from Augustinian piety and redemptive revelation. Soon they lost their sense of solidarity with the historic church in its witness to the historic gospel. At the end of the road they were treading lay Deism, Arianism and the eclipse of the Presbyterian cause in England.

The other group retained the biblical Augustinianism of Geneva, with its stress on fallen man's spiritual blindness, its reverence for God's Word written,

---

114. *Richard Baxter's Account*, 24.
115. *Aphorisms of Justification*, To the Reader.

its vivid sense of the difference between saints and sinners, its demand for radical conversion, its ecclesiasticism, its theological vitality, and its sublime awareness of the transcendence of God Almighty. These were mostly Independents, followers of the great John Owen. They retained the intense, scrupulous piety, often somber, sometimes glowing and passionate, which has always marked British Calvinism, but jettisoned the Platonism of earlier Puritan culture. They were dogmaticians, not rationalists. Revealed truth, they held, was supra-rational, just as regeneration was supernatural. God's elect were convinced and converted through a mysterious, ineffable irruption of His Spirit into their hearts, causing them to find in a message which before seemed foolishness to them the wisdom and the power of God. The transition was as abrupt as that from blindness to sight. It followed, therefore, that an apologetic designed to prove Christianity true was a waste of time and trouble. The unregenerate would not receive it, and the regenerate, to whom the Bible had come to evidence itself as the Word of God, did not need it. It may justly be said of this party that they clung to grace so closely and exclusively as to lose interest in nature. They did not labour to build the synthesis which the Puritan rationalists had projected. They devoted themselves to Biblical theology, and left philosophy and the sciences to go their own way.

The two parties drifted further and further apart, to their mutual impoverishment and loss. But at least one Puritan had a mind sufficiently large and a love of truth sufficiently strong to sustain and develop the synthesis in its full, comprehensive sweep; to evaluate nature positively without under-valuing grace, and to assert grace without denying nature; to invoke reason's authority in order to prove that the Church's gospel and Bible possess God's authority; to take all arts and sciences for his province, so that he might himself construct the hierarchy of truth and show, according to the Puritan blueprint, how all that is comes form God and leads to God. The man in question was Richard Baxter. In his thought we find united and integrated all the separate insights for which each party contended. He stood between both because he embraced both, and asserted, in its place, everything for which either stood. He was a rationalist, sure that the universe was intelligible and all truth demonstrable, and at the same time a dogmatist, teaching and defending Puritan Calvinism and taking his stand on the infallible Book. As a theologian, he was Biblical without being bibliolatrous, rational but never rationalistic, dogmatic without becoming doctrinaire. He faced all the facts, and found a place in his synthesis for them all. And his synthesis was no mere agglomeration of bits and pieces, but a connected, articulated whole, the product of organizing genius. It is a part of this larger system that we are to examine in detail in our present study.

Of Baxter's own intellectual character, little more need be said. It is already apparent that he was *anima naturaliter Puritana*, the incarnation of Puritanism at its purest. Few, if any, of his contemporaries were so passionately devoted to truth, or so tireless in the pursuit of it. "I never discover a Truth in my studies, but it is as sweet to my mind as a feast to my body," Baxter wrote in his third published book; "I spend my time, and strength and spirits in almost nothing but studying after Truth."[116] His was, he admitted, "a mind that would fain know all."[117] Even at the end of his life, William Bates tells us, "His Industry was almost incredible in his Studies: he had ... faint Faculties, yet such was the continual Application of himself ... as if the Labour of one Day had supplied strength for another."[118] The extent of his reading was almost unbelievable. As early as 1653, he could write with reference to theology: "Though I have not read all that hath been written for so many hundred years (sc., since the Apostolic age), yet I have read most of the Writers of great note";[119] twenty years later, he could have made that statement with reference to almost any subject.[120] The love of analysis and "method" was born in him: "I could never from my first studies endure *Confusion* ... I never thought I understood any thing till I could *anatomize* it, and see ... the conjunction of the parts!"[121] It was his passion to know things as they are that led him to the painstaking exactness which his readers found so tiresome. When critics objected to his elaborate definitions and distinctions, because they made his theology hard, without raising the question, whether or not they made it true, Baxter was merciless. He dealt with them as a schoolmaster with lazy pupils. He could sympathize with those whose mental powers were less than his own, but not with those who loved truth less than he did. The doctrinaire theorist who was too proud to check his brain-child by the facts was given short shrift. So was the dogmatism of ignorance and the floundering of incompetence. Baxter's hardest blows were reserved for superficial and muddled thought.

This was not merely because Baxter, an aristocrat by temperament, disliked incompetence as such; though this was true in fact.[122] It was rather because he saw the search for truth as man's first duty, and shoddy thinking seemed to him almost impious. Until one thoroughly understood a subject and knew

116. *Plain Scripture Proof,* 1650, 2.

117. XVIII:314.

118. *Funeral Sermon,* 122; cf. Sylvester's remark in *Elijah's Cry...*, 14: "In his Studying-times ... he could not bear with trivial disturbance."

119 Answer to ... Blake" in *Apology,* 154. Baxter explains that he had only read part of "the most Voluminous," such as Augustine and Chrysostom.

120. Baxter was weak only in mathematics and languages (besides Latin, he was limited to "a mediocrity in Greek," supplemented by "an inconsiderable trial at the Hebrew long after") (*R.B.,* I:6).

121. *R.B.,* I:6.

122. cf. *Poetical Fragments,* 1681, To the Reader: "I have long thought that a painter, a musi-cian, and a poet are contemptible if they be not excellent ..."

how to say what one meant, he held, one should keep quiet. Truth was too sacred to smother under a heap of empty words. To the end of his life he could never understand how his fellow-Christians could love truth so little and seek it so half-heartedly. He himself was absolutely honest and fearless in facing facts, finding truth and following it out, both in thought and practice. He was ready to stand alone, if truth so led. He would not be hidebound by tradition, not even Protestant and Puritan tradition. A majority vote was no substitute for evidence. When he expounded his convictions, he did so in such a way as to make clear the evidence for them. His theological writings were invariably organized as a catena of "self-evidencing coherent propositions."[123] "In all my large writings," he challenged his critics in 1689, "if you find that I call anything certain which is uncertain, that is, which I give not ascertaining evidence of, acquaint me with the particulars, and I shall retract it."[124] What was not evident ought not to be received as true, by Baxter any more than his readers.

After 1647,[125] he saw it as part of his mission to act as peacemaker within the Universal Church, and all his dogmatic and controversial writings were more or less directly designed to promote this end. He "meddled much with Controversies ... to end them."[126] In 1675 he brought out *Richard Baxter's Catholick Theologie: Plain, Pure, Peaceable: For Pacification of the Dogmatical Word-Warriours*, a folio designed to reconcile "Synodists and Arminians, Calvinists and Lutherans, Dominicans and Jesuits." The only real difference between them, Baxter argued, concerns perseverance; all other differences are merely verbal. The book, together with his two other folios, the *Methodus* and *Directory*, embodied his "maturest, calmest thoughts."[127] In 1691, he produced *An End of Doctrinal Controversies .... by Reconciling Explication, without much Disputing*,[128] which covered the same ground more summarily. He was a brilliant controversialist. He could distinguish real from verbal differences; he was exact in definition and accurate in usage; and his respect for truth and sense of responsibility for it kept him from undignified wrangling. He was accused of petty pride, but unjustly; his controversial writings bear witness only to the love of truth and peace which he professed. He believed that he had found the truth that must reconcile a divided Church, and that his opponents, by their misunderstanding and muddle-headedness, were obscuring it, thereby perpetuating conflict. He therefore hurried into battle in order to stop the war,

---

123. *How far Holiness is the Design of Christianity*, 1671, 2.
124. XV:172.
125. "These four and forty years" (*End of Doctrinal Controversies*, 1691, Preface).
126. *C.T.*, Preface.
127. *True History of Councils*, 1682, 240.
128. Written some twenty years earlier, i.e. before *C.T.*; probably immediately after the completion of *M.T.* (p. xxxiv).

as "an Offender of the Offenders of the Church."[129] His aim was to recall all parties to Catholic truth, the faith of the historical witnessing community. His opponents accused him of "singularity," and he recognized, more clearly than they did, that the charge, if true, must utterly discredit him as a Church theologian; but he turned it against those who levelled it, and insisted that it was they, not he, who had left the faith of the Church Universal. His challenge to Dr. Tully is typical of many passages in his controversial books:

> Choose out any one Point of real Difference between you and me about Justification and come to a fair trial, on whose side the Churches of Christ have been for 1500 years after Christ; you bring me but any ... considerable Person, that was for a thousand years for your Cause against mine, and I will say, that you have done more to confute me by far, than yet you have done ...[130]

The truth is, that Baxter held a more just estimate of the importance of the Church's historical continuity than most of his contemporaries. We have already seen one proof of this fact, his remarkably "modern" recognition that the Gospel which created the Church and is preserved within the Church is distinct from the Bible, and that the right way to regard the Bible is as an inspired and normative witness to it. We here see a further illustration of the same insight. Baxter was, *ex professo*, a "meer Catholick." His communion, he claimed, was with the Universal Church, militant and triumphant. His rule, therefore, was: "take nothing as necessary to salvation in point of faith, nor ... of practice, which the universal church in every age since Christ did not receive ... no opinion can be true that condemneth all the church to hell, in any one age ..."[131] Doctrines never heard of before the Reformation he profoundly distrusted. Not that he undervalued the Reformation; but he would not lose his sense of proportion in assessing its significance. The Reformation had purified the Church's life and doctrine (though more still needed to be done), but it had not changed the nature of Christianity. What had been essential before was essential still—the baptismal covenant and the summaries; and what was non-essential before was non-essential still—including all doctrinal novelties of sixteenth- and seventeenth-century origin. True or not, they were not necessary to salvation; they were minority opinions in Christ's Church, and for that very reason it was antecedently likely that they were false. Baxter himself claimed to do no more than "methodize" the faith of the Church Universal, and to guard it against the myopic sectarianism of Protestants who

---

129. *Scripture Gospel Defended*, title-page.
130. "An Answer to Dr. Tullies Angry Letter" in *J.R.*, 20.
131. V:149.
132. *op. cit.*, vii.

in expounding the terms of salvation themselves departed from it. He knew in advance that they must be wrong, and he thought he could show them where they had gone wrong. To this point we shall return when in a later chapter we consider Luther's "articulus stantis vel cadentis ecclesiae," the doctrine of justification by faith.

We here conclude the first part of our study, which was designed to introduce Richard Baxter and to provide some account of the guiding principles of his thought. He has appeared as a Puritan thoroughbred. He endorsed the religious and cultural ideals of the movement and devoted himself with unparalleled energy and versatility to their realization. His eclecticism was inspired wholly by his desire to remain true to the inner logic of the Puritan position. Superficial critics, of his own day and since, have seen him as deviating from it; but the truth is the reverse: Baxter was the most consistent Puritan of them all. His intellectual ideals were inherited, and his originality lay in the "method" which he devised in order to implement them. We have seen something of the magisterial quality of his thought. J. M. Lloyd-Thomas speaks of "his enduring undatedness."[132] Like Calvin, and Bunyan, and very few more, he rose above his age. He took nothing for granted. He tested received opinion and popular prejudice by the touchstone of certain fact and universal principle. He made it his life's work to know and judge of things as they are; and as they were then, so in all essentials they remain. That Baxter's doctrine of the Church has a message for the present day has already been recognized.[133] That his doctrine of man, created, fallen, redeemed and restored, is no less valuable to the contemporary Church will, it is hoped, become clear as we proceed.

133. cf. I. Morgan, *The Nonconformity of Richard Baxter*, 1946; Hugh Martin, *Puritanism and Richard Baxter*, 1954.

PART II

THE RUIN OF THE RACE

"God hath made man upright; but they have sought out many inventions."

Eccl. 7:29

Chapter 5

Man: Created

SYNOPSIS

1. Introduction: the importance of self-knowledge;
    Baxter's diligence in seeking it.
2. Man a rational being with a triple soul.
    Three faculties in the rational soul: vital power
                                     intellect; its activity
                                     will; its appetition
                                     its freedom
    The soul as sensitive; sensitive appetite.

3. The psychology of rational action: a hierarchy of activities.
    Love the distinctively human activity:
        sensitive self-love, rational self-love, rational love of good
            as such:
    man's search for happiness.
    Analysis of the psychology of human action.

4. Man made in God's image; self-knowledge leads to knowledge of God.
    The threefold image: natural
                         moral
                         relative, imaging God's government
                             (*regnum Dei*).

5. God's triple relation to man:
    God as DOMINUS, man's owner;
    God as RECTOR, man's moral governor;
        human nature demands moral government;
        the law of Nature;
        supernatural ("positive") law;
        God's governmental attributes.
    God as BENEFACTOR, man's end;
        man's duty of love.

6. Baxter's natural theology comprehensive but not self-sufficient:
    comparison with Herbert
    resemblance to Cambridge Platonists.

7. Conclusion: these positions fundamental in Baxter's theology.

(Principal Sources: *Methodus Theologiae*, I:1-380; *The Knowledge of God*, in *The Divine Life*, XIII; *The Reasons of the Christian Religion*, XX:441-XXI; *More Reasons of the Christian Religion*, XXI:519 f.; *An End of Doctrinal Controversies.*)

Chapter 5

Man: Created

"Man is the most exquisite piece in the creation. He is a microcosm, or little world … the masterpiece of this visible world … The soul of man …is the man of the man" —Thomas Watson, on the *Shorter Catechism*, Q. VIII

"Very little has been learned in addition to what the sixteenth and seventeenth centuries accomplished in the doctrine of the emotions; whereas, on the other hand, extraordinarily much of it has been forgotten." —M. Steinitzer

In the *ordo cognoscendi*, introspection is the beginning of wisdom; self-knowledge is the road to knowledge of God:

'Prima verae sapientiae pars est, vere scire nosmetipsos. 1. Quia inde certo & finem & Officia nostra, pleraque colligimus: Qui vere novit quid sit Homo, novit etiam vel ad noscendum paratus est, quorsum est conditus? quo tendit? quid amare? quid sperare? quid agere? oportet. 2. Quia in seipso Dei Creatoris Imaginem inveniet & in speculo hoc Deum ipsum pro modulo nostro hic videre, seu nosse, necesse habemus. Et Deum plerique non norunt, qui seipsos non norunt."[1]

Nothing is more certain than the elementary data of self-consciousness, and nothing, rightly understood, bears clearer testimony to man's place in the universe. We are now to examine this witness, and thereby to appreciate the significance of the psychological studies which, as we saw, Baxter thought so necessary for the theologian. And it is important to make clear at the outset

---

1. *M.T.*, I:v.2, 154 f. [The first part of true wisdom is, trulyy to know ourselves …]

that Baxter's studies "de Anima" were genuinely psychological, in the modern sense of that word, though carried on in the vocabulary and thought-forms of Mediaeval physics and metaphysics. Baxter took nothing on trust from his authorities without first testing it and modifying it where necessary in the light of searching self-scrutiny. "Cum non *libros*, sed *animam meam* inspicio, experientia ductus fas esse judico dicere ..."[2] are words which could stand as a preamble to all his exposition; each detail had been checked and cross-checked by introspection into his own Puritan soul. Here, as elsewhere, he was of all the Puritans the most appreciative of others' labors and the least hidebound by them, more a traditionalist and more an eclectic than any of them. His account of man is the fullest and most characteristic that Puritanism produced.

"HOMO est MENS INCARNATA," "Animal Mentale ... Mens incorporata,"[3] Baxter affirmed. Man consists of an inert body indwelt by an active soul. The latter must be conceived (inadequately) as "a *Vital, Intellectual, Volitive Spirit*, animating a *humane organized Body*."[4] It contains within itself three "*general Faculties*, that is, mental, sensitive and vegetative ... distinct, but not divided ... not three *Souls*, but one."[5] By a faculty, power or virtue (virtus), Baxter meant "principium agendi," that is, principle of action; a concept made up of three "inadequate conceptions," the power to act, as such ("potentia-activa"), the capacity to perform a specific function ("vis") and the tendency to pursue a specific goal ("inclinatio"). (This analysis, we may note, retains the teleology of Thomistic metaphysics but replaces the rhythm of *potentia* and *actus* by a doctrine of energy immanent in each spiritual substance.) Each of the three characteristic faculties of man's soul was further trichotomized. The vegetative faculty, shared with plants, involved "three Faculties, Motive, Discretive (differencing its proper Nutriment from other things) and Attractive (which is assimilative)." The sensitive faculty, shared with the animal creation, "hath the Faculties, 1. Vitally active, 2. Sensibly apprehensive, 3. Sensibly appetitive." Mental powers are peculiar to man, making him the noblest of creatures and the rightful lord of the rest of creation. They consist of "three distinct faculties ... *Vital Active Power, Intellect* and *Will*."[6]

Of these three, the first is simply "vita," which, here as at the other two levels of human existence, manifests its presence in the fact that there is some activity as distinct from none. It is "considerable, first as exciting *Intellection*

---

2. I:vii, 195.

3. I:v, 153; I:vii.2, 186.

4. *Of the Immortality of Man's Soul*, 1682, 27. Baxter explains that, strictly speaking, it is its relation to the body that constitutes it a soul: "*separated*, it is not *formally* a Soul, but a Spirit still" (*loc. cit.*).

5. *An End of Doctrinal Conroversies*, ix.

6. *An End of Doctrinal Controversies*, x f.

and *Will*, and after as *Executive*."[7] This power of action in general underlies, and is presupposed in, Baxter's account of the specific potentialities of intellect and will.[8] *Intellect*, the second member of the triad, has as its object "ENS [being, reality] in sua triplice affectione essentiali, viz. ut *Existens* ... Verum, & Bonum":[9] that is to say, as fact in general and as moral value, which is a kind of fact, in particular. External objects are presented to the understanding via sense (the power to apprehend through contact,[10] and "phantasia" (the power to form and retain an image of the content of an act of sense-perception);[11] and the mind comprehends the object through its cognizance of the image.[12] The occurrence and nature of conscious internal acts of sense, thought and will, however, is known directly and immediately, by reflection. "As by seeing, hearing, feeling, we perceive that we *see, hear, feel, &c.* every Sense having essentially a *self-perception*: So by thinking, knowing, willing, nilling, loving, joying, we perceive that we do it ..."[13] Images and reflex perceptions together constitute the raw material of thought, which consists in the apprehension, analysis and combination of this material as a means to the knowledge of things (including things not sensed, but inferred from the evidence of sense) and the attainment of good. "Conscience" is the name given to one particular class of these mental operations. Properly, "the word conscience signifieth ... the knowledge of ourselves and our own matters in relation to God's law and judgment: *Judicium hominis de seipso prout subjicitur judicio Dei*, as Amesius defineth it."[14] This knowledge may consist in a judgment either of desert or of

7. *op. cit.*, xi. The character of "vital power" is more precisely described in a further trichotomy in M.T., I:vi.12, 177; "triplicem habet naturalem inclinationem: 1. Magis inclinatur ad *Agendum* quam ad *Non agendum*. 2. Magis inclinatur ad *Actiones Naturae congruas*, quam ad *incongruas*. 3. Inclinatur *ad Volitiones exequendas*." [It has a threefold natural inclination: 1. It is more inclined to action than to inaction. 2. It is more inclined to actions natural to it than unnatural. 3. It is inclined to execute wishes.]

8. "Intellectus quidem est *Potentia Activa*; sed tantum in specie *Actus Intellegendi*: Et Voluntas est *Potentia Activa*; sed tantum in specie Actus Volendi aut Nolendi: Suntque *Potentia secunda* & *tertia* . . . At *Potentia* Vitalis ab Intellectu & Voluntate distinctum principium est; haec est prima . . ." (*M.T.*, I:vi.7, 177).

9. I:vii.10, 186 f.

10. "Omnis sensus est *per Tactum*" (I:x.32, 227). By what operation of spirits contact was effected, however, in the case of distant objects, Baxter did not profess to know.

11. "Phantasia" includes memory, the storehouse of images: "*Memoria* non est sensus a Phantasia distinctus." Baxter recognised, however, that memory retains thoughts as well as perceptions, and distinguished accordingly: "memoria videtur esse duplex, Intellectus scilicet, & sensitiva" (M.T., I:x.35, 227; 79, p. 232).

12. cf. M.T., I:vi.27, 189: "Res externae corporeae prius a sensu & phantasia percipiuntur quam ab intellectu." [External material things are perceived by sense and imagination before intellect.]

13. *An End of Doctrinal Controversies*, ix.

14. *Works*, VI:96; quoting Ames, *De Conscientia*, I:i.1. Baxter appends an acute analysis of usage: "conscience is taken. 1. Sometimes for the act of self-knowing. 2. Sometimes for the habit. 3. Sometimes for the ... intellect itself, as it is a faculty of self-knowing ... 4. And sometimes ... for the person himself, that doth *conscire*: or for his will (another faculty)."

duty. The mind's practical judgment ("iudicium practicum") is to be distinguished from instinctive and (literally) unthinking reaction, which is an act, not of intellect, but of fantasy and sensitive appetite. Reactions of this kind make up the "thinking" of "brutes."[15] Man's mind must check such pseudo-reasoning as this.

The third rational faculty is *will*: a self-determining appetitive faculty, directed to good as such. "Bonum scilicet, qua Bonum appetit, & nihil nisi sub ratione Boni."[16] 'Good' to Baxter is the proper denomination of any object, experience or idea that presents itself to the mind as in any way attractive and pleasurable, whether as means or end: "both ... that which hath a simple excellency in itself, and which maketh for the happiness of the world, or my own."[17] Following the Greek and Mediaeval tradition, he treats attractiveness as the specific mark of goodness; "Ad *Jucundum*, qua tale, Voluntas omnis humana inclinatur."[18] What attracts and pleases is *ipso facto* good "secundum quid [in some way]," though it may be bad in every other respect. The object of an act of will is first apprehended by intellect. Good must be discerned before it can be desired, and will, as such, is eyeless. "Neque potest Voluntas se determinare ad actum ... sine apprehensione aliquali praevia *intellectus* ... Objectum enim Voluntatis est Bonum ... *intellectum*. Et Voluntas suum objectum non intelligit."[19] "Sine ductu Intellectus nihil appetit [It seeks nothing without the leading of intellect]." Will is naturally free; neither intellect by its apprehensions, nor objects by their attractiveness, nor sensitive appetite by its importunity, nor angelic powers by direct influence on the soul, so necessitate the will as to be the efficient and decisive cause of its acts.[20] Will determines itself, by its own inherent power. God is the first cause of its acts only in the sense that He made it capable of so acting. Baxter constantly stresses this point, on which, as we shall see,[21] he differed from many of his Calvinistic contemporaries. Natural liberty of will, he insisted, consists in freedom from physical constraint: freedom, that is, from such external necessitation as would destroy man's moral responsibility for what he does. "By the Power and Liberty

15. cf. *M.T.*, I:x, 36: "Phantasiae tria sunt officia: Apprehendere res simplices, *Receptive* & *Memorative*, & *Aestimare* vel judicare (ut Lepus aestimat Canem sibi inimicum) & *Practice colligere* quid agendum est (ut Lepus judicat Canem fugiendum esse)"—"Quamvis non proprie ratiocinando" (margin).

16. I:viii.7, 200.

17. *Works*, XX:459.

18. *M.T.*, I:viii. 20, 201.

19. I:viii.88 and 163, 207, 214

20. cf. I:viii.102 f., 208: "Objectum Voluntatem non necessario vel certe determinat, neque *Intellectus* eam ita determinare potest . . . Boni Angeli Voluntatem *juvare* multum possunt; *praedeterminare* autem *motione necessitante* . . . non possunt. Suggestiones & sollicitationes *Diaboli* etiam ad malum *pellicere* possunt Voluntatem; Motione *necessitante determinare* non possunt."

21. chap. XIII.

given by God, the Will can act or not act, or turn itself to this object or to that … And this Power and Liberty is its Nature, and God's Image."[22]

Man's soul, as we saw, is sensitive as well as rational. As sensitive, it has its own vital power, its own capacity for apprehension (sense), and its own "inclinatio," the sensitive appetite. Baxter trichotomized the latter into "Appetitus Animalis," the impulse to gratify the various senses;[23] "Appetitus Naturalis," the urge to absorb nourishment and relieve physical tension; and "Appetitus Vitalis," under which he subsumed the passions. These are emotionally charged reactions, positive and negative, to different objects, according as they appear conducive or detrimental to life, pleasure and health. They are of two sorts, "concupiscibiles" and "irascibiles." Of the former, three are "ad bonum" ("Amare, vel Complacentiam habere; Concupiscere; Gaudere" [love, desire, joy]), and three "contra malum" ("Odio habere; Fugere; Tristari"[hatred, aversion, sorrow]). Of the latter, six are "erga bonum" ("Positive, 1. Confidere, 2. Audere, 3. Sperare [confidence, daring, hope]; Privative, 1.Diffidere, 2. Animo despondere, 3. Desperare" [diffidence, despondency, despair]); three "adversus malum" ("Ira, Timor, Pudor" [anger, fear, shame]); and "Plurimae … sunt Passiones *Mixtae*; ut superbia, humilitas, contentatio, inquietudo, patientia, impatientia, cura, reverentia, admiratio, zelus, contemptus, poenitentia, obstinatio, &c."[24]

Man was made for rational action. The hierarchy of his faculties was designed to this end. "Omnis natura inferior est quodammodo propter superiorem … Appetitus scilicet *Naturalis* (sc. vegetative appetite) ad praeservationem Vitae, & ad *Usum Sensus* factus est: Appetitus autem Sensitivus ad praeservationem Naturae Sensitivae, & ad *Usum* Naturae *Intellectualis*, factus est." Sense, the medium of perception, has its *raison d'etre* as a means to thought and knowledge: man possesses *sense* "propter *Intellectum*."[25] The passions, which, as we saw, canalize the outflow of energy from the soul as sensitive, were also implanted in man to promote rational action, by subserving thought and volition. Some passions were designed to evoke them, and some to be evoked by them. "Deus enim Naturae res ita ordinavit, ut quaedam passiones internae positivae, utilia essent media ad intellectum, Voluntatem & Potentiam superiorem, ad actum suscitandum; quaedam vero intellectionem & Volitionem sequerentur, ad meliorem scilicet decretorum executionem."[26] Baxter made this point over and over again by the use of two images which were themselves Puritan commonplaces: the passions, he said, are "the wheels or the sails of the

22. *C.T.*, I:ii.6, 28.
23. cf. *M.T.*, I:ix, 224, for details.
24. pp. 225 f.
25. *M.T.*, I:v.16-7, 158.
26. I:v.24, 159.

reasonable soul, to speed our motion."[27] Simple apprehension of fact by sense and intellect (both, so far, wholly necessitated by the object)[28] is not in itself moral action, but sets the stage for it. It is the choice by which man responds to known fact that is "actus ... plene humanus,"[29] deliberate and, therefore, responsible. In this choice all his rational powers are involved, intellect and executive power operating at the direction, or misdirection, of will.

Volition and action originate in the promptings of appetite, which in relation to particular objects is denominated *love* ("amor"). "Love is the complacency of the appetite in apprehended good."[30] Love is at the root of all conative action whatsoever. There is in man a double appetite, that of sense and of rational will; consequently, there is a double love.

> Love is either merely sensitive and passionate, which is the sensible act and passion of the sensitive and fantastical appetite; or it is rational, which is the act of the rational appetite or will. The first is called sensitive in a double respect. 1. Because it followeth the apprehension of the senses, or fantasy, loving that which they apprehend as good; 2. And because it is exercised passionately and feelingly by the sensitive appetite. And the other is called rational, 1. Because it is the love of that which reason apprehendeth as good; and, 2. Because it is the complacency of that will which is a higher faculty than the sensitive appetite ... Sensitive love is the complacency of the sensitive appetite in sensible good (or in that which the sense and imagination apprehendeth as good). Rational love is the complacency of the rational appetite in that which reason apprehendeth as good ...[31]

The characteristic human activity, therefore, is a rational love to all good things, proportionate to their goodness: "we should love all that is good, and love that best which is best." To this activity, sensitive love is itself a means. Sensitive love is always self-love, "necessary and not free ... Sensitive self-love containeth in it, 1. A love of life, and that is, of individual self-existence; 2. And a love of all sensitive pleasures of life; and, 3. Consequently, a love of all the means of life and pleasure."[32] As such, it is "planted in man and brutes, as a principle ... to engage the creature in the use of the means of its own preservation, and so to bring it to perfection."[33] But it is not a rational appetite, and must be subjected

27. *Works*, XI:148.
28. cf. *M.T.*, I:viii.85, 206 f.: "Intellectus non est Liber ... nisi quatenus est sub imperio *Voluntatis*: sed movetur per modum naturae, & per necessitatem naturalem. Cogi scilicet quis potest per objecta, ea intelligere, quae intelligere nollet."
29. I:viii (ix).16, 220.
30. *Works*, II:460 f.; cf. XVIII:370. "Pleasure and love are the same thing."
31. II:459 f.
32. p. 461.
33. p. 460.

to reason's control. Sensitive self-love must be subordinated to rational self-love, and this in turn to the love of good as such. In man as God made him, "self-love did subserve the love of the universe and God; and man desired his own preservation for these higher ends."[34] This is still what God and human nature require. When, therefore, sensitive appetite urges the pursuit of its object of desire, the will should first command the intellect to assess whether such action would in fact be a means to the highest good, and determine itself according to the result of the investigation; for rational action consists, not merely in choosing good as distinct from evil, but in choosing the best of possible alternatives. "Bonum ... *simpliciter Volitum comparate* nolendum est ... quando Bono superiori sit oppositum & inimicum."[35]

Often it is necessary and right to deny the cravings of sensitive appetite. In the first place, rational self-love may well direct the acceptance of present sensible evil as a means to future good (e.g. "to take bitter physic" as a means to health).[36] And, in the second place, the satisfaction of sensitive appetite is for rational creatures only one kind of good among many. "The rational soul ... is naturally inclined not only to love itself, and that which is for itself, but also to love extrinsic good," even that which "could be of no benefit to us," such as "the good of posterity of countries, of kingdoms, of the church, of the world ... when we are dead and gone."[37] Furthermore, as we shall see, the highest object of rational love is God himself, and other good things may be loved and sought only as they tend to God's glory and man's enjoyment of Him—i.e., only so far as they are really good. Sensitive appetite is not party at all to love of this sort. "Though I must love greater, simple, extrinsic good above myself, with that love which is purely rational, yet it cannot ordinarily be done with a more sensitive and passionate love."[38] But while Baxter is emphatic that a man can and should take pleasure in good which is not good for him personally,[39] he is equally emphatic that man cannot love anything which is in his apprehension bad for him, nor can it ever be his duty to perform such an impossi-

---

34. XI:xxvii.
35. *M.T.*, I:viii.125.
36. *Works*, XX:460.
37. II:460.
38. p. 462.
39. Baxter denounced the alternative view as a shameless rationalization of sin: "And were not narrow selfishness much of our Pravity, we should take the universal and publick good, and Gods love to it and Pleasedness and Glory in it, to be much more our end, and the object of our desire and delight, than any personal felicity of our own. It is a monster of inhumanity in the Doctrine of the *Sadducees*, i.e., materialists, *Spinosa*, *Hobbes*, and their brutish followers, that they set up Individual self interest as a mans chiefest end and object of rational Love ... and own no Good, but that which Relatively is Good to me ... Though *Grace* only savingly cure this base inhumane maladie, yet *common reason* beareth witness against it, and only sense, and *reason* captivated by sense do patronize it" (*Church-History*, 1680, Preface).

bility. Self-love, sensitive and rational, "is so deeply rooted in nature, that we cannot lay it by, nor love anything that is absolutely and directly against us." For instance, "we conceive of the devil as ... one that seeks our destruction, and therefore we cannot love him."[40] Nor could we love God, if we thought him inimical to our happiness. For man is so made that "in general ... happiness is his end;"[41] he cannot but seek it, and he cannot love what is inconsistent with it. We shall see later that virtue consists in making God our end and loving Him above all things, in the knowledge that here true happiness is to be found; and that sin, rooted as it is in an inordinate and uncorrected love for an unsuitable object, is essentially a matter of seeking happiness in the wrong way. The one is a rational love of God, the other an irrational love of things. The first is wisdom, man's true life; the second is madness, the abjuration of rationality.

Baxter's elaborate analysis of the psychology of human action may here be reproduced in full. It pulls together in summary form all that has been spelled out in the foregoing paragraphs.

1. Voluntatis *Potentia*, *Inclinatio* Naturalis (ad faelicitatem, &c) [i.e. rational self-love] & Libertas supponuntur.
2. Sensus objectum sensibile percipit; & inde Phantasia Bonum imaginarium sensatum.
3. Intellectus Bonum (aut Malum) intelligendo Voluntati proponit.
4. Inde Voluntas Bonum (vel Malum) intellectum complacentia amat (vel odit) simpliciter.[42]
5. Alia item bona competantia Intellectus percipit, & comparanda esse dicit.
6. Voluntas Intellectum comparationem facere jubet; nisi abusu libertatis vel ignavia actum hunc omittit (*sic*), vel adhaesione ad unum impediatur: Et in hisce peccatum incipere videtur.[43]
7. Intellectus cogitando comparationem serie & fideliter instituit (nisi

---

40. *Works*, IX:28.

41. VII:39.

42. cf. I:viii.34, 202: "Primus Actus Voluntatis erga Bonum est *Complacentia*, quae *Amoris forma* est: Et primus actus erga malum est *Displicentia* quae est *Odium* vel *Aversatio Rationalis*."

43. Baxter asserts this view more than once; cf. *C.T.*, I.ii.XIX.23, 60: "It seemeth that *all sin beginneth* in the *wills omission* of what it was able to have done ... this *not-willing what and when it should*, is the beginning of all sin." This failure may be due to "an inordinate inclination to the pleasing of the fleshly (i.e., sensitive) appetite and fantasy" (*Works*, II:238) or to emotional turmoil: "passiones omnes inordinatae aptae sunt Libertatem *impedire*, in quantum scilicet Intellectus & Voluntatis *exercitium* impediunt per *violentiam sensationis*" (*M.T.*, I:viii.96, 207). Fear and pain are instanced; though Baxter notes that some of the actions to which these passions give rise are genuinely involuntary and not, therefore, "*Actus Humani*, id est, *Morales* ... Quando nulla adest *Voluntatis* vel *Actualis Consensus*, vel *Omissio privativa*, sed tantum *Omissio Negativa*" (I:v.31, 159). Not every failure of conscious control is culpable.

ignavia vel malo motu Voluntatis eius exercitatio impediatur vel
omittatur ...).

8. Intellectus Objectum praeferendum Voluntati clare & sine
dubitatione proponit.

9. Voluntas (nisi errore jam dicto praepedita) Optimum tenaciter
amplectitur.

10. Et simul (nisi libere adhaerendo peccans) bonum inconsistens rejicit
vel negligit.

11. Passiones saepissime Voluntatis hos actus vel promovent vel
impediunt praeveniendo.

12. Voluntas Finis Amore mota, Intellectui de Mediis inquirere imperat.

13. Mediorum aptissimum Intellectus invenit, nisi errore & peccato
impeditus.

14. Inventum Medium Voluntas eligit, nisi ignavia, morbo,[44] vel errore
impedita.

15. De Mediis recte utendis consulere Intellectum jubet ...

16. Consilio Intellectus (nisi peccando deficiens) Voluntas consentit.

17. Potentiam executricem ad hunc Mediorum usum suscitat.

18. Opponentibus & impedientibus cunctis adversatur.

19. Ad executionem & contra oppositionem passiones suscitat (nisi
inordinate se ingerant).[45]

20. In Fine comprehenso, Amore delectatur, eoque, Amore adhaerendo,
fruitur.[46]

Such is human nature and human action, as Baxter understood them. His
account consists mainly of traditional material, revised and re-shaped by a
vigorous and independent mind.[47] The hierarchy of faculties within man's soul,
the conception of attractiveness as the mark of goodness and the eudaemonism

---

44. Baxter recognized that mental acts not only conditioned but also were conditioned by the
state of the body; hence he often stressed the fact that "ad Animi salutem plurimum interest,
ipsum *Corpus* . . . in temperamento idoneo & conveniente conservare. Morbi enim Corporei,
praesertim ex Ebrietate, Crapula, Socordia, Venere & aliis peccatis orti, operationibus
Intellectualibus . . . admodum sunt inimici" (I:v.48, 162). [For the well-being of the mind it is
important to keep the body in a fit and fitting condition. For bodily disorders, especially those
arising from drunkenness, intoxication, idleness, sexual lust and other sins, are very hostile to
intellectual activities.]

45. cf. I:v.39: "Voluntas . . . non habet in sensus, Passiones, Phantasiam vel Appetitum
sensitivum, potestatem *despoticam*, sed quam vocant *Politicam*; vel saltem non habet potestatem
in hos nuto unico, vel facile . . . sed tantum per vigilantiam, industriam & constantiam."

46. I:viii, 199.

47. The theological student's book list in *Christian Directory* reflects the width of Baxter's
reading "de anima" and showed his relative valuation of sources. Books of the first importance are
(*Works*, V:588): *D. Francisci Toleti Commentaria una cun Quaestionibus in tres libros Aristotelis de
Anima* (1575); Melancthon, *Liber de Anima* (1540) ("written . . . to furnish a psychological groundwork for ethics," G. S. Brett, *History of Psychology*, 1912, II:164), a treatment which follows Aristotle on every subject but conscience; Vitus Amerbach, *De Anima* (1542) ("merely a transcript of

which finds at the root of love the desire for one's own happiness had been commonplaces in Western thought since Aristotle, and were part of the Neoplatonic heritage bequeathed to the Church by Augustine. If Baxter leaned more heavily on one authority within this tradition rather than another, it was on the "doctor subtilis," Duns Scotus, for whose psychology he had the highest regard ("if I must take any thing in this part of Philosophy on trust, I confess *Scotus* his credit will go as far with me, as any man that ever writ").[48] From Scotus came his insistence that man's soul is one; its faculties are only its powers, not its parts, its forms rather than, as Aquinas held, its accidents; indeed, the whole faculty analysis is nothing more than a series of "partial inadequate conceptions" of a single entity, nonetheless inadequate for being legitimate and illuminating.[49] His conception of will as a power of spontaneous self-determination, and of its freedom as consisting in the absence of coercion, seems to be an echo of the voluntarism with which Scotus opposed the intellectualism of Aquinas. His map of the passions, on the other hand, derives from Renaissance discussion of Scholastic tenets which go back ultimately to the Platonic θύμος and ἐπιθυμία ("passiones irascibiles" and "concupiscibiles," in Mediaeval terminology). What is new and distinctive in Baxter's account is his "method," trichotomy, and his introduction of the third faculty, "vita," [life] at each level of human action.[50] Substantially, however, his views are entirely characteristic of the Reformed Mediaevalism which produced him. For practical

---

Aristotle," Brett, *loc. cit.*); Ludovicus Vives, *De Anima* (1538) ("Aristotelian analyses fill out the programme," Brett, *loc. cit.*); J. C. Scaliger, *Exotericarum exercitationum liber XV de subtilitate* (1557); D. *Sennerti Hypomnemata physica* (1636). Books of secondary value are (V:597): Mamertus Claudianus, *De Statu Animae* (5th cent.) and Nemesius, *De Natura Hominis* (περὶ φύσεως ἀνθρώπου; 4th cent.), both concerned to prove the immateriality and immortality of the soul; Henry More, *The Immortality of the Soul, so farre forth as it is demonstrable from the knowledge of Nature and the light of Reason* (1659); Cicero's Tusculan Disputations (Cicero was in vogue during the latter part of the seventeenth century); the works of Plato and Plotinus. (Baxter gives only the author's name, but these identifications are certain.)

48. *Plain Scripture Proof of Infants Church-membership and Right to Baptism*, 358.

49. Baxter insists that his "many (not feigned or forced, but) real and necessary Trinaries in Unity" (*C.T.*, I:.i.15, 3) are conceptual only; yet they "are not *Fictions*, but as *Scotus* calls them, FORMALITATES . . . as noting only a *fundamentum objectivum distinguendi.*" (*An End of Doctrinal Controversies*, xi). Baxter adduces Scotus, Scaliger, and William Pemble, among others, in support of the view that the faculties are really distinct neither from the soul nor from each other (*Aphorisms of Justification*, 222).

50. When "vita" first found a place in Baxter's psychology is uncertain. Tillotson, writing to Sylvester, records Baxter's statement to him concerning the conversation in which the existence of "vita" as a principle was pointed out to him, but gives no hint of the date or circumstances. (Powicke, *Under the Cross*, 248). In the 1670 *Life of Faith*, Baxter admits, "I was wont to say of both faculties, I now say of the three faculties, which constitute the soul of man" (sc., as rational), as if his change of view had been comparatively recent (*Works*, XII:331). But reference to the three faculties appears as early as *Christian Concord*, 1653 ("Explication," 22), and often in later books.

purposes, Baxter adds little to the standard Puritan and Reformed conception of man's soul as made up of reason, will and affections; nor does he use his refinements upon it to say anything which his predecessors had not in substance said already. It would be wrong, however, for this reason to underrate the uncommon acuteness and ability which Baxter's anthropology displays.

The importance of a true doctrine "de anima," in Baxter's view, was due to the fact that to a unique degree "microcosmus homo"[51] bears the image of his Almighty, Wise, Good Creator, so that his clearest idea of the Divine nature must be formed by analogical predication from his conception of himself. This self-knowledge must be the stepping-stone to knowledge of God.

> God is here seen in the *Glass* of his Works ... And from these *works* we must borrow our conceptions ... the principal Glass in which we must *see God* ... is the *Soul of man* ... which being *our selves*, we can best perceive ... By the knowledge of our own *Acts* we know our *Powers* and the *Nature* of our *own souls* (though imperfectly); And by the Knowledge of our *Souls*, we know the *nature* of other *Intellectual Spirits*; and by the Knowledge of *our selves* and *them*, and the Scripture expressions of his Attributes, we *know* so much of *God* as we can here know ...[52]

As the Bible reveals what man is by showing what God is, so right reason may rise to grasp God by reflecting on man.

Reason and revelation unite to testify that God's image in created man was threefold: natural, moral and relative. "As God is the God of *Nature*, *Grace* and *Glory*, so he hath made on Man the Image of these three: 1. The natural Faculties of the Soul, are his natural Image on Man as Man ... 2. His moral gracious Image is Holiness, of Intellect, Will and Executive Power. 3. The Image of his Majesty, Glory and Greatness is, 1. in all men the Dominion over the lower Creatures: 2. And in Governours a Power over Subjects or Inferiours."[53] The first strand of this triple image has already been examined. Man's faculties reflect God's perfections: power, wisdom, goodness, active towards men as Life, Light and Love. Moreover, the fact that God knows and loves proves the existence in Him of something answering to sense in man.[54] The second strand

---

51. *M.T.*, I:v.1, 156. The Platonic conception of man as μικρόκοσμος ("a little world," *Works*, XIII:18) was common in seventeenth-century Reformed theology; cf. *R.D.*, 220, and Ames, *Marrow* I:viii.61, 37, where man is termed "the *Compendium*, abridgment of all Creatures."

52. *C.T.*, I:ii.7.13.21, 2 f.

53. *An End of Doctrinal Controversies*, ix f.

54. Baxter insisted that, though the nature of particular senses depends on the body, sense as such is essential to the being and activity of rational spirits as such, created and uncreated, human and Divine. God is not to be thought of as impassive: "Talis ... Amor vix nobis notus, qui non est quaedam sensatio. Et *Deus ipse* AMOR a Spiritu Sancto dicitur; Imo & *gaudere* saepe diditur in

consisted in "original righteousness," the form of which, though lost since the Fall, can at once be reconstructed merely by considering the faculties involved, quite apart from the Biblical testimony. Baxter delineates it as follows:

> the souls inclination to God as God; that is in the ... propensity of the soul, to love God for himself, as the infinite good, and also as our felicity. 2. In the understandings disposition to know God as one to be thus beloved. 3. In a holy vivacity Godward. 4. In the ordination and subjection of all the inferior faculties to the understanding and will thus inclined. 5. And *relatively*, in the innocency hence resulting.

This part of God's image was lost at the Fall, though the natural image remained; man continued man, though no longer good. The third strand was a matter of man's relation to the rest of the created order, in particular to animals. This relation "revera continet Relationum *Trium Divinarum* ad Creaturas *Imaginem*, viz. 1. *Sub-domini* sumus inferiorum, & ea *possidere, uti* & *alternare* ... possumus, jure huius sub-dominii. 2. Eorum item sumus sub-gubernatores; & juxta *nostram Voluntatem* (ad Divinum subordinate) hunc usum & dispositionem possumus jure ordinare. 3. Eorum item sumus *sub-Benefactores* .... & *Fines*, (nostri enim gratia & sunt, & agunt, & patiuntur)."[55] To confine the image of God to the first two of these three was the normal Reformed practice,[56] and apparently Baxter's earlier view.[57] The third strand had been rejected by Calvin as no part of the *imago Dei*,[58] but was included in it by one or two early Reformed theologians.[59] Seventeenth-century orthodoxy, however, generally repudiated it, probably because "the Remonstrants and Socinians

---

Sacris Literis." Baxter roundly attacked those who treated sense as evil *per se*, Manichaeans and advocates of "stillness," who "ad vitam perfectam . . . pertinere existimant, ut sensus omnes occludamus . . . Imo ut ipsos Intellectus actus suspendamus, & in silentio mere passivi Dei gratiam expectemus." Sense is only evil when misused. It will continue in the intermediate state, and in heaven and hell: "Imo faelicitatem sine omni sensatione ego concipere non possum:" "si damnatorum animae omni sensu privatae sunt, quinam & quales sunt gehennae cruciatus?" *M.T.*, I:x.70 f., 230 f.).

55. *M.T.*, I.v.12, 157. [This relation truly contains the image of the three divine relations to the creatures: 1. We are sub-lords over lower creatures, and can own, use, and rearrange them by the right of this subdominion; 2. We are similarly their sub-governors, and can by right appoint their use and arrangement at our own will (under God); 3. We ae their sub-benefactors ... and goals too (for it is thanks to us that they exist and act and have their life-experience.] Baxter appears to be thinking of cattle and pets.

56. *R.D.*, 232 f.

57. cf. *Call to the Unconverted*, 1657, Preface: "there is a twofold image of God on man; the one is natural ... reason and free-will ... the other is qualitative and ethical ... our holiness . . ."

58. *Institutes*, I:xv.4.

59. *R.D.*, *loc. cit.*

were disposed to confine the image of God in which man was created to his dominion."[60] To Baxter, however, it was one of the truths of natural religion[61] and of vital importance, for it imaged the *regnum Dei*, God's monarchial government over man, to which we must now turn.

Power, wisdom and goodness, as we saw, are the primary and essential attributes which make up the Divine character. All three were expressed in the act of creation; and it is from the Creator-creature relationship that the *regnum Dei* derives.

> God is related to us as our Maker: from this relation of a Creator in unity, there ariseth a trinity of relations; this trinity is in that unity, and that unity in this trinity. First, God having made us of nothing, is necessarily related to us as our Lord: by a Lord ("dominus") we mean strictly a proprietary or owner, as your are the owner of your goods ...

> Secondly, He is related to us as our Ruler, our Governor, or King. This riseth from our nature, made to be ruled in order to our end, being rational, voluntary agents; also from the dominion and blessed nature of God, who only hath right to the government of the world, and only is fit and capable of ruling it.

> Thirdly, He is related also to us as our Benefactor ... freely and of his bounty giving us all the good that we do receive.[62]

Therefore

> I must next tell you that we also stand in answerable counter-relations to him: and must have the qualities and do the works that answer those relations. 1. As God is our Almighty Creator, so we are his creatures, impotent and insufficient for ourselves. We owe him therefore all that a creature that hath but our receivings can owe his Maker. 2. In this relation is contained a trinity of relations. 1. We are his own, as he is our Lord. 2. We are his subjects, as he is our Ruler. 3. We are ... his obliged beneficiaries, as he is our Benefactor.[63]

God's natural fatherhood, and man's natural sonship, consist in these three mutual relations:

> The term Father comprehendeth in it all his three great relations to us. 1. A father gives being to his children, and therefore hath some propriety in them;

---

60. C. Hodge, *Systematic Theology*, II:97. The idea, however, appears in Ames, *Marrow*, I:viii.74, 38.
61. cf. *Reasons of the Christian Religion*, I:ii, vi-xii.
62. *Works*, XIII:19 (*Divine Life*, I: *The Knowledge of God*, 1663).
63. p. 21.

and God is the first cause of our whole being, and therefore we are his own. 2. A father is the governor of his children; and God is our chief governor. 3. A father tenderly loveth his children ... and seeketh their felicity: and so doth God love ... When I call God our Benefactor, I precisely distinguish the last part of his relation to us, from the rest. But when I call him a Father, I mean the same thing or relation which a benefactor signifieth; but with fuller aspect on the foregoing relations, and connotation of them as they are perfected all in this.[64]

God's threefold relation to man constitutes His kingship or kingdom, the sole absolute monarchy, the archetypal patriarchy ("*Monarchia absoluta Paterna ex pleno Dominio in personas*").[65] We must now examine in more detail the triple relationship which it comprises.

As *Dominus*, God has an absolute right to dispose of His creatures as He wishes; and none may call Him to account. Man must recognize that "it is impossible that God can do us any wrong, or any thing that he can do, can be guilty of injustice"[66]—for man has no claims on Him, "God may do with his own as he list."[67] In actual fact, God "was pleased to make his Creatures of various ranks; and among the Rational to make Man a free undetermined self-determining Agent, not fixed by Necessity in Love and Obedience, but left with a Power of Loving and Obeying, which he could use or not use; that so he might be a fit subject of Gods Moral Government by Laws, and persuasions in this world, in order to a more fixed state of holiness. Not but that Angelical Confirmation had been better for us; But it pleased not God to compose the universe of Creatures only of the noblest order."[68] And we may not criticize or complain; rather, "we must learn to be the more thankful for all our mercies, because they proceed from the absolute Lord, that was not obliged to us. He might have made us idiots, or mad-men; he might have made us beasts or toads, without any injury to us ..."[69] Having made us, God exercised his "dominium" by assuming "the relation of our Governor" ("imperium"), and thereby "as it were obliged himself by his laws and covenants";[70] but He still retains and exercises his absolute right of disposal

64. p. 129.
65. *M.T.*, I:xii.II.3, 250. Cf. M.T. I:12.32, 247: "Divinam hanc Politeiam, aliquando *Regnum*, aliquando *Familiam*, aliquando *Dominatum*, nominamus, & aliquando omnia innuimus per *Theocratiam*"—denominating it according to the various relations between God and man which it includes.
66. XIII:115.
67. *loc. cit.*
68. *C.T.*, I:ii.I.I, 27.
69. *Works*, XIII:117.
70. p. 116.

in abundance of things about his rational creatures, wherein as rector he is not engaged, nor hath in his laws declared his will; as about the various constitutions and complexions of men, their ranks and dignities in the world, their riches or poverty, their health or sickness, their gifts and parts both natural and acquired; the first giving of the gospel, and of special grace, to such as had forfeited them, and had no promise of them; the degrees of outward means and mercies; the degrees of inward grace, more than what is promised, &c.[71]

Baxter thus safeguards the absolute freedom of God in His dealings with man as forthrightly as any Augustinian could desire. Like Augustine he affirms his faith in the goodness of God even when it is out of sight. "Much may be above us, because our blindness cannot reach the reasons of his ways; but nothing is unreasonable or evil; for all proceedeth from infinite wisdom and goodness, as well as from omnipotency." To what is revealed in His Word, "our reason must presently submit, and undoubtedly conclude it reasonable and good";[72] and nothing must be allowed to weaken the conviction that "all his disposals shall work to that end which is the most universal perfect good, and most denominateth all the means."[73] Circumstances may be bad *secundum quid*, but man's part is, as Baxter poetized it, always to

> Take what He gives,
> And praise Him still
> Through good and ill
> Who ever lives,

secure in the knowledge that God only permits evil in order to bring out of it greater good.

The second in the trinity of God's relations to man, that of being his moral governor ("rector, gubernator, rex"), is founded on the first, but is less inclusive; God "is the Lord or Owner of the world ... but he is the sovereign King or Governor only of the reasonable creature; because no other are capable of ... proper moral government."[74] God made man "a rational free agent ... among sensible objects, and out of sight of his invisible Creator, and so infirm and defectible."[75] He also made him "capable of everlasting happiness," with a view

---

71. *loc. cit.*

72 *loc. cit.*

73. p. 120.

74. XIII:120. Baxter defined moral government as: "the exercise of the moral means of laws, and execution by a ruler, for the right ordering of the subject's actions, the good of the society, and the honour of the governor" (XX:495).

75. XX:495.

to his ultimate enjoyment of it. Plainly, therefore,

> his (man's) very nature and the end of his creation required, that he should
> be conducted to that end and happiness, by means agreeable to his nature;
> that is, by revelation of the reward before he seeth it, that he may seek it and
> be fitted for it; and by prescribed duties that are necessary to obtain it ... and
> by threatened penalties to quicken him to his duty.[76]

Having made man a rational, purposive creature, "God ... must move him as
rational by such objects, and such proposals, and arguments, and means, as
are suited to reason."[77] The behavior of "inanimates and brutes" is caused by
the appeal of external objects to their vegetative and sensitive capacities
respectively. But man is such that his action results not from automatic external
necessitation, but from free individual decision. Man, therefore, is to be moved
by "moral suasion." The proper way to make him act is to give him a reason
why. This is God's method. "God would not have made him rational, if he
would not have governed him accordingly."[78] Now, there are two, and only
two, reasons for rational action, love of, and desire for, good, and aversion
from, and desire to escape, evil. At the heart of each lies the strongest human
motive, self-love, the desire for happiness. To these sanctions wise governors
appeal. To make laws for rational creatures without giving them a reason for
obedience in terms of good to be gained and evil to be avoided would be bad
government, for man's natural constitution makes it certain that such laws
would not be kept. "Take away all reward and punishment, and you take away
all duty in effect ... it will not be done, for a rational agent will have ends and
motives for what he doth."[79] No such folly may be attributed to the Only Wise
God, the archetypal moral governor; all his laws include penal sanctions and a
promise of reward.

The facts of human nature reveal, not merely the necessity of Divine moral
government over man, but also the basic content of God's Law. This is the Law
of Nature: "that *signification* of *God's will concerning Man's Duty*, which was
discernible in the *Universa Rerum Natura* in all God's Works; but principally
in *Mans own Nature*, as related to *God* and all *Persons*, and *Things* about him."[80]
By the very fact of being rational creatures, "we ... are ourselves ... objectively
part of the law of Nature; that is, the signifiers of the will of God.[81] God legislated

76. XIII:121.
77. XX:502.
78. *loc. cit.*
79. p. 496.
80. *An End of Doctrinal Controversies*, 113.
81. XIII:18.

for us "by making our nature such as, compared with objects, duty shall result from this nature so related,"[82] and hence the created order can properly be described as "God's statute book."[83] This conception of the law of Nature as the sum of moral obligations intrinsic in a state of affairs became prominent in the early seventeenth century through the work of Grotius, and deeply pervaded the thought of the age. Whereas, however, Grotius had thought of natural law as essentially a norm for man's relations with man in the civil and international sphere, Baxter was wholly concerned with man in relation to God, and with the law of Nature as "*pars* prima & nobilissima"[84] of God's legislation. It was legible in the created order, included in the Decalogue, reaffirmed in Christ's law, and is written more or less plainly in the heart and conscience of every man. It includes (i) man's duty to God—praise, prayer, worship, and a willingness to receive instruction about Him from those qualified to give it; (ii) man's duty to his fellow-men—to exercise and to submit to governmental and parental authority, to be honest, just, truthful and charitable, and to respect rights of property; (iii) man's duty to himself—to live a godly, rational, temperate, contented life. "All this," Baxter insists, "is evidently legible in nature, to any man that hath not lost his reason, or refuseth not considerately to use it."[85]

The law of Nature is immutable. It must continue to be what it is as long as God and man remain what they are. But God has also enacted supplementary laws, founded on natural law, specifying duty in relation to particular circumstances at a particular time; and these may be altered by the Divine Lawgiver as circumstances require. These were Divine "positive" laws, the authority of which derives solely from the personal authority of the legislator. The distinction between "natural" and "positive" law was widely used by seventeenth-century theologians in their endeavors to state the relation between the Jewish and Christian dispensations and to determine the relevance of Mosaic laws for New Testament believers. It represents a further debt to Grotius; for he was the first to transfer Aquinas' distinction between 'lex naturae' and 'lex humanitus posita' to the laws by which God rules men. Baxter preferred to expound it as the distinction between natural and supernatural laws, differentiating them according to the mode of their revelation and

---

82. XII:368.

83. XXI:8; "et Adami quidem innocentis opus fuit, hunc librum mundi quotidie legere, perlegere & meditari" (*M.T.*, I:v.23, 158).

84. *M.T.*, I:xiii.(III).1, 266.

85. XXI:17, at the end of *Reasons of the Christian Religion*, I:x ("Of God's particular laws, as known in Nature"). Baxter continues: "And he that will read but Antonine, Epictetus and Plutarch . . . may see, that he who will deny a life of piety, justice and temperance to be the duty and rectitude of man, must renounce his reason and natural light . . ."

apprehension: whether they were to be read in Nature or to be known only by direct verbal communication from God. At creation, Adam was placed under the law of Nature and three supernatural, 'positive' enactments: that he should not eat the fruit of the tree of knowledge;[86] that he should set apart each seventh day as a day of rest and worship, which was "such a positive, as must be next to a law of nature";[87] and the command to marry ("be fruitful and multiply, Gen. 1:28), which was "partly *supernatural*" also.[88] But these laws were not of perpetual obligation, and each has in fact been amended or repealed in the course of God's later dealings with mankind.

Many of the Divine attributes of which the Bible speaks are governmental attributes, appearing in God's legislation and execution of His laws. This becomes clear in the following extract:

> As he is our Ruler ... it is his principal attribute to be Just or Righteous; in which is comprehended his Truth or Faithfulness, his Holiness, his Mercy, and his terrible Dreadfulness. As his attributes appear in the assertions of his word, he is True (his veracity being nothing but his power, wisdom and goodness expressing themselves) ... For he that is able to do what he will, and so wise as to know all things, and so good as to will nothing but what is good, cannot possibly lie ... As his first properties appear in his word of promise, he is called fruitful, which is his truth in making good a word of grace. As he commandeth holy duties, and condemneth sin as the most detestable thing, by a pure, righteous law, so he is called Holy ... As he fulfilleth his promises, and rewardeth and defendeth men according to his word, so he is called merciful and gracious, as a governor ... As he fulfilleth his threatenings, he is called angry, wrathful terrible, dreadful, holy, jealous, &c. But he is Just in all.[89]

We now can appreciate why Baxter attached so much importance to the study of politics. God's moral government of man, he insisted, is the central subject of the Bible and the central topic of theology. The doctrines of sin and of the unfolding of redemption must be understood, from first to last, within a "political" framework. The alternative was to misconceive and misrepresent the relations of God and man, and inevitably to hold a theology according to which God either did violence to human nature or denied His own. This will appear as we proceed.

---

86. XIII:121.

87. XIII:413. Though the keeping of the seventh day Sabbath was not in the law of nature (Baxter argues this at length in chapters III-IV of his Appendix to *The Divine Appointment of the Lord's day, Proved*: XIII:496 f.), yet "stated days at a convenient distance (for worship) is of the law of Nature."

88. *An End of Doctrinal Controversies*, 118.

89. XIII:20 f.

The third of God's three relations to man is founded on the other two. It is that of being Man's Benefactor, which God became:

> 1. Even in creating us ... giving us the fundamental good of being, and the excellency of manhood. 2. By setting us in a well-furnished world, and putting all things under our feet and giving us the use of creatures. 3. By entering into the relation of a governor to us, and consequently engaging himself to terms of justice in his dealing with us, and to reward if we did obey; and making us capable of everlasting happiness as our end, and appointing us sufficient means thereto. These benefits denominated God the great Benefactor or Father unto man, in the state of his creation.[90]

God's beneficence is the expression of His essential goodness; and, as we saw, the mark of goodness is its *attractiveness* to rational beings. As it is man's nature to love good as such, to feel and respond to its attractive force, so it is his duty to love most what is best. God is the highest good, and therefore must be the ultimate object of man's love. God's end in creation, as in providence and grace, is His own self-display by the revelation of His attributes; which is expressed in the statement that God's end is Himself, or His "glory." All created values are hierarchically arranged, as means to the glory of the Creator on whom they depend for their existence. All come from God, and all are means to God. Man, therefore, must learn to view each good thing in its relation to the rest of the hierarchy and, ultimately, to God, and his love and regard for it must be regulated and proportioned according to its place in the hierarchy. What God created as a means must be used as a means. The alternative is idolatry, which is unworthy of a rational being. God has revealed Himself as the supreme Good, the primal source of all goodness, and has thereby made it man's duty supremely to love Him. "God hath given no command for duty, but what most perfectly agreeth with the nature of the object. He hath therefore bid us love God and delight in Him above all, because he is above all in goodness ... else we could not love him above all, nor would he ever command us to do so. The object is ever as exactly fitted to its part, as to draw out the love and delight of our hearts, as the precept is on its part, to oblige us to it."[91] By loving God, man both promotes the glory of his Creator and discovers his own happiness; and thus he attains his chief end, which is to glorify God and enjoy him for ever. Man's happiness and God's glory are not incompatible goals; for, as supreme goodness is its own end, so love for it as such is its own reward. "Surely, love is both work and wages."[92] Duty and interest coincide. Baxter explains his view of man's destiny as God's rational creature in the following passage:

---

90. XIII:130.
91. IX:28; cf. XXI:40: "Nature hath made love and goodness like the iron and the loadstone."
92. XXII:63.

All the difficulties, *de fine hominis*, are best resolved by understanding that it is *finis amantis*, and what that is. The nature of love is an inclination or desire of union or adhesion; and therefore it includeth the felicity of the lover, together with the attractive excellency of the object ... The lover, withal, intends his felicity in fruition. But if any soul be so far above self-love as to be drawn up in the fervours of holy love, in the mere contemplation of the infinite object, not thinking of its own felicity herein, its felicity will be never the less for not intending or remembering it. Therefore the final act of love hath no fitter name than love itself, or delightful adhesion to God, the infinite Good, with full complacency herein.[93]

The love of God is thus man's true vocation, his highest and noblest duty, the fulfillment of his nature, the perfect use of all his powers, and his supreme and lasting happiness, both here, where love is in the bud, and in its perfect flowering hereafter. It should be his prime occupation. "The love of God should be with all our soul, and with all our might ... the exercise of love to God ... should be the chief employment of our thoughts ... the love of God should employ our tongues," and our lives be spent "to his praise and pleasure ... the streaming effects of inward love."[94] We must love him as our Creator by setting a proper value on His gifts, thanking Him for them and using them in His service ("1. A willing, receiving love; 2. A thankful love; 3. A returning, devoted, serving love ... True gratitude will devote the whole man to his service, will and honour, and bring back his mercies to him for his use, so far as we are able"). We must love him as our Governor by trusting Him and His Word, by joyfully submitting to His rule ("all his instructions, helps, reproofs, and all his conducting means, should be amiable to us"), and by gladly following the path of his appointment ("to love the tokens of his presence, and footsteps of his will, and all the signs of his approbation, and, with an heroic fortitude of love, to rejoice in sufferings, and venture upon dangers, and conquer difficulties for his sake"). We must love him as our Final Good by desiring Him, seeking Him, and, so far as may be in this life, delighting in the enjoyment of Him as He makes Himself known to His lovers.[95] All our love for and delight in created

---

93. XXI:43 f. Baxter versified this doctrine in *Poetical Fragments*, 3:
       Thy *own Perfections* by *Attraction* move,
       As the *chief formal Object* of Man's Love,
       Though our *own Good* we may, and must intend;
       Thy *simple Goodness* is Man's *chiefest End.*
       They that deny this, never knew *Love's* force,
       Which to *meer Excellence* hath its recourse,
       Or never well considered *Love's* end,
       Which unto *God*, for *Goodness* sake doth tend.
94. XXI:47 f.
95. p. 40 f.

things must be "improved," and used as a stairway by which our hearts may rise to love for their Author. It was for this very purpose that God filled the world with so may joys and gave man the capacity to appreciate them so keenly: to add fuel to the flames of man's love for Himself. Not to use them so is to abuse them. For

> God hath planted in our nature the principle of self-love, that he might suit our nature to the mercies of God, and make them sweet to us ... that this sweetness in them, which respecteth ourselves, and is relished by self-love, should lead us to the fountain of perfect goodness from which they flow. Our very senses and appetites are given us to this end, not that we should judge by no higher faculties, but that the delights of the patible or sensible qualities in the creature, by affecting the sense, might presently represent to the higher faculties, the sweetness of infinite goodness ... and so we might by all ascend to God.[96]

Thus, every part of the complex hierarchy of faculties and inclinations which makes up the human soul has its true place as a means to man's ultimate end, the only genuinely rational activity—love, and thereby enjoyment, of God, the activity and perfection, not of a single faculty, but of the whole man. ("I suppose that the *Thomists* grossly err in placing beatitude chiefly in the intellect ... and the *Scotists* are more sound, who place it in the Will, and those others most sound who place it in the perfection of the whole man actively; but objectively in God ...")[97] It is the most intense activity and the most concentrated and sustained joy of which man is capable.

> This life of love should be our chiefest delight ... which all other pleasure should subserve, and all be abhorred which contradicteth it ... This ... should be our work and our recreation, our labour and our pleasure, our food and feast ... Nothing can be so delectable as God ... and no employment can be so delectable as loving him. And here the soul must seek its rest.[98]

It is hard to realize, as we are swept along by Baxter's rough, vigorous eloquence on this theme, eloquence all the more compelling for being unconscious and unstudied, that we are still in the realm of natural religion; yet so it is. The doctrine of God, man and their three basic relationships is written in the book of the creatures, and may there be read by all who will take the trouble to think out the implications of their own self-consciousness. It is more certain than any part of God's supernatural revelation, and is the

---

96. p. 27.
97. *C.T.*, I.ii, "A Premonition," 25.
98. XXI:48.

substructure on which Biblical theology must rest. Baxter's is the most comprehensive and the least self-sufficient of the essays in natural religion which seventeenth century England produced. It is interesting to note his attitude to the pioneer work in this *genre*, Herbert's *De Veritate*.[99] Its basic principles he approved: "I take most of his rules and notions, *de veritate* to be of singular use."[100] He endorsed Herbert's list of five basic *notitiae communes*: "I would they [atheistical sensualists] would learn of him, that the being and perfections of God, the duty of worshipping him, and of holy conformity and obedience to him, and the rewards and punishments of the life to come, with the soul's immortality, are all *notitiae communes*, and such natural certainties, as that the denial of them doth unman them."[101] But he claimed that Herbert's list was incomplete, and added to it the universality of sin and the fact of God's moral government. The second of these was in fact the distinctive feature in Baxter's natural theology, the rest of which was drawn largely from accepted sources, Platonist and Aristotelian, Stoic and Mediaeval.[102] By its introduction, Baxter was able to show the insufficiency of natural theology alone and to bridge the gap between it and supernatural revelation, arguing as follows: If God is man's moral governor, then man must obey His laws; but since men prove so dull in deciphering the book of Nature, they stand in great need of a supernatural revelation of the Divine will, which can be read more easily. That most men are aware of this need appears from the fact that "almost all the world do hearken after oracles, prophecies, visions, or some such further revelation, as conscious of the unsatisfactoriness of their natural light."[103] Again, man needs an answer to the question, how can he expiate and escape

---

99. In the second part of *More Reasons for the Christian Religion*.

100. XXI:522.

101. *loc. cit.* Baxter dissented from Herbert at the one point which was crucial for the establishment of the Deist case; he denied Herbert's assertion that repentance, *per se*, expiated sin without any further objective atonement. To prove that this was not a "natural notice," but the reverse of Nature's teaching, Baxter appealed to the fact that in both public and private law repentance has never been held to remove liability to punishment (p. 572 f.).

102. The Platonists and Stoics, Baxter held, "were the noblest philosophers; because the former studied the highest things, and the other the necessary means of felicity, the amending of men's hearts and lives" (XV:15). His account of the "heavenly Eros," man's love for God, reveals his debt to the Platonist and Neo-Platonist tradition, as mediated by Augustine and his Mediaeval disciples. Stoic influence on Baxter can be gauged from the following comments on quotations from Seneca (of which there are no less than 52 in the margins of the second and later editions of the *Saints' Rest*): "Who would think these were a heathen's words?" (XXII:104, n.); "it is more than probable that he had heard or read Paul's doctrine" (p. 332, n.). But cf. the judgment passed in the Preface to *The Crucifying of the World* (IX:ccxciii): "What excellent precepts hath Seneca? . . . And yet . . . it is self that is his principle, end, and all. For a man to be sufficient for himself, and happy in himself, without troubling God by prayer, or needing man, was the sum of his religion. Pride was their master-virtue." Such was Baxter's opinion of the Stoic ideal of αὐτάρκεια.

103. XXI:574.

punishment for his crimes against God's law. It is a pressing question, for Nature teaches that a good governor will not permit lawbreakers to go unpunished; and it is a question to which Nature gives no answer. Natural religion thus proclaims its own insufficiency, and prepares the mind to seek and to accept further revelation, conveyed by other means. Baxter's natural theology is thus poles apart from the self-sufficient, anti-supernaturalist systems of Herbert and the later Deists; rather, as Powicke pointed out, it resembles the position reached, through an independent study of the same sources, by the Cambridge Platonists.[104]

We have in this chapter examined the foundation on which the rest of Baxterianism was built. The doctrines of sin and salvation which we are now to examine were all fitted into the framework provided by this account of human nature, God's nature and the law of Nature. In Baxter's universe, teleology pervades everything; the human faculties, rational action and right conduct, created things and moral values, all prove on analysis to take the form of a hierarchy of means and ends, the ultimate end of everything being the glory of God. We shall see that the same is true of the economy of redemption. There was nothing original about these positions, save perhaps in the consistency with which Baxter worked them out. He himself did not claim to be doing more then "methodizing" the Church's faith more accurately than his predecessors had done. So far, at least, his claim to catholicity appears well founded.

---

104. *Under the Cross*, 238 f. and 247 f.

Chapter 6

Man: Fallen

SYNOPSIS

1. The covenant of Nature: life promised and death threatened to Adam.

2. Adam created holy and mutable, for probation and development:
    His need of moral government till confirmed in love.
    Adam given necessary (i.e., sufficient) grace to withstand temptation.

3. How Satan tempts in general.
    How Satan tempted Adam and Eve.
    Adam and Eve betrayed into thoughtless action:
        their single sin was virtually total apostasy.

4. Adam's guilt and depravity transmitted to his posterity:
    All parents' sins imputed to children on grounds of physical
        descent.

5. Analysis of human depravity, as derived from Adam:
    Derangement of the will
                        intellect
                        memory
                        imagination
                        sensitive appetite
                        affections

    Consequent action:
        universal selfishness or flesh-pleasing:
            "flesh" defined; physical factors in sin;
                each man tempted according to physical constitution.
            happiness sought only in created things:
                man's will free to do nothing else.
            captivity of intellect, leading to rationalization;
                man's lack of self-knowledge;
                man's consequent rejection of the preaching of sin.

6. Baxter's vocabulary for describing sin's   bestiality
                                               uncleanness
                                               ugliness.
    Wholesomeness of his anatomy of sin.

7. Conclusion: Baxter represents Puritan orthodoxy on man and sin.

(Principal Sources: *Methodus Theologiae* I; *Christian Directory* I (*Works*, II-III); *Self-Denial* (*Works*, XI); *Two Disputations of Original Sin.*)

Chapter 6

Man: Fallen

"The devil would paint sin with the vermilion colour of pleasure and profit, that he may make it look fair; but I shall pull off the paint that you may see its ugly face."—Thomas Watson on the Shorter Catechism, Question XIV.

The Law of Nature, Baxter maintained, proclaimed the reality of rewards and punishments;[1] the wages of sin, it taught, was death, and the issue of obedience was life. "The Law said [in sense] (*Obey perfectly and live; Sin and die*)."[2] As such, the law constituted a *covenant*, a conditional promise, as indeed do all laws that are sanctioned by the prospect of profit or loss.[3] Reformed theologians in the seventeenth century usually denominated it the

---

1. The rationale of punishment which Baxter gives is a revision of Grotius in the light of the rest of his natural theology: "The ends of punishment are, 1. To do justice, and fulfil the law and truth of the lawgiver. 2. To vindicate the honour of the Governor from contempt and treason. 3. To prevent further evil from the same offender. 4. To be a terror to others, and to prevent the hurt that impunity would encourage them to. 5. And if it be but merely castigatory, it may be for the good of the sinner himself; but in purely vindictive (i.e., retributive) punishment, it is the governor and society that are the end" (*Works*, XXI:101). But: "It is a false position, that punishment is only or chiefly to be a warning to others. It is chiefly for the ultimate end of government, which *secundum quid*, among men, is the *bonum publicum*; but *simpliciter*, in God's government, it is the glorifying and demonstration of the holiness and justice of God ... to the pleasure of his holy will" (p. 329).

2. *C.T.*, I:ii.33, 14.

3. cf. *An End of Doctrinal Controversies*, 99: "Though the word (*Law*) do principally signifie the regulating Imposition of our Duty, and the word *Covenant* doth principally signifie a *mutual Contract*; yet it is the same *Divine Instrument*, which is meant oft and usually in Scripture, by both these names ... It is called a *Law* in one respect, and a *Covenant* in another ..." For proof of this, Baxter refers the reader to Grotius' Preface to his *Annotations on the New Testament* (as also in *C.T.*, I:ii, "An Appendix to this Premonition," after p.26, *ad fin.*)

Covenant of Works, but Baxter objected to the phrase, on the ground that the Covenant of Grace is also in an important sense a covenant of works, and preferred to entitle it the Covenant of Nature or of Innocence. The precise nature of the bliss and misery which it set before men he inferred from the New Testament description of the salvation which Christ bestows. For the first: "the titles of (*Redemption Reconciliation Remission*) &c. given in the Gospel to the acts of our Salvation by Jesus Christ ... seem to import that they restore us to that state of Heavenly hope, which we fell from in *Adam*";[4] for the second, "The Penalty is called *Death*, which signifieth *Undoing* and *Misery*. But whether it was only *temporal death* or also *Hell*, Divines are not agreed..." Baxter, however, was not in doubt: "It is the *Wrath to come* that Christ delivereth us from, and *Hell* and the *Power of Satan* that he redeemed us from: Therefore it seemeth that it was no less that our Sin deserved."[5] These sanctions, together with the duties described in the last chapter, constitute the permanent elements in the law under which Adam was created and all his children live.

Adam was made upright: "holiness was the primitive, natural constitution of man, and was before sin, and is the perfection or health of nature, and the right employment or improvement of it, and tends to its happiness."[6] Baxter magnified the glory of man's original righteousness, as Augustinian theologians have always done. Adam's reason ruled his will and passions, he followed with all his heart after good and, therefore, after God, his natural inclination led him to cleave to his Maker, and he found supreme delight in so doing. But he was made *in via*, not *in patria*, not yet mature and confirmed in holy humanity, and therefore mutable. "We deny not but as to degrees, Adam's nature

---

4. *C.T.*, I:ii.12, 31. In the *Aphorisms* Baxter had favored the view held, he claimed, by "most Divines" (p. 15), including three quondam oracles, John Ball, John Cameron and Thomas Gataker (cf. *J.R.*, "Consideration ... of ... Cartwright," 19), that Adam would have lived for ever in Eden; but in 1652 he confessed himself completely undecided (*loc. cit.*), and by 1675 (marginal note, *loc. cit.*) had been "fully convinced, that *Adam* was made for Heaven." This, he tells us, was the result of considering the Biblical terminology of salvation, mentioned in the text, together with "the natural tendency of all the superior faculties of the Soul." But "the matter is the less, because wherever the place be, the same state of Enjoyment would make it a Heaven" (*An End of Doctrinal Controversies*, 116). Neither Nature nor Scripture reveal "*How long man must have obeyed before he had merited the full Reward of his Perfections*. But only that he must conquer all the Temptations that God would try him with, and must persevere till God should please to translate him" (*loc. cit.*).

5. *op. cit.*, 118 f.

6. XIII:236. Baxter goes out of his way to repudiate the view that Adam became holy only by "a superadded gift of grace" distinct from his creation, as belonging to the class of "Popish improved fancies ... contrary to nature and the word of God." To hold it was to "feign that God first made nature defective, and then mended it by superadded grace" (*loc. cit.*). Jeremy Taylor's denial of original sin on the ground that infants *in puris naturalibus* were in the same state as Adam at creation, neither holy nor unholy, must therefore be rejected also (cf. *M.T.*, I:xv, disp. 2, 354). Such was not Adam's original state.

was to grow up to more perfection; and that his natural holiness contained not a sufficient immediate aptitude and promptitude which might afterward be required of him; but this was to be obtained in the exercise of that holiness which he had."[7] God's purpose was to crown his obedience, when his probation was over, by confirming him in the habit of love. Thus he would pass beyond the possibility of sinning, and no longer stand in need of moral government, which is appropriate for rational creatures only so long as they need to be moved to action by a direct appeal to self-love. The Covenant of Nature, with its promise of life and its penal sanctions, was intended both to animate Adam to his duty of free, deliberate, constant love for God as the highest good and, with this, to deepen his appreciation of the Love which made him and set before him such a glorious hope. He was to increase his knowledge of the Giver by meditating on His gifts; and gratitude for personal benefits was to be a ladder up which he should mount to the apprehension of God's essential nature and the exercise of the highest and most perfect love—the love of God for his own loveliness, not for the benefits merely but for the goodness from which they flowed. When he had reached this height of love, he was to be confirmed in it. Thus he was set under moral government in order that by means of it he might outgrow it. Baxter was certain that human nature has always required government by promise and threat; but he was no less certain that this was a sign of the immaturity and imperfection of that nature, and that moral government would have been done away when men had risen above it; for "love … as such, is above obedience as such."

> The difference of understandings and will requireth government and obedience, that the understanding and will of the superior may be a rule to the subjects; but love is a concord of wills; and so far as love hath caused a concord, there is no use for government by laws and penalties; and therefore the law is not made for a righteous man as such; that is, so far as love hath united his soul to virtue, and separated it from sin, he need not be constrained or restrained by any penal laws, any more than men need a law to command them to eat and drink …[8]

But until he reached this point, even Adam, naturally disposed to righteousness as he was, needed a penal law for his effective government.

For this time of testing, his natural faculties and disposition in themselves constituted "Grace Necessary called Sufficient":[9] he could not sin unless he chose to, and was able to choose not to. That he fell was not due to God's

---

7. XIII:240.

8. XXI:39 f.

9. *C.T.*, I:ii.7, 28. "Necessary" is Baxter's term for Augustine's "sufficient," as distinct from "efficient," grace. "By *sufficient Grace* is meant that which is *necessary* to the effect, and without

failure to equip him for his test: "For God took no Grace away from *Adam* before he sinned, nor let out any temptation upon him which he was not able to resist; nor did he sin for want of necessary Grace; but by that same degree of help he might have overcome."[10] If Satan was to make Adam sin, it must be by persuasion, not by force; and his task might at first sight have appeared hopeless.

> Satan dulciorem nullam escam, praemium nullum nobilius offerre potuit, quam voluptatem inanem, sensualem, momentaneam, & phantasticae faelicitatis umbram, qua hominem a Creatoris obedientia, & amore pelliceret; Deo interim mortem peccatori minante, & vitam, & faelicitatem offerente, sub innocentiae facilis & suavis conditione.[11]

But, in the event, Satan was completely successful.

If Baxter's psychology was to stand, it was clearly necessary for him to show how Adam, endowed as he was, could ever have lapsed at all.[12] Although "it is a matter of great difficulty to understand how sin first entered into the innocent soul,"[13] yet it was an issue which, having gone so far, he could not fairly balk; nor did he try to do so. The second and third chapters of Genesis, however obscure they might be on other points, were to his mind clear enough on this.[14] He cast the Biblical material into the psychological mold described

---

which it *Cannot be*, but with it, it may be, though it sometimes be not . . . This *sufficient* Grace consisteth in a *Power* to the act" (I:iii.XV.1.3, 48), the natural freedom of the will: "he that *can do it if he will*, and *also hath power to will it*, is said to have *sufficient Grace*, which if he use not, the fault lieth in his wilfulness" (II:146).

10. *C.T.*, I:ii.7, 28.

11. *M.T.*, I:xiv.55, 274: qu. "facili & suavi"? [Satan could offer no sweeter morsel, no nobler reward, than empty sensory momentary pleasure, and the semblance of fancied happiness, to allure man from obedience and love to the Creator; while God threatened death to the sinner, and offered life and happiness on condition of an innocence that was easy and pleasant to sustain.]

12. Baxter believed that "Adamus aliquandiu integer vixit, in sanctitatis exercitiis, antequam per tentationem lapsus est" (*M.T.*, I:xiv.24, 271).

13. *Works*, II:240.

14. Baxter's comments on some of the less plain details are worth recording. On the two trees: "Sacramenta illa & praecepta de Arboribus horti, Adamo clare revelata fuerunt . . . Nobis autem doctrina de eorum natura & usu, concise & obscure traditur; quia non aeque ad nos . . . eorum clara cognitio pertinet," [Those sacraments and commands about the trees in the garden were clearly revealed to Adam . . . but the doctrine about their nature and use is conveyed to us briefly and obscurely; because clear knowledge about them is not equally relevant for us] (I:13.6, 267)—though he ventures an opinion on the subject in *C.T.*, I:ii, "A Premonition," 5: "No doubt the Trees were symbolical, and the remembrance of them should yet teach us to prefer *living to God*, before a *selfish, distrustful, needless* knowledge." On God's converse with Adam: "Utrum per *Angelum* aliquam, an per *Vocem* jam ab ipso factam, Deus cum Adamo collocutus est, non inter revelata aut cognita invenitur" [Whether God spoke with Adam through an angel or through a voice he himself produced is not among things revealed or known] (*M.T.*, I:xv.3, 336). The narrative is not so full "ut de natura Serpentis Tentatoris nos omnino certos reddere possit," though

in the previous chapter, and there emerged a version of the characteristic Augustinian doctrine of the Fall.

"Here I shall open the methods of the devil," Baxter announces at the beginning of *A Christian Directory,* Part I: "Christian Ethics," chapter 3, Grand Direction IX ("Spend all your days in a skilful, vigilant, resolute and valiant warfare against the flesh, the world and the devil");[15] and it is convenient to review the general account of Satan's activity there given before considering in detail the first recorded instance of it. Baxter's demonology in no way differs from that of Puritan theologians generally, except perhaps in its greater vividness. The devil's existence he believed to be as evident as God's: "He that believeth not this, doth prove it to others, by showing how grossly the devil can befool him. Apparitions, witchcrafts and temptations are full proofs of it to sense;[16] besides what Scripture saith."[17] He is a fallen angel, "the deadly

---

Scripture indicates (2 Cor. 11:3, Rev. 12:9, 14:15, 20:2) that "Serpentem istum fuisse ipsum Diabolum, at probabiliter per Serpentam naturalem loquentem" [The serpent was the devil himself, but probably speaking through a genuine snake (*M.T.,* I:xiv.27, 271). On the cursing of the serpent: "Qualis autem per hanc poenam mutatio sit in serpente . . . & qualis Diabolorum . . . mortalibus vix . . . patescit: (I:xv.13, 337); though he has no doubt that "after the fall, God put an enmity into the nature of man against devils, as a merciful preservative against temptation: so that as the whole nature of man abhorreth the nature of serpents, so doth the soul abhor and dread the diabolical nature" (*Works,* II:258).

15. *Works,* II:258 f.

16. Baxter produced his evidence for "apparitions and witchcrafts" in *Saints' Rest,* II:vii (XXII:319-29), *The Unreasonableness of Infidelity,* III:"the Unpardonable Sin against the Holy Ghost," sects. 4-7 (XX:253-77), and in the last book he published, *The Certainty of the Worlds of Spirits. Fully evinced by unquestionable Histories,* a curious collection of stories of the supernatural. He did not doubt that the evidence was conclusive, and it occupied an important place in his apologetics. In the Preface to the last-named work, dated July 20, 1691, he stated: "I write it for *Practice,* and not to please Men with the Strangeness and Novelty of useless Stories." Having studied the subject "near three score years" and gone to some pains to collect information, in order to strengthen his own faith, he was now publishing "these Historical Letters and Collections: Which I dare say have such Evidence, as will leave every Sadducee that readeth them, either convinced, or utterly without excuse." Baxter was not alone in using ghost stories as ammunition against the materialists of his day; e.g., Joseph Glanvil (an admirer; cf. *Under the Cross,* 49 f.) did the same in *Sadducismus Triumphatus* (1681; 5th ed. of *Philosophical Considerations touching Witches*), on which B. Willey comments: "It may seem a roundabout way of defending religion . . . but . . . believers were just awakening to the possibility that science might abolish the category of the supernatural altogether, and it seemed the shortest way of preventing this to insist upon that class of supernatural phenomena which most of the scoffers themselves acknowledged" (*The Seventeenth Century Background,* 194). On the evidence for Satanic influence in "temptations," cf. *The Certainty,* 171: "multitudes that are melancholy . . . come to me . . . And in almost all I perceive, besides their disease, that a malignant Spirit . . . doth agitate them incessantly against God and Jesus Christ . . . (174) and it is not for nothing, that in the Gospel the Distressed and Epileptick are said to be possessed of Devils: for he may cause the Disease, and work by it accordingly when he hath done it."

17. II:258.

enemy of Christ and us."[18] With Christ and Satan as commanders, "the world is formed into two armies, that live in continual war ... Between these two armies are (sic) the greatest conflict in the world."[19] In "this holy war":[20]

> "Both Christ and Satan work persuasively, by moral means ... Christ forceth not men against their wills to good, and Satan cannot force them to be bad; but all the endeavour is to make men willing; and he is the conqueror that getteth and keepeth our own consent."[21]

And so in Satan's solicitations "self-love and love of good is the principle which he abuseth, and maketh his ground to work upon; as God also useth it in drawing us to good."[22] The anatomy of temptation is always the same; the only difference between one case and another lies in the "officers, instruments and means" employed.

> 1. The devil first worketh upon the outward sense, and so upon the sensitive appetite: he showeth the cup to the drunkard's eye, and the bait of filthy lust to the fornicator ... sensual things, are the baits by which the devil angleth for souls. Thus Eve first saw the fruit, and then tasted, and then did eat ... The sense is the door of sin ...
> 2. The tempter next worketh on the fantasy or imagination, and prints upon it the loveliest image of his bait that possibly he can, and engageth the sinner to think on it and to roll it over and over in his mind ...
> 3. Next he worketh by these upon the passions or affections: which fantasy having inflamed, they violently urge the will and reason ...
> 4. Hence he proceedeth to infect the will, (upon the simple apprehension of the understanding,) to make it inordinately cleave to the temporal good, and to neglect its duty in commanding the understanding to meditate on preserving objects, and to call off the thoughts from the unclean thing: it neglecteth to rule the thoughts and passions according to its office and natural power.
> 5. And so he corrupteth the understanding itself, first to omit its duty, and then to entertain deceit, and to approve of evil: and so the servant is put into the government, and the commanding powers do but serve it.

---

18. *loc. cit.*; cf. *M.T.*, I:xiv.44, 273: "Sicut in Sanctis *Amor Dei* est ordine naturae ante *Amorem Creaturarum* (Deum enim amant propter se at alios propter Deum;) Ita Diabolorum Malitia est *primo* adversus *Deum*, & *secundo* tantum adversus homines." [As in the the saints love of God is in order of nature before love of creatures (for they love God for himself, and others for God's sake), so the malice of devils is primarily against God, and only secondarily against men.]
19. *Works*, II:260; cf. p. 6, *sup.*, for Baxter's use of this principle as a key to church history.
20. p. 262.
21. p. 261; cf. VII:172: "Satan's servants are all volunteers."
22. II:265.

Reason is blinded by sensuality and passion, and becomes their servants, and pleads their cause.[23]

And an act of sin follows.

This was the devil's method with Adam and Eve; whose sin consisted, not in apprehending "the forbidden thing ... [truly] as good,"[24] nor in willing it "by a simple complacency or volition"[25] (these mental acts were necessitated by the object, and were not, therefore, *moral* acts at all), but in what followed, the sixth stage in the analysis of action reproduced in the preceding chapter.[26] Sin began, as it always does, with the failure of the will, "the master-commanding faculty of the rational soul,"[27] to test and rule by reason the non-rational impulse of passion and sensitive appetite. Satan called the attention of Adam and Eve to a lower good,[28] a fruit that was pleasant to look at and to eat, and a source of wisdom into the bargain, and assured them that they could only gain by eating it. Thus he enlisted self-love on his side, and so won his triumph. Thoughtlessness, the practical abjuration of rationality, was man's original sin; Adam and Eve fell because they did not think what they were doing. They accepted Satan's assurances uncritically, omitting to evaluate them in the light of God's warning,[29] and accepted the lower good without question, not setting alongside it the higher good which they thereby forfeited. The comparisons which are essential to rational action were not made.

> 7. And so when the cogitations should have been called off. 8. And the intellect should have minded God, and his command, and proceeded from a simple apprehension to the comparing act, and said, The favour of God is better, and his will shall rule, it omitted all these acts, because the will omitted to command them; yea, and hindered them. 9. And so the intellect was next guilty of a *non-renuo*,—I will not forbid or hinder it (and the will accordingly). 10. And next of a positive deception, and the will of consent unto the sin, and so it being 'finished, brought forth death.'"[30]

23. pp. 263 f.

24. p. 240.

25. Ibid.; cf. *M.T.*, I:xiv.62, 275: "Neque peccavit Adamus . . . Bonum inferius ut tale (*sc.* bonum) *simpliciter apprehendendo* per intellectum; nec *simplici complacentia* Volendo: Quia revera Bonum fuit . . ."

26. p. 117 above.

27. IX:65; cf. *M.T.*, I:xiv.80, 277: "Potentiae abusus vel non usus primum fuit peccatum."

28. Gen. 3:6; cf. *M.T.*, I:xiv.50, 273: "Tentationis maxima pars fuit animum a summo bono avertere; Quod boni inferioris sensibilis & phantastici propositione & ostentatione Diabolus effecit."

29. Gen. 2:17, 3:4-5.

30. II:240. Cf. the analysis of action, 117. "In all this," Baxter notes, "I go upon common principles" (241).

Adam hereby did much more than merely eat an attractive fruit. By this one transgression he changed his disposition, contracting the "disease of selfishness,"[31] and committed, in principle at least, nearly every sin there is. His act contained the seeds of total apostasy. In the first chapter of *Self-Denial*, Baxter expounds something of the significance of this first act of disobedience.[32] Adam hereby ceased to look to God as "his only felicity and ultimate end"; he "was suddenly taken with the creature as a means to the pleasing of his carnal self" and "delivered up his reason in subjection to his sensuality, and made himself his ultimate end." He ceased "to use all creatures in order to God, for his pleasure and glory," for now "all that he possessed was become the provision and fuel of his lusts." Turning away from the Creator to the creature, and from a proper concern for the next life to an exclusive preoccupation with this, he flew in the face of God's *dominium*, rejected his *imperium* and paternal care, and chose instead to look after and fend for himself.[33] He began to play God; "he became regardless of the honour of God, and his mind was bent on his own honour, so that he would have every knee bow to himself, and every eye observe him, and every mind think highly of him, and every tongue to praise and magnify him." And hereby he proclaimed that in fact he had sunk to the level of beasts, deaf to all but the clamour of self-regarding appetite.

The effect of Adam's sin was thus twofold, "Guilt and Pravity"; the latter being part of the punishment due to the former. And this double disability was bequeathed to his descendants, for "he could beget no better than himself."[34]

---

31. XI:59.

32. XI:59-76. In *M.T.*, I:xiv, 269, Baxter lists twenty-seven distinct sins, of each of which Adam's action was the prototype.

33. It was in terms of this changed attitude that Baxter explained the knowledge Adam acquired by eating the forbidden fruit. Adam in innocence was "not to take any thought or care for himself . . . it was his Father's part to preserve him and provide for him, to keep off death and danger, and supply all his wants." "At quando Mens hominis a Deo ad seipsum averti incipit, & sibi ipsi ut fini ultimo adhaerere, & in seipso sufficientiam & faelicitatem quaerere . . . tunc statim sibi ipsi *prospicere* incipit, & vice Dei se curare, & regere, & consequenter Deus quidam esse vellit, quoad cognitionem rerum ad finem suum inordinatum conducentium; & Bonum & Malum sensitivum, & media omnia ad carnis & Mentis superbientis complacentiam, comperta habere maxime cupit. Quorum *plurima* plane *nescire*, & *omnia aliter scire*, optatissimum foret." [But when the man's mind starts to turn from God to himself, and to cleave to himself as his ultimate end, and to seek sufficiency and happiness in himself, then at once he begins to make provision for himself, and to look after and rule himself in God's stead, and thus grabs at being God in knowing what furthers his lawless goal, and greatly desires to have under his control good and evil for his senses, and all the means of pleasing his proud flesh and mind. Most of which it would have been most desirable simply not to know, and all of which to know in a different way.] "Much of this selfish knowledge of the creature he did attain; but with the woeful loss of the divine knowledge of the creature, and of the filial, soul-contenting knowledge of God; yea, and of himself, as in his due subordination to God" (*Works*, XI:65 f.; *M.T.*, I:xiii.14, 267).

34. *An End of Doctrinal Controversies*, 95, 94. "When the soul is depraved by sin, there is no

The New Testament, to Baxter's mind, plainly taught that God imputed Adam's sin to all his children, so that they shared its penal consequences;[35] and the depravity of human nature was to him a necessary inference from everyday experience.

> He that thinks that God made man in this distempered, distracted state, that selfishness doth hold the world in, hath unreasonable thoughts of the workmanship of God. He that seeth even children, before they can speak or go, so selfish as they are, and all mankind, without exception, to be naturally as so many idol gods in the world, and can believe that this is the image of God, in which they were created, doth make the image of Satan to be the image of God. No wiser, no better, is the doctrine that denieth original sin ..."[36]

The grounds which justify the penalizing of the race for Adam's sin must be sought in Adam's natural relation to the rest of mankind; otherwise it cannot but appear an arbitrary and unjust arrangement on God's part. "God doth not impute Adam's sin to us because *he will do it*, without any real participation of ours; nor *beyond* our true natural participation, but according to it; Otherwise *God* should have *made us sinners* ... and not Adam."[37] —a blasphe-

---

virtue left in nature to rectify that by generation, and hinder the propagation of the pravity" (*Two Disputations of Original Sin*, 113). Baxter, following the common Reformed usage, covers both "guilt and pravity" by the phrase "original sin."

35. This is the meaning which Baxter attached to the doctrine of original guilt. "I say not that we sinned in *Adam properly*, but that we received a *guilty nature* from *Adam*, which then began to be a sinful or guilty ... *person*, when it began to be a ... *person*, and before that was but a *guilty seed*." We share Adam's guilt by "*derivation and participation*," and are "justly reputed *odious and punishable*, as being *then seminally in him*" (*Two Disputations*, 218, 227). In the first disputation, "Whether Infants have Original Sin?," reproduced almost exactly in Latin in *M.T.*, I:xv.Disp. 2, 353 f., he set out the standard Reformed arguments for "original guilt" from Rom. 5:12-18. They amounted to this: Death is a penal infliction, the wages of sin; sin therefore must be as universal as death (v. 12); but infants are liable to death from the moment of birth; they, therefore, must be among the "all" who sinned and were condemned by reason of Adam's transgression (vv. 12, 18); and since they have committed no actual sin, their sin and guilt must be derived by imputation.

36. XI:115 f. In this context Baxter had Pelagian and Socinian ideas particularly in view. To the objection that there could be no sin in infants' being ruled by sense while they were too young to have acquired the use of reason, Baxter replied: "If sin had not made the appetite inordinate, infants might have lived till they had outgrown their infancy without transgressing: an ordinate appetite would have carried them to no inordinate acts" (*Two Disputations*, 116). For Baxter's belief about the natural state of infants, cf. VII:88: "I remember what an outcry was once against me (margin, "fifteen years ago"—1642, cf. *R.B.*, I:24) in this town, for saying that children by nature, considered as ... unsanctified, were as hateful in the eyes of God, as any toads or serpents are in ours; so that the people railed at me as I went along the streets; but doubtless the comparison is far too short ..."

37. *An End of Doctrinal Controversies*, 95.

mous idea. It was, therefore, Baxter held, important to see that Adam's 'federal' representation of mankind was nothing arbitrary and mysterious, but merely the archetypal instance of something perfectly familiar both in law and in life: the father acting for his children as well as for himself and involving them in the consequences of his action, and the children inheriting their parent's legal status and natural rights or disabilities. Adam was the progenitor of mankind, both body and soul.[38] Had he stood, his children would have been born holy, as their father was at creation, and, after passing the same test as he, would in their turn have been confirmed in sinlessness and perfect love.[39] As it was, they were born under the same disabilities as their father had incurred. Baxter was quick to see and accept the logical corollary of making physical descent the ground of the imputation of sin: "it seems to me that we are so far guilty both of *Adam's* sin, and of our neerer Parents, committed while we were seminally in them, as that God may ... in positive execution of vindictive justice, punish us ... for such guilt";[40] "I must confess for my part, I am not able to maintain our guilt of *Adam's* sins without this."[41] He found support for the doctrine that children share all their parents' and ancestors' guilt in Scripture;[42] in the

38. Baxter was a convinced advocate of the "*Generative Traduction of Souls,*" which characteristically he sought to synthesize with creationism; cf. *M.T.*, I:xv, Disp. 2, 371 f.: "ipse dico Animam esse simul ex *Traduce* & *Creatam*: substantia tota fit a Deo, at ... per Creationis legem" (i.e., the law of the reproduction of species, cf. Gen. 1:22, 28); "Specificatio autem & Individuatio a Deo & Parentibus, per viam generationis ..." Man is essentially soul and body, and if the soul were excluded from reproductive process man would not in fact reproduce his kind at all: "novis certo constat: Parentes liberos generant; & homines hominem ... ideo plus facit quam bestiae, quae animam generant Vegetivam & Sensitivam; & ideo animam generat etiam qua rationalem: Aliter non hominem generaret."

39. Baxter rejected the idea, not uncommon among Calvinists of his day, that Adam's obedience would have secured the immediate impeccability of his descendants and excused them from individual probation: "I find not but that all *Adam's* Posterity should have ... lived under the same Law ... still their own sinning would have been a *possible thing* ... if our Publick Root had perfectly obeyed, we must also have perfectly obeyed, or die" (*C.T.*, I:ii, "*A Premonition,*" 15 f.).

40. *Two Disputations*, 151.

41. *op. cit.*, 238. Baxter may have reached this position by considering the arguments against original guilt put forward by Joshua Placaeus, the Saumur liberal, in the first volume of *Theses Salmurienses*, 1641. In the second of the *Two Disputations*, "Whether Posterity be guilty of Death, by reason of the Actual sins of their immediate Parents," 213 f., Baxter answers Placaeus' arguments, as the strongest presentation of the case against direct imputation. The first is, that the imputation of Adam's sin is untenable unless one holds the imputation of all parents' sins to their children. Baxter agrees, and points out that he holds both.

42. *An End of Doctrinal Controversies*, 85 (=97): "The Scripture is more copious ... in making punishment due to Children for their *next Parents* sins, as for *Adam's* ... The case of *Cain's* posterity, and *Cham's* and *Ishmael's*, and *Esau's* and *Achan's* Family, and *Ahab's*, and many more do fully prove it: And more fully the Second Commandment, and God's declaration of his Name to *Moses, Ex.* 34 (cf. v. 7) and many a Threatening to the Seed of the Wicked, and Christ's express Words in *Matt.* 23:36 so that Scripture puts us out of doubt."

consensus gentium ("all Common-wealths are directed by the natural light to punish infants for their parents sins, as naturally participant," and "that which all Rulers may do without injustice, that God may do without injustice"[43]); and finally in the hard facts of heredity: "Many of the children of the most vicious people are more vicious than the ordinary sort of man is,"[44] not merely through bad upbringing, but as a result of possessing "a diseased, distempered Body, inclining men to particular Vices, and an extraordinarily vitiated soul ... the plain fruit of the Parents sin,"[45] and a penal infliction for it. In Baxter's view, therefore, "the *English Litany*, (after Ezra, Daniel and others) well prayeth, Remember not, Lord, our offences, nor the offences of our Forefathers ... "[46] This opinion seems to have been peculiar to himself, and his traducianism was a minority opinion among Puritan and Reformed theologians,[47] but in his emphatic assertion of original guilt he is thoroughly representative of the orthodoxy of his day.[48]

The permanent effects on human nature of the first transgression were disastrous. Human behavior became a travesty of what God had intended. "After the preachers had set forth the ideal sequence as God has instituted it," wrote Professor Miller with reference to the Puritan analysis of action, "they could run over each of the phases, from the phantasms to the passions, pointing out how each now failed to do its share, how each rebelled against subordination, stepped out of line, established immoral liaisons with one or another, and threw the whole microcosm into pandemonium."[49] We are now to review Baxter's endeavors in this field. His general account of the disease is as follows:

> The very nature of original sin doth consist in these two things: Privatively, in the want of our original love ... to God as God; I mean ... as the beginning

---

43. *Two Disputations*, 135, 185. Baxter instances the confiscation of a traitor's goods, which penalizes his family as well as himself.

44. *op. cit.*, 169.

45. *An End of Doctrinal Controversies*, 86 (=98).

46. *J.R.*, "Of the Imputation," 35.

47. cf. *R.D.*, 227 f., 343. I know no evidence for traduciaism among Puritan theologians apart from Baxter's marginal note in *An End of Doctrinal Controversies*, 87 (=99); "Mr. W. Fenner" (from whose ministry Baxter seems to have profited as a young man, cf. *R.B.*, I:13, and whose works, published in one volume in 1651, he frequently recommends) "put his Opinion for the Traduction of Souls, into his Catechismes: But the Publisher left that out." (The reference is probably to the posthumous *Spirituall Mans Directory*.)

48. Baxter names the most prominent of those few Reformed theologians who hesitated to affirm original guilt and regarded man's direct inheritance from Adam as a sinful nature only (*Two Disputations*, 144 f.): Peter Martyr, Chamier and the Saumur liberals, John Cameron and Placaeus.

49. P. Miller, *The New England Mind*, 256 f.

or end of us and all things, and the absolute Lord, and infinite, simple, inestimable good. And positively, in the inordinate propensity or inclination to ourselves, as for ourselves ... the disposition suited to the actual sin that caused it, which was a retiring from God to self. He that feeleth not this evil in himself hath no true knowledge of original sin.[50]

More simply, "an inordinate self-love ... is original sin itself, even in the heart of it."[51] The prevalence of such a disposition shows that every faculty of the rational soul has been thrown out of gear. Baxter expands his summary into an exhaustive diagnosis.[52] The root of the trouble is, as we should expect, in the will:

> The diseases of the will, are in its inclination, and its acts. 1. An inordinate inclination to the pleasing of the fleshly appetite and fantasy, and to all carnal baits and temporal things, that tend to please it, and inordinate acts of desire accordingly. 2. An irrational backwardness to God, and grace, and spiritual good, and a refusal or nolition in act accordingly. These are in the will, 1. Because it is become much subject to the sensitive appetite, and hath debased itself, and contracted, by its sinful acts, a sensual inclination ... 3. Because the will is become destitute (in its corrupted state) of the power of divine love, or an inclination to God and holy things, which should countermand the seduction of carnal objects. 4. And the understanding is much destitute of the light that should lead them higher. 5. Because the rage of the corrupted appetite is still seducing it.[53]

The will has accordingly infected the intellect, in which now

> there are defects or ill dispositions, that are sinfully contracted; and though these are now immediately natural[54] and necessary, yet being originally and remotely voluntary or free, they are participatively sinful. Such is the natural man's disability or undisposedness to know the things of the Spirit ... This lieth not in the want of a natural faculty to know them, but, 1. Radically in the will. 2. And thence in contrary, false apprehensions which the intellect is prepossessed with, which resisting the truth, may be called, its blindness or impotency to know them. And 3. In a strangeness of the mind to those spiritual things which it is utterly unacquainted with.[55]

---

50. *Works*, XI:lii.

51. 125.

52. *Christian Directory*, I:3, Grand Direction VIII, dir. I: "Know what corruptions ... have tainted and perverted the several faculties" (*Works*, II:234 f.).

53. 238 f.

54. "Sinful habits are become as it were a second nature to the ungodly" (*Works*, XIII:229).

55. II:236 f.

The upshot is that man believes only what he wants to believe; his will inhibits his intellect from the cognizance of those objects—spiritual things, in this case—which he no longer desires to know. The particular shortcomings of the intellect are consequently these:

> When it should know by the proper evidence of the thing, the privation of its act is called ignorance … and the privation of its rectitude is called error (which differ as not seeing, and seeing falsely). When it should know by testimony, the privation of its act is simply unbelief, or not believing, and the privation of its rectitude is either disbelief, when they think the reporter erreth, or misbelief, when it believeth a testimony that is not the be believed. [56]

Man has lost his respect and concern for truth as such, at least in the spiritual realm. To be mistaken and deluded at this point is now part of man's natural state.

The ruling powers having defaulted from duty, "our faculties that should be commanded and directed, are by sin grown impotent and obstinate, and have contracted a rebelling, disobedient disposition."[57] They act habitually as they began to do when Adam sinned, and are disinclined to do anything else. A moment's introspection cannot but banish doubt on this point. Memory is infected, as appears from "its retentiveness of evil … and its looseness and neglect of better, spiritual, necessary things … our memories are like walls of stone to any thing that is spiritual, and like walls of wax, on which you may write any thing, of that which is secular or evil."[58] Imagination shows symptoms of the same disease, by "its readiness to think of evil, and of common earthly things, and its unaptness to think of any thing that is holy and good; and when we do force ourselves to holy thoughts, they are disorderly, confused, unskilfully managed, with great averseness …"[59] Both memory and imagination are at the beck and call of blind lust (concupiscence), which now runs wild and seeks to whirl the man along in its train. The sensitive appetite has broken loose from reason's control and refuses any more to submit to it, but storms and fumes till its cravings are gratified:

> The sin of the sensitive appetite consisteth in the inordinate rage or immoderateness to its object, which causeth it to disobey the commands of reason, and to become the great inciter of rebellion in the soul; violently urging the mind and will to consent to its desires … a diseased, inordinate, unruly appetite …[60]

56. II:238.
57. IX:144.
58. II:242.
59. *loc. cit.*
60. *loc. cit.*

And the emotions habitually follow its lead:

> The sin of the affections, or passions, consisteth in this:—That they are too easily and violently moved by the sensitive interest and appetite; and are habitually prone to such carnal inordinate motions, running before the understanding and will (some of them), and soliciting and urging them to evil; and resisting and disobeying the commands of reason and the will.[61]

Reason and will have become the slaves of the passion and lust; human nature has been turned topsy-turvy; and in everything he does man sins.[62]

By the light of this diagnosis of the derangement of human nature, Baxter looked out on his fellow-men with understanding eyes. Beneath superficial differences of temperament and character, he saw everywhere the same grim pattern of perversion. No life was free of its tell-tale symptoms. All were fast in the grip of a vicious self-centeredness. "Is not SELF the great idol which the whole world of unsanctified men doth worship? Who is it that ruleth the children of disobedience, but carnal self?"[63] "Selfishness is the soul's idolatry and adultery."[64] Carnal self is precisely the Pauline 'flesh,' which, Baxter tells us, covers

> 1. The sensitive apprehension, imagination, appetite and passion as it is grown inordinate. And, 2. The understanding, will, and executive power as they are corrupted to a sinful inclination to the objects of sense, and become servants of the sensitive part, and is turned from the love of God, and things spiritual.[65]

The term itself indicates where sinful impulse is rooted.

> Do not think that it is only sin, and not the body, that is the flesh, that is called your enemy in Scripture. For though it be not the body as such, or as obedient to the soul, yet it is the body as inclining to creatures, from which the sinful soul cannot restrain it ... Why should sin be called flesh and body, but that it is the body of flesh that is the principal seat of those sins that are so called?[66]

Baxter made this point in order to correct what seemed to him an exaggerated reaction. Because Rome appeared to identify "flesh" with the body, Protestants,

---

61. p. 243.
62. cf. 235: "it is not this or that faculty that is the full and proper subject of sin, but the man ... It is properer to say, The man sinned, than, The intellect or will sinned ..."
63. XI:xxvii.
64. p. 85.
65. *Cure of Church Divisions*, second pagination, 132 f.
66. XI:248.

Baxter thought, were generally over-chary of relating sin to the body at all.[67] But the one view was as much a mistake as the other; for, as has already been indicated, "no small part of the punishment of our original sin (both as from Adam, and from our nearer parents) is found in the ill complexion of our bodies: the temperature of some inclineth them vehemently to passion; and of others to lust; and of others to sloth and dullness; and of others to gulosity";[68] and of others to melancholy; and so on. Temperament springs from a man's physical constitution, and his temperament largely determines which become his besetting sins. Satan's strategy involves the exploitation of temperament. The enemy of souls

> doth what he can to get an ill tempered body on his side; for as sin did let in bodily distempers, so do they much befriend the sin that caused them. A choleric temper will much help him to draw men to passion, malice, murder, cruelty, and revenge. A sanguine and bilious temper mixed, will help him to draw men to lust, and filthiness, and levity, and wantonness, and time-wasting pleasures: a sanguine temper mixed with a pituitous, much helpeth him to make men blockish, and regardless, and insensible of the great concernments of the soul. A phlegmatic temper helpeth him to draw people to drowsy sluggishness, and to an idle, slothful life ... A healthful temper much helpeth him to draw people to gluttony, drunkenness, lust, ambition, covetousness, and neglect of life eternal: a sickly temper helpeth him to tempt us to peevishness and impatience: and a melancholy temper helpeth him in all the temptations ...[69]

Satan adapts his technique to suit each man's natural susceptibilities, and encourages him to express his flesh-pleasing disposition in the manner most congenial to him. Satan is the first cause of temptation and sin, inasmuch as it is he who engineers the coincidence of inordinate desire and provocative object out of which sin grows.[70] The objects of selfish desire vary enormously from

67. Either error had serious practical consequences: those "that think that the Scripture by 'flesh' meaneth only the rational soul as unrenewed, do thereupon cherish the flesh itself, and pamper it, and feed its unruly lusts, and never do any thing to tame the body; but pray daily that God would destroy the flesh within them ... while they ... neglect a chief part of the cure. And on the contrary, some papists that look only at the body as their enemy, are much in fastings, and bodily exercises while they neglect the mortifying of their carnal minds" (III:98).

68. XII:410.

69. II:265.

70. cf. II:258: "The flesh is the end of temptation, for all is to please it ... the world is the matter of temptation; and the devil is the first mover, or efficient of it: and this is the trinity of enemies to Christ and us, which we renounce in baptism, and must constantly resist . . ." The theme of the Satanic trinity recurs with fanciful elaborations in IX:354. A vivid illustration of Baxter's meaning is his remark about evil thoughts in VII:172: "Why, it is he (Satan) that speaks this in you, whenever you have these thoughts ... Your own corrupt hearts are the mother, but he is the father of them all."

man to man. In general, they may be classified as "this trinity ... pleasure, profit, and honour, not spiritual, but carnal ... sometimes (in the Bible) all is comprehended in the term *world* ... the world being the harlot with which the flesh commits adultery."[71] The common characteristic of "selfish" actions, as such, is their motive. Man's goal in them is, not to please God, but to obey the promptings of his own nature. However noble they may be in themselves, therefore, their motive denominates them sin. Each man does what he likes doing for no other reason than that he likes doing it. The glory of God is not his aim, nor the law of God his rule. What he does may in fact partly correspond to God's requirements; but this is mere coincidence, and does not diminish the sinfulness of his sin. A theologian may be as much a flesh-pleaser as a drunkard: Satan "will permit them ... to study the Holy Scripture ...He can suffer them to be eminent divines, so they will not be serious Christians."[72] A man may have a spotless moral and religious exterior; he may have a real measure of love to God; but as long as he remains "unsanctified," his religion is hypocrisy, for his is only interested in God as a means to his own end—to a happiness, that is, which is not God. "If he look for a life to come, he would have it consist of such kind of pleasures as he here enjoyed in this life ...he hath a nature so suitable to them, that he savoureth these as the sweetest delights ... It is some creature, and not God, that hath men's hearts, their care, and diligence ..."[73] And while this is so, men are Satan's slaves still. For this is the essence of sin.

Men spend their lives in an unsuccessful search for happiness in the created order. They run to and fro from one thing to another, but they find the very reverse of satisfaction in their quest. For "the creatures are many, and of contrary qualities ... and the heart that is set on such an object, must needs be a divided heart; and the heart that is divided among so many and contrary ... objects, must needs be a distracted heart ... He that maketh the world his god, hath so many gods, and so discordant, that he will never please them all; and all of them together will never fully content and please him."[74] There is no *quies*, no satisfaction, in a life of flesh-pleasing. "All the pleasure of fleshly things, is but like the scratching of a man that hath the itch; it is his disease that makes him desire it ... Your loudest laughter is but like that of a man that is tickled, he laughs when he hath no cause of joy."[75] We hear the echo of Augustine as

71. XI:159. This classification, based on John 2:15-6, was, as Baxter himself says, a Puritan commonplace (XXIII:18).
72. XIII:253; cf. 235: "To study and know mere notions of God, or what is to be held and said of him in discourse, is not to study to know God ..."
73. "The ungrounded faith and hope of the wicked produceth a slight and common love" (XXIII:40 f.); Baxter instances the Pharisee, Luke 18:10 f.
74. XIII:25.
75. VII:422.

Baxter develops this theme: "The heart he [God] made for himself, and the heart he will have; or else whoever hath it shall have it to his woe. He will be its rest, or it shall never have rest; and he will be its happiness, or it shall be miserable everlastingly."[76] Yet man will not abandon his hopeless search for a Godless happiness. He is adamant in his refusal to repent. And this is what is meant by saying that man lost his freedom of will at the Fall, and is now *unable* to do God's will. His inability is moral, not physical. It consists precisely in *unwillingness*. "*Cannot*" here means "*will* not." Man has not lost his power to make choices (otherwise he would have ceased to be man altogether); what he has lost is his inclination to make right choices. He still makes decisions, but they are no longer sensible decisions. And this very inability to choose God and life actually increases the guilt of his not doing so.

This seeming paradox, Baxter held, was in fact the teaching of "natural light," as appears from its embodiment in legal codes throughout the world. If a man breaks a law because it was physically impossible for him to keep it, Nature teaches that his blameworthiness is nil. But if he breaks a law for no better reason than that he was disinclined to keep it, the matter is very different: in this case, he transgresses by his own deliberate choice, and is therefore guilty. "If you can but prove that a man offended willingly, you have proved him culpable: for nature hath taught all the world to bring the fault to the will, and there to leave it and look no further for the cause."[77] And if he is a hardened, incorrigible offender, his guilt is the greater. Crime is all the more heinous when committed of set purpose by a habitual lawbreaker who has no intention ever to change his ways. But this is precisely man's state; and when theologians of an Augustinian complexion asserted against Pelagians and Arminians man's total inability and the bondage of his will, what they meant to say was that man has sunk so deep in sin and become so inveterate an offender that there is not the slightest possibility of his improving himself. He is in the grip of vicious habits which he has lost the desire to break. And this makes him more guilty, not less so. Baxter's position on this point is summarized in the following extract form the Epistle "To all Unsanctified Persons ... especially my Hearers in the Parish of Kidderminster," which he prefixed to his *Call to the Unconverted*:

> Augustine as well as Pelagius, Calvin as well as Arminius, the Dominicans as well as the Jesuits, do all generally maintain, that man hath free-will. The orthodox say, that free-will is corrupt and disposed to evil ... No man of brains denieth, that man hath a will that is naturally free; it is free from violence, and it is a self-determining principle; but it is not free from evil dispositions. It is habitually averse to God and holiness, and inclined to earthly,

76. IX:351.
77. VII:317.

fleshly things; it is enslaved by a sinful bias ... Alas, we easily confess to you that you have not this spiritual, moral free-will, which is your right inclination ... If you had a will that were freed from wicked inclinations, I had no need to write such books as these ... But ... the want of it is so far from excusing you, that the more you want it (that is, the more you are wilful in sin) the worse you are, and the sorer will be your punishment.[78]

Fallen man, then, is free for sin, but not for holiness; for madness, but not for sanity; for the life of a beast, but not for the life of a man. Sin has dehumanized him. His will has submitted to the rule of sense, and has dragged down his intellect into the same captivity. Man is no longer rational (though he likes to think he is); reason has become the slave of the passions. "Sin hath unmanned us, and lost us the use of our reason ..."[79] The will no longer encourages the intellect to discern truth and direct accordingly, but impels it to justify and subserve its own perverted inclinations. Reason is pressed into the service of unreasonableness, and used to defend irrationality by argument.

Though the understanding naturally be inclined to truth, yet a selfish bias upon the soul, especially on the will, doth commonly delude it, and make the vilest error seem to be truth to it, and the most useful truth to seem an error. The will hath much command over the understanding ... Do you not see that where self is deeply engaged, the judgment is bribed or overmastered, and carried from the truth? [80]

Impartial investigation and objective judgment become impossible in such cases; reasoning gives way to rationalization and wishful thinking. This is continually happening in human life. The real dictator, the will's master, is sense; in the last analysis, "we judge by feeling, which binds our reason."[81] But man remains wholly unconscious of his own intellectual dishonesty, for he lacks self-knowledge. Having chosen to play God and thus live a lie, he naturally has lost his inclination to know the truth about himself. He is not prepared to know himself as a creature and as a sinner. He is willingly deluded as to his

---

78. VII:cccl.
79. VIII:59.
80. XI:94.
81. VII:361. Baxter subjoins some vivid and telling illustrations: "We see in common worldly things, that most men think the cause is right which is their own ... There are few children but think the father unmerciful ... if he whip them. There is scarce the vilest, swinish wretch, but thinketh the church doth wrong him, if they excommunicate him, or scarce a thief or murderer that is hanged, but would accuse the law and judge of cruelty . . ." Cf. IX:vi: "if once you have affections that can master your understanding, you are lost, and know it not, For when you have a resolution to cast off any duty, you will first believe it is no duty: and when you must change your judgment for carnal advantages, you will make the change seem reasonable and right: and evil shall be proved good when you have a mind to follow it."

own real motives. His heart is a closed book to him, and his life a prolonged course of self-deception. He has trained himself to forget that he is the slave of his appetites, and does not want to be reminded that he has ceased to be rational, lest he should lose his self-respect. Men know everyone better than they know themselves. Passion and interest dictate their views for them, and then "some men are so desperately self-conceited that they take every man to be self-conceited that is not of their conceits."[82] A difference of opinion is construed as a personal slight. And when a Christian preacher punctures their self-esteem and tells them the truth about themselves, they take it as an insult motivated by spite. Baxter found this over and over again: "When I come to convince a sinner of his guilt, and show him the heinous nature of his sin, because it is his own, he will not be convinced of it ... They say, it is out of malice, or humour, or pride."[83] Such an attitude must have tragic results:

> Foolish self-love ... makes men unwilling to know the worst of themselves, and so keepeth them from believing their sinfulness and misery; and causeth them to presume, and keep up false deceiving hopes, that they may be saved whether they are converted or not, or that they may be converted, when indeed they are not ... Like many a sick man that I have known in the beginning of a consumption ... they hope there is no danger in it; or they hope it will go away of itself, and is but some cold; or they hope that such and such an easy medicine will cure it; till they are past hope ... Just so do poor wretches by their souls.[84]

Here is a chronic unrealism that is lunacy. Men said of Baxter's sermons: "I think you will make men mad under a pretence of converting them." "Can you be madder than you are already?" the preacher retorted. "A man is never well in his wits till he be converted." And then, with fine sarcasm: "It is a wise world when men will disobey God, and run to hell for fear of being out of their wits."[85]

We cannot here examine in detail the flaming onslaught against sin and sinners which occupies so many pages in Baxter's practical works. What was said of Charles Finney could equally be said of him: others set snares for sinners, but Baxter rode them down with a cavalry charge. When Baxter deals with sin, he is acute but not subtle. Subtlety, he held, would be out of place when the case is so plain. The truth is simply this: that man has chosen to go mad, and become a beast; man was made holy, and has chosen to pollute himself. The beastliness and the uncleanness of sin, as it appears in the light of

82. XI:131.
83. p. 341.
84. VII:288.
85. p. 415 f.

God's goodness and man's created glory and destiny, are two themes on which Baxter continually harped. A review of his favorite descriptions of sin is very revealing on this point. Sin, or "sensuality," is *bestial* and "inhuman" (i.e., sub-human), "beastly," "brutish," "swinish." Sin makes a man a pig. Sin, too, is *unclean*, "loathsome." Baxter was more concerned with truth than with the canons of good taste, and one of his homiletic devices was a calculated coarseness of image and metaphor to express this fact. The following image, in which the ideas of bestiality and uncleanness are combined, is typical: sinners, he says, are like "men in bedlam wallowing naked in their dung."[86] Lust is regularly "filthy"; a whore is "beautiful dirt"[87]; unconverted hearts are "corrupt" and "rotten"; and so on. Again, sin is *ugly* and repulsive. *Ordo*, as we saw, is the mark of beauty, and disorder and deformity, of life and character as much as of body, betoken the opposite. Especially unlovely is blind hatred ("malignity") towards God and goodness in a nature made for rational love. For all these reasons, sin is "odious" and "vile." "Is not a beastly drunkard or whoremonger, and a raging swearer, and a malicious persecutor, a very deformed, loathsome creature?"[88] Baxter's constant use of these epithets gave to his treatment of sin and sins vividness and power unique in Puritan writing. Grosart rightly comments on its essential chastity: "Nowhere else that I know will you find anatomy so trenchant of fallen human nature, and yet so modest."[89] It was the most elaborate, and the least suggestive, of the hamartiologies of his day. Baxter was so sickened by the beastliness, and foulness, and ugliness, of human sin that he could not make it attractive. His heart was too pure. Like every great preacher, he saw what he said, and today, three hundred years after, it is impossible to read his searching, searing paragraphs on the sinfulness of sin without coming to share something of the clarity of his vision.

We may note in conclusion that all Baxter has to say about man, created and fallen, is entirely consonant with the Reformed and Puritan orthodoxy of his day. He parts company with his contemporaries only to surpass them. But on the basic principles of Augustinian anthropology, which is fundamental to all Calvinistic thought, he and they are at one.

---

86. II:253.
87. p. 289.
88. p. 254.
89. A. B. Grosart, *Representative Nonconformists*, 154.

Chapter 7

The Art of Preaching

1. Aim of chapter: to examine the principles behind Baxter's evangelistic preaching.

2. The Puritan preaching tradition:
   Sermons designed to reach the will, via mind and affection.
   Cooperation of listeners required in noting, memorizing and "repeating."
   The large expository treatise.
   "Powerful" preaching.
   Baxter endorsed this tradition at all points.
   His distinctive development of it for evangelism

3. The need for gravity, plainness and prolixity.
   Studied forcefulness of language.

4. The need for apologetics:
   man's unwillingness to be convinced.
   The Spirit's witness by prophecy, miracles and changed lives to
   the truth of Christianity
   the inspiration of the Bible.
   The Christian case unanswerable.

5. The need for "consideration," to awaken conscience.
   Baxter's method of evoking it.

6. The need for "winning motives":
   self-love,
   God and Christ,
   end and means,
   heaven and hell.

7. The need for "powerful preaching."

8. The magnitude of the preacher's task.
   Baxter's distinction as a Puritan preacher.
   His understanding of man, created and fallen, reflected in his sermons.

(Principal Sources: Baxter's evangelistic sermons, especially: *A Saint or a Brute* (X), *A Call to the Unconverted* and *A Treatise of Conversion* (VIII),

Directions and Persuasions to a Sound Conversion, (VIII); *The Reformed Pastor* (XIV); *The Unreasonableness of Infidelity* (XX).)

Chapter 7

The Art of Preaching

"The understanding is the great wheel of the soul … Usually there the business of salvation sticketh." —Thomas Manton, on Is. 53:11.

"It is a principle in Religion that Christians should observe … to call a Spade a Spade" —Walter Cradock.

"Every one must be A SAINT OR A BRUTE." —Baxter.

"King James said of a minister … that he preached as if death were at his back."—William Gurnall, on Eph. 6:19.

The century which followed the work of Peter Ramus was an age of educational theory, and the Puritans, who took very seriously the teaching office of the Church, devoted much thought to determining the correct method of instruction in the school of Christ. Baxter's own first employment was as a schoolmaster, and he brought a schoolmaster's mind with him to Kidderminster. His congregation he regarded as the class which "Christ hath committed to my Teaching and Oversight, as to an unworthy Usher under him in his schoole."[1] It was his part to instruct and discipline them, and theirs to obey and learn from the teacher whom Christ had set over them. More than

---

1. *Aphorisms of Justification*, To the Reader. This is Baxter's regular way of expounding the prophetic (i.e., teaching) office of Christ and of the ordained ministry; cf. *The Worcester-shire Petition to the Parliament for the Ministry of England Defended* (dated March 28, 1653), p.6: "Christs setting Ministers under him in his Church, is no resigning it to them: We are but Ushers and Christ is the only Prophet and chief Master of the School."

once he reminded them from the pulpit of their ignorance and need to keep learning and reprimanded them for inattention to past lessons, in a way which must have been as ungratifying to his hearers then as it would be to a congregation today, but which is still perfectly familiar in most secondary schools. The subject he had been given to teach was Christianity, a gospel which God had designed for fallen man's restoration, "the instrument ... by which he will bring you to repent and believe, and by which he will renew your nature, and imprint his image on you, and bring you to love him, and obey his will."[2] His aim as a teacher must accordingly be twofold: to instruct the mind and move the will. He must not be content merely to impart information; he must labour to arouse the pupils' interest and elicit an active response. "Take heed of those preachers that stifle practice," Baxter urged;[3] such men do not know their job, and leave their work half done. The method which the teacher employs must be evolved in the light of his pupils' condition and capacities, for "recipitur ad modum recipientis" (a favorite tag). Our purpose in this chapter is not to expound Baxter's gospel as such (that will come later), but to examine his method of preaching and teaching it. This method was directly deduced from the account of human nature, created and fallen, which we have already examined, and may therefore be properly expounded as a "use" of it. Moreover, our exposition will incidentally serve to amplify and elaborate that doctrine; for man is never so clearly seen for what he is as when confronted with the gospel of Christ.

We shall take as the text for this chapter a passage from *The Catechising of Families*, chap. XLIV:

> Q. What must Christ's ministers say and do for the world's conversion?
> A. Luke xiv, and Matt. xxii., tell you: they must tell men of the marriage-feast, the blessed provision of grace and glory by Christ, and, by evidence and urgency, compel them to come in ...
> Q. In what manner must Christ's ministers preach all this?
> A. 1. With the greatest gravity and holy reverence; because it is the message of God.
> 2. With the greatest plainness; because men are dull of understanding.
> 3. With the greatest proof and convincing evidence, to conquer prejudice, darkness, and unbelief.
> 4. With powerful winning motives, and urgent importunity, because of men's disaffection and averseness. And O what powerful motives have we at hand, from self-love, from God, from Christ, from necessity, from heaven and hell!

2. XIII:195.
3. XIX:513.

5. With life and fervency, because of the unspeakable importance of the matter, and the deadness and hardness of men's hearts.[4]

This is a typical Puritan statement;[5] and it is well to begin by saying something of the Puritan preaching tradition generally, We saw that from Perkins onward the standard Puritan sermon was made up of doctrine, reason and use. The ultimate rationale of this method (originally suggested, no doubt, by the Ramist insistence on practice as the end of all instruction) was found in the work God meant sermons to accomplish. They were to reach the heart through the head, to move the will by enlightening the mind. "The understanding and memory are ... the passage to the heart,"[6] and it is to the heart that God's word is addressed. The human will was the target on which the Puritan sermon was therefore trained, and everything that might cause the sermon to misfire was ruthlessly excluded. What came to be expected of the preacher appears in the following extract from John Geree's pamphlet, *The Character of an Old English Puritane, or Non-Conformist* (1646):

> He esteemed that preaching best wherein was most of God, least of men, when vain flourishes of wit, and words were declined ... yet could he distinguish between studied plainness, and negligent rudeness. He accounted perspicuity the best grace of a Preacher and that method best, which was most helpful to understanding, affection and memory. To which ordinarily he esteemed none so conducible as that by doctrine, reason and use. He esteemed those Sermons best that came closest to the conscience ...[7]

Rhetorical display must be rejected, and plainness made a matter of conscience. The material should be rigidly and obtrusively subdivided under separate "heads" as an aid to memory.[8] The congregation was expected to

---

4. XIX:254 f.

5. cf. (e.g.) the following excerpt from the Westminster *Directory for the Publick Worship of God*: "the servant of Christ ... is to perform his whole ministry: 1. Painfully, not ... negligently; 2. Plainly, that the meanest may understand ...; 3. Faithfully, looking at the honour of Christ, the conversion, edification and salvation of the people ...; 4. Wisely, framing all his doctrines, exhortations, and especially his reproofs, in such a manner as may be most likely to prevail ...; 5. Gravely, as becometh the word of God ...; 6. With loving affection ... 7. As taught of God, and persuaded ... that all he teacheth is the truth of Christ ..."

6. IV:257.

7. *op. cit.*, 2.

8. By 1641, congregations had come to expect a rigid analytical discourse from their preachers: "old Mr. Lapthorn," the unsuccessful candidate for the Kidderminster lectureship, was turned down "somewhat uncivilly" after a trial sermon which gave offense by its "roughness, and great immethodicalness, and digressions" (*R.B.*, I:20).

remember and to be able to "repeat" the sermon. Note-taking was encouraged.[9] "Repeating" sermons became a regular exercise of both private and family devotion.[10] Where the preachers could rely on this kind of cooperation from their hearers week by week, they frequently preached large-scale expository treatises consisting of several sermons on a single text. This enabled them to "open" passages with an exhaustive, sometimes exhausting, thoroughness. One sermon might be wholly devoted to the exposition of a single doctrine, or the prosecution of a single use. To awaken "affection," preaching needed to be "powerful"; having stated and proved his doctrine, the preacher must become a veritable Boanerges, thundering and lightening in the pulpit as he applied it. A "close" application that should "rip up" the hearers' consciences was thought necessary if truth was to do good.

Baxter grew up in this tradition, and endorsed it in toto. He often made the fundamental Puritan point, that the test of preaching is not its virtuosity but its effectiveness. "Do not think that God is best served by a neat, starched, laced oration; ... he is the able, skilful minister, that is best skilled in the art of instructing, convincing, persuading, and so winning of souls; and that is the best sermon that is best in these."[11] More vigorously and consistently than any, he insisted on the primacy of the appeal to reason: "Reason rectified is the guide of the eye of the soul, the guide of life ... The use of the word, and all ordinances and providences, is first to rectify reason, and thereby the will, and thereby the life. Faith itself is an act of reason ... He that hath the rightest reason, hath the most grace."[12] To try to move man by playing on his emotions before one has convinced his mind is to treat him as less than a rational being— something God never does—and to ensure ultimate failure, for when feelings wear off unbelief reasserts itself. But there is a place for feelings, and the preacher must labour to arouse them when the time comes. "Every reasonable soul hath both judgment and affection; and every rational, spiritual sermon must have both. A discourse that hath judgment without affection is dead, and uneffectual; and that which hath affection without judgment is mad,

9. On this practice, cf. W. Fraser Mitchell, *English Pulpit Oratory from Andrews to Tillotson*, 1932, 30 f., 74 f. The Puritan patriarch, Arthur Hildersham (*D.N.B.*, s.v.), "used often even in his old age to write Sermons in the Church" (Samuel Clarke, *Lives of Thirty-Two English Divines*, 3rd ed. 1670, 122).

10. The practice goes back at least as far as Richard Greenham, who "after Sermon ... used to call his servants together, and examined them of what they heard and what they remembered" (*op. cit.*, 12).

11. XXIII:120.

12. XXII:261 note; cf. VII:25, "No man can have grace without solid knowledge"; VII:496, "Holiness is not blind. Illumination is the first part of sanctification"; VIII:21, "Ignorance is your disease, and knowledge must be your cure"; XIII:238, "God doth renew men by giving them wisdom, and bringing them to a sound mind."

and transporting."[13] Sermons should be noted and repeated;[14] and preachers must do all they can to make their utterances memorable. "Ministers must not only be methodical, and avoid prolix, confused and involved discourses, and that malicious pride of hiding their method, but must be oft in use of the same method ... and choose that method which is most easy for the hearers to understand and remember."[15] Baxter habitually preached sermons in series, and vigorously defended against Quaker sniping the practice of spending "a month, or two, or three, or a year upon a text."[16] His own *Saint's Rest*, delivered in his weekly lecture, must have occupied longer than that. He worked best on the large scale—his single sermons usually contain too much matter insufficiently developed—and the rigidity of the conventional form stimulated rather than stifled his inventive powers; he used it freely and flexibly, and obtrusive subdivision and lists of reasons and uses became in his hand the vehicle for some masterpieces of cumulative effect. If Baxter stands out among Puritan preachers, it is because his mind was better and he used the standard technique to greater effect. It was his distinction to develop and adapt it for specifically evangelistic purposes. The call to examine one's sincerity ("use of trial") had been heard often enough in addresses directed principally to saints, but Baxter was the first to write (and preach) such a "wakening persuasive" as *A Call to the Unconverted to Turn and Live, and Accept of Mercy while Mercy may be Had ... From the Living God.*[17] "In this department of writing, I am not aware that he had properly any predecessor in the English language," is Orme's judgment.[18] Certainly he had no rivals.[19]

13. XXIII:125, Baxter knew something about "mad and transporting" sermons: "I have oft been sorry to see how the people have been moved (in the Army and Countryes) to value a Quaker, a Seeker, an Antinomian, an Anabaptist, a Socinian that preached down the God-head of Christ ... merely for the tone and fervency of their delivery." (*Defence of the Principles of Love*, 109.)

14. There is an interesting discussion of mnemonics and note-taking in the *Christian Directory*, IV:254 f. Mrs. Baker (cf. 43, note 1, *sup.*) "wrote down some of my familiar discourses, with serious application to herself" (XVII:599); cf. the "self-judging paper" which Margaret Charlton wrote on the basis of Baxter's sermon on Rom. 8:9 (*Breviate* . . . , ed. Wilkinson, 71 f). Baxter taught his own congregation to repeat sermons at home, on Sundays; cf. *R.B.*, I:84, quoted p. 45, note 7 *sup.* In the *Christian Directory*, the paterfamilias is advised to make the family repeat the morning sermon after lunch, the afternoon sermon on returning home, and both again before going to bed (IV:250). Cf. the advice given, XIX:512 f: "When you come home, preach over the doctrine again to your own heart, and urge it on yourself. And pray it all over to God . . . "

15. IV:255.

16. VII:257.

17. *Works*, VII:cccxxxi. Though intended for publication (cf. next note), the *Call* was written for the pulpit and preached; cf. the language on pp. 377, 395, 405, 444 f.

18. I:485. Baxter complains, in the Preface to his *Treatise of Conversion* (1657, a year before the *Call*, which is there promised) of "the scarcity of books that are wrote purposely on this subject" (VII:xi).

19. The only comparable work produced in Baxter's lifetime was Joseph Alleine's *Alarm to the Unconverted* (1672), which sold 70,000 copies in a few years (cf. A. Gordon in *D.N.B.*, s.v.). Baxter

He could not have identified himself more unmistakably with the Puritan tradition than by making the preacher's first requirements "gravity" and "plainness." The first needs no separate comment. The need for the second is explained by the following clause: "because men are dull of understanding." They are slow to grasp divine truth, not merely through natural stupidity, but because their wills are fundamentally antipathetic towards it. They dislike it; they do not want to learn it; their thoughts wander during sermons, and what they hear and remember they misunderstand and misapply. "I am daily forced to admire how lamentably ignorant many of our people are, that have seemed diligent hearers of me these ten or twelve years, while I spoke plainly as I was able to speak!" Baxter wrote in 1655.[20] To combat this ingrained, wilful obtuseness, Baxter strove to be as plain and pungent as he could. He described his pulpit technique in the Preface to his *Treatise of Conversion*. "Witty" preaching he renounced, on the ground that its studied artificiality made serious issues seem trivial.

> The plainest words are the profitablest oratory in the weightiest matters. Fineness is for ornament, and delicacy for delight, but they answer not necessity ... It is hard ... to hear or read a neat, concise, sententious discourse, and not to be hurt by it; for it usually hindereth the due operation of the matter, and keeps it from the heart, and stops it in the fancy, and makes it seem as light as the style. We use not to stand upon compliment ... when we run to quench a common fire, nor to call men out to it by an eloquent speech. If we see a man fall into fire or water, we stand not upon mannerliness in plucking him out, but lay hands on him while we can without delay.

Gilded periods and exotic conceits are a sin against gravity as much as against plainness. Such exhibitionist antics do not befit a man who comes from God on an errand of life or death. Baxter had felt this from his teens, perhaps as a result of his experience at Court:

> I shall never forget the relish of my soul, when God first warmed my heart ... When I read such a book as Bishop Andrews' Sermons, or heard such kind of preaching, I felt no life in it: methought they did but play with holy things ... But it was the plain and pressing downright preacher, that only seemed to me to be in good sadness, and to make somewhat of it, and to speak with life, and light, and weight: and it was such kind of writings that were wonderfully pleasant and savoury to my soul. And I am apt to think that it is thus now with my hearers ... And yet I must confess, that though I

---

contributed a long preface (XIII:535 f.) The work is demonstrably a rehash of the *Call, Treatise of Conversion* and *Directions . . .to a Sound Conversion* by a writer of inferior ability.

20. XIV:xix.

can better digest exactness and brevity, than I could ... yet I as much value seriousness and plainness: and I feel in myself in reading or hearing, a despising of that wittiness as proud foolery, which savoureth of levity, and tendeth to evaporate weighty truths ... they deal liker to players than preachers in the pulpit ...

Such a "plain and pressing downright preacher" Baxter aspired to be. "May I speak pertinently, plainly, piercingly and somewhat properly, I have enough."[21] He was willing to be criticized as redundant and inelegant if by repetition and the use of a straightforward colloquial idiom he could make his sermons arresting and effective to the man in the street.

> The more I have to do with the ignorant sort of people, the more I find that we cannot possibly speak too plainly to them. If we do not speak in their own vulgar dialect, they understand us not ... if we speak any thing briefly, they feel not what we say; nay, I find, if we do not purposely draw the matter into such a length of words, and use some repetition of it ... we do but overrun their understandings, and they presently lose us ... [22]

His prolixity and his idiom were the fruit of self-denial, the deliberate crucifixion of his erstwhile aspirations after "literate fame," and something of the struggle which it cost him is reflected in the very frequency and vehemence with which he protests his indifference to the censures of the cultured as long as his books do good to ordinary men and women. He accounted for his diffuseness as follows, in the Premonition to the second edition of the *Saints' Rest* (1651):

> Some, I hear, blame me for being so tedious ... such I would inform, that in thus doing, I have more crossed myself than them, having naturally such a style as, because of brevity, is accused of obscurity; and had much ado to bring myself to this which they blame; and did obey my reason in it, against my disposition. For ... I speak to plain, unlearned men ... as they must be long in thinking, so we must be long in speaking.[23]

As for literary elegance: "humility and self-denial required me to lay by the affectation of that style, and spare that industry, which tended but to advance my name with men, when it hindered the main work, and crossed my end."[24] Not that Baxter would tolerate "negligent rudeness": "How oft have I

---

21. XXII:19. He would rather, he tells us, "be charged with the greatest rudeness of style, than with the guilt of neglecting what (he) might have done for the saving of one soul" (VII:xii).

22. VII:ix f.

23. XXII:19.

24. X:iv.

heard a stammering tongue, with ridiculous expressions, tedious circumlocutions, and unseemly pronunciation, to spoil most precious spiritual doctrine, and make the hearers either loathe it or laugh at it!"[25] When Bates spoke of the "noble Negligence"[26] of Baxter's style, he did not mean that he was gauche and slipshod in his use of words; his point rather was that Baxter cared for words only as instruments for the conveyance of meaning, and was careless what canons of stylistic or rhetorical propriety he violated as long as he "got across" what he was trying to say. That his words should express his meaning as accurately and forcefully as possible concerned him very much indeed. That was why he wrote his sermons in full, as appears from his complaint to his brother preachers: "In the study of our sermons we are too negligent, gathering only a few naked heads, and not considering of the most forcible expressions by which we should set them home to men's hearts. We must study how to ... get within them."[27] Stylistically, he learned most from the homely address of the pioneers of the "plain style," Perkins, Sibbes, Hooker, and their fellows, with their short, terse sentences and vivid imagery, drawn from the Bible and everyday life. But their example did no more than foster the development of his own natural aptitude for colorful, incisive, pithy prose. His style improved as he wrote more. There are pages in the *Saints' Rest* which reveal something less than stylistic integrity: an occasional overdose of imagery, a straining after effects just out of his reach; but in all his later works he is completely master of the language he employs. And he was never anything but plain. Never did he leave room for any possible doubt as to what he meant.

Baxter's third requirement was that the preacher should produce "the greatest proof and convincing evidence, to conquer prejudice, darkness and unbelief." For fallen man distrusts God's word, just because it is God's word ("The first sin of man, in believing the serpent before God, hath left a vicious habit in our nature");[28] moreover, he has become altogether unreasonable, because unreasoning, where spiritual matters are concerned. This makes him very hard to convince.

> Before they know what you will say, they have confuted you. For they have resolved to believe that your reasons are insufficient, and their cause is good ... Had we only their understandings to dispute with, it were the less; but our main dispute is with will and passion, which have no ears, nor eyes, nor brain, though sense enough ... [29]

25. XXIII:124.
26. *Funeral Sermon*, 90.
27. XIV:182.
28. XX:417.
29. IX:426.

Men will believe only what they want to believe. But "man, being a reasonable creature, is accordingly to be dealt with";[30] and God has given him such cogent reasons for believing the gospel as to make unbelief inexcusable. Baxter went into the pulpit to reason a case. He had no illusions as to the difficulty of his task: "We dispute not with them on equal terms; but we have children to reason with, that cannot understand us; we have distracted men (in spirituals) to reason with, that will bawl us down with raging nonsense: we have wilful, unreasonable people to deal with, that when they are silenced, they are never the more convinced."[31] But he was fortified by the certainty that his case was unanswerable. It was infidelity that was unreasonable; all reason was on God's side. "I will undertake to prove the truth of Christianity,"[32] was his challenge to the unbeliever. "I ... dare challenge the wisest of you all to reason the case with me, while I plead my Maker's cause."[33] To expose and sweep away the refuges of lies, and to force men to face truth, was the task to which he set himself and called his fellow preachers. Men must be compelled to listen to reason.

> Satan will not be charmed out ... We must lay siege to the souls of sinners which are his garrison, and find out where his chief strength lieth, and lay the battery of God's ordinance against it, and ply it close till a breach be made; and then suffer them not by their shifts to make it up again, but find out their common objections, and give them a full and satisfactory answer. We have reasonable creatures to deal with; and as they abuse their reason against truth, so will they accept better reason for it before they will obey. We must therefore see that our sermons be all convincing, and that we make the light of Scripture and reason shine so bright in the faces of the ungodly, that it may even force them to see, unless they wilfully shut their eyes ... The great things which we have to commend to our hearers, have reason enough on their side ... we should therefore be so furnished with all store of evidence, as to come as with a torrent upon their understandings, and bear down all before us, and with our dilemmas and expostulations to bring them to a nonplus, and pour out shame upon all their vain objections, that they may be forced to yield to the power of truth ... [34]

30. VII:409.
31. XIV:55.
32. XVIII:258, XI:xiii.
33. VII:410.
34. XIV:226. The removal of objections was part of the standard Puritan technique; cf. the Westminster Assembly's *Directory*, "Of the Preaching of the Word"; "if any doubt obvious from scripture, reason, or prejudice of the hearers, seem to arise, it is very requisite to remove it, by reconciling the seeming difference, answering the reasons, and discovering and taking away the causes of prejudice and mistake."

Baxter's insistence on the necessity and possibility of proving the Christian faith derived, as we saw, from his certainty that the God who made man rational will always treat him as such, and that God's messengers must therefore do the same. The way in which God brings men to faith is by enabling them to apprehend objective evidence; faith can have no other foundation;[35] and the minister's duty is to set that evidence before them. A full critical study of Baxter's "methodus probativa"[36] would here be out of place, and a brief description of it must suffice. The chain of evidence began with the indubitable fact of self-consciousness and, with it, the consciousness of a world that is not oneself. Now, "to see the world, and to know what a man is, and yet to deny that there is a god, is to be mad." Baxter thought it self-evident that everything subject to change and decay must be an effect, formally or eminently contained in its cause, and his certainty of this axiom made him sure that "the great argument from the effect to the cause is unanswerable."[37] This axiom was the lever on which his whole proof depended; for once God's existence was granted, he could demonstrate the law of Nature, the certainty of future rewards and punishments, the reality of sin and man's need of further revelation, and thus lay the groundwork for the gospel. The second part of his apologetic was designed to show that the Christian message, as epitomized in the baptismal covenant and the three summaries and more largely expounded in the Bible, was God's authentic word. That the Christianity of Baxter's day was identical with the original could be shown, as we saw, by tradition, or historical proof (for "tradition, is primarily nothing but the certain history of usage of the universal Christian church; as baptism, the Lord's day, the ministry ..."),[38] and by the Bible, the substantial accuracy of which, as a record of events, was not open to doubt. That this gospel message was of Divine origin was proved by

> the grand evidence, the Holy Spirit ... viz. 1. The antecedent evidence in the spirit of prophecy, leading unto Christ. 2. The inherent, constituent evidence of the gospel, and of Christ, the image of God, in the power, wisdom and goodness, both of Christ and of his doctrine. 3. The concomitant evidence of miracles in the life, resurrection and prophecies of Christ, and in the abundant miracles of the apostles and other of his disciples, throughout the world. 4.

35. Of the serene, untroubled faith which Baxter had seen in "many godly women, that never disputed the matter," he concluded: "the foresaid unlearned Christians are convinced, by good evidence, that God's word is true ... though they have but a confused conception of this evidence, and cannot word it." "Inward perceptions" of the things spoken of in the gospel provide them with "fundamental evidence" (XVIII:257 f.).

36. *M.T.*, Praefatio. The "method" is outlined in *Christian Directory*, III:vi, dir. 5.

37. XII:170.

38. p. 97.

The subsequent evidence of the success of the gospel, in the true sanctification of millions of souls.[39]

In his self-review, written probably in 1665, Baxter speaks of his increasing realization of the need to teach men to recognize "the Witness of the indwelling Spirit," and goes on to make the following admission:

> For I more sensibly perceive that the Spirit is the great Witness of Christ and Christianity in the World: And though the Folly of Fanaticks tempted me long to over-look the Strength of this Testimony of the Spirit, while they placed it in a certain internal Assertion, or enthusiastick Inspiration; yet now I see that the Holy Ghost in another manner is the Witness of Christ and his Agent in the World ... [40]

This passage has often been taken, since Robert Barclay drew attention to it,[41] as a reference to the effect of Baxter's early brushes with the Quakers, and as evidence of a subsequent increase of sympathy towards them. That his attitude toward them did in fact soften may well be true;[42] but there is no reference to the Quakers in this passage. What Baxter here has in mind is the Antinomian doctrine of assurance, which we shall examine later;[43] and his mature account of the Spirit's witness to Christian truth "in another manner"—by prophecy, miracle and, supremely, by the transformation of countless human lives, as he goes on in the next sentence to explain—had been fully expounded in print[44] before ever he had dealings with the Quakers.[45] A similar witness of the Spirit authenticates the Bible as the Word of God written: "our evidence objective of the divinity of Scripture" is partly in the internal light of their own perfections, partly in providential attestations, especially miracles, and partly in the effects on readers' lives.[46] At every stage in the proof, the evidence was overwhelming. Baxter had no doubt of this at all. "I believe that he that will, by just argumentation, follow on the Christian cause with an unbeliever, if he can hold him to the point from rambling, and suppose him capable of historical evidence, may drive him to yield ..."[47] But that was not the end of the teacher's work. A bare assent, unwillingly extorted, does not automatically lead to action.

---

39. XXI:387.

40. *R.B.,* I:127 f.

41. *The Inner Life of the Religious Societies of the Commonwealth* (1876), 332 f.

42. cf. Powicke's account of Baxter's debate with Penn in 1672 (*Under the Cross,* 20 f.).

43. Chap. XV.

44. In *The Unreasonableness of Infidelity,* 1655; the Preface is dated August 20. Cf. especially the first two treatises (XX:l f.).

45. In 1656. Thomas Goodaire first visited Kidderminster Church on March 25, 1655/6.

46. XX:xxxi.

47. XXI:581.

The most cogent reasoning does not of itself move the slaves of appetite. Truth must be driven deep into fallen man's soul if it is to touch his will. Conscience and passion must be roused, for only rational passion will avail to unseat and dethrone irrational passion. Man must be made to feel what he knows, or he will never be willing to act on it.

> There is scarce a more common and powerful cause of men's ... perdition, in all the world, than that sleepiness and stupidity which hindereth reason from the vigorous performance of its office. In this senseless case, though a man both know and consider of the same truths, which in their own nature are most powerful to cleanse and govern and save his soul, yet sluggishness doth enervate them ... Even as a dream of the greatest matters moveth not the sleeper from his pillow. In this senseless state, the devil can do almost anything with a sinner ... [48]

And so, over and over again, when the doctrinal exposition is done, Baxter lifts up his voice and charges his hearers to *consider*.

> The greatest matters in the world will not work much upon him that will not think of them. Consideration opens the ear that was stopped, and the heart that was shut up ... By consideration a sinner makes use of the truth, which before lay by, and therefore could do nothing ... As men are inconsiderate because they are wicked, so they are the more wicked because they are inconsiderate ... it is not the most excellent truths in the world that will change your hearts, if you let them not down into your hearts, and keep them not there by meditation ... The plaster must be laid upon the sore if you would be cured ... It must be truth at the heart that must change the heart. And if you will not think on it, and think on it again, how can you expect that it should come at your hearts?[49]

Consideration, deliberate and sustained reflection on revealed truth, "must be a principal means of your salvation if ever you be saved."[50] "I have no hope of that soul, that will not be persuaded to this duty of consideration."[51] A man who will not *think* cannot be saved: for "sleeping reason is as none ... it is the very art and business of the devil to charm sinners to sleep ... A man is not a man in act till he be considerate."[52] Baxter's usual way of stimulating "consideration" is by a series of interrogatives ("I pray you answer these few questions, and suffer the truth to have its proper work upon your mind ..." "I

---

48. XIII:254.
49. VIII:30 f.
50. VIII:55.
51. p. 61. The Biblical grounds for this assertion are given on p. 58.
52. X:10.

shall yet draw nearer you, and reason the case a little further with you; and to that end I shall propound these following questions, desiring your serious answer ...").[53] In these momentous questionnaires, he turns his doctrine over and over, drawing out its implications, bringing it to bear on his hearers' lives at point after point, forcing them to face its relevance, prodding tirelessly at conscience with ten or a dozen blunt, searching questions, trying all the time to "get within them" and make truth grip. "Oh that I could make every man's conscience a preacher to himself ... !"[54]

Next, desire for the proffered salvation must be awakened, if the will is to be won. "Powerful winning motives" are accordingly the next requirement, "because of men's disaffection and averseness." Man is necessarily actuated by the desire for happiness, and so the first motive in Baxter's list is drawn from self-love. Baxter's most frequent and most powerful appeal is avowedly and deliberately eudaemonistic. He comes from God to tell men what true happiness is, and where it may be found: to impart to them true wisdom. "Nothing will prove a man simply and properly wise, but that which will prove or make him happy."[55] By this standard the unconverted were fools, and Baxter told them so. "It can be no act of wisdom that tendeth to a man's damnation."[56] They were looking for happiness in this world, where it is not to be found, and laying up for themselves a fearful retribution. Suicidal mania had gripped them. "You would think it impossible that any man in his wits should be persuaded for a trifle, to cast himself into the fire or water, into a coal-pit, to the destruction of his life: and yet men will be enticed to cast themselves into hell ... Well, sirs, now we have found out the great delinquent and murderer of souls (even men's selves, their own wills) ..."[57] They were renouncing their own human nature and destiny. "It is the content of the higher faculties, that are the pleasures of a man: the pleasing the throat is common to us with the swine."[58] "If you live by sense and not by faith, on things unseen, you go backward; you stand on your heads and turn your heels against heaven; you cause the beast to ride the man; and by turning all things upside down, will turn yourselves into confusion."[59] "You are but an ingenious kind of BRUTES; exceeding apes and monkeys in the cunning contrivance of your unhappy designs, but incomparably worse in

---

53. XIII:310 f., IX:464. It was of sermons thus composed that Baxter wrote "some sermons are all to work on the affections at present" (IV:256). An excellent example is in *Treatise of Conversion*, chap. VI, "A Use of Exhortation; set on by ten questions" (VII:230-250).

54. XVI:538.

55. XIII:247. This prudential conception of wisdom, common to all the Puritans, clearly derives from Proverbs.

56. XIII:249.

57. VII:435 f.

58. IX:489.

59. XII:45.

your successes ..."[60] Be human, Baxter urged them, and enter into the happiness which God made men to enjoy. "God made you men and if you reject not his grace, will make you saints; make not yourselves like beasts or vermin. God gave you souls that can step in a moment from earth to heaven ... do not you stick then fast in clay."[61] "I dare say," he told them at the end of the sermon which concluded the doctrinal part of the *Treatise of Conversion,* "I have shown you enough to win the heart of any man that is not obstinately blind and wicked. If you would be rich, I have shown you the only riches, if you would be honourable, it is only conversion that can make you so, if you would have pleasure I have showed you the way to pleasure ... In a word, if you would be happy, I have showed you the only way to happiness."[62]

The other motives mentioned in Baxter's list serve only to underline the unhappiness of the unconverted and the wisdom of returning to God. When Baxter speaks of "God and Christ," he reminds the impenitent that deliberate defiance may provoke his Maker to visit him with temporal judgments and take from him even his transient worldly pleasure, to harden him irrevocably in sin, to cut short his life; whereas, the Father and the Son have done everything necessary for his salvation and will receive him without demur if only he will return. "Necessity" is an argument drawn from the connection between means and ends, as he explains: "Whatever is a man's end, he puts a must upon the obtaining of it, and upon all the means without which it will not be attained."[63] Now, happiness is man's end; and that means that he must be converted, for happiness is otherwise out of his reach. Last in the list of motives are "heaven and hell," towards one or other of which all men were hastening. Here Baxter left his fellow Puritans far behind. No man of his age, perhaps no preacher of any age, painted the glories of heaven and the terrors of hell more vividly. Glimpses of heaven through "the prospective of the promise,"[64] and thoughts of hell suggested by the grim Biblical hints on the subject, moved him as nothing else, and inspired his most passionate and powerful appeals. His preoccupation with the next world was not merely the result of precarious health, which made it difficult for him to forget it, but was a matter of conscience. He took care never to let heaven and hell out of his mind; for he held that a man was only sane and wise to the degree to which he had learned to see his daily life *sub specie aeternitatis,* to value this life only in relation to the

---

60. X:26.
61. XIII:211.
62. VII:228; cf. the titles of the following chapters in *A Saint or A Brute*: VI. "Holiness the only way of safety"; VII. "Holiness the only honest way"; VIII. "Holiness is the most gainful way; proved"; IX. "Holiness is the most honourable way"; X. "Holiness is the most pleasant life."
63. IX:383.
64. XII:53.

next and to sit as loose to it as he would on his dying day. Men were pilgrims on earth, traveling to eternal bliss or misery; let them therefore live as pilgrims and take heed which destination they make for. Heaven and hell were realities to Baxter, the weightiest of all realities, and the solemnity with which he thought of them was reflected by the earnestness with which he preached of them. His most elaborate treatment of man's eternal destiny and of the motives to a Christian life thence arising is in the *Saints' Rest*, but in all his evangelistic writing the subject is never far from his mind. Where it is not being directly dealt with, it towers in the background and overshadows everything else.

Baxter had no qualms about thus exploiting the self-regarding motives of gain and loss, reward and punishment, fear and hope. To use them, he considered, was simply to treat man as man—as God does. Indeed, in evangelism fear must normally come first; the law must do its work before the gospel can effect anything. Man must be shocked out of his flesh-pleasing by being forced to see that hell awaits him at the end of it, and until that happens the call to repentance will fall on deaf ears. This does not mean that Baxter supposed that fear alone could convert anyone; he knew that love must draw, as well as fear drive. "Fear is not the principal affection of a true convert ... love must be the predominant affection; and therefore it is the discovery of the amiableness of God, and the wonderful gain that comes by godliness, that must be the principal argument that we must use with you," he told his hearers.[65] But both fear and love must have their place, in evangelism as in Christian experience. Failure to grasp this fact is disastrous, as we shall see later.[66]

But, however lucid and convincing the argument, however pertinent and close the application, however compelling the motives, fallen man continues dull, sleepy and apathetic, and if the preacher is to rouse him he must communicate heat as well as light. This is Baxter's final requirement. God's messenger must be a "powerful" preacher, speaking "affectionately," "in good sadness" (a favorite phrase), manifesting "life and fervency," preaching in "an earnest, persuading, way" so that "the people can feel him when they hear him."[67] For "the best matter will scarcely move them, if it be not movingly delivered ... When a man hath a reading or declaiming tone, like a schoolboy saying his lesson, or an oration, few are moved with any thing that he saith."[68] The hearer's heart will only catch fire as the preacher blazes. His manner is

---

65. VII:189; from a sermon (*Treatise of Conversion*, chap. V) which begins: "Having said thus much to you by way of terror, to drive you from an unconverted state, I ... shall next say somewhat also by way of allurement to draw you to a better state ..." (188).

66. Chap. XV.

67. XIV:183.

68. pp. 225 f. For the positive effect of "powerful" preaching, cf. XIII:168 f: "when a minister of Christ that is truly a divine ... shall copiously and affectionately open to his hearers the excellences he hath seen and the happiness which he hath foreseen and tasted, it frequently ... doth

thus as important as his matter; a lifeless delivery can kill the best material. Baxter noted in his self-review (1665) that his own preaching had been most successful when most "powerful." "When I was young," he recorded, "I was more *vigorous, affectionate,* and *fervent* in *Preaching, Conference* and *Prayer,* than (ordinarily) I can be now;" and though in those days "my Stile was more extemporate and lax" and the material of his sermons, in his own opinion, not so good, "my preaching then did much more affect the Auditory, than many of the last Years before I gave over Preaching" (i.e., 1662).[69] Preaching that lacked "power" would prove ineffective to rouse sluggish sinners. "How many sleep under us, because our hearts and tongues are sleepy; and we bring not with us so much zeal and skill as to awaken them!"[70] Baxter showed his fellow-preachers the royal road to "powerful" preaching in the *Reformed Pastor.* "Preach to yourselves the sermons that you study, before you preach them to others," he advised. "That which is on your hearts most, is like to be most in their ears ... If we let our love go down, we are not like to raise up theirs."[71] And, in the pulpit: "Though I move you not to a constant loudness, (for that will make your fervency contemptible,) yet see that you have a constant seriousness; and when the matter requireth it, as it should do in the application at least of every doctrine, then lift up your voice, and spare not your spirits, and speak to them as men that must be awakened either here or in hell ... O speak not one cold or careless word about so great a business as heaven or hell! Whatever you do, let the people see that you are in good sadness ..."[72]

To practice these principles, Baxter knew, was an exacting business. The ministry of the gospel was a terrible calling, for it demanded so much of a man.

> What skill is necessary to make plain the truth, to convince the hearers; to let in the unresistible light into their consciences, and to keep it there, and drive all home; to screw the truth into their minds, and work Christ into their affections; to meet every objection that gainsays, and clearly to resolve it; to

---

wrap up the hearers' hearts to God ... inflaming their hearts with a heavenly love." Part of the prescribed cure for all sorts of spiritual lassitude and decline is to sit under a "powerful" ministry (II:113 f., 523 f., V:118 f., VIII:351 f., etc.).

69. *R.B.,* I:124.

70. XIV:57.

71. p. 223. Baxter characteristically subjoins his own experience as proof of his point: "when I let my heart grow cold, my preaching is cold ... and so I can observe too oft in the best of my hearers, that when I have a while grown cold in preaching, they have cooled accordingly; and the next prayers that I have heard from them hath been too much like my preaching ..."

72. p. 225. The preacher's feeling, of course, must be genuine: "I know it is not mere noise that will convert a soul: a bawling fervency, which the hearers may discern to be histrionical and affected, and not to come from a serious heart, doth harden the auditors worst of all ..." (II:524).

drive sinners to a stand, and make them see there is no hope, but they must unavoidably be converted or condemned: and to do all this for language and for manner as beseems our work, and yet as is most suitable to the capacities of our hearers: this, and a great deal more that should be done in every sermon, should sure be done with a great deal of holy skill ...It is a lamentable case, that in a message from the God of heaven, of everlasting consequence to the souls of men, we should behave ourselves so weakly, so unhandsomely, so imprudently, or so slightly, that the whole business should miscarry in our hands, and God be dishonoured, and his work disgraced, and sinners rather hardened than converted ...[73]

In fact, his own practice is the finest illustration of his ideals that Puritanism affords. There can be no serious quarrel with Bates' opinion of his early practical writings, all of which, with the exception of the *Right Method*, were sermons before they became books:

'tis a singularity of your owne to excell in every Subject: none so movingly speaks to ye affections or with greater clearnes and power convinces ye understanding: and that wch puts a lustre uppo all your productions is a spirit of holines and zeale which animates them, and fires all those who with attention read them."[74]

For sustained earnestness and energy, for vividness of imagination, for power to catch in words the beauty of holiness and the repulsiveness of sin, I know nothing in homiletic literature to compare with the molten torrent of Baxter's eloquence as he pleads God's cause with the careless and impenitent. The secret of his power lay in the clarity of his vision. With Johannine penetration, he saw human life in terms of absolute and ultimate antithesis: heaven or hell, Christ or Satan, a saint or a brute, this world or the next, the service of God or the service of self. As a preacher, he was utterly loyal to his vision. Purity of heart had enabled him to see it, and purity of heart kept him true to it. He did not speak to entertain, nor to please, but to make his hearers see what he saw so clearly. His sermons reveal no self-seeking, no self-concern, but only the transparent integrity and awful holy passion of the prophet and pastor, burdened with the word of God and with the fear that its recipients would reject it. He told his hearers of heaven and hell, and his descriptions were "powerful" and "affecting" precisely because of their note of authenticity. Like Jonathan Edwards, he had gone to the edge of the pit and forced himself to

73. XIV:56.

74. 59:VI f. 161. The letter is dated July 19th, and the year is fixed by Bates' reference to the appearance of a new book by Thomas Gataker, price twelve shillings. This must be the posthumous folio, *Adversaria Miscellanea*, published in 1659.

look in; with Bunyan, he had gazed across the river and feasted his eyes on the promised land. One of the most searching tests of a man's stature as a Christian and as a preacher is what he says, or omits to say, about heaven and hell. Baxter passed this particular test with flying colors. Here, where most men's sight is most dim, his was clearest; even here, he always spoke with the authority of a man who knew what he was talking about. There is nothing secondhand, nothing cheap or stale or trite, nothing artificial or meretricious, in his handling of such tremendous matters. He never falls into empty jargon. He never sought to do more than deliver an honest report of what he had seen and heard, and as a result he never did less than that. That is why his sermons on heaven and hell, the glory of man and the foulness of sin, and all the topics we shall study in the course of this exposition, are still fresh and "powerful" for modern readers. They, too, can still feel and tremble at the terrible earnestness with which he spoke. He did not pose or rant; he pleaded. He tells us himself that his precarious health was a great help to him at this point. He went into the pulpit Sunday by Sunday at Kidderminster a chronically, sometimes a desperately sick man, knowing that each sermon might be his last, that very soon he might have to give account of his preaching it, and that many of his hearers were not yet converted. This knowledge, he records, a "little stirred up my sluggish heart to speak to Sinners with some Compassion, as a dying Man to dying Men."[75] He thought himself hard and unfeeling:

> I seldom come out of the pulpit, but my conscience smiteth me that I have been no more serious and fervent ... it accuseth me not so much for want of human ornaments or elegancy, nor for letting fall an unhandsome word; but it asketh me, How ... wouldst thou preach of heaven and hell, in such a careless, sleepy manner? Dost thou believe what thou sayest? Art thou in earnest or in jest? ... Shouldst thou not weep over such a people, and should not thy tears interrupt thy words? ... Truly, this is the peal that conscience doth ring in my ears, and yet my drowsy soul will not be awakened. Oh what a thing is a senseless, hardened heart! ... I am even confounded to think what difference there is between my sickness apprehensions, and my pulpit and discoursing apprehensions, of the life to come...[76]

So he felt; but it seems doubtful whether the Christian pulpit has ever witnessed more earnest preaching than his.

It is in his evangelistic sermons that his doctrine of man, created and fallen, comes to life and finds its most convincing expression. Not until he clothes its abstract theological skeleton with the flesh and blood of concrete illustration,

75. R.B., I:21.
76. XIV:284 f; cf., among several similar passages, XXIII:110 and VII:579.

unearthing sin and showing his hearers and readers their hearts in the light of it, does its truth fully appear. But when he applies it in detail to the libertine, the hypocrite, the drunkard, the pleasure-seeker, the time-server, the man who drifts through life, the presumptuous, the censorious, the pig-headed man, the proud man, the ambitious man, the bad-tempered man and a hundred more, it appears how "catholic" and comprehensive his anthropology really is. As a formulation of the Christian view, Baxter's must stand high; for it fits, not merely some of the facts, but all of them, and provides the evangelist with a ready instrument for diagnosis as well as laying for the theologian a firm foundation on which to erect the Biblical doctrine of redemption.

Part III

THE REDEMPTION
OF THE WORLD

"God so loved the world, that he gave his only begotten Son, that whosoever believeth in him should not perish, but have everlasting life."

John 3:16, KJV

Chapter 8

The Growth of the Synthesis

1.   Introduction to Parts III-IV.
      Aim of chapter: to isolate the formative influences on Baxter's thought.

2.   First influence: Puritan doctrine of the covenant of grace.
            "Covenant" defined.
            The covenant of grace described:
                        its promise;
                        ground (Christ's death);
                              four dispensations;
                        condition (faith);
                              true faith works;
                              place of works in the two covenants;
                        its universality.
      The goal in religion: assurance.
      The way to the goal: use of the law, to lead to repentance;
                              use of the gospel, to bring faith and assurance.
      The marks of true repentance and sincere faith.

      Baxter's lifelong loyalty to this doctrine.
      Its dangers no reason for rejecting it.
      The covenants of works and of grace embody law and gospel.
      History of the doctrine:
                  i. The covenant of grace based solely on exegesis.
                  ii. The covenant of works based largely on natural theology.

      Covenant theology involves no substantial departure from Reformers.
      The covenant of grace comprehends the "two wills" of God.
      Two opposed developments:
                  i. Covenant defined in terms of God's secret will alone (Dutch
                        Calvinists).
                  ii. Covenant defined in terms of God's revealed promise alone
                        (Arminians; Saumur school; Baxter).

3.   Second influence: Arminian controversy.
            Arminius' protest and position.
            Baxter's reading on the subject.
            i. Twisse: the Divine decrees
                        justification of the elect before faith
                        (from Pemble).
            Baxter's early acceptance of this view.

Chapter 8

The Growth of the Synthesis

Let not the names of men draw thee one way or the other; nor make thee partial in searching for truth; dislike the men for their unsound doctrine; but call not doctrine unsound, because it is theirs; nor sound, because of the repute of the writer. —Baxter, 1649

There was nothing particularly original or controversial about Baxter's doctrine of human nature. His Puritan critics found fault, not with his anthropology, but with his gospel, the superstructure which he erected upon it. The remaining two sections of our study are concerned with Baxter's gospel. In this part, we shall deal with the work of Christ, and in the next with the work of the Holy Ghost. This division is convenient, for it corresponds both to the distinction between *impetration* and *application* of redemption (axiomatic for all seventeenth-century Reformed thinking about grace) and to that between God's *legislative* and *decretive will* (fundamental to Baxter's system, as we shall see). The distinctive elements in his teaching were born through reaction and received their final form as a result of prolonged theological debate; and we cannot hope to understand him until we know something of those whom he opposed and those who opposed him. From now on, therefore, more attention must be given to those tendencies in seventeenth-century thought which, directly or indirectly, made Baxter's theology what it was. In this chapter, an attempt is made to trace the evolution of his system, and to mark the decisive influences which produced it. It has already been noticed that Baxter was a traditionalist by temperament, and his originality consisted precisely in his power to combine old ideas in a new and suggestive synthesis. We shall, therefore, commence our study of his doctrine of redemption by seeing what in his case the old ideas were.

Baxter learned his first lessons in theology from the "multitude of our English Practical Treatises," which he had already devoured "before I had ever read any other bodies of Divinity, than *Ursine* and *Amesius*."[1] These books had a decisive influence on him. They fixed his approach to theological questions by teaching him to regard theology as a practical science, and furnished the framework of his system by setting before him the doctrine of the covenant of grace, which Professor Miller justly terms "the marrow of Puritan divinity."[2] We shall here outline this doctrine, with illustrations from authors whom Baxter tells us he read and approved.

A covenant, as such, is "*A mutual agreement between parties upon Articles or Propositions on both sides, so that each party is tied and bound to performe his own conditions.* This . . . is common to all Covenants, publike and private, divine or humane. . ."[3] A covenant between God and man is "a certaine transaction of God with the *Creature*, whereby God commandeth, promiseth, threatneth, fulfilleth, and the *Creature* doth tie it selfe in obedience to God thus covenanting"[4] The covenant of grace is described in the Westminster Confession, which Baxter held to be "the most excellent for fulness and exactness that I have ever read from any Church,"[5] as an enactment whereby God "freely offereth unto sinners life and salvation by Jesus Christ, requiring of them faith in him . . . and promising to give unto all those that are ordained unto life his Holy Spirit, to make them willing and able to believe."[6] The Puritans found the *locus classicus* for this covenant in the account of its promulgation to Abraham (Gen. 17), where it appeared as an undertaking on the part of "God all-sufficient" (as *El Shaddai* was universally understood)[7] to give to his elect

1. *R.B.*, I:5. Ursinus' *Corpus Doctrinae Christianae* (expository lectures on the Heidelberg Catechism, 1586) was translated in 1587; its popularity may be inferred from the fact that it was reprinted in 1589, 1591, 1595, 1601, 1611, 1617, 1633. Baxter recommended (*Works*, V:590) and apparently used the revised Latin edition by David Paraeus, 1598. At Cambridge in Thomas Goodwin's time this was "the renowned summaries of the orthodox religion, and the Puritan Fellows . . . explained it to their pupils on Saturday night, with chamber prayers" (Goodwin, *Works*, II:lix).

2. Title of Perry Miller's article on the covenant of grace in *Publications of the Colonial Society of Massachusetts*, XXXII:247 f.

3. Thomas Blake (cf. *D.N.B.* s.v.), *Vindiciae Foederis* (1653), 3.

4. Ames, *Marrow*, I:x. 9, 45.

5. *Confession*, 20. Though Baxter is here labouring to vindicate his orthodoxy, we may trust his statement, for he was too honest to misrepresent his views in order to escape attack. He also praises the Shorter Catechism as "the best Catechism that ever I yet saw" (14) and the Larger as "a most excellent summ of Divinity" (18); and concludes (22) "I take the labours of that Assembly, especially these three pieces . . . for the best Book, next my Bible, in my Study."

6. VIII:iii.

7. So (e.g.) Calvin, "that excellent Expositer" (Baxter, *Of Justification*, 115), *Comm. on Gen.* (*C.T.S.*) I:443 ("in these words (sc. El Shaddai) a promise is included"); John Preston devoted the first five sermons (173 pp.) of his *New Covenant*, 1629, to expounding :Gods All-sufficiency" from the same text.

(i.e., Abraham and his seed) final salvation and all things necessary for its attainment. This was the significance of El Shaddai's promise to be "their God": "here in grace, and hereafter in glory," as Sibbes explains. "There is no phrase in Scripture that hath so much in so little as this ... All other particular promises in the covenant of grace are members of this ... This is the first and fundamental promise ... the life and soul of all the promises ..."[8] The ground of the covenant was Christ's death, which by putting away sin ratified the covenant promises. In virtue of its sacrificial basis, "the covenant of grace is frequently set forth in the scripture by the name of a testament";[9] "for a testament is established by blood."[10] The four distinct dispensations, or editions, of this covenant span the whole of history. The first lasted from Adam to Abraham, during which period the covenant, promulgated in the Protevangelium (Gen. 3:15), "was called a promise of the blessed seed"; next, the covenant promise was explicitly stated to Abraham, "and then it was called a covenant," and so till the Exodus; then, through Moses, the covenant promise was renewed and a typical revelation was made of its sacrificial basis; "But now from Christ's time to the end of the world, the covenant of grace is most clear of all; and it is now usually called the New Testament, being established by the death of Christ himself."[11]

From the first to last, the condition which the covenant requires of man has been the same: "Walk before me, and be thou perfect" (Gen. 17:1); which to the Puritan was an exposition of the nature of faith. Perfection here means perfection of heart, not of performance: "under this gracious covenant sincerity is perfection."[12] Thus, according to Preston's paraphrase, the covenant now

8. *Works*, VI:7 f. The Puritans often expounded this promise in terms of the divine attributes, cf. (e.g.) Thomas Brooks, *Works*, V:308: "that is as if he said, You shall have as true an interest in all my attributes for your good, as they are mine for my own glory ... My grace, saith God, shall be yours to direct you, and my goodness shall be yours to relieve you, and my mercy shall be yours to supply you, and my glory shall be yours to crown you. This is a comprehensive promise ... it includes all ..."

9. *Westminster Confession*, VII:iv.

10. Sibbes, *Works*, VI:4.

11. *loc. cit.*; cf. (e.g.) Musculus, *Common Places* (E.T. 1563)—"extraordinarily clear and sound ... opening the reconciling truth" (Baxter, *Works*, V:591)—f:123b: "there is one onely and perpetuall Couenant of God, made and confirmed with all his electes, and there is but one onely and perpetuall Godlynesse and iustification of beleuers. But the orderyng of this one Couenant, grace, fayth, Churche, religion and Godlines, is ... by the purpose of Gods wisdome, diversly and sondry wayes appoynted, according unto yᵉ qualitie of the times. Onewise before the lawe, an other wise in the law, and an other wise after the lawe."

12. Sibbes, *Works*, I:59; so Calvin, *loc. cit.*: "the eyes of God look for faith and truth in the heart ... the integrity here mentioned is opposed to hypocrisy;" Musculus, *op. cit.*, f:122a (on the words "Walk before me ..."): "This point conteyneth all things belongyng to our trewe fayth, obedience, religion, sinceritie of minde, trust and loue of the hart"; John Ball ("this great learned, holy Divine as almost *England* ever bred," Baxter, *Aphorisms*, App. 182), *The Covenant of Grace*, 1645, 84 (on "be thou perfect"); "God requires not so much the matter, as the forme of obedience; nor so much the thing done, as the affection wherewith we doe it."

runnes in these terms, Thou shalt beleeue, thou shalt take my Sonne for thy *Lord,* and thy Saviour, and thou shalt likewise receive the gift of righteousnesse, which was wrought by him, for an absolution for thy sinnes, for a reconciliation with me, and thereupon thou shalt grow up in love and obedience towards me, then I will be thy *God* and thou shalt be my people.[13]

Faith is no less a walk than a rest; it is a matter of the will, of activity; without works it is dead. "A true, lively, justifying faith, is also a sanctifying faith."[14] "For, you know, there is a false, dead, and counterfeit faith: ... when a man thinkes that he hath Faith in his heart, but yet he finds no life, no motion ... no worke proceeding from his Faith, it is an argument he was mistaken ... For, if it be a right faith, it will worke ..."[15]

> Not that faith, and the works of faith, earn salvation; the saints' obedience to the law of Christ is so imperfect that it could merit only condemnation. Faith secures salvation not by its own intrinsic worth, but simply as the qualification which God has laid down as the condition of receiving the promised good. The Covenant of Grace doth not exclude all conditions, but such as will not stand with grace ... a lively, unfained and working faith is required to receive the promise ... faith ... doth not justifie as it produceth good workes, but as it receiveth Christ, though it cannot receive Christ unless it bring forth good workes ... Good workes of all sorts are necessary to our continuance in the state of justification ... but they are not the cause of, but only a precedent qualification or condition to finall forgiveness and eternall blisse."[16]

Thus, the essential contrast between the covenant of works and the covenant of grace is that "in the latter, the Lord, in stead of requiring perfect obedience ... to our justification ... promiseth to those, who beleeve, redemption and justification without workes; and being redeemed and justified by faith, he promiseth to give them grace to walke in new obedience, as being the unseparable fruit of our ... justification, & as the high-way wherein we are to walke towards our glorification."[17] This new covenant is to be offered to all men; none are excluded but those who by unbelief exclude themselves. But only the elect enter the covenant, for they alone are enabled by God's Spirit to fulfill the condition of faith.

All this being so, each man's supreme concern in religion should be the attainment of assurance that he is one of the elect, with an interest in the

---

13. Preston, *op. cit.,* 317 f.
14. George Downame (cf. *D.N.B.,* as Downham), *The Covenant of Grace,* 1631, 38.
15. Preston, *op. cit.,* 391.
16. Ball, *op. cit.,* 17, 19 f.
17. Downame, *op cit.,* 28.

covenant. This is the only way to happiness and peace of mind.[18] Indeed, God commands it: "strive to make your calling and election sure," is the word of God to the Church visible. Now, election may be inferred from faith, and faith from its works. In order to be assured of his election, therefore, a man must have sincere, working faith. But no man can sincerely receive God in Christ as his Savior, Lord and End while he is ruled by self-will, liking his sins and seeking felicity in flesh-pleasing. Hearty repentance, therefore, must pave the way to faith. He must turn from sin before he can turn to Christ. But he will not turn from it until he has ceased to love it; and he will not cease to love it until he sees that it is leading him to hell. Only when self-love has been enlisted against sin can he come to Christ. To bring him to this point, and thus to make way for faith and assurance, is the "use of the Law."

"The Law . . . hath three workes. 1. It enlighteneth the sinner. 2. It convinceth him. 3. Raiseth up terror in him. But . . . the Law workes no grace, but only prepares for it . . . as Elijah was prepared by a whirle-winde and earth-quake to heare a still voyce, so wee by the terrible voyce of the Law, to heare the sweet voice of the Gospel."[19] To make men hear "the terrible voyce" was the avowed aim of Thomas Hooker, Rogers' quondam assistant, in his *Treatise of Contrition.* "As you desire to have the rich promises of the Gospell put over to you, as ever you would have the Lord Jesus Christ a guest to your soules . . . give your soules no content til you . . . see your sins . . .";[20] "by serious meditation bring thy heart to such a loathing of sinne, that it may never love it more, besiege thy heart with daily meditation . . . if the soule be looking after any sinne . . . then batter that . . ."[21] The burden of sin must grow intolerable.

God must let loose his Law, Sinne, Conscience, and Satan to baite us and kindle hell fire in our soules, before wee will bee driven to seeke to Christ . . . All those who would come unto *Christ* . . . must bee utterly unbottomed of themselves . . . They must bee emptied, First, Of all conceit of any righteousnesse or worth in themselves at all: Secondly, Of all hope of any ability or possibility to helpe themselves."[22]

Sometimes men

shift from the hand of God . . . wrestle with the terrors and beare them out, and resist them . . . Well, these must have the more hammering . . . if God . . .

---

18. cf. *op. cit.,* 39: "the greatest comfort that we can have in this life, is to be assured of our election and salvation."

19. J. Rogers, *The Doctrine of Faith,* 71, 97.

20. Hooker, *op. cit.,* 36.

21. Hooker, *op. cit.,* 111.

22. Bolton, *op. cit.,* 168 f.

purpose their good, then all their striving shall doe them no ease . . . God will lay on more load, terror upon terror, trouble upon trouble, till he have bound him hand and foote, and made him tame: hee will make him yeeld ere he have done with him . . .[23]

There is no other way to conversion; the man who does not go by this road never gets there at all. "Hast thou not had the spirit of bondage? I say, surely, if thou hast not tasted of this, Christ hath not sowne the seede of grace in thy heart: doth any man sow before he hath plowed? . . ."[24] Ministers must understand the "use of the Law" and allow it to do its full work. They must not leave the preaching of God's law and judgment till men are willing to leave the practice of sin. It is disastrous for them to start speaking peace before God speaks it. For "those unskilfull Physitions of the Soule" who gave "comfort" too soon, before repentance was ripe, the Puritans had nothing but condemnation: by their good offices "thousands, are sent hood-winckt to hell, more is the pitty! even in this blessed time of the Gospell."[25] "There are many, who in stead of curing of the soule, kill it, and by popping the Sacrament into a mans mouth, thinke to send him to heaven, but in conclusion send him to hell."[26] Such are "not sound *Comforters*, but true *Cut-throates*."[27] There is a time to pronounce sins remitted and a time to pronounce them retained; a time to calm troubled consciences with hopes of mercy, and a time to trouble them still more with fears of hell. The minister's wisdom is not to console too soon, before he sees that regret has become repentance.[28]

When the terrified soul is fully convinced of its own helplessness, looks to Christ as its only hope and is willing to be saved on any terms, then, seeing that the "soul's preparation for Christ"[29] is complete, the wise minister propounds the promises which the gospel extends to the poor in spirit. Out of the depths the sinner stretches the hand of faith and grasps them. He is at once lifted out of the pit; his chains fall off; he rests on God's word; new life begins. Now he is safe in the covenant, and may assure himself accordingly. "These three workes of GOD" (sc. enlightenment as to the truth, sorrow for sin, and hearty acceptance of Christ—God's work on mind, affections and will), "whosoever findeth to haue been wrought in himself, he may thereby know certainly he hath Faith."[30] Assurance is to be gained and kept by habitual self-examination,

23. Rogers, *op. cit.*, 92 f.
24. Preston, *op. cit.*, 395.
25. Bolton, *op. cit.*, 193.
26. Hooker, *op. cit.*, 240.
27. Bolton, *op. cit.*, 255.
28. Bolton's book is particularly instructive on this point, as containing a catena of Puritan authorities; cf. esp. pp. 137 ff., 251 ff.
29. Sub-title of Hooker's *Treatise of Contrition*.
30. Culverwell, *A Treatise of Faith*, 47.

through which the faithful may discern the evidence of their own sincerity. True faith, which works by love and purifies the heart, can be infallibly discerned by careful introspection. Care, however, is needed to avoid the Scylla of "false," "unsound," peace and the Charybdis of true grace unable or unwilling to see itself for what it is. A principal concern of the Puritan preacher, therefore, was to list the signs ("marks") by which sincere faith may be recognized. Culverwell, for instance, gives the following: "a godly jealousie of being deceived with false Faith, Ioy, and Loue . . . to thinke so meanely of our selues, that wee highly esteeme the graces of God in others, and . . . desire and labour for nothing more, then to haue all these increase in vs . . . hee (a true Christian) is the same inwardly, and in shew . . . the true child of God from his heart hateth all sinne . . . those who make conscience to please God . . . content not themselues with the deed done . . . but they endeavour to doe all these in such a holy manner (especially for the inward affection) as God requireth; and therefore be as much humbled for their defects this way, as if they had not done these duties at all . . . "[31] Finding these marks, a man may follow out the golden chain of Downame's evangelical sorites: "dost thou, professing the true faith, endeavour to keep a good conscience and to walke uprightly before God; then it is certaine, that thou art justified by a true faith; art thou justified? then it is certaine, that thou art effectually called: art thou called according to Gods purpose? then without doubt thou art elected: art thou elected? then undoubtedly thou shalt be saved."[32] Thus solid peace and sound comfort are won.

Such was the doctrine of the covenant of grace in its theoretical and practical aspects as Baxter learned it from his first theological reading. From his own experience, he knew very well what frantic heart-searching and agonies of despair it could cause to the scrupulous, especially if no "great Master in the deepe mystery of dealing with afflicted consciences"[33] was at hand to see them through the slough of despond to the firm ground of faith beyond it. But he never ceased to insist that this was the fault, not of the doctrine or of the books expounding it (which he always praised and recommended), but of the hearers and readers who misunderstood it, and cast anchor under the shadow of the law when they should have sailed on into the sunlight of the gospel, or tormented themselves with doubts because they could not trace in their own conscious experience every minor detail of the change of mind described. The preachers had themselves stressed that humiliation for sin had no value or significance except as a means to an end. "See them (your sins)," says Hooker, "that they may drive thee, and compell thee to seeke unto Christ for mercy: and this is all God lookes for . . . in this preparation or preparative worke . . .

---

31. Culverwell, *op. cit.*, 60 f.
32. *op. cit.*, 38 f. (based on Rom. 8:30).
33. Bolton, *op. cit.*, 273, of Perkins.

For it is not sorrow for sinne, nor humiliation, nor faith it selfe, that can justifie, but onely these must make way for us to a Christ . . ."[34] Bolton makes the same point: "in this Case of legall terrours, humiliations and other preparative dispositions, wee doe not prescribe precisely just such a measure and quantitie . . . But sure wee are, that a man must have so much, and in that measure, as to bring Him to Christ."[35] Hooker and Bolton were very well aware that, as Baxter later put it, "God breaketh not all men's hearts alike."[36] They did not demand that everyone be converted exactly according to the book. They knew that they were elaborating a pattern on which there could be an infinite number of variations. Their point was simply that a heart not broken for sin was incompatible with saving faith, that faith could be not more sincere than repentance, and that therefore the spiritual *praeparatio evangelica* must be the preaching of law, judgment and hell.

In the last chapter we saw how Baxter grounded the order, first law, then gospel, on the facts of human nature. This, however, was a seventeenth-century rationale of something which had been established a hundred years before by straightforward exegesis of the literal sense of St. Paul. And the great Puritan evangelists were avowedly doing no more than to echo and underline the Reformers' insistence that faith in Christ was a mystery incomprehensible to any but convicted sinners. *Tota haec doctrina* (sc., justification by faith) *ad illud certamen perterrefactae conscientiae referenda est, nec sine illo certamine intelligi potest. Quare male iudicant de ea re homines imperiti et prophani* . . .[37] Those who cannot see their sin cannot see their Savior either. The difference between the Puritans and Reformers at this point is not one of substance, but of fuller statement. In the Puritans, the law and the gospel have become two covenants: a covenant of works, broken in Adam, and a covenant of grace, freely offered to sinners through Christ. The second of the two appeared in Protestant theology first. Reformed exegetes had been quick to see that Paul considers the gospel promises to be the meaning and exposition of the covenant promise made to Abraham,[38] and to give due weight to the fact. Calvin and Musculus, as we saw, recognized it, and Bullinger wrote *De Testamento seu Foedere Dei Unico et Aeterno* as early as 1534. The covenant of works did not appear till the end of the sixteenth century. It was first expounded in England by Perkins, in his *Golden Chaine*, and from then on became a standard part of Puritan orthodoxy. Its introduction marks the arrival in Reformed thought of

---

34. Hooker, *op. cit.*, 116.
35. Bolton, *op. cit.*, 261.
36. *R.B.*, I:8.
37. Augsburg Confession (1531), xx. [All this doctrine must be related to the struggle of a terrified conscience, and it cannot be understood without that struggle. So strangers to the struggle, and profane people, judge wrongly about it . . .]
38. cf. esp. Gal. 3.

the kind of natural theology we saw in Baxter. Biblical truth was being anchored in "natural" knowledge. Theologians were looking behind Scripture to see how much of its teaching could have been learned from Nature. The Scholastic synthesis was being revised. Behind the Mosaic code, the theologians found a universal moral law, legible in Nature; a law, therefore, which Adam must have known. In Gen. 2:17, as we saw, they found a promise of life on condition of obedience; and thus the doctrine of the covenant of works came to birth— "Gods covenant, made with condition of perfect obedience . . . expressed in the Morall Law . . ." as Perkins describes it.[39] All men, it was held, are condemned by the covenant of works, for all fall short of its requirements.[40] The covenant of works, therefore, still plays its part in Christian proclamation as the Divine *praeparatio evangelica*. The two covenants "are both in the church, and both taught, one subordinate to the other . . . the covenant of works is taught to show us our failing, that seeing our own disability to perform what the law requireth, we may be forced to the new covenant of grace."[41]

Professor Miller rightly observes that "in the background of Puritan thought, lies the common law conception of the covenant, the idea of a formal agreement of legal validity."[42] To the Puritan, after all, the common law was from God, and, as we saw, it was an axiom of his exegesis that the Bible presupposed natural knowledge. When it spoke of covenants, it assumed that its readers knew what a covenant was. If they did not, then the proper person to ask (we shall see Baxter laboring this point) was a lawyer. But Professor Miller is mistaken in finding here a substantial departure from the Reformers. The Puritans, he says, "practically do away with the conception of God as merely (?) promising, and substitute a legal theory of God's delivering to man a signed and sealed bond." But this, to the Puritan, is a distinction without a difference; for "a promise is as legall a word as a covenant."[43]

Before leaving this subject, it is important to note that the covenant theory admitted of two divergent lines of development. Calvinistic soteriology, based as it is on the Augustinian doctrine of the will's bondage to sin, has a double pivot: promise and election, the secret and the revealed will of God. God's revealed will is that all should believe and be justified in Christ through faith, and the gospel invitation is extended to all; God's secret will is to save his elect, by bringing them to faith through the gospel, and not all are elect. Here, *prima facie*, is inconsistency. Calvin faced the problem of "two wills in God," denied

39. *Workes*, I:32 *(A Golden Chaine)*.
40. cf. Rom. 1, 2.
41. Sibbes, *Works*, VI:5.
42. *art. cit.*, 258 n.2.
43. S. Rutherford, *A Survey of the Spirituall Antichrist*, 1648, II:128.

the inconsistency[44] and asserted that man's present limitations are the sole reason for his inability to reconcile the apparent contradiction: "quamvis multiplex sit Dei voluntas quoad sensum nostrum, non tamen eum hoc et illud in se velle, sed pro sapientia sua . . . attonitos reddere sensus nostros, donec cognoscere nobis dabitur mirabiliter eum velle quod nunc videtur esse voluntati eius adversum."[45] This became the general Reformed attitude to the question. The Christian was thus left with the delicate task of holding together two positions which in this world he was not competent to unite in a single logical whole. Part of God's will revealed in the gospel is that He intends to save His elect through the gospel. But who the elect are, and why they were chosen rather than others, and how and when God will convert each, are mysteries which are only revealed as God unfolds the map of history and works out "his eternal purpose . . . whereby, for is own glory, he hath foreordained whatsoever comes to pass."[46] Man must acknowledge his ignorance at this point, learn his duty from God's revealed will, the rule of duty, and devote himself to doing it, secure in the knowledge that hereby God's secret will is being worked out. "The secret things belong to the Lord our God: but those things which are revealed belong to us and to our children for ever, that we may do all the words of this law" (Deut. 29:29). Now, one reason why the doctrine of the covenant of grace rapidly became central for Reformed soteriology was because it held together in their proper relation both God's revealed and His secret will. By it, as we saw, God "freely offereth unto sinners life and salvation by Jesus Christ, requiring of them faith in him . . . and promising to give unto all those that are ordained unto eternal life his Holy Spirit, to make them willing and able to believe." It thus includes both God's universal conditional promise and His particular, unconditional election. So Baxter's mentors had taught it.[47]

---

44. cf. *Inst.* III:xxiv.17: "videamus iam numquid inter se haec dissideant, quod dicitur ab aeterno Deus ordinasse quos amore complecti, in quos iram exercere velit: et quod salutem omnibus indiscriminatim denunciat. Equidem dico optime convenire: sic enim promittendo, nihil aliud vult quam omnibus expositam esse suam misericordiam, qui modo eam expetunt . . . quod non alii faciunt nisi quos illuminavit. Porro illuminat quos praedestinavit ad salutem. . ." [Let us see whether the fact that God is said to have ordained from eternity whom he wills to embrace with love and on whom he wills to vent wrath, and that he announces salvation indiscriminately to all, are in conflict. I say these facts mesh perfectly. For by so promising he simply means that his mercy is extended to all who seek after it . . . which only those he enlightens do. For he enlightens those he predestined to salvation.

45. *loc. cit.*

46. Westminster Shorter Catechism, Q. 7.

47. cf. (e.g.) Preston, *op. cit.*, 389 f: "The Condition that is required of us, as part of the *Covenant* . . . is to repent and serve the *Lord* in newnesse of life, but the abilitie by which we are able to performe these, is a part of the *Covenant* on the *Lords* part . . ."; Sibbes, *Works* I:59: "in the covenant of grace (God) requireth no more than he giveth and giveth what he requireth, and accepteth what he giveth"; VII:483: "He requires obedience, that he may work it when he requires it . . . When he commands us to believe and obey, he gives us grace to believe and obey."

The point we must notice here is that this comprehensive statement could be whittled away at either extreme. On the one hand, the gospel promise, conditional and universal, could be excluded from the definition. The covenant thus became synonymous with God's decree of election, unconditional and particular. This was the position taken up by certain Continental Calvinists, as Baxter notes:

> Four or five Divines rose in *Holland* . . . who have owned ill Definitions of God's Covenants, and laid the foundations of Antinomian Libertinism, (especially *Maccovius*, and *Cluto*, and *Cocceius*, and *Cloppenburgius* too much consented) making the Covenant in Constitution to be nothing but Election by Eternal Decree, and the Covenant in Execution, to be fulfilling . . . of that decree . . . in all our Mercies . . . with other such confounding Notions.[48]

Baxter found this view objectionable in the extreme, for it meant either that the gospel was quite distinct from the new covenant of grace (which the Bible showed it was not), or that the gospel was essentially a proclamation, not that God would save all who trusted Christ, but that He would save all His elect—an announcement, in other words, not of His revealed promise but of His hidden purpose. The latter alternative, to which the Dutchmen appeared to him to lean, was the one stigmatized by Baxter as Antinomian; in a later chapter we shall see why.[49] On the other hand, the covenant concept could be revised in an opposite direction, and the unconditional electing decree excluded from the definition. The covenant of grace then became a synonym for the gospel promise. This position was taken up by the Arminians, because they rejected the unconditional decree altogether, and also, as we shall see, by the Saumur theologians and Baxter; not because they doubted unconditional election, but because they held on exegetical grounds that the doctrine of grace was exclusively concerned with God's revealed will, and that His secret decree had no place in the definition of it. This was one of the reasons why Baxter was suspected of Arminianism by contemporary critics. It was not, however, till after 1646 that he came to this position.

The doctrine of the covenant of grace was, chronologically, the first great influence molding Baxter's mind, and the Arminian controversy, which raged throughout his youth, was the second. To this we must now turn. The real issue in this controversy was the doctrine of God: whether His love to sinners was equal to all, in which case it was plainly ineffective to most, or whether it was effective for the salvation of His beloved, in which case it must be thought of as confined to those who actually believe. Arminianism began as a reaction against the doctrine of "double predestination." This view, Arminius claimed,

---

48. "Mr. Cartwright . . . Considered" in *J.R.*, 71 f.
49. cf. chap. XIV.

made God the first cause of disobedience and unbelief, the author of sin as much as of salvation; it destroyed man's moral responsibility by making him a puppet, jerked into faith or unbelief at God's whim. It could not, therefore, be true. His own alternative was as follows: Election and reprobation do not cause faith and unbelief, but *vice versa*. Christ died for every man, but it rests with the individual whether he accepts or rejects the proffered Savior. God foresees, but does not foreordain, his decision. God loves all, and has provided a Savior for all; when the gospel is preached, He enlightens all and puts them in a position to choose with understanding; but he does no more. He then, as it were, stands back and leaves the final decision to them.

To hold this position, it was plainly necessary to put a semi-Pelagian doctrine of man in place of the Augustinianism of the Reformers; for, on the latter view, such assistance as the Arminians postulated would be always insufficient. If man's will is not merely weak, as the Arminians held, but evil, in love with sin and at enmity with God, as Augustinians maintain, mere intellectual enlightenment will save nobody. Man's heart must be radically changed before he will believe. If depravity and inability are total, then that grace is ineffective which is less than irresistible. The Arminians commended their scheme on the ground that it represented unbelief as a choice made apart from God; the Calvinists condemned it because it represented faith as a choice made apart from God. This, they held, was both a denial of the truth about man, that his will was in bondage till his heart was renewed, and a dishonor to God, whose gift faith is. In reply to Arminianism, they reargued both the Augustinian anthropology and their doctrine of the Divine decrees.

Into these controversies, Baxter tells us, he entered in about 1640. "All my reverend acquaintance (save one) cryed down *Arminianism* as the *Pelagian* Heresie, and the enemy of Grace: I quickly plunged my self into the study of Dr. *Twisse*, and *Amesius*, and *Camero*, and *Pemble*, and others on that subject: By which my mind was setled in prejudice against *Arminianism*, without a clear understanding of the case . . ." He admitted that until some years later he did not read "much of any *Arminians*."[50] His early judgment was immature, and he swallowed far more than he could evaluate or digest. In particular, the works of William Twisse, first prolocutor of the Westminster Assembly, "a man very famous for his Scholastical Wit and Writings in a very smooth triumphant Stile,"[51] captivated the fledgling theologian. Twisse became the author "whom I most esteemed."[52] His *magnum opus, Vindiciae Gratiae, Potestatis ac*

---

50. *C.T.*, Preface. There are articles on William Twisse, John Cameron and William Pemble in *D.N.B.*

51. *R.B.*, I:73.

52. *C.T., loc. cit.* Baxter tells us in 1650 that he had read "six of Dr. *Twisse* his books again and again (which I think are all)" *(Plain Scripture Proof,* 214 (misprinted in 4th ed. as 124)).

Providentiae Dei, was an eight-hundred-page Latin folio published at Amsterdam in 1632 with a prefatory eulogy by Ames. The sub-title describes it as a "responsio scholastica" to Arminius' *Examen Libelli Perkinsii*, a line-by-line discussion of Perkins' tractate *De Praedestinationis Modo et Ordine*.[53] Twisse quoted both works in full, and re-argued Perkins' supralapsarianism. He was in Cunningham's opinion the ablest of all the exponents of this position;[54] he was certainly the most abusive.

The essence of his view was as follows: God foreordains all things for His own glory, that is, the full display of His attributes, and particularly His justice. His purposes were comprehended in two "decrees," that *de fine* and that *de mediis*. The first comprises election and reprobation, and therefore necessarily includes a decision to create: "decretum creandi neque prius est decreto salvandi . . . neq; posterius . . . sed potius simultaneum et coaevum."[55] Both election and reprobation were designed to reveal God's justice, though in different ways. The reprobating decree includes the permission of the sin which God intends justly to punish: "manifestum fit, praescientiam peccati, nec praecedaneam esse reprobationi, neque succedaneam; sed simul Deo decretum esse, & peccatum permittere, & damnare propter peccatum." The electing decree was designed to display God's justice in remuneration according to promise: "Gloria autem Dei in quam tendit salus hominum . . . non est gloria simplicis misericordiae, sed cum justitia temperatae, ut sic conferatur salus per modum *praemii*." The second decree, *de mediis*, covers the administration of providence and of grace, through Christ, who was sent into the world "ut soli decreto de gloria Dei patefacienda per modum misericordiae cum justitia temperatae subjiciatur [to be subject to the one decree about displaying the glory of God by means of mercy combined with justice]." Twisse was clear and vigorous in arguing this scheme, but he never convinced Baxter that the charge of making God the author of sin could possibly be rebutted on such principles. Indeed, it seemed to Baxter that Twisse rather gloried in admitting its justice. Moreover, Twisse's statement of the doctrine of grace was seriously defective. "He was so taken up with the doctrine of the Decrees and Divine knowledge, and other School-points," Baxter wrote in 1653, "that I more than suspect he was very little seen in this part of Theologie, about satisfaction, remission, justification, as evidently appears in his writings."[56] On the basis of a definition of pardon as *nolle punire*, an eternal attitude in God towards His elect (a basic error, in Baxter's later view, for pardon is an act, not an attitude),[57] Twisse maintained

53. 1598: E.T., *A Christian and Plaine Treatise of . . . Predestination . . .* , in *Works* II:687 f.
54. W. Cunningham, *The Reformers and the Theology of the Reformation*, 371.
55. Twisse, *op. cit.*, "Praefatio ad Lectorem, " from which the following quotations are taken.
56. "Confutation of . . . Ludiomaeus Colvinus" in *Apology*, 276.
57. cf. *op. cit.*, 251: "Do you think that *Non punire* and *Nolle punire* [not to punish, and not to

that the elect were pardoned, reconciled, adopted and justified from eternity, prior to and independent of faith on their part.[58] The justification which faith secures is not *in foro Dei*, but *in foro conscientiae*—is, in other words, no more than a discovery and assurance of the status which one had in reality enjoyed from the moment of birth. This doctrine of justification *in foro Dei* before faith had already been mooted by William Pemble in his *Vindiciae Gratiae: A plea for Grace ... Wherein ... the maine sinewes of ARMINIUS doctrine are cut asunder.*"[59] It is, doubtless, a forceful reply to Arminianism to say, not merely that faith is the gift of God, but also that the justification of the elect precedes faith in any case; but, as Baxter later came to see, the second assertion is not true. In the early forties, however, Baxter embraced this doctrine of pre-faith justification, "taking it upon trust from Dr. *Twisse* and Mr. *Pemble*, (whom I valued above most other men;) and so ... remained long in the borders of Antinomianisme, which I very narrowly escaped ..."[60]

While at Coventry during the Civil War, Baxter defended this opinion in public, an act which he later regretted. "I ... engaged in a dispute against Mr. *Cradock*, and Mr. *Diamond*,[61] to prove *Remission of Sin* (not only Conditional but Actual) to be an *Immediate effect* of Christ's Death, and pleaded for it, *Heb.* 1:3. and *Rom.* 8:32 (and against Universal Redemption) which I since perceive

---

be willing to punish] are all one? I know Dr. *Twiss* talks thus ... I suppose it drew Dr. *Twiss* into many other mistakes about justification, that he knew not the nature of it, or of pardon of sin."

58. Twisse actually argued that the gift of faith itself proved that this was so; cf. *op. cit.*, 322 f: "I know it is ... Dr. *Twisses* Master argument, That God would not have given us faith, unless we were first Pardoned, Justified, and Reconciled? ... And all this because men will not hold to Scripture, but set up their vain reasonings against it, yea when they have received a false Model or Platform of Theologie in their brains, and then will stretch all Scriptures to speak their sence, and serve their turns."

59. Published posthumously, 1627 (Pemble died in 1623): in *Workes* (1635), 1 f: cf. (e.g.) 25: "For 'tis vaine to thinke with the *Arminians*, that Christs merits have made God only *Placabilem*, not *Placatum* ... A silly shift ... No ... the ransome demanded was paid and accepted, the full satisfaction to the Divine Iustice was given and taken, all the sinnes of the Elect were actually pardoned ... This grand transaction betweene God and the Mediator ... was concluded upon and dispatcht in heaven long before we had any beeing ... Yet the benefit of it is ours, and belonged to us at that time, though we never knew so much till after that by faith we did apprehend it." Baxter frequently points out that Pemble himself changed his mind: (e.g.) *Apology, ut sup.*, 323: "its known Mr. *Pemble* was young when he delivered this, (dying about thirty,) and his Treatise of Iustification came from a througher consideration of that point, and in that he wholly lays by ... his former conceit." (This was Pemble's *Vindiciae Fidei; A Treatise of Justification*, 1625.) Baxter often refers to Downame, *op. cit.*,197 f, "An Appendix to the Treatise of the certainty of Salvation" (against eight alleged errors in *Vindicae Gratiae*) as a convincing refutation of Pemble's earlier view (cf., e.g., *Aphorisms*, 190).

60. *Aphorisms*, Appendix, p.163.

61. "two antient Ministers" (*C.T., loc. cit.*); listed among "about thirty worthy Ministers ... who fled there for Safety from Soldiers and Popular Fury ... though they never medled in the Wars" (*R.B.*, I:44). The first is presumably Walter Cradock; for the second, "a profess'd Arminian, in Doctrine," cf. *C.R.*, as Dimond.

I misunderstood and abused."[62] The doctrine of limited atonement or particular redemption—the assertion, that is, that Christ died to save only the elect—had become, thanks largely to Ames' advocacy of it, a further plank in the Calvinist platform against Arminianism. That Christ by his death obtained salvation for every man was basic to the Arminian doctrine of grace. Ames, following his teacher, Perkins, categorically denied it. God, he held, does nothing without a precise end in view. Divine power will apply to those for whom Christ died the benefits of his death; for those who never receive them, we must assume that they were never obtained. The impetation and application of redemption are coextensive.[63] The advocates of this view took in their stride the exegetical difficulties which it involved. When Scripture affirms that Christ died for "all" or for "the world," the meaning, they claimed, was simply "men of all sorts" and "men all over the world"—viz., the elect. To this opinion Baxter subscribed during the early forties, when "my mind was so forestalled with borrowed Notions, that I chiefly studied how to make good the Opinions which I had received, and ran further still from the Truth."[64] His theological interests at this stage were three: predestination and the Divine decrees; the practical theology of the covenant of grace; and, as we shall see later, the work of the Holy Spirit in regeneration.[65] He had not yet, however, seriously asked himself whether his views on these separate topics were consistent with each other. Later, he became convinced that they were not; but that was not until after 1646.

A somewhat different alternative to Arminianism was worked out by the Scotsman, John Cameron, who created the distinctive Saumur theological tradition. Saumur, where Cameron taught form 1618 to 1622, "was, till its suppression by Louis XIV in 1685, the most important and influential of Protestant theological schools in France."[66] Saumur theologians were the black sheep of Continental Calvinism, for they all rejected the dogmas of limited

---

62. *Penitent Confession*, 24. In *Universal Redemption*, 326, Baxter refers to Piscator's exegesis of 2 Pet. 2:1 (that Christ "bought" apostates "κατὰ δόξαν and not κατ᾽ ἀληθείαν" [supposedly and not really) with the comment: "I am ashamed unfeignedly to remember the time when I took up with this interpretation my self, and had the face to maintain it." This may well be a reference to the same occasion.

63. cf. Ames, *Coronis ad collationem Hagiensem . . . adversus Remonstrantium Quinque Articulos*, 96: "Huc igitur tandem redit controveresiae huius summa. 1. Utrum in morte Christi talis impetratio sit, quae nullam applicationem aut intentionem applicandi propositam habet, ut proprium sum finem? 2. An impetratio haec aeque atque indiscriminatim, quoad consilium Dei . . . ad omnes & singulos mortales pertineat? 3. An non omnes illi quibus Christi mors intendebatur, applicatam eam habuerint coram Deo . . . ita ut actualis applicatio certo sequatur . . . ? Nos mortem, resurrectionem, ascensionem, sessionem, & intercessionem aeque conjungendas esse dicimus in fine ac intentione . . ."

64. *Aphorisms*, Appendix, 110.

65. cf. chap. XIII.

66. Schaff-Herzog, IV:33 (s.v. Du Plessis-Mornay, Philippe).

atonement and the double decree. Cameron's successors[67] developed the Saumur system in detail, but the whole of it can be pieced together from Cameron's own writings. Baxter always quoted from the folio edition of his works (*Ioannis Cameronis . . .* ΤΑ ΣΩΖΟΜΕΝΑ, edited by M. Amyraldus, J. Placaeus and L. Cappellus), which was published only in 1642. We may, therefore, infer that Baxter's first acquaintance with them was in that year or soon after. Cameron asserted a double will in God. Conditionally, He wills to save all mankind—that is, if they will believe the gospel and receive Christ, who died for the sins of all men without exception; but His elect He wills to save absolutely, and to them He gives, not merely a promise of salvation if they believe, but the gift of faith itself. This distinction alone, Cameron maintained, accounts fairly for the Biblical evidence concerning the will of God and the death of Christ.[68] It must be held, both that God will infallibly save His elect (and none else will be saved) and that the gospel invitation is a true revelation of God's will for every man. The new covenant, ratified by Christ's death, is simply the gospel.[69] It is enlightening to see Cameron's attitude to the stock Calvinist argument against universal redemption: "Quaerunt, *unde fit quod Christus non offertur, siquidem pro omnibus mortuus est . . .* Hoc est vere εἰς ἄλλο γένος μεταβαίνειν. Nos agimus de patefacta Dei voluntate in Euangelio, illi confugiunt ad arcanum Dei consilium."[70] It was axiomatic to Cameron

---

67. The principal writings of the Saumur school are: P. Testardus ("judicious," Baxter, *Works,* XXII:489), ΕΙΡΗΝΙΚΟΝ *seu Synopsis Doctrinae de Natura et Gratia,* 1633 (the first detailed exposition of the system); *Syntagma Thesium Theologicarum in Academia Salmuriensi . . . disputatarum . . . . (Theses Salmurienses),* four parts, 1641, 1645, 1651, 1665, a complete theological system by Amyraldus, Cappellus and Placaeus, three friends of similar views who were professors at Saumur together, the first two pupils of Cameron (Baxter in *Plain Scripture Proof,* 292, described Amyraldus as "one eye of that University which in Divinity is one eye of the Christian world"); Amyraldus, *Defensio Doctrinae Calvini,* 1634, and *Specimen Animadversionum* (1648); J. Dallaeus, *Apologia . . .* (1655). All these works appear in the reading-list of "theological disputations and treatises which I take to be extraordinarily clear and sound, escaping the extremes which many err in, and opening the reconciling truth," in *Christian Directory* (V:591).

68. cf. ΤΑ ΣΩΖΟΜΕΝΑ, 389: "Scriptura eadem ait & negat Christum mortuum esse pro omnibus . . . Christus ideo pro omnib. mortuus dicitur, quodomnibus datus est redemptor, ea lege tamen vt omnes in Christum credant . . . Ergo Christi mors, sub fidei conditione, ex sequo ad omnes omnino homines pertinet, verumtamen cum omnes . . . non praestent hanc conditionem . . . hinc fit vt Christus pro certo quodam hominum genere, nempe pro Ecclesia, pro fidelibus, mortuus dicatur in Scriptura. Vno verbo, Christus . . . pro fidelibus mortuus est *absolute,* pro omnibus . . . *conditionate."*

69. cf. Samuel Bolton's translation of Cameron's *Theses de Triplici Foedere Dei,* appended to his *True Bounds of Christian Freedom* (1645), 401: "The *Covenant* of Grace is that whereby God, upon the Condition proposed of *faith in Christ,* promises *remission of sinnes in his blood,* and a *heavenly life . . ."*

70. Cameron, ΤΑ ΣΩΖΟΜΕΝΑ, 535. [They ask whence it comes that Christ is not offered (sc., universally) if indeed he died for all. . . . This is truly to move to a different category (a verbal tap from Aristotle). We are dealing with the revealed will of God in the gospel, they have recourse to God's secret counsel.]

that God's secret and revealed will must be clearly distinguished and consistently held apart. The doctrines of the work of Christ and of reprobation fell under the latter: Christ redeemed the world, God offers salvation through Him to the world, and God rejects none but those who first reject Him—in other words, reprobation is conditional upon sin foreseen. But Cameron still held the essential Calvinist position, that God's secret will includes the unconditional particular election of certain men to salvation, and that these, and they alone, are brought, by irresistible sovereign grace, to faith and perseverance.

By denying the "double decree" and asserting universal redemption, Cameron effectively defended himself against the charge of making God the author of sin and unbelief in the reprobate, and after 1646 Baxter made this part of the Scotsman's system his own. He rejected, however, Cameron's doctrine of the will, which, he held, made his theology valueless as a reply to Arminianism. In 1622, Cameron published a debate between himself and the Arminian leader, Daniel Tilenus, *Amica Collatio de Gratiae et Voluntatis humanae Concursu in Vocatione . . .* Here he granted Tilenus that in conversion God's Spirit merely enlightens the mind, but performs no additional operation on the will. Whereas, however, Tilenus claimed that this was so because God would not rob the will of its freedom, by which he meant its natural indeterminism, Cameron attributed it to the fact that the kind of knowledge given by the Spirit, "efficax cognitio summi et veri boni,"[71] determined the will automatically, so that a man thus enlightened would inevitably and irresistibly come to Christ without any further work on the Spirit's part. The seat of freedom, in other words, is not the will, but the mind. What the mind entertains as good, the will necessarily chooses. And God effectively moves the will by presenting objects to the mind. But, Baxter objected, if this were the truth about God's way of making man act, then God was after all the author of sin: for he caused Adam's fall, by withholding knowledge and permitting man to be deceived by the Devil as to the goodness of eating the forbidden fruit.[72] It was, as we saw, an essential part of the doctrine of man, as Baxter understood it, that his will, though not itself a cognitive faculty, has power to command the intellect to institute a comparison between the seeming good presented and the various alternative possibilities resident in the situation. Adam and Eve fell, he held, through failure to do this. Cameron, however, denied the existence of this power altogether. Here Baxter parted company with him. But he came to hold *in toto* Cameron's doctrine of the decrees.

It is no part of our present purpose to evaluate the two answers to Arminianism which we have considered. But it is worth noting that there is at least as much difference between Twisse and Cameron as between Cameron

71. *Amica Collatio*, 1.
72. Baxter develops this criticism at length in his discussion of the Fall, *M.T.*, I.xiv:68 f., 276.

and the Arminians in their doctrine of God. Twisse's whole polemic was concerned with God's secret will: what He chooses to do, and how He does what He chooses. The πρῶτον ψεῦδος of his system, in Baxter's later judgment, was his doctrine on the latter point, that "no act natural or free can be done by any creature, without the Predetermination of God's Physical efficient immediate Premotion, as the first total Cause of that act."[73] Human freedom was a psychological fact ("rational spontaneity"), but not a physical or metaphysical fact. The Nominalist deity enclosed in Twisse's scholastic straight-jacket causes evil as much as good, sin no less than holiness. He is in Himself bare power; no properly *moral* character can be assigned to Him. Baxter came to see that the doctrine of "physical predetermination" carried blasphemous implications. It was a human invention, derived "not from Christ, or *Paul*, but the Dominicans";[74] it was an audacious attempt to pry into things unrevealed;[75] and it involved a fearful picture of the character of God.[76] While most of Baxter's Augustinian contemporaries were exclusively concerned to attack Arminianism as a reappearance of the Pelagian heresy, he himself never lost sight of the original question which the Arminians had raised: how could Calvinism be true, when it made God the first cause of sin? "His reverence of the Divine Purity, made him very shy and jealous of any Doctrines that seemed to reflect a blemish and stain upon it," Bates tells us.[77] It was for this reason that he came to abhor Twisse's views. Cameron's God, on the other hand, was a Deity in whom goodness, purity and love to all His creatures were real qualities, one who neither causes nor delights in sin (Cameron's doctrine of the will was an excrescence on his thought, of the implications of which he had himself been unaware). This was the God of Baxter's natural theology, of the Bible as he understood it, and—a point which the "meer Catholick" came to regard as most important[78]—the God of the Fathers, in particular of Augustine,

---

73. *C.T.*, I.i.XVII.527:84. For elaborate attacks on this position, see "Disputatio Prolixa," *M.T.*, I.xiv:278 f., and *C.T.*, I.i, iii, *passim*.

74. *J.R.*, "Mr. Cartwright . . . considered," 14.

75. Thus, "those leaves of *Bradwardine* and *Twiss* . . . which I was wont to reade with longing and delight, I confess I look on now (1653) with fear . . . " ("Reply to . . . Kendall" in *Apology*, 8).

76. In *C.T.*, I.iii:87 f., "lest any think that none but *Hobbes* hath made the right deductions from it" (p. 80), Baxter drew out the doctrine of God and man as it seemed to him to be implied in Twisse's system. Here are a few specimen sentences: "God's hatred of sin, is no true hatred or nolition . . . but only his prohibiting it to us, and his punishing men for it . . . God causeth and Loveth sin as much as obedience . . . God . . . looketh on *good and bad* but as *modal physical differences* caused by himself . . . God will punish man, not out of any hatred of sin (which he willeth and causeth) but out of a differencing will, as he maketh Toads and Serpents, and causeth Cattle and Fowl to be killed by us . . . "

77. *Funeral Sermon*, 110.

78. cf. "Answer to . . . Blake," in *Apology*, 155: "I shall ever think him more culpably singular, who differeth from Christ, and his Apostles, and all his Church for 1200 or 1400 years, then he that differeth from any party now living, and differeth not from them forementioned."

Prosper and Fulgentius, "than whom none known to us in the whole world went higher for Predestination and Grace."[79] Cameron's views had also been sponsored by the little group of Anglican Calvinists who represented England at the Synod of Dort:[80] Davenant ("the most judicious of English Divines (so far as I can know them by their works)"),[81] Hall (who considered Cameron "the learnedest Divine, be it spoke without envy, that the Church of Scotland hath afforded in this last age"),[82] Ward and Carleton. Archbishop Usher and a number of the most distinguished of the practical Puritans espoused them too.[83] It was not, however, till Baxter had independently reached his final position that he discovered how much support he had among English theologians.

Two subsidiary influences which prepared Baxter's mind at this time for what it was later to bring forth may here be noticed. First was his close contact with Disciplinarians in the late thirties. "Before the Parliament began (i.e., 1640), how frequent and fervent were we in secret! . . . the end of all our prayers was church reformation . . . Oh the earnest prayers that I have heard . . . for a painful ministry, and for discipline! . . . Yea, they commonly called discipline.

---

79. *C.T.*, I.i.XXII.665:123; at the end of nine pages of extracts from them.

80. See *The Collegiat Suffrage of the Divines of Great Britaine (E.T.* 1629).

81. *C.T.*, I.ii.VI.101:54; cf. *Plain Scripture Proof*, 332 f.: "God . . . opened to him (I think) the true middle way in many weighty points . . . 1. The doctrine of universall Redemption . . . 2. . . . the doctrine of Justification . . . how far good works . . . are necessary."

82. *Works*, ed. J. Pratt, VII:59.

83. cf. Baxter's Epistle "To the Associated Ministers of Worcester" prefixed to *Certain Disputations of Right to the Sacraments,* 1657: "I meet with so many of *Amyraldus* mind (i.e., Cameron's) in the point of Universal Redemption, that if I might judge of all the rest by those of my acquaintance, I should conjecture that half the Divines in England are of that opinion"— some "as excellent Divines for Learning, Judgment, holiness and powerful Preaching . . . as ever *England* bred"; such as the British contingent at Dort, Preston, William Whateley, Ball, Culverwell, Richard Vines, one of the two "Learned, zealous, Faithful Ministers . . . my very much valued Friends" to whom the *Aphorisms* were dedicated (cf. *D.N.B.*, s.v.), who "hath often and openly owned *Davenant's* way of Universal Redemption"; and, finally, Usher himself, whose *Judgment . . . of the True Intent and Extent of Christ's Death* (written in 1617, published in 1658; Baxter had a MS. copy) "asserteth this Doctrine in the same middle way as *Davenant* and *Camero* do. And I askt him whether he yet owned it, (not long before his death), and he said, He did, and was firm in that judgment," holding that "we can not rationally offer Christ to sinners on any other grounds." Baxter tells us that Usher had, in his company, "gloried that he was the Man that brought Bishop *Davenant* and Dr. *Preston*" to this view (*R.B.*, II:206). (M. Fuller, *Life of Bishop Davenant*, 1897, 520 f., following J. Allport, "Life . . .," prefixed to his translation of Davenant's *Colossians*, xlviii, queries this statement, supposing the Synod of Dort, at which Davenant maintained the "middle way," to have been "prior to his acquaintance with Usher." But this is a mistake. They first met in 1609 (cf. *D.N.B.*, s.v. James Ussher), when Preston and Davenant, firm friends, were Fellows of Queens' College, Cambridge.) In his "reply to . . . Kendall" in *Apology*, 71, Baxter describes Davenant, Cameron and Robert Baron ("Camero secundus"; cf. *D.N.B.*, s.v." as "the glory of *Britain*, as having hit on that mean, which many others have mist of . . . in this, they have many excellent Companions . . . Our Renowned B. *Usher*, D. *Preston*, and many another famous light in England . . . "

The kingdom of Christ . . . and so preached and prayed for it, as if the setting up of discipline had been the setting up of the kingdom of Christ . . ."[84] The second was his study of the rights and wrongs on both sides in the Civil War.[85] Though he took the Parliament's side, he was a decided monarchist ("I was always satisfied . . . that the Authority and Person of the King were inviolable, out of the reach of just Accusation, Judgment, or Execution by Law; as having no Superiour, and no Judge"),[86] and disagreed with the "democratic" principles of Parker and Richard Hooker.[87] We shall see the fruit of these preoccupations in the "political method" which he came to regard as the key to theology and in the centrality for his system of the kingdom and kingship of Christ.

Antinomianism was the midwife which finally brought Baxter's system to birth. In 1645, finding that in Cromwell's army "Independency and Anabaptistry were most prevalent; Antinomianism and Arminianism were equally distributed,"[88] Baxter became chaplain to Whalley's regiment ("I thought the Publick Good commanded me").[89] His conduct in this position was thoroughly Baxterish: "I set my self from day to day to find out the Corruptions of the Soldiers; and to discourse and dispute them out of their mistakes . . . I was almost always . . . disputing with one or other of them; sometimes for our Civil Government, and sometimes for our Church Order . . . sometimes for Infant Baptism, and oft against Antinomianism."[90] Soon after, John Saltmarsh, one of the "two great Preachers at the Head Quarters,"[91] published *Free-Grace*;[92] "which I saw so exceedingly taking both in the Country and the Army . . . that I fell on the serious perusal and consideration of it: and its palpable errors were a most usefull discovery to me of some contrary Truths."[93] The book is rhapsodic and incoherent. It represents a reaction against the Puritan doctrine

84. XIV:291; partly quoted on p. 43, n. 4, above.

85. cf. *R.B.*, I:30-40, a detailed exposition of the arguments on both sides, complete with references to books and pamphlets; clear evidence of the amount of thought Baxter bestowed upon the issue at the time.

86. *R.B.*, I:39 f.

87. *R.B.*, III:151: "the Observator (*Parker*) almost tempted me to *Hooker's* Principles, but I quickly saw those reasons against them, which I have since published" (in his *Holy Commonwealth*, and *Christian Directory*, IV:3); "for my part I am satisfied that all *Politicks* err, which tell us of a *Majestas Realis* in the People, and distinct from the *Majestas Personalis* in the Governors" (I:41; where Richard Hooker's Christian name is twice given as Thomas). For Henry Parker, author of *Some few Observations upon his Majesties late Answer to the Declaration or Remonstrance of the Lords and Commons*, cf. *D.N.B.*, s.v.

88. *R.B.*, I:50.

89. p. 51.

90. p. 53.

91. p. 81; cf. *D.N.B.*, s.v.

92. Full title, *Free-Grace: Or, The Flowings of Christs Blood freely to Sinners . . . Wherein divers secrets of the Soule, of Sin and Temptations, are experimentally opened* . . . (1st ed. 1645, 6th. (corrected) 1649; all quotations are taken from the latter).

93. *Confession*, Preface.

of the covenant of grace and the pastoral praxis based on it, as described above. It consists of an extended commentary on the case of one who, after years spent in a fruitless quest for peace under orthodox Puritan direction, had come to Saltmarsh for guidance—"a Spirit of Adoption in Bondage, and one made poore in Spirit through the ignorance of the riches of grace, and by a legal faith (as I may say) both under Grace and the Law at the same time."[94] We shall examine Antinomian theology in more detail below;[95] here we shall say no more about it than is necessary for understanding the effect of Saltmarsh's book on Baxter's thought. Saltmarsh sets out a short route to assurance of salvation. The covenant of grace, he tells us, is "free without all condition."[96] Faith is not its condition; faith, defined as "a being perswaded more or lesse of Christs love,"[97] is a state of mind, whose function is merely to assure men that the covenanted blessings are theirs. In the covenant, which God made with His elect from all eternity, "Christ is ours *without faith* . . . but we cannot here know him to be ours, but by *believing*"[98]—i.e., believing that He is. The mark which distinguishes the elect from other men is that God enables them to perform this feat. "There need no more on our sides to work or warrant salvation to us, but to be perswaded that *Jesus Christ died for us* . . . they, and they onely are justified, who can believe . . ."[99] None need question their interest in the covenant through doubts as to the sincerity of their own repentance; for "Christ hath *believed* perfectly, he hath *repented* perfectly, he hath *sorrowed* for sin perfectly, he hath *obeyed* perfectly . . . we are to believe our repentance true in him, who hath repented for us."[100] Nor need daily shortcomings, however grievous, worry the believer: "that soule can never fall away that can believe; and no sin can damn it, if it will but believe the pardon of that sin . . ."[101]

Whether Saltmarsh really meant to say that faith was no more than taking for granted, whatever the evidence of one's life may be, that one is safe in Christ for ever, we need not here determine; certainly that is what he did say; and Baxter recognized in his teaching the lineaments of a religion he had met before.

> Truly I finde as farre as I can discern, that most of the prophane people in every Parish where yet I have liv'd, are Antinomians; they are born and bred

94. Saltmarsh, *op. cit.*, "To the Reader."
95. See chap. XIV.
96. p. 197.
97. p. 95.
98. p. 189.
99. p.194.
100. Ibid., 84—quoted by Baxter, *Aphorisms*, 113, with the comment: "What unsavory stuff." Saltmarsh was "the first that I remember that taught" such a doctrine ("Admonition to . . . Eyre" in *Apology*, 18).
101. p. 76 f.

such; and it is the very natural Religion of men, that have but the advantage to believe traditionally in Christ: I mean, their corrupt nature carrieth them without any teaching to make this use of Christ and the Gospel. And almost all the success of my Labours which hath so much comforted me, hath been in bringing men from natural Antinomianism or Libertinism, to true Repentance and saving Faith in Christ . . . [102]

His study of Saltmarsh, however, revolutionized his own thought; for he began to see that Saltmarsh's gospel was an inescapable deduction from two doctrines he held himself—limited atonement and justification before faith. If it were true that there were some for whom Christ in no sense died (and that was what Baxter understood limited atonement to mean), then the preacher dared not assure his hearers indiscriminately that upon repentance and faith Christ would receive them; how could he tell the elect from the reprobate? Again, if it were true that the elect were justified from the moment of birth, while the reprobate were not and never would be, then the preacher had no right to assure his hearers that upon repentance and faith they would be justified. If these doctrines were accepted, then the old paths marked out by Hooker, Bolton and Rogers must be abandoned, and men must be told instead exactly what Saltmarsh was telling them—namely, that the elect were justified already; that all men should believe themselves to be among that number, for none ought to doubt his election; that the very ability to believe oneself justified and bound for heaven, whatever one's life was like, was itself evidence of election; and that no reason could be given why any Christian should forsake sin beyond the fact that, as experience proved, it is more difficult to believe oneself justified when engaged in the practice of sin than otherwise. Sin would thus rob the Christian of his "comfort" and assurance; but it could never affect the status before God of a man who could go on believing himself elect. But this was neither the Puritan nor the Biblical gospel. The doctrines which implied it, therefore, must go. Baxter now remembered that Twisse, his oracle, had himself asserted that Christ had died for all in such a sense that salvation could be offered to all without exception, on condition of faith (though, plainly, he had failed to integrate this idea with the rest of his soteriology),[103] and, reviewing the case, was converted to a belief in universal redemption. Later, replying to the charge that "Amyraldus Baxterum Anglum . . . peperit proselytam," Baxter wrote:

this *unus Baxterus* did write a Book for Universal Redemption in this middle sense, before he ever saw either *Amyraldus, Davenant*, or any writer (except

102. Baxter, "Admonition to . . . Eyre" in *Apology*, "Preface."
103. In *Universal Redemption*, 287 f., Baxter quotes a passage that shows Twisse "industriously explaining" John 3:16, in proof of his claim that Twisse taught this doctrine.

Dr. *Twiss*) for that way, and was ready to publish it, and stopt it on the coming forth of *Amyraldus*, and was himself brought to this judgment, by reading Dr. *Twiss*, and meditating of it.[104]

As for the doctrine of a double justification, *in foro Dei* and *in foro conscientiae*, Baxter recalled that Downame had attacked it and Pemble himself had abjured it, and followed the latter's example: "now I saw, that neither of these was the Justification which the Scripture spake of."[105] The discovery that the views he had so zealously canvassed really subverted the gospel marked Baxter for life. He had burned his theological fingers, and he never forgot it. In 1653, he put on paper the following solemn warning:

> All young Students that will deigne to take advice from so mean a man as I, as ever you would preserve your graces . . . preserve your Judgements; and as ever you would maintain the Doctrine of Christ, take heed of the Errors of the Antinomians . . . That Christs satisfaction is ours . . . before the Application; and that . . . we are actually Pardoned, Justified, Reconciled and Adopted by it before we were born, much more before we believe . . . That pardon of sin is nothing but *Velle non Punire*: That Justification by Faith is nothing but Justification *in foro conscientiae*, or the sense of that in our hearts, which was really ours from eternity . . . That justifying faith is the feeling or apprehension of Gods eternal Love, Remission and Adoption. I say, take heed of these master-Points of Antinomianism. And as ever you would avoid these, take heed how you receive them on the reputation and plausible words of any Writer: and especially of Dr. *Twiss*, who is full of such passages . . . For you know, if you receive these, then you must receive the rest, *if you discern the concatenation.*[106] For if all your sins were pardoned as soon as Christ died, then what need you pray for pardon, or Repent or Believe . . . for pardon? then God loved you as well when you were his enemies, as since; and then how can you be restrained from sin? . . . I speak . . . mainly for Gods glory and Truth, and for the love of souls. I take my self the rather bound to it, because I was once drawn my self to some of these opinions by the meer high estimation of Mr. *Pemble* and Dr. *Twisse*.[107]

Baxter had himself "discerned the concatenation," and he wrote with feeling. He felt he had had a narrow escape.

In later life he looked back to his reading of Saltmarsh as the time when he was not merely shaken out of error, but guided towards the truth. The

---

104. *Certain Disputations of Right to the Sacraments, loc, cit.*; cf. 39 f., above. The charge had been leveled by Ludovicus Molinaeus (Louis du Moulin) in the Preface to his *Paraenesis ad aedificatores Imperii in Imperio* (1656).

105. J.R., "Of the Imputation of Christ's Righteousness," 22 f.

106. My italics.

107. "Reply to . . . Kendall," in *Apology*, 13.

experience led him "to study better than I had done the Doctrine of the Covenants and Laws of God, of Redemption and Justification,"[108] and light began to dawn. Meanwhile, at the end of 1646, his health broke, and the doctors gave him up for lost. Thinking he was dying, he turned his thoughts to "the Everlasting Rest which I apprehended myself to be just on the Borders of. And that my Thoughts might not too much scatter in my Meditation, I began to write..."[109] A few weeks later found him in convalescence at Rous-Lench, still writing. Then the revelation came, and "I discovered more in one weeke, than ... in seventeen yeares reading, hearing and wrangling."[110] Since this proved the turning-point in his theological career, we may quote his account of it in full.

> The points, or method, or termes in that book of Aphorismes, which cause the great offence ... I did not to my utmost remembrance receive from any Book or Person in the world; but only upon former study of the Scriptures, some undigested conceptions stuck in my minde, and at the time of my conceiving and entertaining those Notions ... I was in a strange place, where I had no book but my Bible (and a Concordance, I think and two or three Physick books were with or near me,) ... in extream weakness, I ... began ... *The Saints Rest*; and ... when I came to that place which is now at *pag.* 68 ... I was urged, partly by the occurring difficulty, and partly by a question put to me, to resolve, In what sense it is that men are called Righteous, and publikely Justified at the day of Judgement in reference to the Improvement of their Talents, and the feeding, visiting, cloathing, &c. of Christ? ... The expounding of *Matth.* 25. was the task ... which as I seriously set my self to understand, I found so great difficulties as drove me to God again and again; and thereupon so great light that I could not resist; so that I solemnly professe that it was partly on my knees, and partly in diligent consideration of the naked Text ... that I received ... the forementioned particulars. An overpowering Light (I thought) did suddenly give me a clear apprehension of those things, which I had often reached after before in vain. Whereupon I suddenly wrote down the bare Propositions ... and so let them lye by me long after. And then falling into ... more confident expectations of death, I revised them, and thrust them out too hastily and undigested.[111]

108. "The Preface long ago written" prefixed to "A Breviate of ... Justification" in *Scripture Gospel Defended.*

109. *R.B.*, I:108.

110. *Aphorisms*, App., 110 f.

111. "An Unsavoury Volume ... Anatomized" in *Apology*, 5. Baxter completed the Aphorisms (there are 80 altogether) after his return to Kidderminster, intending them as "an Appendix to another Treatise going to the Presse on a more excellent Subject" (i.e., the *Saints' Rest*): but when he showed them to friends, "they complained of obscure brevity, and desired some fuller explication; which when I had done, that which before was but two or three leaves ... did swell to this bignesse, that I was faine to let it goe alone" ("To the Reader").

And so *Aphorismes of Justification, With their Explication annexed. Wherein also is opened the nature of the Covenants, Satisfaction, Righteousnesse, Faith, Works, &c.* came into the world. The preface "To the Reader" is dated Nov. 11th, 1648. The new "political method" is here plain: the two covenants are presented as successive enactments of the Divine legislator, and God's government is expounded in terms of the legal principles which "natural light" afforded. For some of the details, he tells us, he drew on the two pioneers of this method, John Bradshaw[112] and Hugo Grotius. "Where I say I used no Authors . . . for the forementioned Theses, I say not so for all in the explications: Two I must confess my self much to have profited by in that doctrine; the one is Mr. Bradshaw, the other is *Grotius de satisfactione* . . . Yet I had almost finished those Aphorismes before ever I read a leaf of Grotius . . ."[113] The book caused a considerable stir. "I put into it many uncautelous words (as young Writers use to do,) though I think the main doctrine of it sound.[114] I intended it only against the *Antinomians*; But it sounded as new and strange to many. Upon whose dissent or doubtings, I printed my desire of my friends Animadversions," and received a number of elaborate comments, to which he spent the best part of three years writing replies.[115] In later years he acknowledged his debt to these correspondents: "the great Learning of their various Writings, and the long Study which I was thereby engaged in, in answering and rejoyning to the most, was a greater advantage to me, to receive accurate and digested conceptions on these subjects, than private Students can expect."[116] He was particularly grateful to George Lawson, rector of More,[117] "from whom I learned more than from any man." In particular, "his instigating me to the study of Politicks . . . did prove a singular Benefit to me";[118] for it showed Baxter the full significance of the method he had adopted and enabled him to draw out in detail its implications. By 1653 his system of theology was complete, and it remained unchanged for the rest of his life.

We have taken some pains to trace out the various factors which, by their action on Baxter and his reaction to them, went to produce his mature theology, for, as with all eclectic thinkers, the finished product is scarcely intelligible

---

112. cf. *D.N.B.*, s.v. The work here referred to is *A Treatise of Iustification* (1615). A revised Latin version, *Dissertatio de Justificationis Doctrina*, was printed at Leyden in 1618.

113. *Apology, loc. cit.* The passage continues: "being at that time in speech with Mr. *Tombes,* upon his high commendations of it, I borrowed it of him . . . and I confess, I learned more out of it, than I did out of any book except the Scriptures, of many a year before." Baxter quotes Grotius' book on pages 39, 55, 80, 94 f., and 146 of *Aphorisms.*

114. cf. App. II.

115. cf. App. I.

116. *C.T., Preface.*

117. cf. *D.N.B.*, s.v.

118. *R.B.*, I:108.

without some knowledge of the raw material of which it was made. We can now see why Antinomianism became a *bete noire* which Baxter thought he saw round every corner, and why a philosophical theologian of such gifts spent so much of his time decrying philosophical theology. And we are now in a position to evaluate the system we shall study in the following chapters. Only when we appreciate how much Baxter was a man of his time, how deeply he was immersed in the thought-currents of his own day, shall we be able to see how far he rose above the limitations of his age. Not till we can strip his thought of its transient and inevitably dated form can we adequately appraise the permanent worth of its substance. Baxter claimed to do no more than state the old faith in a new and, he hoped, final form. It was a sufficiently daring claim, and his dream of finality has proved delusive. The seventeenth century has passed away, and Baxterianism with it. But the first part of his claim was warranted. He did re-state the old faith. The subsequent chapters will show how broad, balanced and discerning that re-statement really was.

Chapter 9

The Kingdom of Christ

1.   Aim of this and the next chapter: to expound Baxter's doctrine of
         redemption and show its controversial relevance.

2.   Distinction between God's laws and decrees:
         God works out the second through the first.

3.   Three epochs of God's kingdom: nature, grace, glory.
         Importance of political and legal knowledge for studying the
           first and second.

4.   Upon the fall, The Law of Nature ceased to be a covenant:
           the promise withdrawn;
           the precept augmented.
         The Law of Grace (first edition) given to Adam:
           Providence proves this.
         Christ's satisfaction presupposed in it;
         God's glory the end of it.
         Successive promulgations of it.

5.   Christ's mediatorial vocation;
         satisfaction for sins;
         Christ's kingdom set up over a redeemed world.
         The covenant of grace (second edition) its law;
           terms of the covenant.
         The last judgment: all men judged by the law of grace.

6.   Christ gives the law (as *Rector*) and causes the elect to obey it
           (as *Dominus*).
         The precise effects of Christ's death.

7.   Baxter's debt to Grotius *De satisfactione*;
         Baxter's originality on the kingdom of Christ;
         Baxter's claims for his synthesis.

8.   Baxter's reply to the Arminians:
           agrees with their doctrines of universal redemption and
            conditional reprobation;
           corrects their doctrine of universal sufficient grace;
           asserts against them unconditional election and irresistible grace,
            following Saumur school and Synod of Dort.

God more gracious than Arminians allow.
None but the elect will in fact be saved.

9.   Baxter's objections to Limited Atonement:
                i.   An innovation
                ii. A misrepresentation of Christ's death
                iii. Exegetically untenable
                iv. Harmful to religion: undermines evangelism, faith and
                        assurance
                v.   Destroys the doctrine of hell.

10.   Criticism of Baxter's polemic:
                attacks a man of straw
                obscures the basic issue (nature of atonement)
                fails to appreciate the positive content of the doctrine attacked.

(Principal Sources: *Aphorisms*; *Catholick Theologie*; I.ii, II; *Of Justifying Righteousness*; *God's Goodness Vindicated* (VIII); *Universal Redemption.*)

Chapter 9

The Kingdom of Christ

We have somewhat else to think of, than only to fly from Arminianism. Truth borders close to error, and therefore to Arminianism. To be near to error is a sign of Truth. If you will fly further and go to Antinomianism to avoid Arminianism, you will go out of the ashes into the fire. —Baxter

Baxter's soteriology was a reformulation of the covenant theology of the Westminster Confession according to a "political method." Theology was to him, as we saw, "doctrina de regno Dei." The present age is the period of the "regnum Christi." In this chapter, we shall review his doctrine of God's kingdom as a whole, and consider it as a reply to Arminianism and a correction of Calvinist extremism. In the next chapter, we shall focus our attention on the *articulus stantis vel cadentis ecclesiae*, justification by faith, and consider his statement of it as an answer to its Antinomian counterpart. As we saw, his theology was hammered out on the anvil of these controversies, and will be best appreciated when seen in the context of them.

The linch-pin of his doctrine was a clearly drawn and consistently maintained distinction between God's will as *dominus* and as *rector*, "God's Decrees and his Laws."[1] In his first Aphorism he draws the distinction as follows:

God hath first a Will of purpose, whereby he determineth of events: what shall be, and what shall not be, *de facto*; secondly, And a Legislative, or Preceptive will, for the government of the Rationall Creature: whereby he determineth what shall be, and what shall not be, *de jure*, or in point of duty; and in order thereto, concludeth of Rewards and Punishments.[2]

---

1. *Confession*, 290.
2. *Aphorisms* (I), 1. The first three deal with this distinction.

The first is God's will as *dominus absolutus*, disposing of His creatures at His pleasure, answerable to none for what He does. It covers "Predestination, Election, Reprobation, or Preterition . . . the Covenant betwixt the Father and the Son[3] . . . the absolute Promises of Regeneration and Perseverance (sc., made in Scripture to the elect as such) . . . the fulfilling of those Promises by differencing Grace."[4] The second expresses God's mind as man's moral governor. It is propounded "in his written Laws . . . promulgate and established by way of Covenant."[5] In Scripture God proclaims Himself *just*. This means that he never transgresses the rule of His own enactments. Justice is a rectoral attribute. The theologian, therefore, must start from the axiom that, while God's legislative will is one thing and His decretive will another, His decrees are performed through the execution of His laws and never at their expense. God never wills to act otherwise than in His law He said He would. Not to grasp this point was a high road to error.[6]

All Reformed thought, as we noticed, is founded upon this distinction in some form or other. Baxter found Twisse the most helpful in showing him how it should be formulated; although, even so, "his Notions were very imperfect of it, and his Improvement very short, in respect to its desert and use."[7] And clarity here, Baxter held, was of the very highest importance. The Biblical doctrine of the kingdom of God could not be understood without it.

The covenant theology of the seventeenth century, as has often been pointed out, was a philosophy of history, according to which the successive dispensations of the covenant of grace gave the historical process its meaning. In stating it, its exponents put forward, not merely an interpretation of the whole Bible from Genesis to Revelation, but of all history, from the Creation to Christ's return. This historical perspective was part of Baxter's inheritance, and his statement of the doctrine of God's kingdom was made in terms of it.

---

3. i.e. the so-called "Covenant of Redemption"; cf. Westminster Confession, VIII.i, and *R.D.*, 376 f.

4. *Aphorisms*, (II), 7.

5. *op. cit.* (III), 11. The Laws, as we have seen, are written in both Nature and Scripture.

6. cf. the following observation, from the "Admonition to . . . Eyre" in *Apology*, 38: "It is a most dangerous mistake for Divines to set Gods Decrees, Foreknowledge or Disposal of Events, in opposition to his Moral Rectorship, (as) if the acts of one must be inconsistent with the acts of the other. Let me speak it out . . . this one grand mistake, hath introduced most of their Errors, and feedeth most of your (sc. Eyre's) contentions. They cannot reconcile the acts of Gods Absolute Dominion, with the moral acts of Regiment (i.e., government); nor can they see in what a distinct series they stand."

7. "Mr. Cartwright . . . Considered" in *J.R.*, 8. Twisse failed, in Baxter's judgment, to do justice to the fact that God's published laws really signified His wishes concerning human behavior. He did not allow that they were "properly the . . . signification of his Will" (14). God's will, Twisse maintained, was expressed only in His secret decree—that the elect should believe and be saved, and the reprobate sin and perish; and His laws and promises were published only as means to bring about that end. They could only, therefore, be termed His will *metaphorically*.

The subject, he tells us, divides into three, according to the three successive stages in God's dealing with mankind:

> God hath three Kingdoms, in *specie*, over mankinde, whereof the first two are on earth and the third in heaven (though in regard of the Identity of the Soveraign, subjects, &c. they may be called all one:) These are grounded on a threefold *Jus Dominii & Imperii*, Right of Propriety and Government: *viz.* His Creation, Redemption, and Raising and Glorifying us. The first was the Kingdom of God over Perfect man, and is never called the Kingdom of the Son, or the Mediatour . . . This endured but till the fall of man. The second is the Kingdom of the Son, or Redeemer, which is distinguished from the rest by the Foundaton of Right (General Redemption) by its Ends, Laws, State of the subjects, &c. The work and end of this Kingdom, is to effect mans cure and recovery, and to bring the lapsed disobedient creature, to a perfect Conformity and Obedience to God again: so that this whole Kingdom, from first to last, will be imployed in Recovery and Cure, and when that is finished, the Son shall then deliver up the Kindgom to the Father[8] . . . not laying by his humane Nature, Authority or Honour, but that *species* of Government which was Medicinal, Restorative, and for the Reduction of the disobedient to God . . . ; and so as a Conquering General, as a Physitian that hath finished his Cure, so will the Kingdom of Christ then cease, his work being done, and the Restored delivered Spotless to the Father: And then it shall be the Kingdom of the Father, of God again, in the fullest sense.[9]

In the first kingdom, the instrument of government was the Law of Nature, which we have already considered. In the second, this was supplemented by a new remedial covenant of grace, the law of Christ. In the kingdom of glory, the redeemed will be confirmed in the habitual holiness which grace began to create in them on earth, and will need no law. Our present concern is with the second of these three. Here familiarity with the general principles of law and politics, as Nature teaches them, is essential. "Theologus est jurisconsultus Christianus.[10]" Kingship is the fundamental idea for the description and interpretation of the Divine dealings with man, and the regulative concept in theology must be royal government by law. Whatever God does in other capacities and relations, he does *as King*. We are now to study Baxter's outworking of this axiom in his account of the inception, progress and consummation of the kingdom of Christ.

When man fell, the law of innocent Nature ceased at once to be a covenant of life to him:

8. Baxter quotes I Cor. 15:24 f.

9. "An Unsavoury Volume . . . Anatomized" in *Apology*, 26.

10. "Reply to . . . Kendall" in *Apology*, 99. Baxter continues: "I could wish men would lay by their over-bold enquiries into Gods Decrees . . . and study this intelligible and necessary part of Theology a little more."

the *premiant* part of the Law of Innocency, from whence it is named a *Covenant*, is now *truly null* . . . This was not done by GOD but Man, who *ceased* to be a *capable subject* of that *Covenant, Promise* or *Reward*: And so the Condition (*Innocency* or *Perfect Obedience*) being become *naturally impossible*, we must not feign God to say to Sinners (*On condition you be not Sinners* you shall live)."[11]

"God maketh not Promises and Covenants upon *Natural* impossibilities . . . When the Condition is once totally violated, all sense and civil Law saith, *Res transit in judicatum, & Lex Sententiam*; and the Promise ceaseth *Cessante capacitate promissarii*."[12] The promise was withdrawn, but the Law of Nature, as a statement of man's duty and of his desert if he transgressed, remained unaltered. Indeed, it was enlarged:

as soon as ever Man was faln . . . the Law of Nature obliged faln man to repent and *return* to God. But it gave him no hope of pardon on his Repentance. So that it would have been but a despairing Repentance. Yet hereby it is apparent, that the Law of Nature maketh us new duties, as our case changeth . . . [13]

This Law, as we have seen, comprehends all the duties which result from man's actual relationship to God and the universe, and changes as that relationship changes.[14] It continues to condemn the transgressor, but no longer carries with it a promise of life to those who keep it; for none can keep it.

According to the terms of God's first covenant, man should have died, physically and spiritually, the day he fell. Part of the penalty was in fact inflicted:[15] but not all. For God suspended its full execution, and at once in the

---

11. *End of Doctrinal Controversies*, 120. In his *Confession* (106) Baxter stated that Lawson's animadversions convinced him of the error of "what I first in terms asserted, *viz.* The continuation of the whole Covenant, Promise and All" (cf. *Aphorisms*, 78 f. (XI-XIII)). For "the name (i.e., covenant) is given from Gods promise of life in that Law . . . and . . . it is not fit to denominate the law A *Covenant* from that only part which is null . . . " He approved the titles "law of works," "law of nature," "moral law," for the original law as it still exists for fallen man, but rejected "covenant of works" altogether.

12. *C.T.*, I.ii.12:29-30. The legal tags are common in Baxter's discussions of this subject after the *Aphorisms*; probably he learned them from Lawson.

13. "Mr. Cartwright . . . Considered," in *J.R.*, 145. Baxter marked this addition by distinguishing between the law of *innocent* and of *fallen* Nature.

14. Thus, this Law (which "is so far *mutable* as *Nature* it self is mutable," *C.T.*, I.ii.28:33) was enlarged again when it became clear that God was dealing with fallen man on terms of grace: it "now obligeth him to *love* and *thankfulness* . . . to seek to him for Mercy, and to use all possible means for further hope of pardon" (*End of Doctrinal Controversies*, 127).

15. cf. *Aphorisms*, 69: "we feel part of the curse fulfilled on us: We eat in labour and sweat; the earth doth bring forth thorns and bryars; women bring forth their children in sorrow; our native pravity is the curse upon our souls; we are sick, and weary, and full of fears, and sorrows, and shame, and at last we dye and turn to dust." Cf. Gen. 3:16-19.

Protevangelium promulgated a new law, the Law of Grace:

> When God judged man for sin, at once he promised him a Saviour, and
> through him as promised, made a new Law of Grace with man.

> This Law giveth pardon of the Spiritual and Eternal Punishment . . . upon
> certain *terms*: And with pardon a free gift of *Life Spiritual and Eternal* . . . on
> the said conditions.

> The Promise *Gen.* 3:15 is plain as to *Mercy* and *Salvation*, and darker as to the
> *promised seed*, and his *mediation* . . . But this is clear, that by this new Covenant
> God becometh man's *Merciful Redeemer* and *Pardoner*, and *Ruler on terms of
> Grace* in order to *recovery* and *Salvation*; And that man was to *Believe in God
> as such*, and accordingly to devote himself in Covenant to him. *This Law* or
> *Covenant* was made with *all Mankind in* Adam: For all were in his loins . . . [16]

Both Scripture and providence throughout man's history bear witness to
the fact that the world has been put under grace.

> Seeing Life, Health, Food, Hope, and all that is truly good, were forfeited by
> Sin, and none of them can be due to us by the *Law of Innocency*, it followeth,
> that wherever they are given, it is upon other terms . . . those of the *Law of
> Grace*, as fruits of our Redeemer's Mercy . . . And where the *Fruits* are apparent,
> we may know the *Cause*.[17]

This law of grace was promulgated on the basis of a decision which the
Creator had taken before the world was made, that His Son should become
man and by dying satisfy for the sins of the race. To pardon sins without
satisfaction would reflect upon the character of a ruler who had previously
threatened sin with death, and God would not do it. "*Stante rerum natura* he
cannot make those things fit, which *ex natura rei* are unfit: Nor can God do
that which is unfit.[18] And if it had not been unfit for the supream Rector of the
World to pardon Mans Sin without satisfaction, God would not so dearly have
satisfied his own justice . . . "[19] God was under no obligation either to provide
or to accept satisfaction as an alternative to the sinner's death; but He

---

16. *C.T.*, I.ii.13-16:31.

17. *End of Doctrinal Controversies*, 98; cf. Acts 14:17. That God has made a law of grace with
mankind is thus among the "natural notices": "all the World that never heard the Gospel, do yet
take God to be a *merciful, forgiving God*, and take themselves to be under some duty for the obtaining
of further mercy, recovery and felicity" (*op. cit.*, 128).

18. cf. *Universal Redemption*, 104 f: "When I say (God cannot) I mean not, that he cannot for
want of Power, but because of his Wisdom, Goodness and Justice, He cannot (being Rector . . .) do
that which is . . . such a Monster in Government, and so destructive to the ends of his Government."

19. *op. cit.*, 125 f.

did of his free abundant Mercy undertake the saving of sinful Man, and
notwithstanding his Threatning and Man's Defect, resolving to make
advantage of our Sin and Misery, for the Glory of his Wisdom, Love, Mercy
and Justice, he promised that the Eternal Word should in due time assume
Man's nature, and therein do and suffer that which should glorifie him more
than Man's Perdition would have done, and which should make it just and
meet for him to save the Guilty both inceptively . . . under the Promise (for
4000 years) and afterward more fully at Christ's Incarnation, and finally to
perfect all in Glory.[20]

The redemption and restoration of man through Christ, involving as it does a
fuller manifestation of the Divine attributes, will bring more glory to God
than summary execution would have done; and this, in the last analysis, must
be given as God's reason for undertaking it. His end in it is His own glory, "the
. . . glorious *impress* or *appearance* of himself communicated to his Creatures";[21]
and this supremely in the case of the Incarnate Son. "The Glory of our *Redeemer*
is more excellent than *mine* or *yours*."[22] And so the law of grace was first given
by God to Adam, and renewed "with some positive Additions"[23] to Noah. These
two editions of it were universal in scope. After this, an amplified version was
promulgated to Abraham and his seed,[24] and renewed, with additional elements,
to the same group through Moses.[25] In due time, the Mediator came.

20. *End of Doctrinal Controversies*, 94 f.

21. *How Far Holiness is the Design of Christianity*, 10.

22. *End of Doctrinal Controversies*, 215; cf. *Works*, XIII:97: "here a very great truth appeareth,
which very many overlook, that the exaltation of the person of the Redeemer, and the glory that
God will have in him is a higher and more principal part of God's intent in the sending of him to
. . . redeem us, than the glorifying of man, and of God by us. Christ will be more glorious than men
or angels, and therefore will more glorify God; and God will eternally take more complacency in
him than in men or angels; and therefore . . . we are more for Christ, as a means to his glory, than
he for us . . . "

23. *End of Doctrinal Controversies*, 131: "because he was as a second Head . . . of all Mankind,
all coming from his Loins as they did from *Adam's*." The "positive additions" are in Gen. 9:4.

24. "The Promise to *Abraham* was, besides the Common Covenant of Grace, renewed, 1. A
promise of *peculiar Favour* to his Seed . . . 2. A promise that the *Messiah* should be of his Seed! . . .
The *peculiar Precept* of that Covenant was, That by Circumcision as a Seal and Symbol . . . they
should difference themselves from others, as God's *peculiar People*" (*op. cit.*, 132 f).

25. "The gathering of *Israel* into a Policy (i.e. polity) by *Moses*, as a Theocracy . . . was but the
full Establishment of what God had promised to *Abraham* . . . This Law of *Moses* therefore must be
considered as an Affix or Appendix to the Common Law of Grace . . . The Common Covenant of
Grace was the *Soul* as it were of this Political Jewish Law; and therefore was really expressed in it."
(*op. cit.*, 134). "The entire Law of God which the Israelitish Nation was under had all these parts. 1.
The remaining preceptive and directive part of the Law of Nature. 2. The Universal Covenant of
Grace made with all mankind in *Adam* and *Noah*, and personally renewed to *Abraham* . . . 3. The
special promise to Abraham and his seed as a *peculiar people* of whom the Messiah should come.
4. The body of the *Law of Moses* as a *Law for* that Common-wealth . . . " (*C.T.*, I.II.33:35).

"Christ as man was under a Law, yea and a Law peculiar to himself, . . . even the Law of Mediation, which deserves in the body of Theologie a peculiar place . . ."[26] God's overall plan of redemption was as follows:

> The Father giveth up to Christ as Redeemer the whole lapsed cursed reparable world . . . and especially his *chosen* to be *eventually and infallibly saved*, and promiseth to accept his *Sacrifice and performance*, and . . . by him to establish the *Law of Grace* (in its perfect Edition) and to give him the Government respectively of the Church and World, and to Glorifie him for this work with himself for ever.[27]

The law of his mediation prescribed "1. That habitually and actually he *perfectly fulfill all the Law of Nature*, which he was capable of. 2. That he fulfill also the Law of *Moses*. 3. That he also do those things proper to the *Mediator*, in his *Miracles, Sacrifice, Resurrection, Intercession, Teaching, Government, &c.*"[28] The focal point of his mediatorial work was his sacrificial death, by which he made satisfaction for the world's sin. In view of the importance which Baxter attached to the doctrine of the death of Christ[29] and the detailed study which he devoted to it ("I have bestowed more consideration about it, then about any other point in Divinity"),[30] it is proper for us to consider his account of it in full.

Satisfaction, though not a Biblical word,[31] is the proper legal term for the thing in question.

> Satisfaction is commonly by Lawyers and Schoolmen defined to be *Redditio aequivalentis, alias indebiti*: or *solutio vel Redditio tantidem*: and it is contradistinguished from *solutio stricte sumpta*; which is *ejusdem quod debetur*. And so in Criminal Cases, the Punishment of the Offender is the *Ipsum Debitum* . . . But if any other sufficient means be found which, without the

---

26. "Answer to Blake," in *Apology*, 115.

27. *C.T.*, I.ii.38:38.

28. *End of Doctrinal Controversies*, 121 f.

29. cf. *Of Justification*, 382: "The right understanding of it, is the main Ground of our safety and comfort: The wrong understanding it, is the vety (*sic*) turning point to Antinomianism . . . the Heart of the whole System of their Doctrine;" "Confutation of Ludiomaeus Colvinus" in *Apology*, 262: "The not understanding of Christ's satisfaction . . . leadeth men into the Antinomian doctrines above anything." Baxter remained convinced that (as he had asserted in the *Aphorisms*, 67) it was "one of the greatest and noblest questions in our controverted Divinity, *What are the immediate effects of Christs Death?* He that can rightly answer this, is a Divine indeed; and by the help of this, may expedite most other controversies about Redemption and Justification."

30. *Of Justification*, 383.

31. cf. *Universal Redemption*, 392: "Some very Wise, Godly and Learned men that I have spoke with, wish that the word . . . had been never here used, but instead . . . (an Expiatory or Propitiatory sacrifice:) because the last is the Scripture phrase and the first is not: But yet Satisfaction is no such unfit term but that it may well be used, though still Scripture phrase I confess is better."

Punishment of the offender, may provide for the Indemnity of the Lawgiver, and the publick good, and this both for what is past by reparation, and for time to come by Prevention, that so the main ends of the violated Law may yet be attained, this is satisfaction to the Lawgiver; Satisfaction alway supposeth the non-payment of the debt. And in Criminal Cases (as our is) satisfaction still supposeth the Duty, or Punishment, or both to be overpassed which the Law required."[32]

Christ's death was fully satisfactory according to the terms of this definition:

the equivalency lay not in the proportion of Punishment (pain or loss) equal to that which was due to all or to the Elect; but in the sufficient aptitude of that Degree or (i.e. of) Punishment, which Christ bore (becoming a publick spectacle of shame, for the demonstration of Justice, &c.) from the exceeding Dignity of the person, to be a means to Gods obtaining the remote ends of his Law, (viz. the demonstration of Justice, and right governing of the Creature, and preserving the Authority of the Lawgiver) . . . Many Learned Divines have written largely to prove that Christ did not properly suffer the pains of Hell on his Soul; I will not meddle much with the question; But doubtless it was a very great part of our punishment which Christ was uncapable of undergoing . . . The Death due to us was Temporal, Spiritual and Eternal . . . The Spiritual Death, so far as it consisted in the loss of Gods Image, and privation of Holiness, and Dominion of Sin and Slavery to Satan, Christ bore not at all. Nor yet as it lay in any Torments or Gripes of Conscience, which are the fruits only of personal proper guilt . . . Christ had no sin of his own to look on to torment him: and other mens Sins could not procure to him the gripes of a Guilty Conscience. Nor yet was his Soul or Body so deprived of Gods Love as are the wicked, nor so hated by God, nor at all disunited from God: . . . nor yet were any of Christs sufferings Eternal. Yet did he endure that debasedness and publick shame, and that forsaking of God by the denial of Spiritual Comforts, and by giving him up to the Will of his Enemies, and by an inward sense of Gods displeasure,[33] in trouble of Soul, which was a full satisfaction to Justice, or a Sacrifice sufficient for God to do what he did, upon the reception of it.[34]

The Father now accepted the satisfaction which He had Himself provided, and installed the Son, "God-Redeemer,"[35] in the kingdom prepared for him. All power and authority was given him, and he became the world's ruler and

32. op. cit., 378 f.
33. Sc. "the sorrowful sense of Gods hatred of sin and wrath against Sinners, though not properly terminated on himself" (C.T., I.ii.51:40).
34. Universal Redemption, 390 f.
35. This is almost a technical term in the vocabulary of Baxter and Lawson, referring to Christ as ruler in the kingdom of grace.

lawgiver ("for the Legislative-Power is the principal efficient part of Soveraignty").[36] As creation had been the ground of kingship in God's first kingdom, so redemption became the ground of it in the second. "God being minded to change the Government of the World, did lay the whole Foundation of the New Government in Christ's Universal Redemption, even as he laid the Foundation of the Old Government, in the Creation of Man after his Image."[37] "The maker becomes the repairer; Christ redeemeth the World: And hereby hath first a *novum jus Dominii*, a new Propriety in it. 2. A *novum jus imperii*, a new right to Govern it. 3. And hence he is *novus Legislator*, he doth make new Laws, even the laws of Grace and Faith."[38] "As Christ the Anointed and Soveraign Redeemer, he made *Legem Remediantem*, An Act of Oblivion, A new Law, *viz.* A Law of Grace; thereby Granting free pardon, Justification, Adoption and right to Glory to all that will sincerely Repent and Believe in him; and Peremptorily Concluding those to everlasting death that will not."[39] This is the covenant of grace, "the Law of Liberty, and the Law of the Spirit of *Life*,"[40] in its final edition. It may properly be termed "the Law of Nature and Grace,"[41] for it consists of two parts: the Law of (fallen) Nature plus a supplementary statute which, on the basis of Christ's satisfaction, relaxes and dispenses with the penal provisions of the original Law and "appointeth us the terms and means of our recovery."[42] These are, properly two laws—(One *in this forme, Perfect Obedience is thy Duty (or obey perfectly): Death is thy Due for every sin.* The other in this forme, *Repent and Believe, and thou shalt be saved (from the former curse): Or else damned.*"[43] But they can be stated as one, thus:

> Though thou have sinned, and art condemned, yet obey me perfectly for the future . . . and if thou disobey in any thing, for that also death shall be thy due: Yet for the sake of him that Redeemed thee, if thou wilt believe in him

36. *C.T.*, I:ii.60, 42.

37. *Universal Redemption*, 446 f.

38. *op. cit.*, 187.

39. "Admonition to . . . Eyre" in *Apology*, 25.

40. *C.T.*, I.ii.60:43; cf. James 1:25, 2:12, and Romans 8:2

41. *Confession*, 129.

42. *C.T., loc. cit.* Baxter carefully states the legal basis for the change: "A Dispensation is (as *Grotius* defineth it) an act of a Superior, whereby the obligation of a Law in force is taken away, as to certain persons and things" (*Aphorisms*, 80 f.). It must be effected by *ad hoc* legislation: "It is a Rule in the Civil Law (as *Ulpian*) that *By the same way as an Obligation is induced or caused, it must be removed or destroyed*: But by the curse of the Law . . . was our obligation to punishment . . . caused; therefore by way of Law dissolving that cause, must it be taken off" (*Of Justification*, 334). Accordingly, "the New Law of Grace is but *Lex particularis*, and the Law of Nature is *Lex universalis*, and the Law of Grace is but subservient to the Law of Nature, being *Lex Remedians*, purposely ordained for the dissolving of its obligation to punishment" ("Confutation of . . . Ludiomaeus Colvinus" in *Apology*, 184).

43. Answer to Blake, in *Apology*, 146.

and Repent, then thou shalt be pardoned and saved; but if thou wilt not, thou shalt be remedilessly damned.[44]

Christ's new law does not provide for any lessening of temporal affliction for sins, whether Adam's or one's own (such a course would encourage further transgression and thus be manifestly bad government), but it confers eternal life and hope of glory upon those who submit to it, who will be justified and accepted when the Redeemer returns in visible, bodily form to judgment. This, the closing event of human history, will terminate the kingdom of grace and usher in the kingdom of glory. The procedure that will be followed on that day may be deduced partly from its issue, the separation of sheep from goats, sincere believers from hypocrites, and partly from the composite nature of Christ's law. Satan, the Accuser, is cast for the role of prosecuting counsel, and the trial will proceed as follows:

We (i.e., believers) are liable to all these following *Accusations* . . .

1. It may be said by the Accuser of the Brethren, (*Thou art a sinner* . . .) He that denieth this is a Lyar: Against this charge there is no *Justification* for ever. But we must in Heaven confess that *we have sinned*: but Glory be to him that *washed us from our sins in his blood* (by Pardon and Sanctification.)

2. Next it may be said that, (*We did deserve Hell by our sin.*) This also is to be confessed for ever.

3. It may be said, that by Gods *Law of Innocency* Hell is our *due*, and therefore we are to be *condemned to it*. To this, we deny the *consequence*; because *we have right to Impunity and to Glory, freely given us by God our Redeemer by a Covenant of Grace* . . .

. . . But the turning point of the day is yet behind; Our allegation of Justification by Christ and the Covenant may be denied. It may be said by the Accuser, that the Covenant justifieth none but *penitent believers* . . . and that *we are none such*. Against this accusation we must be justified or perish . . . Christs merits and Satisfaction is not the Righteousness . . . which must justify us *against this Accusation*; But our *own personal Faith, Repentance, sincere Holiness and Perseverance* . . . wrought by the Spirit in us, but thence, *our own acts*. He that cannot truly say, *The Accusation is false. I am a true Penitent, sanctified persevering Believer* must be condemned and perish. Thus Faith and Repentance are our Righteousness by which we must thus far be justified.[45]

44. *Confession*, 107.
45. *C.T.*, I.ii.163-6:70 f.

Christ's satisfaction effects nothing for those who lack faith. But all in whom is found the latter will be accepted on the ground of the former, whether they had ever heard of Christ or not. Those who never knew of the final edition of the covenant will be judged according to the earlier version, given to Adam and Noah and legible in the book of Providence, which "is still in force, and the Law by which the world shall be *governed and judged*: They are all possessors of *Mercy which leadeth to Repentance,* and *bound* to use *the means* afforded them in order to *Repentance and Salvation,* and it is their sin that they do not: For which it is ultimately that they are condemned."[46] Towards the end of his life, Baxter openly voiced his confidence that some, perhaps many, who never heard of Christ but lived under the Noahic covenant will in that day be found penitent believers.[47]

So far, we have been exclusively concerned with Christ's exercise of his *imperium.* But he is more than *Rector,* he is *Dominus* also, and his kingship involves a right of disposal as well as of government. "He purchased all men from the Legal necessity of perishing that they were in, into his own Power, as their Owner and Ruler, that so he might make over Reconciliation, Remission and salvation to all, if they will believe; and might send forth sufficient means and help of Grace to draw all men towards him: resolving to draw his Elect Infallibly to him."[48] His infallible drawing of the elect, by which He brings them to faith,[49] the covenant condition, is no part of moral government, as such, but the act of a Divine Proprietor "as absolute Lord above Laws."[50] Nor is Christ's statement of His intention thus to draw them any part of the law of his kingdom, the covenant of grace. Those who included absolute promises to the elect in their definition of the covenant, Baxter held, were confusing the exercise of *imperium* and *dominium,* which must be held apart. In fact, Christ bestows varying degrees of grace and opportunity upon different individuals, according to the dictates of infinite wisdom. But this is something quite distinct from his legislation, by which he offers salvation on equal terms to all.

The answer to Baxter's "great and noble question" as to the effects of Christ's

---

46. *C.T.,* I.ii.82:47.

47. In *Universal Redemption* (?1648; see App. I), Baxter wrote cautiously: "whether any Heathen be ever saved? I cannot find that he (God) hath revealed" (474). But in *C.T.,* I.ii.88:49, he is more positive: "when the Scripture assureth us that it is the *Law of Grace* . . . which all the world is *governed by,* and shall be judged by . . . there is so great a probability, that this Covenant, and the mercies of it, are not in vain to *all* of them that are under it alone . . . that an impartial considerer of Gods Nature and Government, may easily see what to think most probable . . . " The same confidence is expressed in *End of Doctrinal Controversies,* 198 f.

48. *Universal Redemption,* 430.

49. "Faith is the effect of that degree of Grace which from his Plenipotency he (Christ) giveth, lest his chosen should miss of the intended salvation" (*op. cit.,* 431).

50. p. 305.

death is therefore as follows: (i) Satisfaction to God's justice; (ii) Consequent benefits to men: (a) "general and common, (as the freeing of all Men from the necessity of perishing, which lay on them by the Curse of the first Law) . . . ," through the promulgation of a new law; (b) special blessings confined to the elect and given to them upon their believing, "Pardon, Justification, Adoption, Sanctification, Glorification."[51] The gift of faith itself, however, is a fruit of election rather than of redemption. All men were redeemed, in the sense that they live under a law of grace in virtue of Christ's death; but only the elect believe and are saved.

In his account of Christ's death as a satisfaction to rectoral justice and a ground for the relaxation of the original penal law, Baxter, as he admits, followed Grotius. But his debt must not be exaggerated. He merely incorporated Grotian detail into a fundamentally Anselmic outline. The essential difference between a Grotian and an Anselmic approach to the atonement lies in what the former overlooks. According to Grotius, satisfaction must be rendered to God, not as God, but merely as governor, *princeps supremus*. But Baxter, a true representative of the Augustinian tradition, saw that God's rectorship was a derived relation to man, grounded on the much more fundamental relation of ownership. Baxter insisted that Christ offered satisfaction to God as God. In all his relationships to man He had been dishonored, and in all of them reparation was necessary if man was to be restored. He criticized Grotius for not making this plain:

> Though I owe much thanks to God for what . . . I learned from *Grotius de satisfact.* yet I must say that in this great question, whether Christ *satisfied* God for sin as *Domino absoluto, vel ut parti laesae, vel ut Rectori*, which (latter) he asserteth *alone*, I take him to come short of *accurateness* and *soundness* . . .

> God is to man, 1. *Dominus absolutus* . . . 2.*Rector supremus*. 3. *Amicus, Benefactor. vel Pater & finis.* Sin is against God in all these *three Relations*. . . . For 1. As our *Owner*, we owe him *total resignation* and *use* as such. 2. As our *Ruler*, we owe him *Subjection* and *Obedience* a such. 3. As our *Friend* . . . we owe him *Gratitude* and *Love* as such . . . Now *Sin* being the privation of *all this*, God is to be satisfied for it as such, in all these three Relations; And he is *pars laesa* in all these three Relations, that is, he is *injured*, though not *hurt*. It is true, that *Government* and *Punishing* Justice, formally as such, belong to God only as Rector. And *satisfaction* is made to him *eminently in that Relation*; yet also to compensate the injury done by sin to him in the other two Relations also.[52]

---

51. pp. 134 f.
52. *C.T.*, I.ii. 150-51:69.

In fact, the basis of Baxter's account of satisfaction had already been put forward in Bradshaw's *"reconciling Tractate of Justification,"*[53] which he probably read long before he studied Grotius. Also, the substance of his doctrine of the new covenant of grace had already been mooted by Arminian and Saumur theologians, one of whom, Placaeus, had already printed an identical account of the last judgment.[54] But it would be a mistake to treat his synthesis as a mere collection of snippets from the writings of others. It had come to him with the force of a new revelation as he brooded over Matthew 25 and "set to study the truth from thence, and from the nature of things, and naked evidence."[55] And the distinctive, integrating idea of the synthesis, the kingship of Christ, was derived from this source. The subject of Christ's kingdom, in one form or another, was "in the air" during most of his life. It was a theme prominent in Scripture, and a topic of peculiar appeal to the seventeenth-century English mind, for which the whole idea of monarchy had a limitless fascination.[56] That Christ was King of his Church, as well as its Prophet and Priest, had been a Protestant commonplace since Calvin. That His crown rights over it must be secured and enforced was the Disciplinarian war-cry. That He would soon return to rule the world was the faith of the Fifth-Monarchists. But that he was enthroned as its ruler already was a position stressed by Baxter. Matthew 25 showed him the King of Kings judging all nations. This convinced him that the Christian theologian moves in the sphere of criminal and constitutional law, and must, therefore, adopt a "political method." The passage told him also that all men, whether or not they had heard of Christ, would at the last day be found in one or other of two

53. *End of Doctrinal Controversies*, 266. Cf. the following extracts: "Satisfaction is, when sufficient amends are made to the party offended for the fault done, by meanes whereof, freedome from punishment is merited . . . Sufficient amends are then made, when the offended partie . . . reapeth as much benefit, at least, as hee should have done if the fault had not been committed . . . Satisfaction made by another . . . may bee eyther by doing or suffering the same kinde of things that the offender ought to have done; or such things as are of another kinde, if of the same worth and value . . ." (Bradshaw, *op. cit.*, vi.1, 2; vii.6, 7; pp. 25, 29).

54. *Theses Salmurienses*, I:32 (1645): "Opponitur justificatio accusationi: a duabus autem accusationibus premimur in foro divino. Primum objicitur, nos esse peccatores: hoc est, reos violatae conditionis quae foedere Legali lata est. Deinde objicitur nos esse infideles; hoc est, non praestitisse conditionem foederis gratiae: videlicet fidem. Ab accusatione priori, sola fide justificamur, qua Christi gratiam et justitiam amplectimur. A posteriore, justificamur etiam operibus, quatenus iis fides ostenditur. A posteriore, justificationem respiciens Jacobus affirmavit merito, ex operibus justificari hominem et non ex fide tantum. Paulus vero respiciens ad priorem, sola fide hominem sine operibus justificari." This way of reconciling Paul and James was also substantially Baxter's; cf. Note B, pp. 263 ff. Baxter does not quote this passage in the *Aphorisms*, but it is often referred to in his later writings on justification.

55. *Aphorisms*, App., 110. Baxter adds: "Not that I therefore repent of reading other mens writings: for without them I had not been capable of those later studies."

56. cf. G. F. Nuttall, *The Holy Spirit*, 121f.

classes: sincere believers, or formal hypocrites, whose works would reveal their real impenitence. All, therefore, must have received some grace; all must have been really invited to faith and obedience; all must have lived under a law of grace. This discovery was the foundation on which everything else in Baxter's system was built. And "when I have oft studied how to forsake my present Judgement, the bare reading of the 25 of *Matthew* hath still utterly silenced me."[57]

The new synthesis, Baxter claimed, was Scriptural.[58] It was the doctrine of the early Church. It was a reconciling doctrine, in terms of which all Papists and Protestants could be brought together; this he tried to show in *Catholick Theologie* and *An End of Doctrinal Controversies.* It was the true corrective, he held, to Arminianism, and equally so to the extremes of those Calvinists who, by their eagerness to deny what Papists and Arminians asserted, had themselves run into error over the doctrine of redemption. We are now to examine these last two claims more fully.

The Arminians, Baxter held, were right in maintaining that redemption is universal in scope, that the whole world is under a law of grace and that reprobation is conditional upon the foreseen rejection of grace offered. They were also right in thinking that a Calvinism which denies any of these positions does in fact represent God as the first cause of the reprobate's sin. But he considered that they "over-did" when they claimed that every man, whether he knows the Christian gospel or not, possesses sufficient grace to make him capable of immediate salvation. This seems to him obviously false. The truth was, rather, that every man has *some* grace, and that if he used it aright he would have more. Baxter states his position carefully in the following passage:

> God hath appointed to the World some means which they are to use for their recovery. I avoid the Remonstrants extream: I say not that all have sufficient means or Grace to believe, or to Salvation. And I avoid the fouler extream, which saith that Heathens are under the meer Law of works . . . and have no Means appointed them, or helps afforded them towards their recovery . . . But he prescribeth some means to all men in the World which they are to use, to bring them nearer Christ and to remove impediments: As to consider of what the Book of Nature and daily providences teach them of God: To study him in his mercies and Judgements. To study their own heart till they find their Sin and misery: To use all their interest and utmost endeavours to enquire what remedy God hath revealed to the World: To continue in Prayer, fasting

---

57. *Of Justification,* 171.

58. "Christ's sermons . . . with all the Sermons in *Acts,* and all the Catholick Epistles of *Peter, James, Jude* and *John,* and *Paul's* Epist. to the *Rom.* . . . and a great part of the rest of his Epistles, are made up of this Doctrine of Grace which I have asserted" (*C.T.,* I.ii.366:123).

and Alms deeds as *Cornelius* did, and to break off their sins by repentance. These are their duties; and for not doing these, in the improvement of their Talents, they shall be condemned by Christ the Redeemer at the bar of grace ... I doubt not but they have sufficient help which is not effectual to the doing of more in these means then they do; and so they will be left unexcusable, at Judgement. Even as the Ignorant and ungodly where the Gospel is preached, have sufficient power (which is not effectual through their own wilfulness) to hear the word ... and to use more means to get Faith then they do, though they have not power or grace sufficient to believe.[59]

All men are far from Christ Naturally, and ... must be brought divers steps or degrees nearer him, before they are brought to the very act of Faith which unites men to him; specially Heathens that are at the remotest distance.[60]

God's sovereignty appears in this inequality of opportunity, while His mercy appears in the fact that the opportunity is real in every case. Again, Baxter held, the Arminians "over-did" in their rejection of unconditional election and irresistible grace, and their refusal to allow that Christ died to save one man more than another. Universal grace was part of the counsel of God for man's salvation, but was not the whole of it. "The Arminians give too little to Christs death, as well as they do to Gods decree, while they make both the elected, and the redeemed to infallible pardon and salvation, to be no Individuals, but Believers in general, assuming that Christs death may have its full end, though none were saved by it."[61] God has done all that the Remonstrants allowed, and more, as Baxter explained in *God's Goodness Vindicated ... with respect to the Doctrine of Reprobation and Damnation*:

And if besides all the mercy that God showeth to others, he do antecedently and positively elect certain persons, by an absolute decree, to overcome all their resistance of His Spirit, and to draw them to Christ ... by such a power as shall infallibly convert and save them, and not leave the success of his mercy, and His Son's preparations, to the bare uncertainty of the mutable will of depraved man, what is there in this that is injurious to any other? or that representeth God unmerciful to any but such whose eye is evil because he is good ...? If they that hold no grace but what is universal, and left, as to the success, to the will of man ... do think that this is well consistent with the mercifulness of God; surely they that hold as much universal grace as the former, and that indeed all have so much, as bringeth and leaveth the success to man's will, and deny to no man any thing which the other give, do make God no less merciful than they, but more, it they moreover assert a special decree and grace of God, which with a chosen number, shall ... infallibly

59. *Universal Redemption,* 117, 122.
60. *op. cit.,* 469.
61. "Confutation of ... Ludiomaeus Colvinus" in *Apology,* 261.

secure his ends in their repentance, faith, perseverance, and salvation. Is this
any detraction from, or diminution of, his universal grace? or rather a higher
demonstration of his goodness; as it is no wrong to man, that God maketh
angels more holy, immutable, and happy.[62]

This was the position held by the Saumur school and the British deputies at
the Synod of Dort.[63] Baxter considered it to be the true interpretation of the
"sound and moderate Doctrine"[64] contained in the Synod's findings
(subscription to which "is my test of the (Calvinist) party"),[65] and defended
the Synod against Arminian attacks as follows. The divines, he insisted,

> give more to Christs death for the Elect then you, but no less that I know of,
> to his death for all then you . . . the Synod thought that Christ purchased
> more for some, then you do; but no less for others . . .

> And seeing this is (I think) undenyable, judge . . . whether it is Christian
> dealing to give out, that they do by restraint of Grace, make God a Tyrant,
> Cruel, not lovely to man, a Dissembler, with abundance of the like; when
> they come not a step behind the Jesuites or Arminians in setting forth Gods
> Love to All, but go beyond them in Extolling his special Love and Grace to . .
> . his Elect . . . they make God more Gracious, and man more sinful and
> impotent then you do, and do not say that which is not so, that they make
> God less Gracious, because they make man more sinful.[66]

As an *ad hominem* reply to Remonstrant criticism, this is clearly unanswerable.

We may here correct a traditional misunderstanding of Baxter's theology
which is found even in so accurate a book as Dr. Irvonwy Morgan's *The Nonconformity of Richard Baxter* (1946). Baxter, it is said, mediated between the
Calvinist and Arminian doctrines of grace by maintaining that each was true
in some cases. The elect would be brought to heaven in the Calvinist way, by an
infallible communication of grace to believe, but others would arrive there by
the Arminian route, having received "sufficient" grace (enough to save them, if
they would use it) and of their own free will made the most of it. Dr. Morgan
affirms that Baxter parted company with Amyraldus on this one point: whereas

62. *Works*, VIII:529 f.

63. cf. *The Collegiat Suffrage*, 47 f: "Christ therefore so dyed for all, that all and every one by
the meanes of faith might obtaine remission of sins, and eternall life by vertue of that ransome
paid once for all mankinde. But Christ so dyed for the elect, that by merit of his death in spirituall
manner destinated unto them according to the eternall good pleasure of God, they might infallibly
obtaine both faith and eternall life."

64. *Confessions*, 23.

65. *C.T.*, I.i.666:124.

66. *The Grotian Religion Discovered*: "The Preface, to the Reverend Mr. *Thomas Pierce*," 9, 35,
36. For Pierce, a convert from Calvinism to Arminianism, cf. *D.N.B.*, s.v.

Amyraldus' universalism was strictly hypothetical, Baxter held that "the elect were lucky, but many others would be saved by taking it."[67] This is a complete mistake. Baxter constantly insisted that God has given every man an opportunity of salvation and that everyone could be saved if he would. But he knew in advance that all but the elect, whom Baxter makes willing, would in fact deliberately reject the Gospel offer. This certainty gave a tragic undertone to his evangelistic preaching, as appears in the following remarkable passage:

> I can foresee the certain damnation of all unconverted sensualists and worldlings . . . but to prevent it is not in my power. For I cannot make you willing to prevent it . . . So that with all sorrow I must say, that now I have said all, and delivered my message, I fear the most will still be the same . . . Though our heart's desire, and prayer, and endeavour must be that the professed Israelites may be saved; yet we must take up our comfort shorter, that the elect shall obtain it, though the rest are hardened. For it is God's will, not ours, that must be done. If Christ be satisfied in the salvation of his little flock . . . even so must we; and though as Samuel did over Saul, so we may mourn over the rest that God hath forsaken, yet that sorrow must know its reason and its measure . . . I shall therefore, according to my duty, beseech you to review and practice the directions which are given you . . . But if you will not hear and take warning, it is because the Lord will destroy you, and because you are not the sheep of Christ.[68]

There the sermon ends; Baxter turns and walks sadly down from the pulpit. He had an evangelist's heart, and his very certainty that none but the elect would ever be willing to turn and live oppressed and burdened him. Elsewhere, with characteristic honesty, he goes out of his way to face the question: "if God were as infinite in mercy as you say, why doth he not make all these men willing, that so they may be saved?" He confesses in effect that he does not know, but has no doubt that there is a good reason.[69] He cannot tell why the elect are so few;[70] but he may not and will not doubt God's wisdom and goodness on the basis of his own ignorance.

Arminianism, Baxter held, represented an extreme of reaction against

---

67. Morgan, *op. cit.*, 79. Stoughton justly observed (*History of Religion in England*, 4th ed., IV:383 f.), "I find no trace of such an opinion in Baxter's books."

68. *Works*, IX:509 f. (from *The Crucifying of the World by the Cross of Christ*).

69. cf. *Works*, IX:32.

70. It is noteworthy that in his later works Baxter records his conviction that the number of the elect will prove greater than was sometimes supposed in Calvinist circles; cf. (e.g.) *C.T.*, I.ii.368:123: "its very probable that (this Earth being a very little *punctum* of the Creation) taking all God's rational Creatures together, the number of the damned will be very small in comparison of the blessed; even as the Malefactors in the Jailes are to the Subjects of the Kingdom . . . Though the proportions be unknown to us, I speak this again, that mistakes tempt not men to unworthy thoughts of the infinite amiable goodness of God, or of the Christian Faith."

Calvinism; and the doctrine of limited atonement represented an extreme of reaction against Arminianism. (Actually, Beza had propounded it before the Arminian controversy began; but Baxter is right so far, in that this controversy gave it a prominence it would otherwise not have had and won it most of its adherents.) Both extremes, in Baxter's judgment, involved the denial of half the doctrine of God's grace: Arminianism denied special grace to the elect, limited atonement denied general grace to the world. The latter doctrine was introduced into England by Perkins and expounded during the 1640's by a number of able writers. Baxter understood it as an assertion that there are some for whom Christ is no sense died, and after his change of view opposed it inflexibly. His *Universal Redemption of Mankind by the Lord Jesus Christ* was written almost at the same time as the *Aphorisms*, though it was not published till 1694.[71] It had the advantage of several revisions, and is one of the most closely knit of his controversial productions. The view that God's saving acts had no reference to any but the elect was a theory attractive for its simplicity and economy; but Baxter had a number of objections to it.

First, it was a novelty within Protestantism, the property (so he informs the Arminian in his "Pacifying Praxis or Dialogue" on the point) of "a few odd conceited persons, driven by you into extreams."[72]

> Our Ancienter Protestant Divines . . . use ordinarily this distinction to solve the doubt, whether Christ died for all? *viz.* he died for all sufficiently, and for the Elect only effectually. And indeed this one distinction . . . is most full and apt for the resolution of the question. The Schoolmen go the same way.

But "our late most rigid Anti-Arminians . . . new moddel their Doctrine . . . and . . . say only that (Christs Death was sufficient to have procured pardon for all men, if he (God) would have suffered it for all)."[73] However, they quickly add, God had no such intention. Baxter's comment is caustic:

> And I will give them this encouragement so far to innovate, *viz.* Though they speak not only against Scripture and the Primitive Fathers, and the Church of Christ in all ages, and the generality of our most severe Protestant Divines; yet because, 1. It is against *Arminius,* an adversary: 2. And tendeth to extreams. 3. And so is agreeable to Nature; they shall perhaps with applause, at least with far less wounding of their Reputation, raise up these novelties, than a Sober, Moderate, Judicious Divine shall bear them down again . . .[74]

71. cf. App. I.

72. *C.T.*, II:63.

73. *Universal Redemption*, 133 f., 141 f.

74. *op. cit.*, 142. Baxter adduces an impressive array of Protestant advocates of the older position in *C.T.*, II:50 f.

Secondly, limited atonement was based on a misconception of the true doctrine of Christ's death:

> Redemption doth not suppose all the redeemed to be Elect by decree, and therefore doth not necessarily infer the Salvation of all the redeemed. They do therefore sorely mistake that suppose Redemption hath this for its direct end, viz. The Salvation of the Redeemed; or that it is its end at all . . . But Redemption lays the first ground of Christs new Empire . . . Upon this groundwork is the whole government of the World built, and all the Judicial proceeding, and execution at the last day: And therefore they that deny Universal Redemption know not what they do: They deny the Foundation of Gods Dominion as Redeemer . . .

> Special differencing Grace begins, in the execution (sc., of the electing decree, whereby the Spirit brings God's chosen to faith); and it confoundeth men in the whole body of Theology when they will needs suppose it to begin where it doth not, that is, in Redemption by Sacrifice.[75]

Christ's redemption includes all men; it is the Spirit's regeneration that is confined to the elect. This was standard Saumur doctrine,[76] interpreted in the light of Baxter's "political" understanding of redemption. Thirdly, limited atonement was exegetically untenable: "the Scripture itself . . . makes it as clear as the light, the Christ died for ALL."[77]

But it was not enough to dismiss the doctrine as a freak. It must be fought tooth and nail, for if taken seriously it undermined Puritan religion in two distinct ways. First, it hamstrung evangelism. Baxter thought of evangelism as the proclamation to every man of the rule of the Redeemer and His deed of gift in the gospel, followed by a demand for submission to the world's rightful Lord. God-redeemer commands all men everywhere to repent, promising them salvation if they do. This is the law of His kingdom, and it is every man's duty, as well as his wisdom, to comply with it. Now it cannot be supposed that God demands the universal acceptance of a salvation which in reality is not universally available. "God doth not offer that which he cannot give (for his offer is a gift, on condition of Acceptance: and we must not dare to charge God with illusory or ludicrous actions.)"[78] But the doctrine of limited atonement, Baxter insisted, represents God as doing precisely that, and turns the preaching of the gospel into hollow histrionics.

---

75. *op. cit.*, 189 f., 347.
76. cf. B.B. Warfield, *The Plan of Salvation*, 93 f.
77. *Works*, IX:35. *Universal Redemption*, 269-376, contains detailed expositions of the controverted texts.
78. *op. cit.*, 104.

Now what ground can a Minister have to press all Men to believe in Christ as
their Redeemer, when they know he redeemed but the smallest part? ... Yea
how can he urge any to rest on Christ at all? For till they know that they are
Elect, they know not that Christ died for them ... And then for the duties of
repentance, Love and Thankfulness to Christ for redeeming them ... this
Doctrine evacuates them all, and so that no Minister can groundedly press
them. And ... how can any Minister in Christs Name assure a sinner of pardon
by that Blood which was never shed for him ... And ... with what Heart can
a Minister tell Sinners, (Christ is a Redeemer but to the Elect, yet all the rest
of you shall perish for not taking him for your Redeemer ...) ... How will
the divulging of these, glorify God? When he has purposely designed the
glorifying of Love and Mercy ... by this great work of the Redemption of the
World ... [79]

In fact, Baxter claimed, the theory's keenest advocates themselves tacitly
abandoned it in the pulpit:

It is the usual way of Preachers in their popular Sermons to speak far more
soundly in these points than in their disputations: ... For they use to lay all
the blame on the Wills of Sinners (and justly) as that only which can deprive
them of the benefit of Christs sufferings, and to urge them to accept him ...
Which is in other words, to say (Christ hath satisfied for all). So that upon
these right grounds they use to bring men to believe and love Christ.[80]

Which, if they squared practice with theory, their own principles would not
permit them do. In the second place, it made faith, love and assurance
unattainable. "As for the act of affiance or recumbency, commonly called the
justifying Act, no man can groundedly or comfortably rest on Christ for
justification by his Blood, who doth not first know that his Blood was shed for
him";[81] "The Soul is never closed to Christ sincerely, till it close in Love ...
Now it is Love that must cause Love ... no man can soundly love Christ as
Redeemer, that knows not Christs love to him ... "[82] Limited atonement thus
introduces a paralyzing ἀπορία into religion; no man can love and trust Christ
till he knows that he is among the elect, and so Christ is available as an object
for his love and trust; but he cannot know that he is elect except by inference
from his love and trust towards Christ. This is a circle out of which it is
impossible to break. And the message of God's love to mankind in general
becomes a hollow mockery when no man can know whether it applies to him
in particular.

79. p. 223 f.
80. p. 153; on p. 176 he illustrates this by a long extract from Perkins ("who hath writ more
confidently against Universal Redemption than he?")
81. p. 168 f.
82. p. 225.

But there was a further consideration against the doctrine: if it were true, hell would be no more hell. "It is generally granted . . . That the Torment of Hell lieth much in the Horrors and Accusations of Conscience."[83] "Do not the consciences of the damned grind and tear them for the contempt of goodness, and setting against mercy . . .? This is the fuel that feedeth hell, not by way of delusion, but experimental conviction . . . For hell and damnation is a state of misery and torment, in the loss, and in the conscience and sense of refused and abused mercy . . . all confess, in heaven and hell, some with joy, and some with self-tormenting anguish, that God was unconceivably good and merciful."[84] Condemned souls are thus their own tormenters:

> I am persuaded, as it was none but themselves that committed the sin, and themselves that were the only meritorious cause of their sufferings, so themselves will be the chiefest executioners of these sufferings. God will have it (so) for the clearing of his justice, and the aggravating of their distress; even Satan himself, as he was not so great a cause of their sinning as themselves, so will he not be so great an instrument as themselves of their torment.[85]

But if Christ died only for the elect, then the damned are in hell, not because they refused what God had provided for them, but because He had provided nothing for them. That they had not striven to enter in at the strait gate was beside the point; they could not have done so if they had. No strait gate exists for any but the elect. "And thus it is evident that on the grounds opposed, the Gospel would causally *per se*, unavoidably be the greatest plague

83. *Universal Redemption*, 251. This conception of hell was common both to Catholic and Protestant thought.

84. *Works*, VIII:517.

85. XXII:377 f. (*Saints' Rest*, III.ii; cf. the whole chapter). Powicke wrongly supposes that this picture of hell (which he illustrates by an extract from *Reasons of the Christians Religion*) "marks an advance" in Baxter's thought (*Under the Cross*, 243). It appears fully developed in his earliest book; cf. 373, a few paragraphs before the passage quoted in the text: "it is by understanding their misery, and by affections answerable, that the wicked shall endure the most of their torments." "Once he had pictured Hell in terms of material fire," Powicke asserts, and quotes part of an assize sermon ("Of the Absolute Sovereignty of Christ") preached c.1648 (*teste* Baxter: *Works* XVII:380) and published in *True Christianity or Christ's Absolute Dominion* (1654); but the key to this imagery is given in the words put into God's mouth at the beginning of the passage in question: "Go seize upon him justice, let my wrath consume thee, let hell devour thee, *let thy own conscience for ever torment thee* . . . " (400: my italics). The passage is admittedly cruder than is usual in Baxter's mature writing. To the question, "An Ignis Infernalis sit noster materialis?" Baxter gave the following characteristic answer: "Animas cruciari per *Ignem Metaphoricum* certum est; id est, Irae Divinae & Reatus sui Dolorosam perceptionem: At non improbabile videtur corpora Igne materiali crucianda. Sapientis autem est huius Ignis cruciatus cura omni potius devitare, quam de natura eius inaniter disputare" (*M.T.*, IV.vi, q. 2:395). [It is certain that souls are tormented by metaphorical fire, that is, sad perception of divine anger and their own guilt. But it does not seem improbable that bodies are to be tormented by material fire. However, the way of the wise is with all care to avoid the torments of this fire, rather than argue uselessly about its nature.]

on earth to all where it comes, except the Elect: and not only accidentally by their own sin":[86] for it would increase condemnation without holding out to the non-elect "any possiblity (*sic*) either of escaping former misery, or this additional misery."[87] The sentence which Christ passes on them at the last judgment, would then take the following form: "I adjudge thee to Hell Fire, for not being redeemed by my blood, and consequently for not having that faith which might have been a sign that I redeemed thee."[88] Now,

> if the damned should then truly know that there was never any possibility of their recovery; and that Christ never died at all for them; nor was their Redeemer; and that if they . . . had believed, it would not have saved them . . . yea that God could not give them pardon and Salvation as purchased by that Blood that was never shed for them, had they believed never so much; will not this take of(f) all the accusations of conscience, and turn all their clamors against God himself? And so make Hell thus far to be no Hell? . . . for an excusing conscience tormenteth none. But whatever Men may say now, I am certain that those miserable damned Souls will have no such alleviation of their misery . . . [89]

But Scripture, reason and present experience unanimously testify that there is no such relief in hell. To the challenge, "How know you what thoughts the damned in hell will have?" Baxter replies thus:

> First: Why read but the 16th of Luke, and you shall there find some of their thoughts mentioned.

> Secondly: I know their understandings will not be taken from them, nor their conscience, nor passions. As the joys of heaven are chiefly enjoyed by the rational soul, in its rational actions, so also must the pains of hell be suffered. As they will be men still, so will they act as men.

> Thirdly: Besides, Scripture hath plainly foretold . . . that their own thoughts shall accuse them, (Rom. 2:15) and their hearts condemn them, I John 3:19-21; *and we see it begun in despairing persons here.*[90]

The last words are important. Following the Puritan tradition,[91] Baxter saw the Spirit's conviction of sin as a case of realized eschatology: "If it (God's

---

86. *Universal Redemption*, 236.
87. p. 233.
88. p. 244. Baxter adds, "But who dare feign Christ Jesus to pass such a sentence?"
89. p. 252 and 254.
90. *Works*, XXII:395. My italics.
91. cf. (e.g.) T. Hooker, *A Treatise of Contrition*, 55: "judge the Lyon by the pawe, judge the torments of hell by some little beginnings of it . . . When God layes the slashes of hell fire upon thy

wrath) seize on the conscience, what torments doth it cause, as if the man were already in the suburbs of hell! ... he is weary of living, and fearful of dying ... Oh! what a pitiful sight is it to see a man under the wrath of God! And are these little sparks so intolerably hot? What then do you think are the everlasting flames?"[92] Every Puritan pastor knew that souls in this condition did not blame their sins upon God, but upon themselves. And so it would be in hell.

Despite its vigor, Baxter's assault on limited atonement cannot be called a success. It is largely an attack on a man of straw. For the advocates of this doctrine never denied that in the gospel Christ is freely offered to all who believe, repent and turn to Him. No one who desired to come would be excluded because he was not of the elect; indeed, this very desire was evidence presumptive that he was one of that number, now being drawn to the Saviour by the Holy Spirit. The certainty that, had they turned to Christ, He would have saved them according to His promise, would be sufficient to feed the recrimination of the reprobate in hell. Baxter's thunderbolts were wide of the mark. In fact, the difference between the two sides concerning the extent of redemption was a corollary of divergence as to its nature. Baxter, basing himself on such passages as Rom. 14:9 ("to this end Christ both died, and rose, and revived, that he might be Lord both of the dead and living"), understood redemption as constituting the ground for an offer of salvation to the world, on condition of faith. Hence he held it to be no less inclusive than the kingdom and law based upon it. His opponents understood redemption as the endurance of vicarious penal suffering, securing to those whose place Christ took a right to both faith and salvation, according to the terms of the covenant of redemption. Hence they concluded that, since God certainly bestows these gifts upon those who have a right to them, Christ could have died for no more

---

soule, thou canst not endure it ... witnesse the *Saints* that have felt it, as also wittnesse the wicked themselves that have some beginnings of hell in their consciences ... If the droppes be so heavy, what will the whole sea of Gods vengeance be?" A famous cautionary tale on this subject was *A Relation of the Fearful Estate of Francis Spira in the Year 1548* compiled by Nath. Bacon Esq., 1649. This was based on *Francisci Spierae ... historia, A quatuor summis viris ... conscripta* (Basle, 1550), part of which had been translated in the year of its appearance as *A notable ... epistle of the famous Dr. ... Gribalde ... concerning the terrible judgement of God upon hym that ... denyeth Christ ... with a Preface of Dr. Caluine,* by E(dward) A(glionby). The Preface, dated Dec. 12th, 1549, shows that the book was published at Calvin's instigation, that men might see God's judgments, and take warning. "The reading of Spira, was almost a tradition in certain Puritan circles" (H. Talon, *John Bunyan,* 1951, 70, n.128). Spira, an Italian lawyer who had been forced by Papal legates to recant after embracing Lutheran views, suffered agonies of remorse for the rest of his life and died convinced that he had sinned away any hope of mercy. In later years Baxter criticized the book: "The reading of Spira's case causeth or increaseth melancholy in many; the ignorant author having described a plain melancholy, contracted by the trouble of sinning against conscience, as if it were a damnable despair of a sound understanding" (*Works,* III:220). Bacon's book was reissued as late as 1688.

92. XVII:402.

than those who actually are brought to faith. A comparison between *Universal Redemption* and John Owen's *Sanguis Jesu Salus Electorum: The Death of Death in the Death of Christ* shows the authors moving in two different worlds of ideas. The real difference between them concerned the true nature of atonement, the proper thought-categories for interpreting the Biblical concept of sacrifice. As long as the nature of atonement remained unsettled, there could never be agreement about its extent. And Baxter was quite wrong in treating the doctrine of limited atonement as a blind reaction against Arminianism. It was, as Owen's book makes clear, an attempt to give its full positive content to the love of the Father and the Son. If Christ's love is equal to all, then it is ineffective for most. Not all believe; few are saved; for many, therefore, He must have died in vain. But the love of God is not impotent; nor will Christ's purpose in dying be thwarted. Therefore, He cannot have died to save any but those whom He saves in fact. This is a clear and positive doctrine of God's saving love and demands consideration as such.

Chapter 10

Justification by Faith

SYNOPSIS

1. Baxter's judgment on the justification controversy:
    errors largely verbal, but dangerous.

2. Historical review of the controversy:
    Loose statements by Luther and Calvin on imputed
       righteousness of Christ:
    the issue whether His sufferings were penal or compensatory
       left open.
    Positions developed in answer to Roman attack:
    (i) Christ's passive righteousness alone personally imputed.
    (ii) Christ's active and passive righteousness personally imputed.
    (iii) Christ's passive righteousness imputed, but not personally
       (Wotton).
    (iv) Christ's active and passive righteousness imputed, but not
       personally (Bradshaw).
    Baxter endorsed Bradshaw's view.

3. Antinomian doctrine of justification (Crisp, Eaton, Saltmarsh):
    (i) Justification analyzed: personal imputation of
       Christ's righteousness to believers,
          their sins to Christ.
    (ii) Justification unconditionally given, before faith: faith
       evidences it.
    (iii) Justification unconditionally continued.

4. Baxter's doctrine of Justification:
    (i) Justification analyzed: constitutive:
                                 faith imputed for righteousness;
                                 how Christ's righteousness is imputed;
                                 judicial;
                                 executive.
    Justification secured and bestowed by Christ.
    (ii) Justification given on condition of a life of faith;
          faith analyzed;
          faith and assurance: Puritan advance on the Reformers;
             Antinomian appeal to the Reformers;
    (iii) Justification continued on condition of a life of faith.

    Corollaries (unacceptable to Protestants generally):
          (i) Twofold righteousness (Christ's and one's own) needed for

present and future justification;
(ii) Faith and works needed for future justification.

5.   *Aphorisms* accused of Socinianism, Arminianism, Popery.
      Baxter not substantially unorthodox;
      why so many of his controversies were futile.
      Fundamental difference between Baxter and other Calvinists: idea of
          law.
      Calvinism: how the law was satisfied;
      Baxter: how the law was changed.

6.   Baxter's motives in arguing his views.

(Principal Sources: *Aphorisms*; *Apology*; *Confession*; *Of Justification*; *A Treatise of Justifying Righteousness*; *Catholick Theologie*, I.ii, II; *Life of Faith*, III.viii (Works, XII); *An End of Doctrinal Controversies*, XXI-XXV; *Scripture Gospel Defended.*)

Chapter 10

Justification by Faith

This, and nothing less than this, is the matter of the gospel . . . God in, and through Christ, will pardon sin to all that leave off sin, and ask him forgiveness, and return to duty. This is the true explication of justification by imputed righteousness; and whatsoever is beyond this is imaginary, and will deceive any man —B. Whichcote, *Aphorisms*, iii:75.

Choose out any one Point of real Difference between you and me about Justification, and come to a fair Trial, on whose side the Churches of Christ have been for 1500 years after Christ —Baxter

I had rather have a Contention that promiseth Holiness and Salvation, then a Peace that doth destroy it —Baxter

B axter's theology came to birth as an answer to mistakes about justification, and he wrote more on this *locus* than on any other. It was here that his orthodoxy was most suspect among his fellow-Puritans, and it was here that he supposed himself to be making his most valuable contribution to theology. The plain truth on the subject, he held , had been needlessly obfuscated by its incompetent friends. He claimed to have disentangled it from their misrepresentations. We may begin by recording his considered opinions on the controversy as a whole. The differences, he came to believe, were more verbal than real:

I believe that yet most of those that . . . err in notions, are not so bad in their *Judgment* of the *matter it self* as their *words import*; but that want of *Skill in Terms* and *Method* hath seduced men of dull wits, slight popular studies, and undigested thoughts, to speak worse than they think.

Error had arisen because the dust of controversy got into men's eyes: "I believe that unskilful contending with the Papists hath occasioned all this . . ."[1] And professional theologians were the worst offenders:

> I am perswaded the common sort of honest unlearned Christians, (even Plowmen and Women) do better understand the Doctrine of Justification, than many great Disputers will suffer themselves or others to understand it, by reason of their forestalling ill-made Notions.[2]

The practical outcome of "notional" errors on justification could, however, be so serious—legalism at one extreme and Antinomianism at the other—that Baxter though it an inescapable duty, though he found it an unpleasing one, actively to oppose such errors as long as they had adherents.

In order to appreciate his doctrine of justification, we must first fill in the background of controversy. He knew that he was joining in a discussion that had been in progress for over a century, and put forward his own position as an answer to questions which others had asked and a settlement of issues which others had raised. We shall, therefore, begin this chapter by reviewing part of "The History of the Controversie,"[3] underlining those aspects of it which to Baxter seemed most significant and which, either by winning assent or provoking reaction, decisively molded his own views.

The seeds of error were sown, Baxter held, in Luther's first proclamation of the truth:

> And when Church-Tyranny and Ignorance, had obscured the Christian Light, the true sence of Justification . . . was much obscured with the rest, and a world of humane inventions under the name of Good works,[4] were brought in to take up the peoples minds . . . Luther . . . did labour to reduce mens minds and trust, from humane fopperies and merits, and indulgences, to Christ, and to help them to the Knowledg of true Righteousness: but according to his temper in the heat of his Spirit, he sometimes let fall some words which seemed plainly to make Christs own personal Righteousness in it self to be every Believers own by Imputation, and our sins to be verily Christs own sins by Imputation . . .[5]

1. "A Breviate" in *Scripture Gospel Defended*, 115 f.
2. "Of . . . Imputation" in *J.R.*, 290.
3. Title of first chapter of the first part of *J.R.*, "Of the Imputation of Christ's Righteousness to Believers . . ."
4. i.e., "Popish bad Works, called *Good* (as Pilgrimages, hurtful Austerities, &c.)" (*J.R.*, "Of . . Imputation," 161).
5. *op. cit.*, 15; cf. (e.g.) Luther, *Galatians*, tr. E. Middleton (1864 ed.), 213: "all the prophets did foresee in spirit, that Christ should become the greatest transgressor, murderer, adulterer, thief, rebel and blasphemer, that ever was or could be in the world": and 220: "they which do believe in Christ, are no sinners, are not guilty of death, but are holy and righteous . . ."

And Calvin, though he had no formal doctrine of imputed righteousness and often defined justification as remission of sins simply,[6] echoed Luther's "dangerous" language.[7] This occasioned a remark which is worth quoting:

> he writes so moderately oft of this very point, that I think his judgment was in sense, in the main, the same with mine. Yet I think his apprehensions of the Doctrines now in dispute, and his expressions of them, were not so clear, distinct and orderly, but that some that come after may see further, and redress those oversights . . . I hope God hath showed me somewhat further in this point, . . . than Calvin hath taught or discovered . . . I hope when the Master-workman hath built the House, his Boy may say, without the imputation of Arrogancy, I have driven two or three pins which my Master oversaw.[8]

The truth about the Reformers seems to be this: They habitually spoke of atonement in the language of legal representation. Christ, they said, *personam nostram sustinuit* at the bar of God, enduring the penalty of the broken law in man's place. But they did not distinguish the two possible ways in which this notion could be developed, nor opt for one rather than the other. The transaction as they described it could be thought of after the analogy either of civil or of criminal law. In the first case, Christ would have paid our *debt*, in the second our *penalty*. In the first case, his righteousness would be imputed to the believer in its effects: to say that Christ's righteousness is reckoned his would then be merely a way of saying that he receives the benefit of legal immunity as a result of Christ's intervention on his behalf. Christ paid the debt; therefore he himself need never pay it. Such a conception is simple. But if the transaction were interpreted in the second way, as a case of penal substitution, the idea becomes more difficult and the pitfalls more numerous. This was in fact the main strand in the Reformers' thought. On the first view, the ground of the

---

6. cf. (e.g.) *Inst.* III.xi:21: "justitiam fidei esse reconciliationem cum Deo, quae sola peccatorum remissione constet . . . ut talis justitia uno verbo appellari queat peccatorum remissio"; 4: "Quarto autem capite ad Romanos (v. 6), primum appellat justitiae imputationem; nec eam dubitat in peccatorum remissione collocare." [The righteousness of faith is reconciliation with God, consisting solely in the remission of sins. In the fourth chapter of Romans (v. 6) he first calls (justification) the imputing of righteousness, and then does not hesitate to resolve it into remission of sins.]

7. cf. (e.g.) *Inst.* III.xi:2; "Christi justitiam per fidem apprehendit, qua vestitus in Dei conspectu non ut peccator, sed tanquam justus apparet." [He lays hold of Christ's righteousness by faith, and clothed in it appears in God not as a sinner, but as righteous.]

8. J.R., "Mr. Cartwright . . . Considered . . ." 227. It is interesting that John Wesley, whose views were similar to Baxter's on this subject, could write: "I think on justification . . . just as Mr. Calvin does. In this respect I do not differ from him an hairsbreadth" (*Journal*, ed. N. Curnock, 1909-16, V:116). It is interesting to find that Baxter does not quote the *Institutio* as a primary authority and did not think it necessary for a student to read it in full. "Calvin's Institutions, or Colonius's abbreviation of him" (*Disputationes Theologicae in quatuor libros Institutionum Joh. Calvini* (1628)) appears among "methods of divinity" of the second rank in Baxter's reading-list (*Works*, V:590 f.). Perhaps Calvin was not sufficiently "methodical" for Baxter.

sinner's acquittal from liability to punishment (i.e., his justification) is the fact that Christ paid the debt he had incurred. On the second view, the ground of justification is God's attribution (*imputation*) of Christ's obedience and suffering to the guilty sinner. The notion is Biblical, but demands careful statement, which in the early days of Protestant theology it did not always receive. In those days, the two lines of thought existed side by side in the minds of the same men without any awareness of inconsistency. Both served to illustrate the position which it was the Reformers' supreme concern to demonstrate and defend, that the sinner's justification is secured, not by his own work, but by his faith in the work Christ did on his behalf. To illustrate this point yet further, they sometimes permitted themselves to speak as if Christ became a sinner in fact at Calvary, and a man becomes righteous in fact when he believes. During the century which followed, Protestant theologians devoted themselves to the task of systematizing, polishing and defending the Reformers' teaching. One of the results of these analytical labors was the discovery of inconsistency between these two lines of thought concerning Christ's satisfaction for sin. Hence arose controversy concerning the nature of imputed righteousness. Moreover, the history of the period reveals how dangerous it was to speak of a real *communicatio idiomatum* between the sinless Son of God and sinful men. This gave rise to Antinomianism. To Baxter's mind, Antinomianism was inseparably linked with one of the two rival views concerning imputed righteousness, and, as we shall see, he was firmly convinced that to fight the one he must fight the other. But this is to anticipate.

To return to the history of the controversy: Protestantism was soon shrouded in the dust-clouds of war, for the Council of Trent declared against justification by Christ's imputed righteousness alone.[9] Baxter reports the subsequent campaign as follows:

> the Papists fastening upon those Divines who held Imputation . . . in the rigid sence . . . abundance of very Learned Godly Doctors fell to distinguish between the Active and Passive Righteousness of Christ; and not accurately distinguishing of Imputation . . . they principally managed the Controversie, as about the sort of Righteousness Imputed to us: And a great number . . . maintained that Christ's Passive Righteousness was imputed to us . . . but that his *Active Righteousness* was not . . . but was *Justitia Personae* to make Christ a fit Sacrifice for our Sins.[10]

---

9. "Si quis dixerit, homines justificari . . . sola imputatione justitiae Christi . . . anathema sit" (Sess. VI, can. xi). By "justify," of course, the Council meant what the Protestants meant by "sanctify."

10. *J.R.*, "Of . . . Imputation," 17. In "A Breviate . . . " (*Scripture Gospel Defended*: 109), he lists "a great part of the famousest divines of the last Age" who took this view, including Ursine, Paraeus, Piscator (with whom it is usually associated, though in fact it goes back to Melanchthon; cf. A. Ritschl, *History of the Christian Doctrine of Justification and Reconciliation*, E.T. 1872, 248), "and Camero, with his most Judicious and Learned followers in France." Lawson held it too; Baxter quotes and discusses the relevant passage from *Theopolitica* in *J.R.*, *ut sup.*, 75 f.

Thus, Baxter observed, error led to error. Roman writers had anticipated Socinus' attack on "Imputation in the rigid sence" (i.e. the reckoning of Christ's whole performance to the Christian's account) as making needless both the pardon of sin and the necessity of personal obedience to the moral law. This forced Protestants to analyze the idea of imputation more closely. Instead of abandoning the "rigid" notion of it, some tried to defend themselves by drawing an artificial distinction between Christ's perfect fulfillment of the precept of the law and his vicarious endurance of its penalty. The explicit denial of imputed active obedience certainly disposed of the objections, but, Baxter held, it was neither intellectually satisfying nor Biblically based.[11] Others, both Lutheran and Reformed, met criticism by providing a positive rationale for the imputation of Christ's active as well as passive obedience; "inasmuch as God in the justification of sinners could not contravene the eternal rule of the law, it was necessary that the justification should proceed upon a perfect fulfilment of the law; and this fulfilment, not being possible for the sinner, had to be accomplished by Christ in his room and imputed." Justification, therefore, was by this party explicitly defined as having two parts: it consisted, they claimed, "*not merely* in the forgiveness of sins, *but also* in the imputation of Christ's righteousness,"[12] founded upon His active obedience. Beza sponsored the innovation, Perkins popularized it in England,[13] and it rapidly gained its place as part of Calvinistic orthodoxy. This view, to Baxter, was worse than the other; not only did it involve the false conception of imputation, but it rested the case for it on a false premise. Man is not justified, Baxter insisted, by a fictitious, imputed fulfillment of the law of works, but in virtue of a real, personal compliance with the terms of the new law of grace. Moreover, the original

11. Cf. the criticism in *End of Doctrinal Controversies*, 125: "it is abusive subtilty to divide *Christ's Performance* into little Parcels, and then say, *This* Parcel is imputed to me for this use, and that for that use, and by one he merited this, and by the other that, when . . . it was only the *entire performance* that was the *Condition* of the *Benefits* . . ."

12. A. Ritschl, *op. cit.*, 250. The argument for imputed active righteousness is stated in a passage which Baxter partly quotes (with disapproval) from Beza (Beza, *Epistolarum Theologicarum liber unus*, 2nd ed., 1575, 248: Baxter, "An Answer to Dr. Tullies Angry Letter" in *J.R.*, 63): "Quid vanius est quam Justum arbitrari, qui Legem non impleverit? Atqui lex non tantum prohibet fieri quod vetat . . . verum praecipit quod jubet . . . Ergo qui pro non peccatore censetur in Christo, mortem quidem effugerit; sed quo jure vitam praeterea petet, nisi omnem justitiam Legis in eodem Christo impleverit?" Paraeus ("Epistola . . . de Justitia Christi Activa et Passiva" appended to his son's revision of his edition of Ursine, 173 f.) says that the question "sitne remissio peccatorum tota an dimidia nostra justificatio" was first discussed "inter Marchiacos (Danish) quosdam theologos" about 1564; "prius vero Ecclesiis Euangelicis ignota fuit." Anthony Wotton (*De Reconcilatione*, 111 f.) attributes the view to Illyricus originally, and its revival to the Danish Lutheran, Nicolaus Hemmingius, whom Paraeus probably has in mind.

13. Perkins echoed Beza in this, as in his supralapsarianism and assertion of limited atonement. Cf. *A Golden Chaine* (*Workes*, I:8): "Iustification hath two parts: Remission of sins, and imputation of Christs righteousness."

criticisms of imputed active obedience remained unanswered. "Inculpability Imputed" "seemeth to me to leave no place or possibility for Pardon of Sin";[14] and an imputed holiness takes away any need for a real one, so that the doctrine must inevitably prove Antinomian.

The true reply to criticism of the Protestant view was, Baxter held, a better and truer analysis of the idea of imputation. This was provided in 1611, when "Mr. *Anthony Wotton* a very Learned and Godly Divine of *London,* wrote a *Latine* Treatise *de Reconciliatione,* one of the Learnedest that hath ever been written of that subject . . . and irrefragably overthrew the rigid Imputation."[15] The book was not published till 1624, but was circulated in manuscript. As might have been expected, the author was accused of Socinianism for his pains.[16] He argued that justification consisted in remission of sins simply and that Christ's passive righteousness was imputed to the believer in the sense

14. *J.R., ut sup.* 102, 99: the twenty-second of forty-three objections brought by Baxter against this theory.

15. *J.R.,* "Of . . . Imputation," 19 f. For Wotton, cf. *D.N.B.,* s.v. The full title of his book, published at Basle, was: *Antonii Wottoni Londinatis Angli de reconciliatione peccatoris, ad Regium Collegium Cantabrigense, libri quatuor. In quibus doctrina ecclesiae Anglicanae de justificatione impii explicatur et defenditur: adversus cum Protestantium quorundam de illis non satis recte, judicantium sententiam, tum pontificiorum, ac praecipue concilii Tridentini, de re ipsa errores.*

16. By George Walker (cf. *D.N.B.,* s.v.), in *Socinianisme in the fundamental point of Justification discovered and confuted,* 1641. This was his reply to *Impedit Ira Animum, or Animadversions vpon some of the Looser and Fouler passages in Mr. George Walker's discourse,* 1641, by John Goodwin (cf. *D.N.B.,* s.v.). Goodwin at that time "(not yet turned *Arminian*) preached and wrote with great diligence . . . against the rigid sence of Imputation" (*J.R., ut sup.,* 21), maintaining that faith, and not Christ's obedience or suffering, was imputed as the sinner's righteousness. Walker accused "Socinian John" of following Wotton. An apologia by Wotton's son Samuel, *Mr. Anthony Wotton's Defence against Mr. George Walkers Charge,* was immediately published in the name of Thomas Gataker, who in fact wrote only the Postscript. In 1642 Walker replied with *A True Relation of the cheife Passages between Master Anthony Wotton and Master George Walker in . . . 1611, and . . . till 1615* (wrongly ascribed to Gataker in *D.N.B.,* s.v.), which Gataker at once met with *An Answer to Master George Walkers Vindication.* Goodwin replied to Walker in *Imputatio Fidei, or a Treatise of Justification,* a full exposition of his views which he had projected before the controversy began, and (a particular answer) *Christ set forth.* Both came out in 1642. Goodwin admitted following Wotton so far, but argued that since the imputation of Christ's active obedience does away with the need of satisfaction for sin, Walker was the Socinian rather than he. On the controversy and Goodwin's doctrine, cf. T. Jackson, *Life of John Goodwin,* 1822, 32 ff. Baxter passed an acid comment on Walker's performance in the *Aphorisms* (53), for which he apologized in his "Admonition to . . . Eyre" in *Apology,* 13 f., "as having no cause to meddle with him . . . I hereby revoke it." He adds by way of explanation that he was provoked by Walker's "exceeding hard language to his Brethren . . . when in discourse and Pulpit he hath done so much for above 20 years, against . . . Mr. *Wotton,* Mr. *Bradshaw, &c."* H. J. McLachlan, who notices the controversy (*Socinianism in Seventeenth-century England,* 1951, 45 f.). thinks it "safe to conclude that Anthony Wotton was rather Arminian in theology than Socinian" (49). But this is false. Wotton was denying one tenet of Bezan Calvinism, with Bradshaw, Gataker, and Baxter. But this did not make any of them Arminians. Justification was not one of the Five Articles. Wotton in fact takes pains to show that Calvin, Luther, Melanchthon and most reformed divines had been on his side (*op. cit.,* 41 f.).

that it was the ground of this remission. In 1615, Bradshaw "attempted a Conciliatory middle way, which indeed is the same in the main with Mr. *Wotton's*: He . . . maintaineth that the Active and Passive Righteousness are both Imputed, but not in the rigid sence."[17] On the basis of a careful Ramist analysis of the notion of satisfaction, which anchored it firmly in the thought-world of civil rather than criminal law,[18] Bradshaw formulated a position which Baxter echoed in the *Aphorisms* as follows:

> though Christs Righteousness be not imputed to us in that strict sense . . . but is ours under the fore-explained notion of Satisfaction only, yet the Active Righteousness considered as such, is part of this Satisfaction also, as well as his [Christ's] Passive . . . and though the Law do not require both obeying and suffering, yet Christ paying not the *Idem*, but the *Tantundem*, not the strict debt itself, but a valuable Satisfaction, might well put the merit of his works into the payment.[19]

In the same passage (1648), Baxter confessed himself a recent convert from the opinion of Wotton and John Goodwin to that of Bradshaw on this point:

> . . . I think it is the truth, though I confess I have been ten years of another mind for the sole Passive Righteousness . . . till discerning more clearly the nature of Satisfaction, I perceived, that though the sufferings of Christ have the chief place therein, yet his obedience as such may also be meritorious and satisfactory.[20]

Baxter was by now convinced that the first of the two accounts of imputation mentioned above was correct. Christ's righteousness, i.e. his satisfaction, was imputed to the believer only in the sense that he reaped the benefits of it. The fact that Gataker, Bradshaw's "bosom-friend . . . a man of rare Learning and Humility," one of "those three persons whom I most highly

---

17. *J.R., ut sup.*, 20. Bradshaw's account of his book's origin is interesting: "I first penned this Treatise to teach my selfe, and have herein opposed my self as much as any man else . . ." He sent written copies to "sundrie Reuerend and learned Divines . . . from whom I receiued . . . divers materiall Animaduersions" which caused him to revise the phraseology (Preface). Wotton was one of the animadverters. The book won high praise, notably from L. Cappellus of Saumur (Life of Bradshaw, by Gataker, in S. Clarke, *Lives of Thirty-two English Divines*, 53 f.).

18. cf. the passage quoted, 225, note 53, *sup.*

19. *Aphorisms*, 54. The *idem* was the statutory penalty, payment of which is *solutio*; the *tantundem* was an acceptable equivalent, payment of which is *satisfactio*. This distinction, borrowed by Baxter from Grotius, caused controversy between himself and Owen, who, in the interests of a rigid doctrine of penal substitution, argued that Christ paid the *idem* in man's place. (See *Aphorisms*, App. 137 f., and Owen, *Of the death of Christ*, 1650, *Works* X:437 f.).

20. *Aphorisms, loc. cit.*

valued for judgment,"[21] "next set in to defend Mr. *Bradshaw's* way, and . . . wrote with great Learning and Judgment in that cause,"[22] may have had something to do with his change of mind, though direct evidence is lacking. Certainly, its immediate cause was his contact with the Antinomians.

About 1640, "the Doctrine of personal Imputation in the rigid sence began to be fully improved in *England*, by the Sect of the *Antinomians* . . . of whom Dr. *Crispe* was the most eminent Ring-leader, whose books took wonderfully with ignorant Professors, under the pretense of extolling Christ and free Grace."[23] Chronologically, the first printed exposition of Antinomian theology had been *The Honey-Combe of Free Iustification by Christ alone*, by John Eaton,[24] "the first founder of this *faction* among us."[25] This was published posthumously in 1642, a year before Crisp's first volume. These books, together with Saltmarsh's *Free-grace*, became the fountain-head of Antinomian theology for the next decade. Their doctrine of justification, which, in view of its importance for the study of Baxter's thought, we shall here expound in some detail, may be summarized in three propositions:

(i) One who is "justified" is "in Christ" in such a sense that both Christ's expiatory suffering and his perfect obedience are accounted by God as done in the sinner's own person. This is God's imputation of righteousness. It is not based on a legal fiction, but on a spiritual fact. The sinner has really become righteous in Christ; for "understanding the course of scripture . . . you shall find that *imputing* is nothing but God's determination and conclusion that he passes upon things, as really and truly they are."[26] Now Christ's righteousness is imputed to man only because man's sins were first imputed to Christ; which, if imputation be thus defined, is as much as to say that Christ became a sinner on behalf of the elect. This Crisp asserted again and again. "It is iniquity itself,

21. *J.R., ut sup.*, 32. The others were Usher and Richard Vines. Baxter met Vines at Coventry (*R.B.*, I:44) and out of respect addressed the *Aphorisms* to him; whereupon he "wrote to me applaudingly" (*R.B.*, I:107).

22. His relevant works were: *Francisci Gomari Disputationis . . . Elenchus . . .* , 1640; *Animadversiones in J. Piscatoris et L. Lucii . . . de causa . . . justificationis . . .* , 1641—Lucius "erred on one side for rigid Imputation" while Piscator "was for Justification by the Passive Righteousness only" (*J.R. ut sup.*, 21); the defense of Wotton and reply to Walker, mentioned on p. 246, note 16 *sup.*; *An Antidote against Errour concerning Justification* (an unfinished exposition of Rom. 3:28).

23. *J.R., loc. cit.* ("Improved" in Puritan jargon means "applied.") For Tobias Crisp, cf. *D.N.B., s.v.* His published works were all posthumous sermons, produced in several volumes under the general title *Christ Alone Exalted*: fourteen in 1643, seventeen in 1644, eleven in 1646, two in 1683, and a collected edition including eight more in 1690.

24. cf. *D.N.B., s.v.*

25. Gataker, *Gods Eye on His Israel*, "To the . . . Reader"; cf. Joseph Hall, Eaton's diocesan, *Works*, 1808, VIII:58: "And what success the dangerous fancies of one Eaton, the father of Antinomianism in this Diocese, hath had, I would rather bewail, than express."

26. Crisp, *Christ Alone Exalted* (reprint of 1832), I:289.

as well as the punishment of it, that the Lord laid upon Christ . . . this is a real transaction; Christ stands as very a sinner in God's eye, as the reprobate . . ."[27] The Son of God became at Calvary "as really and truly the person that had all these sins, as these men who did commit them really and truly had them themselves."[28] Similarly, Eaton speaks of "our sins being imputed to Christ, and he hereby made a sinner."[29] And as Christ became a sinner, so the believer ceases to be such. He is no longer "an idolater, a persecutor, a thief, a murderer, an adulterer, or a sinful person . . . you are all that he was, he is all that you were."[30] Eaton likens a man in Christ to water in a colored glass: "wilst it doth abide in the glasse, it becomes communicatively and passively as blue, or red, as the glasse it selfe."[31] "*A justified person is a perfect Person*," Saltmarsh maintains, "as pure in the sight of God as the righteousness of Christ can make him . . . because God sees him only in Christ, not in themselves . . . *his eyes are purer then to behold iniquity*, or to love a sinner as a sinner."[32]

Baxter accepted the Antinomian analysis of imputation. God judges according to truth; He accounts nothing to be other than it is. But he rejected this theory out of hand. It was philosophical nonsense, since "it feigneth the same Numerical Accident . . . which was in one subject to be in another (*sc.*, Christ's righteousness, transferred to man), which is impossible;"[33] and to suppose Christ "to have been incomparably the worst man that ever was in the World by just reputation . . . guilty of all the sins of all the Elect that ever lived, and reputed one of the Murderers of himself . . . : and the language that *Luther* used Catechrestically, to be strictly and properly true"[34] was the acme of blasphemy. Such a doctrine of atonement must finally discredit the theory of justification which implies it. And every version of "rigid imputation," as far as Baxter could see, implied it of necessity. Its intolerable crudity was due, not to the incompetence of the Antinomians, but to their very consistency. If one held that such a text as 2 Cor. 5:21 speaks of Christ's personal righteousness (as distinct from its fruits) attributed by God to the sinner, one must also maintain that it speaks of the sinner's personal disobedience (as distinct from its consequences) similarly attributed to Christ. The Antinomians were logical, and did so. Nor was this all. Worse was to come.

(ii) According to the Antinomians, the elect are in Christ, and therefore justified, *before* they believe. Faith "serves for the manifestation of that

---

27. *op. cit.*, I:353.
28. *ibid.*, 283.
29. Eaton, *op. cit.*, 363.
30. Crisp, *op. cit.*, 273.
31. Eaton, *op. cit.*, 274.
32. Saltmarsh, *Free-Grace*, 129.
33. Baxter, *J.R.*, "Of . . . Imputation," 94.
34. p. 93.

justification which Christ puts upon a person";[35] "God's love shall not be known to particular men, till they believe; but, considering their real condition, the Lord hath not one sin to charge upon an elect person, from the first moment of conception . . . the Lord hath laid it on Christ already . . . when he paid the full price . . . every elect vessel of God, from the first instant of his being, is as pure in the eyes of God, from the charge of sin as he shall be in glory."[36] The new covenant is, as far as man is concerned, unconditional; it is "*no Covenant, properly with us, but with Christ for us.* . . God agreed to save man, but this *agreement* was with Christ, and all the conditions were on his part; He . . . performed the conditions for life and glory."[37] The elect are consequently in a state of salvation from the moment of birth. Crisp seems to have been the first in England to assert unconditionality of the new covenant.[38] He put it forward as a novelty.[39] Whence he derived it we do not know. We may hazard the guess that he learned justification before faith from Twisse, his neighbor at Newbury,[40] but we cannot prove it.

35. Crisp, *op. cit.*, I:91. He frequently alleges Heb. 11:1 ("faith is . . . the evidence of things not seen") as proof of this position.

36. Crisp, *op. cit.*, I:359 f. Dr. Morgan incorrectly asserts that the Antinomian mistake, in Baxter's eyes, was "emphasizing the all-exclusive necessity of faith without works, as the precondition of justification" (*op. cit.*, 80). His phrase would fit Baxter's own view. The mistake Baxter attacked was the idea that there was no precondition of justification at all, but that justification was rather the precondition of faith.

37. Saltmarsh, *op. cit.*, 125 f. Such remarks prompted Baxter's comment: "Distinguish carefully between that Decree, Law or Covenant . . . whereby the Father did, as it were, appoint unto his Son both his work and Reward; and that Law, or Covenant by which both Father and Son do govern the Church, and make over to us the parts of our own salvation. Confounding these hath lost the Antinomians their Theologie . . . they do take notice of . . . little more than the Promise of the Father to the Son" (*Confession*, 290).

38. Baxter thought so: "All Divines, ancient and modern, reformed and unreformed, that I know of, agreed with us in the conditionality of the said Promise . . . till *Maccovius* in *Holland* and Dr. *Crispe* and other Antinomians in England . . ." ("A Breviate . . ." in *Scripture Gospel Defended*, 20). J. Maccovius had put forward his views in *Collegium disputationum . . . de justificatione peccatoris coram Deo* . . . , 1637. Whether Crisp depended on this book is not known. Baxter dismissed it as "wilde stuff . . . which I had once thought to have confuted" ("Confutation of . . . Ludiomaeus Colvinus" in *Apology*, 301).

39. cf. Crisp, *op. cit.*, I:86 f. The Antinomians found the exegetical basis for this assertion in Jer. 31:31 f. (quoted, Heb. 8:8 f.) and Ezek. 36:25 f. They held that these passages depicted the covenant as an unconditional promise of regeneration for the elect (Crisp, *loc. cit.*; Saltmarsh, *loc. cit.*) Baxter disagreed, "the context satisfieth me, that these Texts speak not of the first Grace" (*J.R.*, "Mr. Cartwright . . . Considered," 65, cf. *Aphorisms*, 91). In these passages, faith (which the "first Grace" creates) is presupposed, as the condition of the benefits there specified.

40. Twisse certainly approved of Crisp's theology; Samuel Crisp, *Christ made Sin*, 1691 (a defense of his father's positions), Preface, quotes his encomium of them. He "had read Dr. Crisp's sermons, and could give no reason why they were opposed, but because so many were converted by his preaching, and (said he) so few by ours." Baxter records an interesting snatch of gossip from an unnamed member of the Westminster Assembly (?Richard Vines or Anthony Burgess?) which

(iii) The third Antinomian position followed from the two already laid down. As justification was given unconditionally, no qualification in the subject being required, so it is unconditionally continued. "The sins of God's peculiar people, that have God for their God, can do them no hurt at all."[41] God never has seen sin in His elect and never will. When He looks upon them, He sees only the perfect righteousness of His Son. No amount of actual carelessness and sin on the part of a believer should therefore be allowed to unsettle his assurance of final salvation.

We shall now set out in three corresponding positions the doctrine of justification to which Baxter came as he sought the Biblical answer to his Antinomian opponents.

(i) The definition of justification which legal and political science provides, represents it as a forensic act involving three distinct operations:

1. Making us righteous and judicially justifiable.
2. Judicial justification (1. By Plea. 2. By Evidence and Witness. 3. By Sentence.)
3. *Using us* as righteous by Execution.[42]

The first (*constitutive* justification) is effected by the lawgiver through his law. A law constitutes a man righteous as he keeps it. "Righteousness" means, simply, a relation of conformity to the law. A man who keeps the law is righteous and, therefore, "judicially justifiable": he has acquired a right to acquittal if accused of breaking it (*judicial* justification) and to the treatment proper to law-abiding persons (*executive* justification). In the light of this analysis, Baxter understood the sinner's justification by grace as follows: (a) His initial act of faith, forsaking sin and receiving Christ, is an act of compliance with the precept of the Divine law now in force, the law of grace which commands all men everywhere to repent and promises an amnesty to those who do. It is thus an act of righteousness, and God imputes it to him as such. Paul states that faith is reckoned for righteousness (Rom. 4:2, 9), and this, Baxter insisted, is what he means. The Antinomians were correct when they insisted that imputation must not be thought of as a fiction or a mistake on God's part. God reckons a man to be nothing more nor less than what he is. "God never judged a man righteous that was not righteous."[43] But a believer is righteous, for he has obeyed the law; and therefore his faith is counted as righteousness. The assertion, "Christ's

perhaps points to dependence: "the Antinomians being questioned, did plead Dr. *Twisses* authority; and the Assembly questioning him ... (while he was Moderator) he was able to say little ..." This must have been late in 1643, when a committee was preparing a report on Antinomianism for the Commons.

41. Cisp, *Christ Alone Exalted*, II:119.
42. *End of Doctrinal Controversies*, 242.
43. p. 243.

righteousness is imputed to believers" is not a Scriptural form of expression, but is "tolerable" if carefully glossed: it must be taken to mean, not that believers are in any sense supposed to have done and suffered what Christ did and suffered ("that rigid Imputation"), but that they benefit from Christ's obedience. Christ by dying procured the new covenant, by which they are justified when they believe. This is, of course, a loose use of the word "impute"; in the strict sense, all that is imputed to them is their own faith. Constitutive justification is actually effected through faith: thus, "we are justified by faith, as soon as ever we beleeve."[44]

(b) Judicial, or, as Baxter sometimes calls it, "sentential" or "declarative" justification, to which the believer has by his faith acquired a right, takes place at the last day. We have already seen what will occur on that occasion. Satan accuses; each man's life is examined; the Christian's faith is proved to have been genuine by the evidence of its works; and the Father and Son together pronounce him not guilty of breaking the law and acquit him accordingly. It is with reference to this process that the Bible sometimes represents justification as future.[45] Baxter took the distinction between constitutive and declarative justification and his analysis of the former from John Goodwin's *Imputatio Fidei*. Lawson would have had him amend it: "I have sore contest with Mr. *L.* and all will not convince him, that *any but sentential* is properly *Justification;* and that which I call *Constitutive* . . . [he thinks] is but *Right to Justification,*"[46] he wrote in 1652. But he continued to maintain the propriety of his usage.

(c) As for executive justification, the bestowal of the benefits and rewards promised in the law upon those who obey it, this "is partly in this life, *viz.* in giving the spirit, and outward mercies, and freeing us from judgements (And thus sanctification it self is a part of Justification)[47] and partly in the life to

44. *Aphorisms*, 184. Baxter instances Rom. 4:2, 5:1, 9, and James 2:21, 25 as referring to present justification. (On the latter, cf. Note B, 263 *inf.*)

45. Baxter instances Rom. 3:30, 2:13, and Matt. 12:37, with the comment: "I think the word in Scripture hath most commonly reference to the Judgment day" (*op. cit.*, 184 f.).

46. *J.R.*, "Mr. Cartwright . . . Considered," 165. Lawson's position, as Baxter summed it up in his manuscript review of their differences, was that, as soon as a man had by believing acquired a right to it, justification followed, i.e. "a sententiall Act of God as Judge in the Soule as his Publique particular Bar" (Mss. 59.xiii, f. 333a). Baxter found the idea unconvincing.

47. This ("reconciling") assertion was founded on Rom. 8:30, 1 Cor. 6:11 and Tit. 3:7, which texts "Many Protestants, and among them *Beza* himself, expound (in the Papists and *Austins* sense of Justification) as including Sanctification also, as well as Absolution from the Curse: And so Arch Bishop *Usher* told me he understood them" ("Of . . . Imputation . . . " in *J.R.*, 134). Baxter accepted this view, and adduced Rom. 8:33 and Rev. 22:11 as cases of the same usage (*loc. cit.*) This interpretation of the texts cited was widely accepted in the seventeenth century (cf. M. Pool, *Synopsis Criticorum*, 1684-86, V. col. 394, on I Cor. 6:11). The case for it was most fully argued in a book which Baxter often praised (and with specific reference to this point, cf. *Works*, XII:317), Ludovicus Le Blanc's *Theses Theologicae* "which I published (he sent them to me to publish, and I gave them to my Bookseller to print, and he sold his Copy to another)," *End of Doctrinal Controversies*, 21.

come, in freeing us from Hell, and possessing us of Glory."[48] It is begun as soon as a man believes. Thus, justification appears, not as a single momentary event,[49] but as a complex, tripartite Divine act, which begins with a man's first faith in Christ and is not completed till he has received his whole reward in the world to come.

Justification, in each of its parts, was secured for and is conveyed to the believer by Jesus Christ. He made it available by offering satisfaction for sin and so obtaining the right to enact the law of grace; He published that law, the new covenant; and now, as the world's King, He rules by it, condemning the disobedient and justifying the righteous. In the first place, He

> made the Law of Grace . . . As it is a Law, it is the Act of a King . . . as it is founded in his death . . . it is called his Testament . . .

> Secondly, Justification by sentence of Judgement is undeniably by Christ . . . For God hath appointed to Judge the World by him . . . To deny these things, is to deny Principles in Politicks.

> Thirdly . . . the Execution of the sentence by actual liberation, [is] . . . the act of a Rector . . . So our actual Justification in all three senses is by Christ as King.[50]

This is presumably a reference to the English edition, published by Moses Pitt in 1683, in which the relevant passage is p. 255 f. Owen confuted Le Blanc's exposition (in *The Doctrine of Justification by Faith*, 1678, *Works*, V:130 f.), and it seems to have been generally abandoned after that.

48. *Of Justification*, 72. The third element in justification is first distinguished in this book. The passage quoted in the text was probably written in 1657, but the distinction appears in the earlier dispute with Blake, dated November, 1656 (65). In the *Aphorisms*, Baxter had dichotomized the concept, and merely noted of the second member (in which the execution of the sentence was included), "The title of Declarative is too narrow for this last" (185). Late in 1653, he reproduced the dichotomy but observed that to do justice to all the Biblical evidence each member must be taken in a larger sense, "putting us into a right to . . . felicity . . ." being included in the first, and "adjudging . . . to a greater glory" in the second. He saw that Paul treats justification as more than the negative blessing of acquittal and non-liability to punishment, associating it with a positive bestowal of new privileges and rights, but he accounted for the evidence as follows: "I suppose that the term *Justification* is Scripture, is commonly taken in the . . . strict sense, for meer remission of sin, or making us relatively righteous . . . ; yet so as to connote, or imply the concurrence of some special Gospel-priviledges; which when particularly intended, are rather expressed by *Adoption, Membership of Christ* &c. then by Justification" ("Confutation of Ludiomaeus Colvinus" in *Apology*, 235). This bestowal of new blessings became "executive justification" when Baxter trichotomized the concept.

49. On this point Baxter acknowledged a debt to George Downame's *Treatise of Justification*, 1633, a broadside against Bellarmine: "it was not so clearly discerned by Divines till Dr. *Downham* had evinced it, that Justification is a continued Act, and not . . . so *simul et semel* as to be ceased, as was before taught" (*Plain Scripture Proof*, 194; cf. Downame, *op. cit.*, I.i.6-7:5 f.).

50. *Of Justification*, 24.

No other doctrine in Baxter's opinion exalted Christ more than justification, and no other version of that doctrine more than his own.

(ii) The condition upon which justification is given to the elect (for "Eternal Electing to Justification, is not Justifying")[51] is faith. Baxter defines it with some care:

> The faith by which we are justified[52] ... is best understood by the Baptismal Covenant, and is essentially a *Believing Fiducial consent* to our Covenant relation to God the Father, Son, and Holy Ghost, as our Reconciled Creator and Father, our Saviour, and our Sanctifyer, connoting the forsaking of all inconsistents ... [53]

It is analyzed in terms of the doctrine of human nature as follows:

> Justifying faith hath three Parts, ASSENT, CONSENT, and AFFIANCE ... ASSENT is but initial and introductory to the rest, as all acts of the Intellect are to those of the Will. CONSENT is the same which we here call ACCEPTING (*sc.* in the phrase, "accepting Christ"), which is but the meer VOLITION denominated from its respect to the offer and thing offered. This, as it is in the will, the commanding Faculty, so it is as it were the Heart of Faith; the first act being but to lead in this, and AFFIANCE the third, being commanded much by this, or depending on it: For as it is seated in the Affections, so far it is distinct from this *Velle* or CONSENT. Now when ever we name *Faith* by one of these three acts (as the Scripture doth from every one) we include them all ... by one word we express the whole. And all those Acts have whole Christ in all the essentials of his Person and Office for their object.[54]

To believe the gospel, commit oneself to Christ and ground all one's hopes upon Him involves a number of physical and psychological events, but is a single, simple moral action, performed, not by this or that faculty (the faculties, as we saw, are abstractions, not parts of man), but by the man himself. It is the

---

51. "A Defence" in *Scripture Gospel Defended*, 61.

52. Baxter characteristically notes that the phrases "justifying faith" and "faith justifying us" are not Scriptural; "and though they may be well used with explicatory caution" (he used them so himself) it is better to follow Biblical usage and speak simply of justification ἐκ or διὰ πίστεως (*C.T.*, I.ii.107:55). For faith is not the *efficient cause* of justification, nor is it the *instrumental cause*, as Protestants had traditionally held. In the only appropriate sense of instrumentality, i.e. the legal sense, the new covenant is the instrument of justification. Faith is simply the *condition* (*causa sine qua non*) upon which God's performance of His promise depends. "The receiving of Christ, is as the silver of this coine: the Gospell-promise is as the Kings stamp which maketh it currant for justifying" (*Aphorisms*, 230 f.).

53. *C.T.*, I.ii.106:55.

54. *Of Justification*, 302 f.

response of the whole man to the whole Christ. Repentance, "our consent to return to God, and the change of our minds, by turning from former sin that was our Idol, and being willing by Christ to be restored to obedience,"[55] is the obverse of faith. Baxter habitually illustrates faith by the Biblical analogies of a woman giving herself to a man in marriage and an invalid putting himself in the hands of the doctor. Sometimes he pictures it as the act of a rebel accepting a pardon offered him on condition of enlistment in the royal army. Central to faith is the act of will, to which assent leads and from which affiance flows. Baxter thus rejected the Antinomian idea of faith as assurance of one's own justification and election in favor of the standard Puritan view ("our English divines in this point are the most sound of any in the world").[56] Puritan teaching seemed to him greatly in advance of what had been said by the Reformers and their Continental successors, to whom the Antinomians made appeal. They had (he was sure) here misstated their own mind:

> Do you think that *Calvin* . . . with the stream of great renowned Forreign Divines (specially the first Reformers) did none of them know *what justifying faith was?* . . . And yet did these men take justifying Faith to be either *Assurance* or *Perswasion* of the *pardon of a mans own sins in particular,* and say, He that hath not this *Certainty* . . . hath no Faith; and even lay a mighty part of Doctrinal Reformation and difference between us and the Papists in this? And yet almost all our English Divines (except Antinomians) and most others, do now generally disclaim that Doctrine as erroneous, and place justifying Faith in Affiance, Recumbency, Assent or Acceptance . . . confessing that *Assurance* . . . to be a separable fruit.[57]

This, to Baxter, was another instance of the dismal effects of controversy. To counter the Roman demand for *implicita fides* in the Church's teaching as such, the Reformers had maintained that *fides divina* was an intelligent assent to the Biblical gospel as true because God-given, together with a firm confidence that the mercy therein declared extends to oneself—i.e., that one's sins are forgiven and one's hope of glory certain, which the Papists denied that a Churchman could ever know. This *fiducia*, the Reformers argued, marked off the faith of true Christians from the dead faith of devils (and, of course, Papists). These polemics, in Baxter's judgment, necessary and valuable as they were in many ways, had obscured the truth about faith in two respects.

In the first place they had focused attention exclusively on the area of disagreement. The Reformers had written as if they accepted the adequacy of the Roman view of faith as assent on authority, and differed only as to what

55. *Confession,* 39.
56. *Works,* XXII:489 note.
57. *J.R.,* "Mr. Cartwright . . . Considered," 228.

must be believed and whether the proper authority was the Church or the written Word. But in fact part of the Reformers' case was that the Roman conception of faith was seriously incomplete. Faith was more than mental assent on God's authority; faith was action as well as belief. Faith, as they made plain in their sermons, lays hold of Christ, and works by love. It is a matter of the will as well as of the intellect. But this was not always made clear in their formal, controversial discussions. In the second place, they met the Roman denial of the ordinary possibility of assurance by speaking as if assurance was essential to faith.[58] But this assertion would not bear examination. Faith rests upon God's written Word; but the proposition that one is elect and justified is no part of that Word, and so it can be no part of faith to believe it. Assurance, as we have seen already, is in reality an inference, faith's fruit. Here, as on the subject of imputation, the Antinomians had taken up the Reformers' looser statements and treated them as the whole truth. Faith, they held, was simply and solely mental assent to the proposition, I am a justified and elect child of God. They made great play with excerpts from the Reformers which, isolated from their context, appeared to assert as much.[59] Long before Antinomianism emerged, however, Puritan pastors had discovered and corrected the Reformers' mis-statements. "Practice discovereth some truth, which mere disputing loseth."[60] Practice brought Baxter to endorse the Puritan account both of the nature of faith and of its relation to assurance.

> I do contradict both the Papists that deny assurance, and many foreign writers, who make it far more easy, common and necessary than it is . . . But I stand in the midst between both extremes; and I think I have the company of most English divines. I come not to be of this mind merely by reading books, but mainly by reading my own heart, and consulting my own experience, and the experience of a very great number of godly people of all sorts, who have opened their hearts to me, for almost twenty years' time . . . See whether all those divines that have been very practical and successful in the work of God, and much acquainted with the way of recovery of lost souls, be not all of the same judgment as I in this point, (such as T. Hooker, Jo. Rogers, Preston,

---

58. Calvin (e.g.) defines faith as *fiducia*, making assurance essential to it: *Inst.* III.ii.7.16: "justa fidei definitio nobis constabit, si dicamus esse divinae erga nos benevolentiae firmam certamque cognitionem, quae gratuitae in Christo promissionis veritate fundata, per Spiritum Sanctum et revelatur mentibus nostris et cordibus obsignatur;" "vere fidelis non est, nisi qui solida persuasione Deum sibi propitium benevolumque patrem esse persuasus, de eius benignitate omnia sibi pollicetur . . . Fidelis, inquam, non est nisi qui suae salutis securitati innixus, diabolo et morti confidenter insultet."
59. Eaton made great play with testimonies from Luther and Calvin in *The Honey-combe*: in 1645 Saltmarsh declined to quote Luther in his favor, as he might have done, because "hee is now lookt on by some, as one that is both over-quoted, and over-writ free-grace" (*Free-Grace*, 210).
60. Baxter, *Works*, XXII:489.

Sibbes, Bolton, Dod, Culverwell, etc.) And whether the confidentest men for the contrary be not those who study books more than hearts, and spend their days in disputing, and not in winning souls to God from the world.[61]

Faith may well be present without any assurance of its presence; the man who knows that he has sought does not always know whether he has yet found: but reliance on Christ as Savior was inseparable from submission to Christ as King. Without this, a profession of faith was hypocrisy and a hope of heaven was presumption. "What is the reason," Baxter inquires rhetorically, "that *Perkins, Bolton, Hooker, Preston, Taylor, Elton, Whately* ... spend most of their labour to bring men to obey Christ as Lord, and not the hundredth line or word to press them to Trust that he will pardon and save them? All the powerfull Preachers that ever I heard ... zealously cry down laziness, lukewarmness, negligence, unholyness ... As that which would be the liklyest cause of the damnation of the people ..."[62] The answer is plain. Full assurance of faith was not needed for final salvation, but the obedience of faith was salvation's *sine qua non.*

(iii) The continuance of justification depends, according to Baxter, on the sincere discharge of the duties implicit in the relationship to Christ which the first act of faith created.

> In our first Believing we take Christ in the Relation of a Saviour, and Teacher, and Lord, to save us from all sin, and to lead us to glory. This therefore importeth that we accordingly submit unto him, in those his Relations, as a necessary means to the obtaining of the benefits of the Relations. Our first faith is our Contract with Christ ... And all Contracts of such nature, do impose a necessity of performing what we consent to and promise, in order to the benefits ... And in humane contracts it is so. Barely to take a Prince for her husband may entitle a woman to his honours and lands; But conjugal fidelity is also necessary for the continuance of them: for Adultery would cause a divorce ... Covenant-making may admit you, but its the Covenant-keeping that must continue you in your priviledges ...[63]

Much more is therefore required for final, declarative justification than for the initial, constitutive justification: "Faith, Repentance, Love, Thankfulness, sincere Obedience, together with finall Perseverance, do make up the Condition of our final Absolution in Iudgement, and our eternal Glorification."[64] To the

---

61. *Works,* IX:96f (1653). In 1648, Baxter wrote of Preston's doctrine of faith: "*I* find him speaking my own thoughts in my own words: and begun to think when *I* read him, that men would think *I* borrowed all from D. *Preston*" (*Aphorisms,* App., 110, 112, where Baxter adduces detailed testimonies from Preston's writings).

62. *Of Justification,* 174.

63. p. 123 f.

64. *Confession,* 56.

first act of faith must be added a life of faith; and final perseverance is not only a gift of God to His elect, but a stipulated condition of justification at judgment. Constitutive justification lasts no longer than faith. "The Law of Grace . . . is . . . not changed by our believing, and therefore continueth to justifie only Believers: and should we cease believing that promise would cease justifying." Baxter adds, however, that since God has "decreed to maintain the faith of this chosen people to the death," "the conditionality of the promise is nothing against the Certainty of perseverance."[65]

Over and over again, through his "more explicate, distinct, necessary delivery of common Truths,"[66] Baxter outraged Protestant susceptibilities, but never more completely than by two of the positions involved in the doctrine expounded above. The first was the doctrine that "as there are two Covenants, with their distinct Conditions: so there is a twofold Righteousness, and both of them absolutely necessary to Salvation."[67] The first is *legal* righteousness, so denominated from the law of works. "Our Legal righteousness is not personall . . . (For we never fulfilled, nor personally satisfied the Law;) but is wholly without us in Christ. And in this sence it is that the *Apostle* (and every Christian,) disclaimeth his own Works, as Being no true legall Righteousness."[68] Had it not been for Christ's obedience, the new covenant would never have been made, the law of works would be still in force, and all would be condemned under its terms. Christ's fulfillment of that law was therefore essential for the justification of anyone. But a man only qualifies for pardon under the new covenant when he believes. And his faith, as such, as we have seen constitutes him righteous. This is *evangelical* righteousness. Unlike the first, it is the believer's own: "all out of Christ in ourselves (though wrought by the power of the Spirit of Christ)."[69] It qualifies a man for the salvation which the new covenant offers, and is thus no less necessary for his salvation than the righteousness of Christ which procured that covenant in the first place. Baxter was in later life willing to term the believer's "rewardableness" or "Evangelical worthiness" *merit*. About 1670 he wrote:

> I have formerly thought, that though we agree in the thing, it is best to omit the *name* (i.e. merit), because the Papists have abused it; And I think so still . . . where the use of it not understood will scandalize men . . . But in other cases I now think it better to keep the word, 1. lest we seem to the ignorant to be of another Religion than all the ancient Churches were. 2. Lest we harden Papists, Greeks and others, by denying sound Doctrine in *terms*, which they

65. "An Unsavoury Volume . . . Anatomized" in *Apology*, 48.
66. *Of Justification*, p.176.
67. *Aphorisms* (XVII), 102.
68. *op. cit.* (XVIII), 103 f. Baxter cites as proof of his statement Phil. 3:7,8.
69. p. 121 f.

will think we deny in *sence*. 3. Because ... I remember no other word so fit to substitute instead of (Merit) or (Worthiness). The word (Rewardable) is long and oft harsh: And what other have we?"[70]

Baxter used his doctrine of the need for a twofold righteousness as a weapon against the Antinomians. He warned them that their neglect of the second would leave them sadly unprepared for the last day, when they would have to answer Satan's charge of hypocrisy. "It will be but a senceless shift in such an accusation," he told them, "to show Christs Legall Righteousness in stead of our own Evangelicall Righteousness. To tell Satan, that Christ hath fulfilled the law for us, when he is accusing us of not fulfilling the Gospell; ... Satan is a better Logitian than to take *quid pro quo*, and to be baffled with such arguing ..."[71]

The second position involved in Baxter's doctrine was even more shocking to his Protestant contemporaries. A man, Baxter held, is justified (sententially, at judgment) *by faith and works*. "Both justifie in the same kinde of causality, *viz.* as *Causae sine quibus non* ... Faith as the principal part; Obedience as the less principall. The like may be said of Love, which at least is a secondary part of the Condition."[72] He put this thesis forward with some trepidation:

> I know this is the doctrine that will have the loudest out-cries raised against it: and will make some cry out, *Heresie, Popery, Socinianism*! and what not? For my own part the Searcher of hearts knoweth, that not singularity, affectation of novelty, not any good will to Popery, provoketh me to entertain it; But that I have earnestly sought the Lords direction upon my knees, before I durst adventure on it: And that I resisted the light of this Conclusion as long as I was able. But a man cannot force his own understanding, if evidence of truth force it not ..."[73]

The Bible, he held, was unambiguous as to the necessity of "evangelical obedience" for justification at the last day:

> It seemeth strange to some, to find the whole Old Testament, and all Christ's Sermons, and all the other Apostles, inculcating *inherent* and *performed* Righteousness, as that which Men must be judged about, to Life or Death, and yet to find *Paul* so oft pleading against Justification by Works. But if we will take the Scripture together, and not by incoherent scraps, the reconciliation is evident ...

---

70. *End of Doctrinal Controversies*, 295. He had already expounded his sense of "merit" in the *Aphorisms* (XXVI), 137 f.

71. *Aphorisms*, 204.

72. *Aphorisms* (LXXIV), 290.

73. pp. 290 f.

Works of Evangelical gratitude, love, and obedience, according to the Law of Grace, subordinate to, and supposing Redemption and the free gift of Pardon and Life to penitent believing Accepters, are those that Christ and *James* and all the Scripture make necessary to Salvation; and our Consent and Covenant so to obey is necessary to our first or initial *Justification*; and our *actual Obedience* to the *Continuance* and *Confirmation* of it. But a Task of Works either of *Moses's* Law or any other set against Redemption and free Grace, or not as aforesaid, duly subordinate to them, is disclaimed by Paul and all Christians, as that which can constitute no man just in God's account.[74]

We can now see why the *Aphorisms* caused such a furor when first published. For his denial of "rigid imputation," their author was duly accused, as he had expected, of Socinianism.[75] John Owen observed darkly in 1653 that there was "too great evidence of very welcome entertainment . . . given by many to an almost pure *Socinian Justification*, and *Exposition of the Covenant of Grace*,"[76] and when in his *Confession* Baxter "opened the weakness of Dr. *Owen*'s Reasonings for Justification before Faith . . . he wrote an Answer, annexing it to his Confutation of *Biddle* and the *Cracovian Catechism* (to intimate that I belonged to that Party)."[77] The answer itself broadly hinted as much. The general antipathy to Baxter's insistence that the reception of Christ as Lord was an essential part of faith seems to have been due to fear that this was the thin end of the Socinian wedge. His insistence that faith was imputed as righteousness, coupled with his advocacy of universal redemption, a semi-Grotian theory of atonement and the conditionality of the new covenant, exposed him to the charge of Arminianism. His assertion of justification by faith and works and the merit of a believer's own righteousness so misled John Crandon (a complete stranger) that he "got a deep conceit that I was a Papist, and in that persuasion wrote a large Book against my *Aphorisms*, which moved laughter in many, and pity in others."[78] Crandon's friend Eyre had already stigmatized Baxter's doctrine as Roman,[79] and in fact the suspicion persisted

74. *End of Doctrinal Controversies*, 252 f. On the reconciliation of Paul and James, cf. Note B, *inf.*
75. Not that this meant much in 1648: "In some mens mouths, *Socinianisme* is but . . . a stone to throw at the head of any man that saith not as they . . . But I had rather study what is Scripture-truth, then what is *Socinianisme*: I doe not think *Faustus* was so *Infaustus*, as to hold nothing true: That which he held according to Scripture is not *Socinianisme*" (*Aphorisms*, 306).
76. Epistle prefixed to William Eyre's *Vindiciae Justificationis Gratuitae*, which Baxter answered in *Apology*.
77. *R.B.*, I:111; referring to Owen's *Of the Death of Christ, and of Justification* appended to *Vindiciae Evangelicae* (1655).
78. *R.B.*, *loc. cit.* Crandon's book, *Mr. Baxters Aphorisms Exorized and Anthorized*, was the "unsavoury volume" which Baxter anatomized, partly in his *Confession* and more fully in his *Apology*.
79. *op. cit.*, "To the Christian Reader": "I am sure he (Baxter) gives as much unto Works and lesse unto Christ then the Papists do." Eyre tries to prove this by comparing Baxter's theology with Stephen Gardiner's, as reported by Foxe.

throughout his life. His denial of the Reformed view that faith is not the condition, but the instrument of justification lent color to all these charges. But in fact Baxter's alleged heterodoxy amounted merely to this: he had assimilated the four characteristic Protestant positions concerning justification (that it is a forensic act, done in this life; that it is grounded on Christ's satisfaction; that it is secured through faith; and that a dead faith justifies nobody) to his "political" doctrine of the new covenant as a legal instrument for its conveyance; and he had distinguished two decisive moments in justification, one present and one future, where other Protestants recognized only the first. The charges brought against him were ludicrous. But we can see why they were made. His readers were completely bewildered by the "political method." It involved re-definition right and left: terms like law, works, merit, righteousness, justification, imputation, instrument, all meant something different in Baxter from what they meant in the rest of Protestant literature. Few had the patience or the ability to master his method and definitions; consequently, a great deal of breath and ink were wasted in confuting what he would have meant had he been using these key words in their accepted sense.

The controversial wranglings between Baxter and his critics on justification make tedious and unprofitable reading, for the two sides make no intellectual contact at all. Both Baxter and the orthodox Calvinists had perfectly consistent positions, granted their first principles, and constructive discussion between them could only take place at the level of their first principles. But their endless acrimonious dissections of each other's statements never got down to this level. The only issue of these exchanges was that each side learned to state its own position more accurately. The root difference between Baxter and orthodox Calvinism, from which all their other disagreements sprang and to which they can all be reduced, may here be pin-pointed. It concerned the idea of law. We will conclude this chapter by setting side by side the two contrasting conceptions.

To orthodox Calvinism, the law of God is the permanent, unchanging expression of God's eternal and unchangeable holiness and justice. It requires perfect obedience from mankind, on pain of physical and spiritual death, and confers salvation and eternal life only upon those who perfectly obey it. God could not change this law, or set it aside, in His dealings with men, without denying Himself. When man sins, therefore, it is not God's nature to save him at the law's expense. Instead, He saves sinners by satisfying the law on their behalf, that He might continue just when He becomes their Justifier.[80] In the covenant of redemption, made from all eternity on the foresight of man's sin, Christ undertook to become man, and, as man, to fulfill the law's demands in place of the elect. This he did by bearing its penalty, the price of disobedience,

80. Rom. 3:26

and by fulfilling its precept, the price of life. His performance was imputed to the elect, not as something which God falsely supposed them to have done in their own person, but as a covenanted grant. By the covenant of redemption, the Son had become surety for them.[81] He was to represent them in the eyes of the law, and what He did in their name was to be reckoned to them. The Father had undertaken to treat Christ and the elect as one mystical person, which in time they actually become when Christ by His Spirit unites His own to Himself. Thus, the covenant of redemption bestowed upon the elect a right in the Father's sight to the same glory that Christ as man was to merit for Himself, and a right to justification in virtue of Christ's pledged vicarious obedience and death. This right was theirs from eternity. The actual imputation of Christ's righteousness to them, and their consequent actual justification (i.e., their acquittal by God from all liability to punishment—Baxter's "sentential" justification) takes place when they come to faith. Faith is not their righteousness, nor is it imputed as such, for it does not satisfy God's law in any sense. The office of faith is simply to unite them to Christ, in whom justification is found. Faith is God's gift. Psychologically, it is man's act of leaving sin and closing with Christ, but theologically it is to be thought of as God's implanting of the capacity to receive what He has prepared for His people. Justification is a single event. It will be manifested and confirmed at the last day, but not repeated nor re-enacted, much less called in question. God's law has been fully satisfied.

Baxter's "political method" led him to a very different idea of God's law. To him, God's justice is precisely a rectoral attribute, a characteristic quality of His government, and His laws are no more than means to ends. Like all laws, they may under certain circumstances be changed, if the desired end is attainable by other means. When man had fallen, and God purposed to glorify Himself by restoring him, He carried out His plan, not by *satisfying* the law, but by *changing* it. God's law is thus external to Himself. The penal law of works, with its sanction of death for sin, was enacted, not because it was a natural and necessary expression of the Divine character, but rather because efficient government required it. The demand for retribution was grounded in the nature of government rather than in the nature of God, and could be dispensed with if it seemed wise. Where orthodox Calvinism taught that Christ satisfied the law in the sinner's place, Baxter held that Christ satisfied the Lawgiver and so procured a change in the law. Here Baxter aligns himself with Arminian thought rather than with orthodox Calvinism. And from this source, as is now clear, all his differences with orthodoxy on the subject of justification took their rise.

We may think that Baxter was wrong; we may even judge him wrong-headed; but we must recognize that it was not gratuitous pedantry that drove

81. Heb. 7:22.

him to new ways of stating old truths. He was sure that they were Scriptural and necessary for the Church's holiness and peace. He had come to them— perhaps we should say, they had come to him—on what he thought was his deathbed, and he believed that God had sent him back from the grave's mouth to spread them. More and more he came to see himself as a chosen vessel, charged to teach the doctrine which alone could reconcile the Churches and save Reformed religion from an Antinomian landslide. When the "dogmatical word-warriours"[82] of his own day refused to hear him, he put it in print "for the times to come, when Fruits of malignant faction and Wars, have disgraced them, and made the world aweary of them."[83] The success of the *Aphorisms* and *Saint's Rest* had led him to suspect this wider vocation. For three years he tested it against doubts born of diffidence, wringing animadversions out of his friends and driving his "restless uncessantly-pained Sceleton"[84] to compose an almost endless succession of replies; by 1653 he was sure of it. We may disagree with him, but at least we need not mistake his tireless zeal in propagating his views for mere arrogance or cantankerousness.

NOTE B: PAUL AND JAMES ON JUSTIFICATION. (cf. p. 252)

Baxter's reconciliation of Paul's assertion of justification without works in Romans and Galatians with James 2:14-26 is worth quoting in full:

> 1. They (Paul and James) debate different questions. 2. And that with different sorts of persons. 3. And speak directly of different sorts of works. 4. And somewhat differ in the sense of the word Faith. 5. And somewhat about the word Justification. 6. And they speak of works iu (*sic*) several Relations to Justification.

> I. The Question that *Paul* disputed was principally Whether Justification be by the works of the *Mosaical* Law, and consequently by any mercenary works, without Christ, or in Co-ordination with Christ ...? The question that *James* disputed, was, Whether men are justified by meer believing without Gospel-obedience?

> 2. The persons that *Paul* disputed against, were, 1. The unbelieving *Jews*, that thought the *Mosaical* Law was of such perfection to the making of men righteous, that there needed no other . . . Where specially note, that the

---

82. *C.T.*, title-page.

83. *End of Doctrinal Controversies*, Preface (dated Jan. 21, 1691). The title-page of *C.T.* proclaims that the book was "written chiefly for Posterity ..." The title-page of *M.T.* (1681) directs it to the rising generation of theological students. Baxter had retired to Acton in 1663 "that I might set myself to writing, and do what I could for Posterity" (*R.B.*, II:440).

84. *Of Justification*, 181; from a letter to Anthony Burgess in 1650.

righteousness which the *Jews* expected by that Law, was not (as is commonly imagined) a righteousness of sinless obedience . . . but a mixt Righteousness, consisting of accurate Obedience to the *Mosaical* Law in the main course of their lives, and exact sacrificing according to the Law for the pardon of their sins committed . . . so that these two they thought sufficient to justifie, and lookt for the *Messias* but to free them from captivity, and repair the Temple, Law, &c. And 2. Paul disputed against false Teachers, that would have joyned these two together (the Righteousness of *Moses* Law, and faith in Christ) as necessary to life. But *James* disputed against false Christians, that thought it enough to salvation barely to believe in Christ . . .

3. The Works that *Paul* speaks of directly, are the services appointed by *Moses* Law supposed to be sufficient, because of the supposed sufficiency of that Law . . . yet by consequence, and a parity of Reason, he may well be said to speak against any works imaginable that are set in opposition to Christ . . . and that are supposed meritorious, and intended as Mercenary. But *James* speaks of no works, but Obedience to God in Christ, and that as standing in due subordination to Christ.

4. By *Faith* in the Doctrine of Justification, *Paul* means our Assent to all the essential Articles of the Gospel, together with our Acceptance of Jesus Christ the Lord, as such, and affiance in him; that is, To be a Believer; and so to have faith, is with *Paul*, to be a Disciple of Christ, or a Christian . . . But *James* by faith means a bare ineffectual Assent to the Truth of the Christian Religion, such as the Devils themselves had.

5. *Paul* speaks of Justification in its whole state, as begun and continued. But *James* doth principally, if not only speak of Justification as continued...

6. ...*Paul* speaks of works as the immediate matter of a legal personal righteousness, in part or whole. But *James* spoak of Works, not as answering the Law, but as fulfilling the condition of the Gospel, and implyed (as promised or resolved on) in our first believing...[85]

Though this exposition involved Baxter in much controversy, it is not substantially different from the normal Reformed view, as expounded by (e.g.) Owen and Thomas Manton.[86] All agree in stating the questions to which Paul and James address themselves, and in differentiating their usage of "faith." Owen and Manton understand James to be referring (v. 21, 23, 24) to the manifestation (by its fruits, good works) of that justification which Abraham had received thirty years earlier (cf. Gen. 15:6). Baxter objects that James is talking about the *occurrence*, not the manifestation, of justification, and understands James

---

85. *Of Justification*, 153 f.
86. See Owen, *The Doctrine of Justification by Faith*, XX, *Works*, V); Manton (for whom, cf. *D.N.B., s.v.*), *Practical Commentary . . . on . . . James, ad loc.* (*Works*, 1873, IV).

to be defining the condition of continued justification as works of "evangelical obedience." By these, faith is made "perfect" (v.22), i.e., effective to its proper end, the attainment of sentential justification at the last day. Each fresh work of faith may be said to "justify" a believer inasmuch as it keeps him in a justified condition. But the difference between Baxter and the others is for practical purposes non-existent; since all agree that James is warning "gospel hypocrites" against expecting final salvation without works, and reminding them that a barren profession saves nobody; a point on which Manton and Owen insisted no less than Baxter. This is a good illustration of Baxter's exegetical ingenuity and of the substantial agreement on practical issues which underlay his verbal dissent from his fellows.

Chapter 11

The Seals of the Covenant

SYNOPSIS

1.   Aim of chapter: to study Baxter's teaching as to the meaning and subjects
      of the sacraments.

2.   Evolution of Baxter's views on   baptism
                                       the Lord's Supper.

3.   Baxter's definition of sacraments:
             mutual seals and pledges
             signifying faith in Christ
             sealing a relation to the Trinity.

4.   Credible profession of faith admits to the sacraments.

5.   Baxter's defense of infant baptism against Baptists:
             a question comparatively unimportant primarily concerning
                   infants' church membership.
             Infants' church membership proved from
                   Nature (legal analogies)
                   Scripture
                   incredibility of alternatives.
             Infants' right to baptism depends on
                   parents' faith
                   parents' dedication of children themselves.
             Children's salvation depends on parents' duty and
                   their own faith, when capable of faith.

6.   Effects of infant baptism:
             not spiritual regeneration
             not bare signification without sealing
             but public investiture into a state of privilege
                                                     acceptance.
             Salvation of believers' children dying in infancy certain;
                   no certainty as to other infants so dying.

7.   Baxter's objection to Anglican rite of infant baptism:
             references to spiritual regeneration;
             part played by godparents.

8.   Conclusion: Baxter ably states the Reformed position.

(Principal Sources: *Plain Scripture Proof of Infant Church Membership and Baptism; More Proofs of Infants' Church Membership and Right to Baptism; Review of the State of Christian Infants; Christian Directory*, "Christian Ecclesiastics" (V); *Confirmation and Restauration, the means of Reformation and Reconciliation* (XIV); *Catechising of Families*, XLV-XLVI (XIX).)

Chapter 11

The Seals of the Covenant

A sacrament is an holy ordinance instituted by Christ; wherein, by sensible signs, Christ, and the benefits of the new covenant are represented, sealed and applied to believers. —Westminster Shorter Catechism, q. 92.

W e have already seen that Baxter's theology was built on the axiom that God's published laws must be kept distinct from His secret decrees. We have seen him re-shape the Puritan doctrine of the covenant of grace so as to confine it to the first of these two categories. We are now to watch him do something similar with the Reformed doctrine of the significance and proper subjects of the sacraments.

Both sacraments had caused him prolonged doubts and scruples in the early years of his ministry, in the days when "I considered not the Tenor of the Covenants distinctly."[1] In "The History of the Conception and Nativity of this Treatise" prefixed to his *Plain Scripture Proof of Infants Church-Membership and Baptism* (1650), he recounts the development of his views on baptism as follows:

> By that time I had baptized but two Children (at Bridgnorth) I begun to have some doubts of the lawfulness of Infant-Baptism. Whereupon I silently forbore the prastise (*sic*), and set my self, as I was able, to the study of the point. One of my temptations was the doctrine of some Divines, who run too far in the other extream. I had read Dr. *Burges*, and (some years after) Mr. Bedford for Baptismal Regeneration,[2] and heard it (in) the common prayer,

---

1. *Aphorisms*, 160.
2. Cornelius Burges (cf. *D.N.B.*, *s.v.*), *Baptismal Regeneration of Elect Infants professed by the*

that God would bless Baptism to the Infants Regeneration (which I thought they had meant of a Real, and not a Relative change). I soon discerned the error of this doctrine, when I found in Scripture that Repentance and Faith in the aged were ever prerequisite . . . and that signs cannot . . . be the Instrument of a reall change on Infants . . . and that to dream of a Physical instrumentality, was worse than Popish, and to do that in Baptism, which Transubstantiation hath done in the Lord's Supper; even to tie God to the constant working of a miracle . . . [3]

If this was the doctrine of infant baptism, Baxter would have none of it. For a time he reacted violently towards believer's baptism, as the simple way out. "And I was unhappy also in my acquaintance (as to this) conversing (*sc.*, at Bridgnorth) with those only whose hearts were better than their heads, suspecting things because imposed . . ."[4] Further study convinced him that the case for infant baptism was probably sound. "Yet did I remain doubtful some time after, by reason the Scripture spoke so sparingly to the point, and because my apprehensions of those things which in themselves were clear and certain, remained crude and weak till time had helped them to digest and ripen . . . And being more in doubt about the other Sacrament than this, I durst not adventure upon a full Pastoral Charge, but to preach only as a Lecturer, till I were fully resolved." At Coventry in 1644 he gave a series of lectures on the

---

Church of England, according to the Scriptures, the Primitive Church, the present Reformed Churches . . . 1629; T. Bedford (*D.N.B., s.v.*), *Vindiciae Gratiae Sacramentalis . . . I. de efficacia sacramentorum in genere; II. de effectu baptismi quantum ad parvulos; quibus praefigitur epistola Joan. Davenantii . . .*, 1650. This volume consists of Bedford's B.D. thesis, with the "determination" of the Moderator, Samuel Ward (*D.N.B., s.v.*) the then Lady Margaret Professor, to the effect that "sacramenta non ponentibus obicem conferunt gratiam" (33 f.), plus a thesis and its defense by Ward, "Omnes Baptizati Infantes sine dubio justificantur" (115 f.), and preceded by a letter from Davenant, Ward's predecessor, on infant baptism. (This, translated by J. Allport, was published separately in 1864. In it, Davenant maintains that all children rightly baptized receive the "relative grace" of a justified status and right to glory, but not spiritual renewal.) Usher had sponsored the publication, and provided Ward's contributions from the latter's papers. Bedford had himself copied Davenant's letter when Ward showed it to him in Cambridge years before ("Praefatio ad Lectorem"). Bedford also published *A Treatise of the Sacraments*, 1638, and *Some Sacramental Instructions*, 1649, on this same subject. "Till of late, I scarce ever spoke with any Divine of note but misliked Dr. *Burges,* and Mr. *Bedfords* doctrine, and it gave general distast to the godly Ministers and People," Baxter commented in 1650 (*Plain Scripture Proof,* 336).

3. "The true History . . . " prefixed to the *Plain Scripture Proof,* (2); cf. *Second True Defence,* 168: "I did in 1640 Baptize two by the Liturgy, (without Crossing) and never more in six or seven years after, because of the imposed corruptions." Actually, Baxter's scruple went deeper than this; see the text.

4. *loc. cit.* It was at this time that Baxter was impressed with the idea that infant baptism was a possible disadvantage to children, as encouraging them to take their salvation for granted: "I once inclined to these thoughts my self"—"about 23 and 24 years of age" (*More Proofs of Infants-Church-Membership,* 107, 101).

subject, which "cost me more labour than ever I am like to bestow upon any again." On that occasion, "I read all the Books for Rebaptizing that I could get," and as a result "arrived at a full Resolution,"[5] which the subsequent overhaul of his theology served only to confirm.

The nature of his "doubt about the other Sacrament" appears from the following passage in the *Aphorisms*:

> But the great Question is, Whether the Sacrament doe seal . . . (That I am justified, and shall be saved)? . . . No . . . Otherwise . . . no Minister can groundedly administer the Sacraments to any man but himself, because he can be certain of no (other) man's justification and salvation, being not certain of the sincerity of their Faith . . . every time he mistaketh, he should set the seale of God to a lye . . . I confesse ingenuously to you, that it was the ignorance of this one point which chiefly caused mee to abstaine from administring the Lords Supper so many yeeres . . .

He goes on to diagnose the reason why such mistakes as this should ever be made:

> one errour drawes on many, and leadeth a man into a labyrinth of absurdities . . . our Divines being first mistaken in the nature of justifying faith thinking that it consisteth in (A Beliefe of the pardon of my own sinnes) . . . have therefore thought that this is it which the Sacrament sealeth.[6]

In the days when Baxter had distinguished justification *in foro dei* and *in foro conscientiae*, and so had confused faith with assurance, the problem of discerning the proper recipients of the Lord's Supper had seemed insoluble. How could Baxter pick out the elect? So he abstained from sacramental ministrations altogether, and waited for more light.

It is evident that when he left Kidderminster in 1642 his mind was very hazy on sacramental subjects. But he returned (in June, 1647) with a revised theology and a new understanding at this point. The first Easter Sunday after his return he commenced regular celebrations of the Lord's Supper, as appears from the following intriguing testimony to the effect of the "Fasting and earnest Prayers" of his "poor, honest, praying Neighbours" on his own behalf:

> Once when I had continued three Weeks, and was unable to go abroad, the very day they prayed for me, being *Good-Friday*, I recovered, and was able to Preach and Administer the Sacrament the next Lord's Day; and was better after it: (It being the first time that ever I administered it): And ever after that

---

5. "The true History . . .", (4).
6. *Aphorisms*, App., 69 f.

whatever Weakness was upon me, when I had (after Preaching) administered the Sacrament to many hundred People, I was much revived and eased of my Infirmities.[7]

Next, on January 1st, 1649/50, he nailed his colors to the mast in the matter of infant baptism. This was the date of his great debate with Tombes at Bewdley, "in the open church, and that fasting, from before ten of the clock till between four and five."[8] Hitherto, "I had never baptized an Infant (but the two fore-mentioned)"—i.e., none at Kidderminster—"till some of my own hearers began to suspect me to be of his (Tombes') judgment (though I testified my approbation by my presence at the ordinance)."[9] The outcome of the day's battle was the publication of his *Plain Scripture Proof*, his third book, which put his position out of doubt.[10] It is the doctrine of the sacraments expounded there and in his later writings that we are now to examine.

Baxter defines a sacrament as "A solemn dedication of man to God by a vow expressed by some sacred ceremony, signifying mutually our covenant to God, and God's reception of us and his covenant with us."[11] Each sacrament is a "mutually engaging sign,"[12] the seal of a mutual compact. "Sealing testifyeth the full consent of the party sealing... that no Adversary may have any exception against the parties right to whom it is sealed: And this full Testimony of the Sealers Consent doth stronglier oblige himself to the performance of his promise."[13] Thus the sacraments serve to strengthen faith; they assure the recipient that God will do His part in the covenant and pledge him to do his own. "Both Sacraments rightly used are a mutual Sealing to the mutual Covenant.[14] God does not by them seal absolute, unconditional promises of grace to the elect, as Tombes maintained ("a strange wild Doctrine ... liker to Mr. Saltmarsh and the Antinomians");[15] they are sacraments of the gospel, not of God's secret decree. "It is only the conditional promise which God sealeth

---

7. *R.B.*, I:80 ("we had 600 that were Communicants," 85). The passage quoted above from the *Aphorisms*, written late in 1648, refers to Baxter's abstinence as a thing of the past and thus enables us to identify the Easter Sunday in question. Perhaps bad health has prevented him from beginning a sacramental ministry earlier.

8. For the debate, cf. *R.B.*, I:96 (quoted in Orme's "Life," *Works*, I:681 f.) and the "True History ..." There is a full account in Powicke, *Life*, 224 f.

9. "True History ...," 9. Presumably his assistant, Sergeant, had officiated on these occasions.

10. Baxter's other books on infant baptism are: *More Proofs*... (1675); *Review of the State of Christian's Infants* (1676); and "Ecclesiastical Cases of Conscience," nos. 33-51, in *Christian Directory* (V:318-370).

11. V:449; Baxter there observes that the word derives from the Roman military oath.

12. *Plain Scripture Proof*, 113, *et al.*

13. p. 324.

14. "Answer to ... Blake" in *Apology*, 91.

15. *Plain Scripture Proof*, 223; cf. the whole section.

by the Sacraments (*If thou believe in the Lord Jesus, thou shalt be saved*)."[16] On God's part, they certify and guarantee the promise of the new covenant. On man's part, the reception of them publicly signifies acceptance of the terms proposed. Receiving a sacrament is an act that expresses faith in Christ.

> It is Christ himself first in order, and then his benefits that are offered in the Sacraments. The main business of them is to exhibit Christ himself to be received by a marriage Covenanting. The signs are but means and instruments, as a twig and turfe and Key in giving possession; When the minister in Christs name saith, Take, Eat, &c. it is not only bread he bids men take, but first and principally Christ by Faith . . . It is one of the greatest errors that can be committed in the Sacraments, to overlook Christ himself who is offered, and to look only either to the signs or to his other gifts . . . it is saving faith that is called for to the due receiving of the Sacraments.[17]

As Baxter often describes faith as a marriage-covenant, so he habitually thinks of baptism as a marriage-ceremony, "the solemnizing of our marriage with Christ"[18] by visibly and publicly professing faith in Him; and this profession is renewed each time the baptized person partakes of the Lord's Supper. Faith is a necessary part of the definition of a sacrament, for "the internal covenanting of a penitent, sincere believer, is necessary for the being of it."[19] Of baptism, therefore, Baxter maintains:

> The word baptism is taken but equivocally or analogically at most, when it is taken for the mere external administration and action;

> Whenever baptism is mentioned in Scripture, it means (The Engagement of the Person to Jesus Christ by solemn Covenant, which Washing is appointed to solemnize).[20]

The believer's covenant with Christ is thus the primary and central significance of baptism. But one who receives Christ thereby enters into covenant with the whole Trinity, as the baptismal formula declares, and a Trinitarian form of statement is needed for a full exposition of the sacrament's meaning, thus:

---

16. p. 223.

17. "Answer to . . . Blake" *ut sup.*, 101; cf. XIX:515 (*Poor Man's Family Book*): "Here Christ for life is delivered to us, and we accept him; and man delivereth himself up to Christ, and Christ accepteth him."

18. "Answer to . . . Blake" *ut sup.*, 86; cf. XIX:274: "baptism is to Christianity what public matrimony is to marriage, ordination to the ministry, enlisting to a soldier, and crowning to a king."

19. V:45.

20. *loc. cit.*; R.B., App., 55.

> In baptism, it is our very relation to God, as our Father and God, to Christ as
> our Saviour, and to the Holy Ghost as our Sanctifier, that is sealed to us, and
> we are invested with . . . As in marriage the persons in relation are given to
> each other for marriage ends; so in baptism, God the Father, Son, and Holy
> Ghost, one God in three persons, are solemnly given to us in relation to
> themselves, for Christian baptismal ends.[21]

The sacraments seal and confirm this relationship, which faith creates.

Sacraments, therefore, both express and confirm man's faith. To receive
them is to profess faith in and acceptance of Christ as Lord and Saviour, God
as Father, and the Spirit as Sanctifier. No adult, therefore, should be admitted
to them without a "credible profession" of such faith; that is, one which is
intelligent, serious, voluntary and not contradicted by the rest of the applicant's
words and life.[22] Since baptism is the appointed rite of admission into the
household of faith, the visible church, this is as much as to say that no adult
may be admitted to church membership without such a "credible profession."
Two extremes must here be avoided: on the one hand, the opinion of Thomas
Blake, who argued that "dogmatical" or "historical" faith, i.e. mere belief that
the Gospel is true, as distinct and divorced from personal committal to Christ,
qualifies a man for church-membership and baptism;[23] and on the other, the
practice of most of the "gathered" churches of Baxter's day, who regularly
conducted a detailed inquisition into the evidence for a candidate's election
before admitting him to membership. This, Baxter held, was unwarrantable
from Scripture and tended to exclude humble saints whose faith was no less
genuine for being tongue-tied. He was never at a loss for a word himself; but
one of the most endearing sides of his character was his deep sympathy for
saints less articulate than himself, and he often rises to their defense against
"church-gatherers" who would not look twice at a person unless he could give
an eloquent testimony concerning his spiritual experience.[24] In fact, Baxter
maintained, a simple profession of consent to the baptismal covenant was all

---

21. XIV:461.

22. *Confirmation and Restauration, the necessary means of Reformation and Reconciliation*
(sc., of Episcopal, Presbyterian, Erastian and Independent disagreement as to the proper
qualifications for church membership), 1658, Prop. VI (*Works*, XIV:425 f.); *Certain Disputations
of Right to the Sacraments*, 1656, 9 f.

23. Argued by Blake in *Vindiciae Foederis*, 1653, ch. XXXII, 241 f.; *The Covenant Sealed*, 1655;
attacked by Baxter in "Answer to . . . Blake" *ut sup.*, 58 f., and in *Certain Disputations, passim* (a
reply to *The Covenant Sealed*).

24. cf. his warning to the Associated Ministers on the occasion of instituting church discipline
(*Christian Concord*, "Explication . . . ," 40): "Above all take heed (in the Name of Christ I warn you)
that you be not cruel to Christs Lambs: that you shut them not out for want of meer words.
Experience hath ascertained me, that there are Christians that are much with God, powerfull in
secret grones and strivings, and do understand the substance of the Fundamentals and much
more . . . who yet are not able to give a Minister or understanding friend any considerable account

that a minister was entitled to require in such cases.

> The case stands thus. God saith in his covenant, He that believeth shall be saved, and ought to be baptized, to profess that belief, and be invested in the benefits of the covenant; and he that professeth to believe, (whether he do or not,) is by ... baptism to be received into the visible church. Here God calleth none but true believers ... and so I say that none other have right *in foro coeli.* But yet the church knoweth not men's hearts, and must take a serious profession for a credible sign of the faith professed, and for that outward title upon which it is the duty of the pastor to baptize the claimer. So that the most malignant, scornful hypocrite, that maketh a seemingly serious profession, hath right *coram ecclesia,* but not *coram Deo,* save in this sense, that God would have the minister baptize him.[25]

For

> Christ hath so contrived in it (*sic*) the Gospel, that every man shall be either the Introducer of himself by Profession, or the Excluder of himself by the rejection of Christianity.[26]

How, on these principles, was it possible to maintain against Baptist attack the propriety of baptizing infants, who were incapable of any profession at all, credible or otherwise? We may premise our exposition of Baxter's answer to this question by noticing, first, that he thought the whole question of the subjects of baptism comparatively unimportant. "Baptism is not in the Apostles Creed."[27] Disagreement in baptismal practice, therefore, was no ground for separation. Baxter's chief objection to Baptists was, not their antipaedobaptism, but their schismatic tendencies, which had alienated him from them even when he sympathized with their theology.[28] If they were heretics, it was schism which

---

of their Faith: Partly through bashfulness, but most through some secret natural unreadiness of speech ... Take heed what you do with poor ignorant men and women that live well ... "

25. V:326 f.; with a reference to the first of *Certain Disputations* ("Whether Ministers may baptize upon a bare Verbal Profession ... without ... requiring any further evidence of sincerity? *Aff.*")

26. *Certain Disputations*, 38.

27. *Plain Scripture Proof*, 329.

28. Already in his debate at Coventry (1643?) with Benjamin Coxe (*D.N.B.*, *s.v.*), who un-churched all Christians that had not been baptized at age, prior to his "full resolution," "my zeal for unity and Peace was so much greater then my zeal against Rebaptizing, that I resolved to dispute the case of separation first ... professing, that if they did not ... sin against the plain word by Divisions, I should easily bear with any that differed from me in the point of Baptism" ("True History ... ," 4 f.). When in 1659 "there was a Treaty in *London* for the Reconciling of the *Presbyterians* and *Independents*, I did first at home to the Ministers of *Worcestershire*, maintain by a set disputation, that it was our *Duty to seek Peace and communion with the Anabaptists*; and after sent up the *Terms* ... to *London*" (*Review* ..., 2; for Baxter's proposals, cf. *R.B.* II:180 f.).

made them so: "I take not a meer Anabaptist for a Heretick: no nor those that hold greater errors then they, except they also divide and rent the Church ... Scripture and Fathers place very much of the nature of Heresie in Schism and separation."[29] In the second place, we must observe how Baxter formulated the issue between the Baptists and himself. The questions, how much water and how soon, were secondary and ancillary issues; what mattered was the status of Christians' children in the covenant and the Church. Baxter always formulated the *status quaestionis* between himself and the Baptists as follows: "we are first to agree, *Whether Infants may be Church-members, and under the Covenant of Grace with their Parents?* And then we shall next consider, at *what age*, and in *what manner* they should be _solemnly invested_."[30] Baxter thought that he could prove infants' church membership to be a fact. With Baptists who granted it, but postponed their children's baptism until the latter were old enough to make the solemn profession of faith which Baxter himself required at confirmation, he had no quarrel at all, any more than with the liberty allowed in the early Church at this point;[31] although, once children's church membership and hence their right to baptism had been granted, he himself saw no good reason for this delay, and held that "the practice of the Church" was "an excellent Exposition, and confirmation of the Scripture herein."[32]

He proved the Church membership of Christians' children from both Nature and Scripture. As elsewhere, so here, their testimony coincides. Both bear witness to the principle that from birth children share the status, privileges and responsibilities of their parents. (We have met this principle already, in connexion with original guilt.) Nature teaches that rights of citizenship or inheritance belong to children from birth, and that parents may undertake at law on their behalf. By parity of reasoning, the same must apply in the case of God's covenant.

> Parents have naturally so great an interest in their children, that by this they are authorised to make covenants in their behalf. The law of Nature is the Law of God. Nay, it is a plain natural duty of parents to covenant for their

---

29. *Plain Scripture Proof*, 259.

30. *Review* . . . , 16 f.

31. cf. *op. cit.*, 3: "I have oft told the World that though the Ancient Churches denied not their *Childrens part in the Covenant of Grace* ... yet the *Time* when Children themselves should be *solemnly Baptized*, was left in the Churches for above 200 years to every ones *free choice*; some (and the most Christians) usually Baptizing them *quickly*, and others thinking as *Tertullian*, that it would *bind them faster* if they *stayed somewhat longer*; or, as *Nazianzene* thought, till they were *3 or 4 years old*: even as one that hath *right to a Crown* in his *Infancy*, may have his *Coronation* performed either *then*, or *afterward*."

32. *Plain Scripture Proof*, 305.

children when it is for their good . . . Nay, were it not a sin in that parent that would refuse to covenant in behalf of his child, when else the child should lose the benefit of it? . . . Who buyeth not Lands for himself and his Heirs?[33]

In such cases, the child undertakes by his parents, who as such are entitled to act for him. We should expect, therefore, to find in God's covenant also that "infants are . . . in covenant with their parents, because reputatively their parents' wills are theirs, to dispose of them for their good. And therefore they consent by their parents, who consent for them."[34]

And this is precisely what in Scripture we do find; for circumcision, the seal of the covenant and the analogue of baptism in the Old Testament church, was by God's express command administered to Abraham's male descendants in infancy. Now, "*Moses* Church and *Christs* Church according to Gods institution are not 2, but one Church. For *Moses* was *Christs* Usher, and his ceremonies were an obscurer Gospel to lead men to Christ."[35] To deny the continuity between the Old and the New Testament at this point was to fall into historical absurdity,[36] and a sort of Marcionism as well. Baxter was emphatic here:

> The New Testament speaketh more sparingly of that which is more fully discovered in the Old. What need the same thing be so done twice . . . ? The whole Scripture is the perfect Word and Law of God . . . This also is the very case in the question in hand. The main question is not, by what sign members are to be admitted into the Church? . . . but, At what Age are they to be admitted Members? Now this is as fully determined in the Old Testament as most things in the Bible: and therefore what need any more? . . . it deserves tears of blood, to hear how light some Christians make of the Old Testament.[37]

Here was the basic difference between Baxter and the Baptists whom he met prior to 1650:

---

33. *op. cit.*, 103; cf. 324: "Do wee not make and Seal Deeds of Gift to Infants ordinarily? and Tastaments (*sic*) wherein we bequeath them Legacies, and put their names in sealed Leases, wherein we engage ourselves to them . . . "

34. V:334. Baxter had not always been clear on this point: cf. *Plain Scripture Proof,* 112 f.: "I was once so ignorant . . . that I adventured . . . to tell others, (long ago) that I did not perceive that we could be said to make any Vow in our Infant-baptism: Therefore I am bound to unsay it & right those that heard me . . . "

35. *More Proofs . . .* , 27.

36. Cf. *op. cit.*, 147: Baxter asks "Whether it be credible that he who came not to cast out Jews, but to bring in Gentiles . . . making of 2 one Church, would have such a Linsey Woolsey Church, of party colours . . . so as that the Church at *Hierusalem* should have Infant members, and the church at Rome should have none? Jews Infants should be members and not Genties (*sic*)?"

37. *Plain Scripture Proof,* 3 f.

All (that ever I spoke with) do deny all Infants their Membership and room in the visible Church; and that is another matter than to deny them Water. They deny them (usually) any part in the Covenant of God . . . They repeal a very considerable part of the Old Testament, which they can never prove that God hath repeal'd.[38]

This, as Baxter forcefully pointed out, is to say in effect that the New Covenant is not a better, but a worse, covenant than the Old.

You cannot yet drive it into my head, that it is a mercy to be out of the visible Church of Christ, nor a misery to be in it; nor that it is a benefit to the Parents that all their children are kept out: Nor yet that Christ is a harder master than Moses . . . nor have you proved to me yet that he hath Repealed the Church-membership of Infants; nor shewed me the Scriptures where any such thing is written . . . He that made his Covenant so large, and his grace so free, hath not left out the Infants of his people who as is confessed, were once in.[39]

The positive testimony of Nature and Scripture, together with the conclusive objections to which the alternative view was exposed, seemed to Baxter to put the question out of doubt; and so he affirmed without hesitation that "it is a most obvious truth, That God Sealeth his Covenant to Infants, and the contrary gives too much advantage to the Anabaptists."[40]

As in other legal agreements, so in God's covenant, parents are entitled to pledge their children as well as themselves. The child's right to baptism has thus a double foundation: his parentage, the fact that he is a child of professing Christians, which makes him eligible for it, and his parents' actual decision to dedicate him to God, which makes it his due. Thus to dedicate him, and to bring him to baptism in order publicly to declare and transact that dedication, is the parents' prerogative and responsibility: they ought to do it, and baptism may not otherwise be administered to their child. From their standpoint, his baptism is an act whereby they acknowledge it their duty and proclaim it their intention to bring him up as one who is with them committed to God in covenant. That baptism is the parents' dedication of their child to God and themselves to its Christian training is stressed by Baxter again and again. We may quote his summary of the task to which they thus commit themselves:

Even before children are capable of instruction, there are certain duties imposed by God on the parents for their sanctification; viz. 1. That the parents pray earnestly and believingly for them. 2. That they themselves so live towards

38. p. 12.
39. p. 283 (addressed to Tombes).
40. p. 325.

> God as may invite him still to bless the children for their sakes, as he did
> Abraham's . . . (marginal note: "Second commandment. Prov. 20:7.")

> It is certain that the church ever required parents, not only to enter their
> children into the covenant, and so to leave them, but to do their after duty for
> their good, and to . . . educate them according to their covenant.

> It is plain that if there were none to promise to educate them, the church
> would not baptize them . . . [41]

If they omit to dedicate their child to God, or if they neglect to use the appointed
means for his Christian nurture, they *ipso facto* penalize him. Christ has
promised to receive their children from birth into His covenant, publicly to
invest them at baptism with a right to the fulfillment of the covenant promise,
and to bless them for the parents' sakes; but only on condition that the parents
cooperate; and

> He that considereth the woful unfaithfulness and neglect of most parents,
> even the religious, in the great work of holy educating their children, may
> take the blame of their ungodliness on themselves, and not lay it on Christ
> . . . seeing he promised but conditionally to give them the sanctifying heavenly
> influences . . . in their just use of his appointed means, according to their
> abilities.[42]

And even when the parents do their part, their child may never enter into
his covenanted inheritance. For "as soon as children come to a little use of
reason, they stand conjunctly on their parents' wills and on their own."[43] Since
they now can, therefore they now must, endorse the decision made for them
by their parents, that they should live to God. And vicarious undertakings count
for nothing if the children concerned repudiate them. Unbelief at age loses all
the benefits of baptism in infancy.

> Remission and Justification are given by a Morall Act of God, even by the
> promise or grant of the new Covenant, which Covenant is conditionall and
> universal: when any performeth the condition (as Infants do by their parents
> faith) the Covenant presently pardoneth and justifieth them without any new
> Act of God . . . & if this person doth by unbelief after deprive himself of the
> benefit, the Covenant which still remaineth Conditional, will condemne him,
> as before it did justifie him; and all this without any change in God or the
> Covenant, but only in the party.[44]

41. V:355.
42. p. 356.
43. *Loc. cit.*

Baptism in infancy must be complemented and completed at age by a personal profession of the faith to which the child was by baptism committed. This is reflected in the fact that the Church admits children to infant membership by baptism only in order that they may at age proceed to full, adult, communicant membership by a personal confession of faith at confirmation, or some equivalent rite of "solemn transition."[45] Where this transition is not sincerely made, the baptized person forfeits his inheritance, which the covenant conveys to none but believers. Many rightly baptized and carefully educated children do in fact repudiate their baptismal covenant at age: "the most holy, skilful, diligent Parents that ever I knew, who have taken pains with their children night and day by fair means and foul, have yet had wicked children."[46] When children thus fall from grace, it is not God's fault, nor their parents' fault, but their own fault.

Thus it appears that the effect of infant baptism is not the spiritual regeneration either of elect infants, as Burges held (else "we must either Baptize all, that we may meet with the Elect among the rest; or Baptize none, because we know not the elect"),[47] or of all infants as such, as Ward and Bedford maintained (for "it is very plain in Scripture, that all the Infants Right is for the sake of the Parent ... there are no promises to them meerly as Infants, but as the seed of the Righteous ... and consequently, the whole of their condition is, that their parents be believers").[48] Baptism does not effect spiritual regeneration in adults; indeed, adult baptism presupposes it, being conditional on repentance and faith, the fruits of it; and there is no reason to think "that God hath instituted Baptism to Infants to one end, & to the aged to another, when the aged are capable of both."[49] Nor, on the other hand, is a child's baptism a "bare sign": "I own not the Doctrine *de nudis signis*; I acknowledge an efficacy to the uses which they (sacraments) are appointed to; that is, As Moral Instruments to

44. *Plain Scripture Proof,* 315 f.; cf. 321: "do but suppose a falling from the Condition, and it is evident that all the forgiven sin returns; because Conditional forgiveness is of no force longer than we have the Condition." He quotes as teaching this doctrine the parable of the unmerciful servant, Matt. 18:23 f.

45. XIV:cccciii. Baxter stressed the need for keeping adult and infant members distinct in the Church; cf. *Christian Concord,* "Explication ...," 10: "I intend to have the Names of all the Members in a Church-Book (the Adult in one Colume and the Infants in another)."

46. *Plain Scripture Proof,* 314; cf. XI:411 (1683): "when I see how many children of excellent men prove wicked, and scourges in the church ... I have many times rejoiced, but never grieved, that I never had a child ... " There is a penal element involved in cases when God is pleased to "deny his saving grace to our ungodly children": it is "a heavy judgment of which we must be sensible" (XIII:120).

47. p. 297.

48. p. 359.

49. p. 300.

convey relations and right, though not as Physical Instruments to make real mutations; But this conveyance I take to be by obsignation, and solemnization ... of that which was before conveyed by the Covenant effectually."[50] That God may spiritually regenerate infants is true, but not relevant to the doctrine of the efficacy of baptism. Baptism does not bring about an internal change, but seals an external relation to God. It proclaims the child to be a beneficiary under the new covenant. "I think ... that all the children of true Christians, do by baptism receive a public investiture by God's appointment into a state of remission, adoption and right to salvation at the present."[51] Though baptism does not confer spiritual renewal *ex opere operato*, it so relates the child to the Spirit of God as to assure him and his parents that he will certainly receive the Spirit in new birth if he duly employs the appointed means of grace; and meanwhile, during the time when the child is incapable of faith, baptism proclaims God's present acceptance of his person. Here, then, was a source of comfort for Christian parents bereaved of young children:

> I believe the Synod of Dort said truly ... that Faithful Parents need not doubt of the Election and Salvation of their Children dying in Infancy, (before the violation of the Baptismal Covenant).[52]

Such children are regenerated, not in or before baptism, but *in articulo mortis*: "an Infant cannot enjoy God in Glory without real sanctifying Grace, and therefore it must be given them at Death." These privileges, like the sacrament which sealed them, belonged to believers' children alone. Baxter had no doctrine of universal infant salvation:

50. p. 365.

51. V:327 (*Christian Directory*). He was more positive here than he had been in 1650, when he had regarded this view as merely probable (*Plain Scripture Proof*, 315). He professed himself a follower of Davenant (cf. 272, n. 2 *sup.*) in his conception of the blessing which baptism conferred on infants.

52. *Review* ... quoting the Synod's Acts, I:xvii. This, as Baxter noted in *Plain Scripture Proof*, 338, was a reformed version of Augustine's position: "*Austins* judgment is, That if he dye before the use of reason, after Baptism, it is a certain sign that he is Elect; and so that no Reprobate shall so dye." Baxter and the Synod, however, did not think that the baptismal rite, as such, had anything to do with his salvation: for "I take it ... for certain, that the children of true believers ... are as certainly saved if they die before baptism as after" (V:335). (Here he differed from Davenant, who appeared to argue in the letter published by Bedford that the benefits which baptism seals belonged to all children rightly baptized, whether their parents were sincere or hypocrites. Baxter held that hypocrites' children should be baptized if their parents' profession of faith remained credible, but limited these blessings, which, he insisted, were actually conferred by the covenant, rather than by baptism, to the children of true believers, those who were themselves really in covenant with God.) On these grounds, Baxter had no qualms in opposing lay baptism, even in cases of emergency (cf. I. Morgan, *op. cit.*, 169 f.) He knew that the child would lose nothing by dying unbaptized. ("I lay not so much as some do on the *meer outward act or water of Baptism*," *Review* ..., 39.)

Most of the anabaptists, that I hear of, do hold that all the infants in the world are pardoned by Christ, and shall be saved if they die in infancy, and run in the downright Pelagian road. But this is not only utterly unproven, but contrary to Scripture . . . Now the gospel no where gives out pardon to every infant in the world; nay it frequently and plainly maketh a difference. The (Christian) parents' will doth . . . choose for them that cannot choose for themselves; for others, whatever God will do with them, doubtless they have no promise of mercy.[53]

Whether there was uncovenanted mercy for unbelievers' children Baxter did not know. But he was sure that mercy was covenanted to the infants of Christians, and that baptism publicly signified and sealed it.

It is of interest in this connection to note Baxter's attitude to the Anglican rite of infant baptism, as recorded in the "Exceptions" which he drew up in the name of the Presbyterian party for the Savoy Conference.[54] He had two main objections to it. First, "the ascribing of the Gift of the Holy Ghost to Infants by their Baptism, as its ordinary effect" was "to bring an undetermined uncertain Opinion into our Liturgy,"[55] and was therefore undesirable. This was a reference to the language of the prayers, which strongly implies in more than one place that spiritual rebirth is the baptismal blessing. To speak of "regeneration," however, did not seem to Baxter objectionable in itself, in view of the scope of the Biblical idea:

Regeneration is not usually taken in Scripture in the Precise sense as our Divines usually take it, for the implanting only of the first habits of Grace; but as *Paul* expoundeth it, he that is in Christ, is a new creature . . . all things are become new, A new Father, new Head, new Lord, a new Body . . . new Hopes, new State, new Rights, &c. Regeneration signifieth all or most of this new State. Now Baptism giveth much of this, and the rest it signifieth.[56]

Certainly, one of the privileges which Baxter held that baptism publicly confirms is a right to the sanctifying operations of the Spirit through a right use of the means of grace. But his is a very different thing from the suggestion that baptism is the physical instrument whereby the Spirit begins to renew the child's nature. Secondly, Baxter disliked the part given to godparents in the rite. He had no

---

53. XIV:408 f. (1658) Baxter adds: "it is strange that they should deny baptism to infants that deny not salvation to them . . . If they have original sin . . . pardoned to them by Christ, then how can men deny them the sign and seal of pardon?" It seemed to him absurd to assert infant salvation and deny infant church membership (cf. the quotation is from *Plain Scripture Proof*, 12, 283, on 280 *sup.*)

54. Printed, *R.B.*, II:308 ff.

55. p. 312.

56. *Plain Scripture Proof*, 358.

objection to godparents' presence, provided that they did no more than he believed them to have done in the early Church—" viz. that they witnessed the probability of the parents' fidelity; but promised that if they should either apostatize or die, they would see that the children were piously educated."[57] But when "Sureties that have not the Parents power . . . are unjustly and irregularly required, to profess present Actual Faith in the Infant's name, when it is a thing not required of the Infant,"[58] then the case was different. Here were Baptist principles creeping in at the back door:

> We know not by what right the Sureties do promise . . . in the Name of the Infant: it seemeth to us also to countenance the Anabaptistical opinion of the necessity of an actual Profession of Faith and Repentance in Order to Baptism. That such a profession may be required of Parents in their own Name, and now solemnly renewed when they present their Children to Baptism, we willingly grant; but the asking of one for another is a Practice whose warrant we doubt of . . .[59]

Here, we may observe, Baxter speaks not merely for the Presbyterian party which he led, but for the whole Reformed tradition.

It has been our exclusive concern in this chapter to see how Baxter integrated his sacramental teaching with his doctrine of the new covenant. We have therefore confined our attention to the objective significance of the sacraments, leaving aside the question of their subjective efficacy as aids to faith; and we have said little about the Lord's Supper, because there was no argument as to its meaning within Puritanism and no detailed treatment was therefore needed. We may note in conclusion that Baxter's precise and detailed outworking of the legal analogies on which Reformed sacramental doctrine is based made him an extremely clear and effective expositor of it. His "political method" here stood him in good stead. The positions he argued were the classical Presbyterian positions, and his orthodoxy at this point was never questioned. Indeed, in the Baptist controversy, his fellow-Puritans regarded him as a champion of their cause.

57. V:338.
58. *R.B.*, II:313.
59. p. 327.

Chapter 12

The Law of Christ

1. Aim of chapter: to show how Christian duty is deduced from the doctrines of man and redemption.

2. Summary of the law of Christ.
   Its contents: law of nature plus new remedial law.
   Its scope: a law for   the whole of man
                           the whole of life
   A means to God's glory and pleasure;
         hence its rigorism, for God cannot be pleased and glorified by sin.
   A means to man's recovery:
         commanding the knowledge of God, the rational creature's end;
         the recovery of rational self-control as a means to it.
         Recovery begins with the thoughts;
         Baxter's directions for "heart-work."
   Corollary: no place for irrational elements in Christianity.
         Baxter's opposition to "enthusiasm."

3. The law of Christ requires a life of faith.
         Faith in its intellectual aspect: acknowledgment of truth
               on God's authority.
         What faith apprehends.
         The duty and means of increasing knowledge.
         Faith in its volitional and vital aspect: first exercised in
               covenanting with Christ.

4. Internal fruits of faith (graces) required by Christ's law:
         Love: an element in faith;
               the end and issue of faith;
               gratitude and thankfulness;
               praise and joy;
   The positive elements in holiness.
   Holiness must be even and comprehensive.
   The negative elements in holiness: self-denial, mortification of sin.

5. External duties of faith required by Christ's law:
         (i) Obedience to Christ's authority in society:
               Authority in church, state and family: its nature and scope.
               The Christian must acknowledge authority in each
                     sphere.
         (ii) Good works:

Necessity of a "calling";
Rules for doing good: which good, and to whom;
Use of time and money.

Conclusion: Christ's law prescribes
            a serious, energetic life
            but not a strained, gloomy legalism.
            Three facts make this clear.

(Principal Sources: *Christian Directory* (II-VI); *Life of Faith* (XII), *Divine Life* (XIII), *Self-Denial* (XI), *The Crucifying of the World by the Cross of Christ* (IX).)

Chapter 12

The Law of Christ

Sound doctrine maketh a sound judgment, a sound heart, a sound conversion and a sound conscience. —Baxter

Christianity is more than a theology. It is a religion and a life. Accordingly, the body of divinity has two parts: theoretical and practical, the second being deduced from the first. Our study of man, created and fallen, and of Christ's redemption and rule, has put us in possession of all the relevant information for formulating the principles of Christian practice, as Baxter understood them. Duty is deduced from the gospel. In this chapter, we are summarily to examine these principles. We cannot hope in so small a compass to convey an adequate impression of the power and mastery which he reveals in dealing with practical Christianity. To do justice to the contents of the Practical Works, that "treasury of Christian wisdom,"[1] would require a volume. Here we shall merely describe the skeleton Baxter there clothed with flesh and blood.

In a large sense, the whole Biblical revelation is included in the law by which Christ rules the world. More than once Baxter describes the Bible as His statute-book.[2] His law embraces both κήρυγμα and διδαχή. Summarily expressed,

---

1. William Wilberforce, *A Practical View of the Prevailing Religious System . . . contrasted with True Christianity*, 1797, ch. 6.

2. Cf. "The Substance of Mr. Cartwright's . . . Exceptions Considered" in *J.R.*, 31: "All the Doctrines, Narratives, Historical and Prophetical found in Scripture, are *Adjuncts* of God's law in the strictest sense; and *parts* of it in a *larger sense*; yea, they are *signa Constituentia Debitum*, and so true parts of Law . . . even as Narratives of the matter and occasion, are in many Statute-Laws of this Land."

291

it is as follows: Understand man's nature and need, and God's redemptive action in Christ; renounce the dominion of sin by repentance, and submit to Christ as Lord and Savior, for these are the terms of salvation under the new covenant; live henceforth in subjection to His will, for He is man's King by right; live in love and gratitude towards Him, for this is the response which redeeming love demands; abound in good works, for they please and honor Him; avoid sin, for sin displeases Him; seek communion with Him in all things, for the knowledge of God is the destined end of man. The various clauses of this law form the subject-matter of Baxter's practical writings. All his expositions of them, even in the systematic *Christian Directory*, are evangelistic or pastoral in intent, and are therefore cast into an appropriate homiletic form. That Christ's law is at each point a corollary of the doctrines of man and of redemption is basic to his thought, but is always taken for granted rather than stated and proved. Our present task, however, is to uncover and make explicit this fundamental assumption.

We have already seen that Christ's law is composed of the original Law of Nature together with a supplementary remedial enactment, the new covenant. It includes both *law* and *gospel*, in the sense in which the Reformers and Puritans used those terms. The new part of it is a means to the attainment by fallen man of the standards prescribed and the reward proposed in the old part. Christ's law is therefore no less universal in its scope than the Law of Nature was. It prescribes for man's heart, his temper and motives, no less than for his outward actions. It requires "graces" (habits of thought and desire) no less than "duties" (specific courses of action); indeed, "graces" are themselves "duties," for the law requires them. Hence "the first and great work of a Christian is about his heart";[3] for action cannot be more right than the heart from which it proceeds. "All outward duties must begin at the heart, and it must animate them all; and they are valued in the sight of God, no further than they come from a rectified will."[4] Accordingly, most of Baxter's homiletic writing is concerned with the care of the heart. Moreover, it covers the whole of life. It imparts to all action a moral significance by demanding that it be made a means to a moral end. Baxter states this point with some care:

> Mere natural actions . . . belong not to our present subject; as being not the matter of rational . . . choice. Such as the winking of the eye, the setting of this foot forward first . . . But every act that is to be done deliberately and rationally, as a matter of choice, must be moralized, or made good, by doing it, 1. To a right end; 2. According to the rule. "Whether we eat, or drink, or whatsoever we do, (that is matter of rational choice,) must be done by us to

3. II:531.
4. XII:382.

the glory of God," 1 Cor. 10:31. All works tend not alike to his glory, but some more immediately and directly, and some more remotely; but all must ultimately have this end . . . All the comforts of good, or rest, or recreation, or pleasure which we take, should be intended to fit us for our Master's work, or strengthen, cheer and help us in it. Do nothing, deliberately, that belongs to the government of reason, but God's service in the world; which you can say, He set me on.[5]

The "rule" to which Baxter refers is simply this: "that is the best good, as to means, which most conduceth to the end."[6] Anything less thwarts it, and is *ipso facto* wrong.

Man's duty is a means to God's glory. "All that God commandeth us to do, is both a duty and a means; it is called a duty in relation to God the efficient Lawgiver, first; and it is a means next in relation to God the End . . . whose will is pleased by it." And we must always respect it in both these notions inseparably.[7] God's written Word is the sole rule of duty, to which man must hold fast even when he cannot see the reason for it and the wisdom behind it. Actions not sanctioned there often "seem to man to have the aptitude of a means, which are no duty but a sin; because we see not all things . . . Nothing must be thought a true means to any good end, which God forbiddeth; for God knoweth better than we." And, on the other hand, "whatsoever we are certain God commandeth, we may be certain is a proper means, though we see not the aptitude."[8] Here, we may note, is the basis on which the rigorism of Baxter's casuistry rests. He is emphatic that no known or suspected sin may be committed under any circumstances. "If it were the saving of the lives of all men in the country, I could no further take it to be my duty, than I take that to be no sin by which it must be done, it being a thing past controversy, that we must not sin for the accomplishing of any good whatsoever."[9] Sin is never a duty, for disobedience and distrust cannot possibly glorify God. Man must obey the Divine law implicitly, however foolish and unreasonable such obedience may appear, and however much it may cost. God knows better than we what makes for His glory and His creatures" good; and He does not need man's sin for the accomplishment of His purposes. This rule has no exceptions.

But man's duty as prescribed in Christ's remedial law is also a means to his recovery. The law is designed for his rehabilitation as a rational creature. It sets before him his proper end, "the manlike noble life; the life which the rational

5. II:325.
6. XVII:295.
7. XII:385.
8. *loc. cit.*
9. II:350.

creature was made for"[10] —the knowledge and love of God. "It is ... the greatest duty of a Christian to know God as revealed by his Son; and it is such a duty about our ultimate end as is also our greatest joy and felicity."[11] Man is commanded to take the knowledge of God as his goal, and to direct his whole life with a view to its attainment. As we have already seen, knowledge of God must be "affectionate" and "practical." God is not properly known till the perception of His desirability has aroused love, joy, delight and desire in the heart and moved the will: "nor is it clear and solid knowledge, if it do not somewhat affect the heart, and engage and actuate the life."[12] It must be "deep, effectual, heart-changing knowledge,"[13] the exercise, not of a single faculty (faculties are abstractions), but of the whole person; not of the mind alone, but of the man. But this end is only attainable insofar as man behaves rationally, and will and affection follow the dictates of intellect. Where intellect is the slave of sense, God can neither be known, nor loved, nor obeyed. In fallen man, however, as we have seen, intellect is a mere figurehead; sense has usurped the government and become the power behind the throne, and the appearance of rationality is a sham. The gospel, Christ's law, addresses this puppet reason accordingly, and commands it to reassert its lapsed authority. The rebel faculties must be recaptured. This is the necessary means to the prescribed end. Man's life on earth must be a continuous campaign for the re-imposition of reason's rule. Rational self-control must be restored. All the inferior faculties must be brought into subjection to the intellect, and so to the law of Christ which demands this subjection. And Christ's law is so designed that a right performance of each particular duty prescribed is a step forward in this process, as the following quotation indicates:

> [Christ] first revealeth saving truth to the understanding, and affecteth the will by showing it the goodness of the things revealed; these employ the thoughts, and passions, and senses, and the whole body, reducing the inferior faculties to obedience, and casting out by degrees those images which had deceived and prepossessed them.[14]

This process, which Christ effects by His Spirit, He commands in His law, and it is necessary in its measure for the right performance of any duty. Christ

10. XIII:v; from the Epistle before *The Divine Life*, 1664, an exposition of the duty, privilege, means and method of knowing God. It contains three parts: I. "The Knowledge of God," an exposition of the Divine nature and attributes; II. "Walking with God"; III. "The Christian's Converse with God . . . in Solitude."

11. p. 10.

12. p. 183.

13. p. 250.

14. II:274. "Senses" here are the inner senses, memory and imagination, not the sensitive appetite.

demands that His will be done gladly and whole-heartedly. Obedience that is not hearty is not acceptable. Obedience to Christ's law must therefore begin with constant, disciplined "heart-work." The prime necessity is the recovery of control over one's thoughts. It is in thought that sins are born: "The fancies of men are the gardens of the devil, where he soweth and watereth the plants of impiety . . . it is his shop in which he forgeth most vices, and doth a very great part of his work."[15] And it is by thought that graces grow: "our thoughts are the bellows that must kindle the flames of love, desire, hope, and zeal. Our thoughts are the spur that must put on a sluggish, tired heart."[16] Where thoughts lead, feelings follow and usually actions too.

Thoughts must not therefore be allowed to wander, and the first part of obedience to Christ is to bring them to heel.

> Our thoughts should be at the direction of our reason, and the command of the will, to go and come off as soon as they are bid. As you see a student can rule his thoughts all day . . . so can a lawyer, a physician, and all sorts of men about the matters of their arts and callings. And so it should be with a Christian about the matters of his soul.[17]

Evil thoughts can be kept out by prepossessing the mind with something better: "If they [thoughts] prove corrupt, sweep clean your fantasy and memory of them, that they . . . take not up their lodgings in you, or have not time to spawn and breed. And fill up the room with contrary thoughts, and useful truth, and cherish them daily, then they may increase and multiply."[18] By the constant consideration of gospel truth, knowledge turns into affection, the mind is cleared, the heart is fixed, holy desires awake and the Christian is equipped for joyful obedience. In this manner, "meditating on great and weighty truths, makes great and weighty Christians."[19] And without such a foundation of "heart-work," no duty will ever be gladly done. Accordingly, whenever Baxter teaches a point of conduct, his "directions" normally include "motives"—i.e., food for such thoughts as will arouse the desire to obey—and a double set of rules: one, for performing the acts prescribed, and the other for keeping the heart right while one does so. The central chapter of "Christian Ethics," the first part of the *Christian Directory*, "The General Grand Directions for Walking with God . . . containing the essentials of godliness and Christianity" (iii), is an exposition of seventeen "great internal duties" concerned with the care of the

15. IX:506.
16. XIII:221.
17. III:199.
18. II:283.
19. III:206.

heart;[20] then comes chapter iv, "Subordinate directions against the great sins most directly contrary to godliness"—unbelief, hardness of heart, hypocrisy, man-pleasing, pride, covetousness and sensuality—and this in turn is followed by six more chapters devoted to "Further subordinate directions for the next great duties of religion, necessary to the right performance of the grand duties": redeeming time (v), the government of the thoughts (vi), of the passions (vii), of the senses (viii), of the tongue (ix), and of the body (x). There "Christian Ethics" concludes. It deals with "heart-work" from beginning to end. This is sufficiently clear testimony to the primacy of "heart-work" in Baxter's conception of the law of Christ.

We may here call attention to an important corollary of Baxter's position. Christ's law, as we have seen, presupposes, requires and produces rationality in man. It addresses him as a rational being, temporarily lapsed, and tells him to become what he once was and by grace may be again. It is indeed man's dignity and glory that the God who made him a rational being, capable of government by moral means, will never govern him in any other way as long as He maintains him in existence. He will move him by a word addressed to his mind, giving him reasons for action and thereby eliciting a free, self-determined act of will, or not at all. It is inconceivable that God should move him by mere physical force, as one kicks a stone, or by a direct appeal to his senses, as one allures an animal, for thus He would dishonor His own image. If man insists on becoming a beast, God will not consent to treat him as a beast; He will still speak to him, judge and punish him as a man. God will not treat man as less than man, nor govern him by means that are less than rational, and there is therefore no sanction in Christ's law for any non-rational elements in religion. Sin and Satan are out to smother and suppress reason, but not God.

Baxter was therefore the diligent foe of "enthusiasm." He rejected its axiom, that sometimes Christ's Spirit works in believers independently of, even in defiance of, their reason, and impels them to action by quasi-physical impulse. Quakers, Ranters, Antinomians, as we shall see, and a hundred and one other sects of the Commonwealth period, were all "enthusiasts" in this sense, all sure that sometimes Christ spoke and moved them apart from His written Word and in a way that by-passed the intellect altogether. They claimed that revelation thus given was more certain than the conclusions of rational exegesis; that action thus prompted by imperious inner constraint was more certainly God's will than that done according to the dictates of rational conscience. Its very immediacy proved that it was wholly and purely Divine. Baxter rejected this claim entirely. Such experiences, he held, were less than rational, and could not therefore originate with the God whose whole aim is to restore man's rationality to him. God reveals His will by causing man to understand the law

20. II:170.

that He published in His written Word, and He evokes action by giving men reasons for it. To do otherwise would be to insult His own image. God does not, for instance, convince men that the Bible is His Word without evidence, but as we saw, mediately, by showing them how convincing the evidence for the claim really is. Nor does He make known new prophecies, apart from Scripture, to latter-day saints.[21] Nor does he inspire a "particular faith" in prayer, more specific than Scripture warrants.[22] Nor are transports and ecstasies to be hailed as God-given because they come suddenly and unaccountably; at best they have a physical, at worst a Satanic, origin.[23] Spiritual affections are not irrational affections.[24] Nor is it of God when texts leap to mind in new and arresting senses; misunderstanding and misapplication do not originate with the Spirit of Truth.[25] Such "enthusiastic" notions, common in mid-seventeenth-century England, were utterly unfounded. To embrace them was to make

21. cf. *Defence of the Principles of Love*, p.55 f., where Baxter describes some Millenarian visionaries whom he had encountered, and puts their visions down to melancholy.

22. This was a widespread opinion, held among others by Cromwell; John Howe (cf. *D.N.B.*, s.v.) earned his displeasure by preaching against it ("*Cromwel* heard him with great Attention, but would sometimes knit his Brows, and discover great Uneasiness ... he afterwards observ'd, *Cromwel* was cooler in his carriage to him than before," Calamy, *Life of Howe* (1724), 22). Baxter described this "common error" as he had met it: "many think that ... if they pray for the recovery of one that is sick, or the conversion of one that is unconverted, and can but believe that it shall be done ... God is then obliged by promise to do it." The promises alleged (in Mk. 9:23, 11:23 f.) Baxter explained thus: "the Spirit of miracles was then given to confirm the Gospel ... the Spirit, whenever he would work a miracle, would first work an extraordinary faith to prepare for it" (XII:239). But the age of miracles is now past, and "a strong conceit (though it come in a fervent prayer) that any thing shall come to pass" beyond what is explicitly promised should not be trusted (IV:303).

23. Baxter often tells the story of "one Dishforth" who went "for Novelty" to a meeting of the "followers of *Hacket* and *Coppinger*, called, *Grundletonians* ... they breathed on him, and he came home so transported, that he left his former way of Praying in his Family ... and did all by Extasy ... and so continued about a Fortnight, and then returned to Humility, and repented (himself and his Son were my Informers)" ("To the Teachers of Dr. Crispe's Doctrine" before "A Defence ..." in *Scripture Gospel Defended*). Baxter asserts that this was a Satanic delusion in XX:296.

24. cf. XXIII:229: "if I find a great deal of comfort in my heart, and know not how it came thither, nor upon what rational ground it was raised, nor what considerations do feed and continue it, I should be ready to question, How I know whether this be from God? ... a Christian's joy should be grounded, rational joy ..."

25. cf. XII:240: "many and many an honest, ignorant, melancholy woman hath told me what abundance of sudden comfort they have had, because such a text was brought to their minds, and such a promise was suddenly set upon their hearts, whenas they mistook the very sense of the promise ... it was nothing to their purpose." Baxter adds, characteristically, that if he saw that they had "true right to sounder comforts" he did not disillusion them: "it is not at all times that we are bound to rectify other men's mistakes, viz. not when it will do them more harm than good." Bunyan's *Grace Abounding* illustrates the kind of experience Baxter has in mind. As he observes, it is dangerous when men "think in their troubles, that every text of Scripture which cometh into their mind ... is a special suggestion of the Spirit of God ... Satan can bring a text or truth to our remembrance for his own ends ..." (495 f.).

Christianity a sub-human, because sub-rational, religion. Enthusiastic experience savored more of demon-possession than of the Spirit's leading. It was by no means self-evidently Divine. The truth was that there was no room in Christianity for these arbitrary intrusions. God had designed the Christian religion to turn sinners into reasonable people through a course of obedience to Christ's law, which demanded the universal rule of reason and forbade non-rational habits and behavior altogether. The ideal for rational living which it commanded man to take as his goal was the complete conscious organization of life as a hierarchy of means to a single supreme end—the knowledge and love of God. It thus demanded the extension of conscious self-control, and called for deliberate self-determination at every point in the light of the end. Mysterious demonic irruptions which sweep away that control and suspend the process of rational choice necessarily thwart this process, and cannot therefore be of God.

We may therefore be sure *a priori*, merely from considering the nature of man and of God and the ends to which Christ's law is a means, that we shall find prescribed in that law an integrated and intelligible hierarchy of duties, each having its place as a means to man's supreme end, the knowledge and enjoyment, and thereby the glorifying, of God. And this is in fact what we do find. We shall now proceed to review the more important of these duties.

The requirements of Christ's law may be summed up in the single phrase: a life of faith.[26] Faith, as we saw, is "an act . . . of the whole man . . . most properly called, a practical trust;"[27] "the practical belief and acceptance of life, as procured by Christ, and promised by God in the Gospel."[28] In its intellectual aspect, faith is an acknowledgment of truth on God's authority. As it is an apprehension of God's love, Jesus Christ is its object: "it is the chief part of the office of faith, to see God's love and goodness in the face of Christ."[29] As it apprehends God's offer of salvation, the promises are its object. As it apprehends the promised hope, "the everlasting fruition of God in heaven"[30] is its object. Faith begins as knowledge of Divine fact, and the Christian's first duty throughout his life is to strengthen faith by increasing and deepening knowledge.

Accordingly, the first Grand Direction in "Christian Ethics," iii, is: "Labour to understand well the nature, grounds, reason and order of faith and godliness," the fourth inculcates "a true, orderly and practical knowledge of God," and the

---

26. Title of a treatise which, in its enlarged form (1670), was designed as a complete *vade-mecum* for the believer, "a breviate and substitute, for the families and persons that cannot have and use so large a volume" (as the *Christian Directory*), II:ix.

27. XII:249.

28. XII:9.

29. XII:181.

30. XII:9.

seventh calls us to "learn of Christ as our teacher." To learn, in a correct method, all that God has revealed of Himself through Nature, Scripture and Providence (i.e., history), to grasp the evidence for each truth and to keep it fresh in the memory, ready for instant use, is a life's work, by reason both of the vastness of the syllabus and of the incessant opposition of Satan and the flesh to the acquisition of this knowledge. The Christian needs to make assiduous use of every means of learning truth that God has provided. The first of these means is the ministry of the Word, audible and visible, public and private, both by prayer and by preaching.[31] This must be supplemented by fellowship; he should cultivate "the company of serious, lively Christians" and learn from their "holy conference."[32] He must learn too from "holy society in Christian families, and family instructions."[33] In addition, he must assiduously study his Bible. ("You come not to the school of Christ to be idle. Knowledge droppeth not into the sleepy dreamer's mouth. Dig for it as for silver, and search for it in the Scriptures as for a hidden treasure").[34] Two subsidiary helps to make one's hearing and reading profitable are, first, to "learn some catechism that is sound and full . . . keep it in memory while you live,"[35] and, second, to read "the solid, lively, heavenly (Puritan) treatises, which best expound and apply the Scriptures."[36] He must go over all that he hears and reads in his mind afterwards ("let the end and order of your meditations be first for the settling of your judgments").[37] His general reading must be governed by the principle that other knowledge is desirable only as a means to the knowledge of God and to the performance of Christian duty. It will include "credible histories, especially of the church, and tractates upon inferior sciences and arts;" but fiction will find no place in it: "vain romances, play-books, and false stories . . . bewitch your fantasies, and corrupt your hearts."[38] The Christian may not read to satisfy idle curiosity, or to while away time. Time is too precious for that. Moreover, he must take care,

---

31. The work of ordained ministers stands at the head of Baxter's list of "outward means of grace under Christ" (XII:377), next only to the written Word which they are to minister. Baxter specifies that he thinks of "all their office" as a means of instruction: "preaching for conversion, baptizing, preaching for confirmation and edification of the faithful, praying and praising God before the Church; administering the body and blood of Christ in the sacrament of communion; and watching over the flock, by personal instruction, admonition, censures, and absolutions."

32. II:523.

33. XII:378.

34. II:223. Detailed instructions for Bible study are given in the *Poor Man's Family Book*: "Read most the New Testament, and the most suitable parts of Scripture. Expound the dark and rarer passages by the plain and frequent ones. Read some commentary . . . as you go . . . Ask your pastor of that which you understand not" (XIX:503 f.).

35. II:97.

36. II:150.

37. III:207.

38. II:150.

not merely to learn the right things, but to learn them in the right way. The increase of knowledge must not increase pride. The more he knows, the more clearly he should be able to see how little he knows. Nor must he permit himself to imagine that the acquisition of knowledge is an end in itself. Knowledge is for use, and the possession of it imposes the responsibility of using it for its proper purpose—the evoking of action. Faith is essentially choice and action, and is seated in the will.

The first act of faith which the new law requires is a personal covenanting with Christ, whereby the penitent believer receives him as Lord and Savior. This, for most of Baxter's hearers and readers, would be an endorsement of the baptismal covenant, by which, as we saw, their parents had committed them to this faith. "Write it out on thy heart, and put thy heart and hand to it resolvedly, and stand to thy consent . . . conversion is wrought when this is done."[39] The decision should be made public, both to one's friends[40] and, ideally, to the local church as well.[41] This covenant should thenceforth be frequently reaffirmed, both to remind oneself of one's obligations to God and as an expression of thanks for redemption.

> This covenant should be actually renewed frequently in prayer and meditation . . . Especially when after a fall we beg the pardon of our sins . . . and on days of humiliation and thanksgiving, and in great distresses, or exhilarating mercies. And the Lord's supper is an ordinance instituted to this end.[42]

The law requires a twofold fruit of faith: internal, in the grace of love and the pursuit of holiness, and external, in good works and obedience to Christ. We must briefly refer to each. There is a sense in which love, the will's closure with proposed good, is not merely a fruit of saving faith, but also a part of it and a mark of its genuineness. The first act of faith is an act of love towards God. Faith works by love. But faith, as such, is no more than a means, the way to the promised land, whereas love is the end, begun here and perfected in the life to come, when faith is lost in sight. Man was made to love, and he is redeemed to love. The law of grace reaffirms the law of nature at this point. Love to God is man's highest duty and his noblest activity, and all the knowledge that faith

---

39. p. 44.

40. "When you have escaped the greatest misery in the world, and obtained the greatest mercy in the world . . . give glory to God. Go to your old companions in sin, and tell them . . ." (VIII:245).

41. "I must say, that it is a shame that we hear no more in public of the conversion of sinners. As baptism is to be in public, that the congregation may witness your engagement . . . so the solemn renewing of the same covenant by repentance after a wicked life, should ordinarily be public, to give warning to others to avoid the sin, and to have the prayers of the church, and to satisfy them of our repentance, that they may have communion with us" (VIII:245 f.).

42. V:47 f.

brings in must be turned into fuel for love.

> Remember, that . . . the kindling of love to God in the soul, is the principal
> use and effect of faith; and to live by faith, is but to love . . . by faith. Faith
> working by love, is the description of our Christianity . . . the true use of faith
> in Jesus Christ is to be as it were the bellows to kindle love . . .

> Faith is the burning glass, which, beholding God, receiveth the beams of his
> communicated love, and inflameth the heart with love to him again; which
> mounteth up by groans and prayers till it reach its original, and love for ever
> rest in love.[43]

Grand Direction XI directs Christians "To love God as our Father, and Felicity,
and End." Love is the sum and substance of the life which Christ's law requires
in the redeemed.

As love must be the Christian's primary activity, so gratitude must be his
principal motive. All God's dealings with him in grace, from his initial
humiliation onward, are designed to evoke gratitude,[44] and his life can only
conform to Christ's law insofar as it is a hearty expression of gratitude and
thanks.

> The design of God in the work of redemption, is purposely laid for the raising
> of the highest thankfulness in man . . . It is a great truth, and much to be
> considered, that gratitude is that general duty of the Gospel, which containeth
> and animateth all the rest, as being essential to all that is properly evangelical.
> Thankfulness is a powerful spring of obedience . . . A thankful obedience and
> an obedient thankfulness are a Christian's life.[45]

Thankfulness is an index of grace: "the more believing and heavenly the mind
is, the more thankful."[46] Grand Direction XIV is an elaborate enforcement of
the injunction, "Let thankfulness . . . be the very temperament of thy soul."

The verbal expression of thanks in "that angelical work of praise"[47] is a
further requirement of Christ's law. Man is to use his lips continually to give
glory to God. This, again, was a part of the law of creation, now reaffirmed in
the new law of the Redeemer. Like the other graces already mentioned, a spirit
of praise is God's gift as well as man's duty, and is itself a blessing to the man

---

43. XII:153, 68.
44. cf., on the subject of humiliation, II:426 f: "This is the main end why God will humble
those that he will save; not to drive them to despair of mercy, nor that he taketh pleasure in their
sorrows for themselves; but to work the heart to a due esteem of saving mercy . . . The humble soul
is the thankful soul, and therefore so greatly valued by the Lord."
45. p. 423, 432.
46. p. 429.
47. XXIII:302.

who has it. Praise is a tonic, bracing and invigorating sluggish spirits. Baxter admonishes "uncomfortable, troubled souls" as follows:

> A life of praise bringeth comfort to the soul . . . as labouring doth warm the body: or as the sight and converse of our dearest friend, or the hearing of glad tidings, doth warm the heart . . . This is the way to have comfort by feeling, to be much in the hearty praises of the Lord . . . if you would taste the heavenly joys on earth, you must imitate them in heaven as near as possibly you can; and this is your work of nearest imitation.

> This life of praise is a continual pleasure to the soul; clean contrary to a melancholy life. It is recreating to the spirits, and healthful to the body . . . and is an excellent cordial and companion in the greatest sufferings.[48]

The exercise of love by thankful praise is the way to joy, and joy is no less a Christian duty than a Christian privilege. Christ's law lays it down more than once that every Christian must rejoice in the Lord. Grand Direction XIII is as follows: "Diligently labour that God . . . may be thy chief delight: and this holy delight may be the ordinary temperament of thy religion." Baxter rejected the idea that mourning and groveling before God was Christianity at its most characteristic. This is the devil's picture of Christianity, not Christ's. It is in reality the believer's privilege and duty to enjoy his religion.

> Penitent sorrow is only a purge to cast out those corruptions which hinder you from relishing your spiritual delights. Use it therefore as physic . . . turn it not into your ordinary food. Delight in God is the health of your souls . . . holy delight adjoined to love, is the principal part of our religion, and . . . they mistake it which place it in anything else.[49]

There is no place in Christianity for the morbid streak which marked the seventeenth-century English mind and cast its shadow over a good deal of Puritan religion:

> Many Christians look upon broken-heartedness, and much grieving, and weeping for sin, as if it were the great thing that God delighteth in, and requireth of them; and therefore they bend all their endeavors this way; and are still striving with their hearts to break them more and wringing their consciences to squeeze out some tears; and they think no sermon, no prayer, no meditation, speeds so well with them, as that which can help them to grieve and weep . . . Do you think that God hath any pleasure in yours sorrows

---

48. II:444; from "Directions for glorifying God with our Tongues in his Praises," the second division of Grand Direction XV, "For Glorifying God."
49. p. 420 f.

as such? . . . O Christians, understand and consider, that all your sorrows are but preparatives to your joys . . . [50]

Joy is the fruit of praise; and therefore praise must have a prominent place both in private prayer and in the Church's public worship on the Lord's day. Baxter often makes this point; we here quote a striking, yet typical passage, written in 1653:

> Never take it [your heart] to be right till it be delighting itself in God. When you kneel down in prayer, labour so to conceive of God, and bespeak him, that he may be your delight; so do in hearing and reading; so do in all your meditations . . . Especially improve the happy opportunity of the Lord's Day, wherein you may wholly devote yourself to this work. And I advise ministers and all Christ's redeemed ones, that they spend more of those days in praise and thanksgiving . . . or else they will not answer the institution of the Lord. And that they keep it as their most solemn day of thanksgiving, and be briefer on that day in their confessions and lamentations, and larger at other times! . . . And truly let me tell you, my brethren of the ministry, you should by private teaching and week-day sermons, so further the knowledge of your people, that you might not need to spend so much of the Lord's day in sermons as the most godly use to do; but might bestow a greater part of it in psalms and solemn praises to our Redeemer.[51]

The Lord's Supper should be celebrated each Sunday, as an act of praise for grace received, as was done in the primitive church:

> the celebrating of the sacrament . . . (which is therefore called the Eucharist,) was part of these laudatory exercises, and used every Lord's day . . . It is not only a holy day, separated to God's worship in general; but to this eucharistical worship in special above the rest . . . and thus all Christians (ordinarily) should use it.[52]

Love, thanksgiving, praise and joy are the positive graces and duties which make up holiness. Holiness in man is an inclusive concept, which Baxter analyses as follows:

---

50. IX:278 f.; cf. XXIII:304: "oh the sinful folly of many of the saints, who drench their spirit in continual sadness."

51. IX:283 f. The passage continues with a plea for a new metrical version of the Psalms ("not neglecting the poetical sweetness under pretense of exact translating") and for hymn-singing. Most Puritans distrusted this practice, as implying the insufficiency of Scripture; Baxter, however, thought hymns to be "no sinful, human invention" but, rather, "next to a necessity in Christian worship." His *Reformed Liturgy* retained all the Psalms and Canticles set in the Book of Common Prayer, added some extra alternatives, and prescribed a third canticle for Evening Prayer "if time allow" (XV:471). Cf, Powicke, *Life*, 95 f., 48, n. l.

52. II:446.

Holiness consisteth in, 1. Our resignation of ourselves to God as our owner
. . . 2. And our subjection to God as our ruler . . . 3. And in thankfulness and
love to God as our chief good, efficiently and finally.
Love is that final and perfective act, which implieth and compre-
hendeth all the rest; and so is the fulfilling of the law, and the true state of
sanctification . . .

Heaven itself, as it is our ultimate end and perfection, is but our perfect love
to God maintained by perfect vision of him, with the perfect reception of his
love to us . . .

Accordingly the greatest use of faith in Christ is to subserve and kindle our
love to God . . .

Our whole religion, therefore, consisteth of two parts: 1. Primitive holiness,
restored and perfected; 2. The restoring and perfecting means: or, 1. Love to
God, the final and more excellent part; 2. Faith in Christ, the mediate part:
faith causing love, and love caused by faith.[53]

Holiness includes the whole of what Christ's law requires. It is the *imitatio
Christi* in intention and the *imago Christi* in effect. It is the subjective aspect of
salvation; so that "to be saved without holiness, is to see without eyes and to
live without life."[54] Baxter often refers to true believers as "the sanctified," those
in whom holiness has begun to appear. Holiness must not be partial and lop-
sided, but even and comprehensive ("universal" was the common Puritan term
for this idea, though never, I think, Baxter's). Scripture and Puritan aesthetics
united to proclaim that its proportion was its beauty.

Carry on the work of holiness and obedience in harmony . . . Every grace and
duty is to be made a help to all the rest, and the want or neglect of any one, is
a hinderance to all: as the want of one wheel or smaller particle in a clock or
watch, will make all stand still, or go out of order . . . The soul is as a musical
instrument, which must neither want one string, nor have one out of tune,
nor neglected, without spoiling all the melody . . . the beauty of a holy soul
and life, is not only in the proportion of each grace and duty, but much in the
proportion, feature and harmony of all.[55]

Holiness will not in this life be perfected at any point, but it must be begun at
every point. Equal regard must be paid to all that the law prescribes.

The negative counterpart of the positive graces and duties of holiness is the
removal of obstacles to their exercise by self-denial and mortification of sin. "I

53. XII:353 f.
54. X:79.
55. XII:362.

take the love of God and self-denial to be the sum of all saving grace and religion ... and I judge of the measure of my own, and all other men's true piety, by these two."[56] The latter is necessary as a means to the former. Baxter deals with it in full in *The Crucifying of the World by the Cross of Christ* (1658) and *Self-denial* (1659), and, more summarily, in Grand Directions VIII ("To obey Christ our Physician ... in his repairing, healing work") and IX ("Of the Christian Warfare under Christ"). (XVII, "For Self-denial," is merely a cross-reference to the two books named above). These titles sufficiently indicate how Baxter understood this part of Christian obedience. "Carnal self," the sum of all lust and affection that is inordinate and self-centered, must be put to death by restraining its outward expression, withholding tempting objects, starving each unruly appetite, and— the heart of the matter—alienating affection from sin. "Bestow your first and chiefest labour to kill sin at the root; to cleanse the heart, which is the fountain."[57] Sin must first be recognized for what it is. Then its guilt must be "aggravated" by assiduous meditation upon the various factors that determine it, until the Christian is adequately aware of its heinousness in the sight of God. He must force himself to realize, what fallen man is notoriously unwilling to realize, how serious and horrible a thing his sin is. Then he must contrast with it the true life and destiny of the children of God, and thus throw into relief the madness, repulsiveness and "malignity" of the sin that would keep him from it. As this "heart-work" proceeds, a new affection will expel the old; the Christian grows more and more disgusted with sin, and more and more impervious to its allurements. Baxter's practical advice for mortifying sin is accordingly made up, first, of preparatory directions concerning outward self-discipline and, second, of "particular directions ... to help you think of sin as it is, that you may hate it; for your cleansing and cure consist in this: so far as you hate sin it is mortified, and you are cured of it."[58]

Here we must conclude our sketch of the internal duties of holiness and pass on to the external duties which Christ's law requires of the Christian as a member of society. We may conveniently begin with a reference to Baxter's doctrine of society. His conception of its structure is hierarchical and theocratic. All authority is ultimately Christ's, and Christ rules through His official representatives in three distinct spheres of delegated authority: Church, State and family. In these three societies, governmental power is directly delegated from the Father, through the Son, to ministers, magistrates and the *paterfamilias* respectively. Each of these, in his own proper sphere, is to be respected and obeyed as Christ's deputy; and each must ultimately answer to Christ for the way he has used his authority. The three spheres are delimited as follows.

56. XI:3.
57. II:256.
58. p. 251.

Ministerial authority relates to private and public instruction and discipline within the Church. It is the moral authority of the prophet who declares the mind of God. It is exclusive to ordained ministers; no layman shares it.[59] All civil power belongs to the magistrate. As a citizen, the minister is subject to the magistrates' jurisdiction; as a church member, the magistrate must be ruled by the will of God as the minister states it to him. "Ministers are as truly the magistrates' teachers, as magistrates are their governors."[60] "Our (ministers') power is but *Perswasive*. It is but, *By the Word*; It is but on the *Conscience*; It is under the Magistrates coercive Government . . . But . . . God hath *described our office, and limited the Magistrates office*, so that he hath no power from God to *hinder the Ministry*."[61] Neither minister nor magistrate has any warrant from God to inhibit or intrude into the other's sphere of jurisdiction. Church-power and civil authority have been independently delegated in order that they might be mutually complementary. The magistrate and the minister are to work together for a common end. Thus,

> the king and Magistrates have *curam animarum*, though not in the same sense as the Pastors have. They have the charge of Government . . . in order to men's holy, sober and religious living, and to the saving of mens souls . . . The same points of Religion, the same sins and duties, come under the judgement of the Magistrate and the Pastor . . . the *Magistrate is Judge, who is to be corporally punished for Heresie and Murder, and Adultery*, &c. And the *Pastors are Judges, who is to be excommunicated as Impenitent in such guilt* . . . [62]

The civil governor's responsibility in ecclesiastical affairs includes the seconding of church censures by civil penalties,[63] the provision of adequate maintenance

---

59. Here, as A. Gordon notes (*Heads of English Unitarian History*, 65 f.), was the essential difference between Parliamentary and Baxterian Presbyterianism, the former modeled on the Scottish system, the latter inspired by the English Puritan tradition and Usher's *Reduction of Episcopacy*. Baxter had no place for "lay elders." Cf. "Explication . . . " in *Christian Concord*, 34: "I confess I take it for a clear truth, that one single Pastor may . . . properly Excommunicate and may Govern a Church . . . though there were a Presbytery in that Church, and the *major* Vote were against him."

60. XVII:408.

61. *The Difference between the power of Magistrates and Church-Pastors*, 1671, 21.

62. *op. cit.*, 43. In thus demarcating the limits of civil and ecclesiastical authority, Baxter followed Grotius' *De Imperio summarum potestatum circa Sacra*, 1647, which he thought settled the question (33): "it is as a shame to us all that we need any more, and a shame to me to trouble the world after him, with Writings on that subject . . . were it not that renewed occasions require it."

63. This, rather than the imposition of Confessions, was in Baxter's view the right way to keep heresy out of the Church: "the remedie for Heresie is not to impose another Rule of Faith than Scripture (as if this was insufficient and we could mend it) but to exercise Church Government carefully, and if any be proved to teach any Doctrine contrary to the Scripture, that Magistrates and Pastors do their parts to correct such and restrain them" (*The Judgement and Advice of the . . . Ministers of Worcester-shire . . . Concerning the Endeavours of Ecclesiasticall Peace . . . which Mr.*

for the ministry,[64] and the ejection of the scandalous and incompetent. Generally, rulers must be guided in legislation by the broad principles laid down in Scripture, for "all human laws are but by-laws, subordinate to God's."[65] Within the sphere in which their competence can be proved from Scripture, they must be implicitly obeyed. The third sphere of authority that Baxter specified is the family. The *paterfamilias*, who *ex hypothesi* belongs both to the Church and to the State, must exercise patriarchal government within the limits lawfully set by the rulers in each to the same end as they—the material and spiritual good of those over whom he has authority. He is both pastor and magistrate to the little church and society in his house, and must teach, rebuke, exhort, lead them in worship and exercise discipline where necessary, so that God may be glorified, as in a holy Church and Commonwealth, so in a holy family. In a Preface that he wrote for the complete edition of the Westminster Assembly's works, Baxter touched on the father's duty in this respect:

> Families are societies that must be sanctified to God as well as Churches; and the governors of them have as truly a charge of the souls that are therein, as pastors have of the Churches . . . But while negligent ministers are (deservedly) cast out of their places, the negligent masters of families take themselves to be almost blameless . . . [66]

—although, as Baxter goes on to lament, they omit the government and instruction of their families altogether. As we saw in the previous chapter, such negligence, besides dishonoring God, may well jeopardize the children's souls.

The law of Christ demands that the Christian should understand his obligations in all three spheres, domestic, ecclesiastical and political, whether as ruler or as subject, and conscientiously discharge them. They are permanent features of the moral landscape, and may never be ignored. He is to recognize that authority in each sphere derives from Christ, to respect those who exercise it as Christ's representatives, and to treat their injunctions, if lawful, as Christ's word. He must honor the office even where he finds it hard to honor its

---

John Durey doth present, 1658, 5.). In his *Humble Advice* . . . preached to Parliament on Dec. 24, 1654, Baxter asks that it should be made illegal to preach "against the Essentiall, (Fundamentall) Truths . . . Thousands might curse you for ever in hell, if you grant such a Liberty to men to . . . entice them thither" (2).

64. cf. *op. cit.*, 7, and (e.g.) *The Humble Petition of Many Thousands . . . In behalf of the Able, Painful, Godly Ministry of this NATION* (Presented to Parliament on Dec. 22, 1652), of which "take special care of their competent maintenance" is a principal theme (6, etc.).

65. XVII: 350; cf. *The Worcester-shire Petition . . . Defended*, 1653 (dated March 28), 36: "What is your (magistrates') office and Power, but as Ministers of God to see his Lawes executed, as far as you can? . . . Your own Lawes are but the determinations of Particulars which God hath determined only in General . . ."

occupant. He must learn the limits of authority in each field, and whom to obey when claims clash: "civil power is to be obeyed before ecclesiastical, in things belonging to the office of the magistrate; and ecclesiastical before the civil, in things proper to the ecclesiastical governors only. And family power before both, in things proper to their cognizance only."[67] The second, third and fourth parts of the huge *Christian Directory* are concerned with the detailed casuistry of obedience to Christ in these three spheres. Part II, "Christian Economics," is concerned with domestic issues—marriage, servants, children, poverty, old age, home life, family prayers; Part III, "Christian Ecclesiastics," covers the duties and problems of church membership; Part IV, "Christian Politics," deals with man's social, economic and professional relationships as a member of society, as well as with political principles in the stricter sense. Space does not permit us, however, to follow Baxter further as he "opens" these complicated topics. It must suffice to have indicated what they are.

The general rule governing the Christian's conduct at all times and in all relationships must be this: *do as much good as possible.* It is not enough to do the minimum that the situation requires; Christ's law demands that one should always aim to do the maximum that time and ability allow.

> We have greater work here to do than mere securing our own salvation. We are members of the world and church, and we must labour to do good to many. We are trusted with our Master's talents for his service.[68]

> He is called our Master, and we his servants . . . (he) doth not give us laws to obey, while we do our own work, but giveth us his work to do, and laws for the right doing of it.[69]

The Christian has no other task in the world but to work the works of God. Baxter scouts the monastic ideal.[70] Christians are in the world to serve their fellows there. "Public service is God's greatest service."[71] Accordingly, the tenth Grand Direction is "For serving Christ our master in good works." Its theme is this:

---

66. Incorporated eventually into Thomas Manton's "Epistle to the Reader," prefixed to most editions of the Westminster documents; cf. *R.B.* I:122.

67. XII:388.

68. XVIII:245.

69. II:320.

70. In his sermon on Gal. 6:10, *How to do Good to Many; or, the Public Good is a Christian's Life*, 1682, Baxter criticizes those "who think that their business is only with God and their own hearts . . . Among the papists, multitudes, by this conceit, turns friars and nuns. Among us, such spend all their time in hearing sermons . . . and such-like exercises . . . if they are but rich enough to live without bodily labour . . ." But God calls all to work (XVII:301).

71. II:334.

Study to do good, and make it the trade or business of your lives...Acquaint yourself with all the talents which you receive from God, and what is the use to which they should be improved...Every day is given you for some good work. Keep therefore accounts of every day (I mean, in your conscience...).[72]

Laziness and inactivity, Baxter insists, are contrary both to human nature and to the Word of God. Work is a universal duty, for man was made to work. As Puritan moralists from Perkins onward had insisted, each must choose and follow a "lawful calling," "such work as is serviceable to God, and the common good."[73] God commands it,[74] the public welfare requires it, and (by no means the least consideration) physical and mental health and efficiency will be lost without it.[75] Each man must lay himself out for the good of his fellows. There are priorities among the alternative goods at which we may aim, and we must always choose the best: "the choosing or using of the lesser (good) at that time, is to be taken for a sin."[76] *Ceteris paribus*, this will mean that spiritual good is given preference over material good. The rule of estimation is that a good "is not to be measured principally by the will or benefit of ourselves, or any creature; but by, 1. The will of God in his laws; and, 2. By the interest of his pleasedness and glory: but secondarily, human interest is the measure of it."[77] Again, there are priorities among the various classes of people to whom good may be done; and here the order must be:

1. That we do what good we can to our own souls. That we first pluck the beam out of our own eyes ...
2. Next we must do good according to our power to our near relations.
3. And next to our whole families ...

---

72. II:324, 326.

73. II:333; Baxter gives directions for choosing and changing callings II:333, III:582 f. R.H. Tawney, *Religion and the Rise of Capitalism*, Pelican ed., 239 f., expounds the Puritan doctrine of "callings." Tawney obscures, however, the fact that in Puritan teaching the believer is to work, not for private prosperity, but for others' good. Private self-seeking, according to Baxter, is precisely what believers are freed from.

74. Baxter quotes 2 Thes. 3:6, 10-12, 14; 1 Thes. 4:11; Gen. 3:19; Eph. 4:28; Prov. 31:32-33; and the fourth commandment ("six days shalt thou labour") to prove that God commands all to work. ("*Quest.* But will not wealth excuse us? *Answ.* It may excuse you from some sordid sort of work, by making you more serviceable in other; but you are no more excused from service and work ... than the poorest man ... *Quest.* Will not age excuse us? *Answ.* Yes, so far as it disableth you; but no further ... ! (II:333). Those who can work, must work.

75. Cf. III:580 f. "Next to abstinence, labour is the chief preserver of health ... for want of which abundance grow melancholy, and abundance grow sluggish and good for nothing, and abundance cherish filthy lusts, and millions yearly turn to earth before their time ... " "Idleness breedeth melancholy, and corrupteth the fantasy and mind ... the constant labours of a lawful calling is one of the best cures of melancholy in the world" (XII:476).

76. XII:380.

77. p. 381; cf. XVII:295.

4. And next them, to our neighbours.
5. And next, to strangers.
6. And lastly, to enemies of ourselves and Christ.
7. But our greatest duties must be for public societies: Viz. 1. For the commonwealth (Both governors and people). 2. And for the church.
8. And the next part . . . must be for the whole world (whose good by prayer and all just means we must endeavour).[78]

With so much to be done, no time may be lost; time is a talent to be used for God. Indeed, as Baxter constantly insisted, "redeeming time" is the duty that sums up all duties: "therein the sum of a holy, obedient life is included."[79] A man who used all his time for God would be a perfect Christian. Baxter himself, living most of his life at death's door, as he supposed, was oppressed by a sense of the shortness of time. "Live as those that are certain to die . . . and you will say (as I have long been forced to do,) Oh how short are the days! How long are the nights! How swift is time! How slow is work! How far am I behindhand! I am afraid lest my life will be finished before the work of my life . . . "[80] He learned to value time by being always forced to work against it. Money also, like time, must be used to the full for God. Extravagance in money matters is a sin to which it is easy to be blind; therefore, "keep an account of your expenses, and peruse them before a fast or sacrament; and ask conscience how it judgeth of them . . . "[81] To tithe one's income for charitable purposes is a useful rule of thumb, but not an infallible one: "the tenth part is too much for some, and much too little for others."[82] The only principle of universal application is: give all you can. Generosity was a Puritan virtue. Baxter catalogues "seasonable good works" for the rich.[83] Every penny must be used for God. And so it must be with all one's other gifts and resources.

In the light of our summary review of the contents of Christ's law, we may now characterize the general temper of the life which it requires. First, it calls

---

78. p. 378.

79. II:vi; "Christian Ethics," I:v, is an elaborate treatment of the subject. In 1673 Baxter reissued William Whateley's sermon on *Redemption of Time*, with a prefatory "Address to the Sensual Gentry" by himself (XIII:517 f.).

80. XII:477.

81. VI:377; from "cases and Directions about prodigality and sinful waste" (*Christian Directory*, IV:xxi).

82. VI:493; from a letter originally written to Thomas Gouge (cf. *D.N.B.*, s.v.) and printed in the latter's *Christian Directions . . . whereunto is added his Sermon of Almes . . . with a Judicious Discourse of Mr. Rich. Baxters*, 1664, second pagination, 79 f., and republished in the *Christian Directory*, IV:xxx. Baxter often expresses admiration for the philanthropic and educational work in Wales done by Gouge (who "got 4score reading schools there set up," *The Poor Husbandman's Advocate to Rich Racking Landlords*, Baxter's last treatise, published by F.J. Powicke in *Rylands Bulletin*, Jan. 1926, 181); cf. *R.B.* III:147 f., 190.

83. Cf. Note C, p. 312 *inf*.

for a *serious* life. Baxter (who was himself, Sylvester tells us, "sparingly facetious; but never light or frothy")[84] makes this point over and over again. "If thou art not serious, thou art not a Christian."[85] "Christianity without seriousness is not Christianity."[86] He preached and published *Now or Never* "to open to you the Necessity of SERIOUS DILIGENCE."[87] Flippancy and superficiality were deadly enemies to Christian religion; "good sadness" was the only proper frame of mind when heaven or hell was the issue at stake. Moreover, Christ's law demands a *disciplined* life, rigidly and ruthlessly organized as a hierarchy of means to man's great end. It calls for intense, directed, unremitting effort; the Christian needs to think harder, work harder, feel more strongly and live at a higher tempo than other men. Men may laugh at this earnest "preciseness," but "I had rather the world should call me Puritan in the devil's name, than conscience should call me loiterer in God's name . . ."[88] Idleness and sloth are fatal; there is no hope for the "sleepy," happy-go-lucky, improvident sinner. "God hath resolved that heaven shall not be had on easier terms . . . he that strives not shall not enter."[89] Yet Christ's law does not commit the Christian to a life of strain and gloom, nor does it lead him into a legalistic wilderness. For, in the first place, the form of the law precludes the possibility of legalism. It sets before him an ideal for heart and life and tells him to pursue it. It calls him to reach for something which at present exceeds his grasp. It does not hedge him in with a network of prohibitions, but shows him a path and tells him to run along it as fast as he can. In the second place, the terms of the law exclude legalism, for it is a law of grace, which requires and accepts sincere endeavor in lieu of perfect performance. Fallen man's sincere endeavour does not enable him to attain the ideal standard, but—paradoxically enough—it does keep the law of Christ. He may not, therefore, pride himself on his achievement, but he may comfort his heart with the thought that he is accepted for his attempt. In the third place, the works commanded by the law are themselves a source of delight to the man who performs them. This is as true of well-doing in the world as of "heart-work" in the closet.[90] These activities are the life of Heaven begun on earth. There is no happier life than the holy life which Christ prescribes. Christ's law is a law of liberty, and Baxter's teaching on the Christian life is as far as possible from the legalism which his fellow-Puritans feared that they found in it.

84. *Elisha's Cry*, 14.
85. XXII:469.
86. VII:518.
87. p. 577.
88. XXIII:468.
89. p. 469.
90. cf. XVII:321: "There is a present pleasure in doing good, which is itself a great reward. The love of others . . . the pleasing of God, and the imitation of Christ, and the testimony of conscience, make it delightful . . . The believing giver hath more pleasure than the receiver."

NOTE C. "SEASONABLE GOOD WORKS" (cf. 310, n.4).

"A probability of doing or receiving good, is to me a call to action."[91] It is of interest to analyze the three catalogues of good works which Baxter drew up at various times for the guidance of the rich: the first (A) at the end of the Preface "To the nobility and gentry, and all that have the riches of this world," before *The Crucifying of the World . . .*" (1658; IX:cccxxxi f.); the second (B) in *Christian Directory*, IV:xxx, "Cases and Directions about works of charity," Tit. 1, answering question 3 (1673; VI:480 f.); and the third (C) in *How to do Good to Many; or, The Public Good is a Christian's Life* (1682; XVII:287 f.); a sermon addressed "To the Truly Christian Merchants and other Citizens of London." They constitute together an impressive program of Christian philanthropy, and reveal Baxter as a Christian strategist of a high order.

(i) Promoting personal religion in others.

(a) Charity "with a view" ("Do as much good as you are able to men's bodies, in order to the greater good of souls"):[92]

1. In general: relieve "the most needy which are next at hand . . . seconding all with spiritual advice and help";[93] "if you give them any annual gift of clothes, bread or money, engage them to learn some catechism withal . . . Some I know that set up a monthly lecture . . . and give sixpence or twelvepence to a certain number of poor that hear it."[94] (A 1, B 12).

2. To landlords: "As far as law will enable you, bind all your tenants in their leases to learn a catechism, and read the Scripture . . . It is very much that landlords might do for God if they had hearts . . . give them back some little, when they pay their rent, to hire them to some duty. And think not too much to go to their houses for such ends."[95] (A 2; B 11)

3. "Set poor men's children apprentices to honest, religious masters;"[96] "if you

---

91. *More Proofs*, 13.

92. XVII:303. Baxter reckons "that small relief which my low state enabled me to afford to Poor . . . Three pence or a Groat to every poor Body that askt me" as one the causes of his success at Kidderminster, as also "my Practice of Physick among them . . . doing it for nothing so obliged them, that they would readily hear me" (*R.B.*, I:89).

93. VI:482.

94. IX:cccxxxi.

95. *loc. cit.*, On the landlord's duty, cf. *The Poor Husbandman's Advocate, passim*.

96. VI:481 f.

are able, settle a perpetual allowance for this use,"[97] to be used at the minister's discretion (A 4, B 8).

4. "Set up free-schools in populous and in ignorant places, especially in Wales"[98] (as Thomas Gouge did) so that children may learn to read the Bible and be taught the fundamentals of Christianity. "A poor honest man, or a good woman, will teach children thus much for a small stipend, better than they are taught it in most grammar schools"[99] (A 6, B 5, C).

(b) Distributing Bibles, catechisms, Puritan treatises and tracts ("plain and rousing books")[100] or, at least, buying them for the minister to distribute (A 3, B 7, C). The latter "are good catechisms . . . it is the catechetical truths which . . . our English sermons press; and the lively pressing maketh them pierce deeper than a catechism."[101] Baxter practiced what he preached; cf. 53 n. 42, *sup.*, and so did others; cf. (e.g.) a letter from Thomas Jackman of Newent (Glos.), dated July 24, 1672, concerning "the charitable Designe of placing pious books in prisons": "I do resolve by Gods assistance, that the prisons in yᵉ 3 adjacent counties, shall not want such a book as your Call to the unconverted whilest I live tho I am att the Charge of renewing them every yeare."[102] In (B) and (C), Baxter advocates leaving "a settled revenue for this use, (naming the books and choosing meet trustees,) that so the rent might every year furnish a several parish,"[103] thus making the benefit more widespread.

(ii) Maintaining the ministry.

(a) Maintaining assistant ministers in large parishes ("What minister can well oversee and watch over more than a thousand souls? Nor I think so many.")[104] "Impropriations may be bought in to that use."[105] (A 5, B 4.)

(b) Sending "some of the choicest wits, among the poorer sort in the country schools"[106] to the university, to study for the ministry. (Conversely, nobody, not even one's own son, should be sent there "who doth not first show these

97. IX:cccxxxii.
98. VI:481.
99. XVII:304.
100. IX:cccxxxi.
101. XVII:304 f.
102. Mss. 59. vi. f.7.
103. VI:481.
104. XXIII:89.
105. IX:cccxxxii.
106. VI:481.

three qualifications: a capable, natural wit and utterance; a love to serious, practical religion; a great desire to serve God in the ministry.")[107] (A 7, B 6.) (In 1658, Matthew Poole issued the prospectus of a trust fund for giving poor students grants (*A Model for the Maintaining of Students of choice Abilities at the University . . . in order to the Ministry*; date misprinted on title-page as 1648), to which Baxter contributed a prefatory appeal for contributions, "To the Rich that love Christ." He alludes to the forthcoming project in A 7. The scheme was short-lived; cf. *D.N.B.*, *s.v.* Poole, for some account of it.)

In 1657 (A 9) Baxter appealed for a college to be built" (at Salop I think the only fit place . . .) for the education of scholars for the use of Wales . . . Too few will send their sons to our present universities, and too few of those that come thither are willing to return."[108]

In 1682, Baxter declared it "a work of great importance, for religious gentlemen to buy as many advowsons or presentations as they can,"[109] so as to secure a competent ministry.

(c) Relieving the impoverished families of ministers ejected in 1662 (B 9).

(iii) Social amelioration.

(a) Advancing capital for the small business man: "It is a good work of them who give stocks of money, or yearly rents, to be lent for five, or six, or seven years, to young tradesmen, at their setting up, upon good security, choosing good trustees, who may choose the fittest persons; and if it be a rent, it will still increase the stock"[110] (A 8, B 10).

(b) "Setting all the poor on work, and building hospitals for the impotent, &c."[111]

(c) Promoting missionary work abroad ("the most eminent work of charity.")[112] Baxter admired the example set by John Eliot and the Jesuits and lamented the general neglect on the churches' part of the missionary task ("the Christian princes and people are exceedingly to blame, that they have done no more.")[113] In 1681, he professed: "For my own part, had I strength and any vulgar tongue,

---

107. XVII:306.
108. IX:cccxxxiii.
109. XVII:306.
110. VI:482.
111. XVII:329.
112. VI:480.
113. IX:cccxxxiv.

which I might use in Preaching in other lands, I think I should have left *England* long ago;"[114] for "No part of my Prayers are so deeply serious, as that for the Conversion of the Infidel and Ungodly World."[115]

"Is it not possible to send some able, zealous chaplains to those factories which are in the countries of infidels . . .?. . . Might not something be done in . . . plantations . . . towards the conversion of the natives there . . . Is it not possible to do more than hath been done, to convert the blacks that are our own slaves, or servants?"[116] (C).

Baxter suggested founding a missionary training college, and procuring "one or two of the natives out of the countries whose conversion you design, to teach the students in this college their language."[117] (A 10, B1).

(d) Translating and circulating Bibles and Christian books (B 1, C).

Part IV

THE RESTORATION
OF THE ELECT

"Whom he did predestinate, them he also called; and whom he called, them
he also justified; and whom he justified, them he also glorified."

—Rom. 8:30

Chapter 13

The Work of the Holy Spirit

"new creature" implanted after faith, as part of covenant promise: Baxter's change of view here;

> necessity of subsequent cooperation with the Spirit, especially at times of special assistance.

6.   The Spirit's work in assurance:

> Assurance desirable and a blessing; "false peace" a curse;
> Assurance an inference from observed sanctification;
>> marks of true faith;
>> Baxter's own assurance imperfect.
> Inordinate preoccupation with assurance discouraged;
>> holiness more important than assurance.

7. Conclusion: Baxter at one with Puritan tradition;

> Common emphasis on the freedom of the Spirit through the means.

(Principal Sources: *Catholick Theologie*, *Saints' Rest*, esp. III:vii-xi (XXII:482-XXIII:53); *Right Method* (IX); *Christian Directory*, I:iii, *Grand Direction* III (II:188 f.); *Life of Faith*, III:iii (XII:210 f.)).

Chapter 13

The Work of the Holy Spirit

The whole work which we assign unto him, is nothing but that whereby we are enabled to perform that obedience unto God which is required in the Scripture, in the way and manner wherein it is required.
—John Owen, *Pneumatologia*, "To the Reader."

The ministry of the word is the pipe or organ; the Spirit of God blowing in it, effectually changes men's hearts.   —Thomas Watson on the *Shorter Catechism*, Q:XXXI.

The doctrine of the work of the Holy Spirit," wrote B.B. Warfield, "is a gift from John Calvin to the Church of Christ."[1] It was Calvin's distinction "to replace the doctrine of the Church as sole source of assured knowledge of God and sole institute of salvation, by the Holy Spirit."[2] The subject of the Spirit's activity in the sinner's salvation occupies only one short chapter (four paragraphs) in the *Institutio*. But this chapter (III.i, "Quae de Christo dicta sunt, nobis prodesse arcana operatione Spiritus") is the key to the whole third book ("De modo percipiendae Christi gratiae"). It states the double principle which guides Calvin throughout his exposition of the manner in which redemption is applied to the individual: that the elect benefit from Christ's

1. "Introductory Note" prefixed to A. Kuyper, *The Work of the Holy Spirit*, 1900, xxxiii. In *Calvin and Calvinism*, 1931, 21, Warfield claims for Calvin, as the Theologian of the Holy Spirit, a place beside Augustine, Anselm and Luther, the Theologians of grace, atonement and justification respectively.
2. Warfield, *Calvin as a Theologian and Calvinism To-day*, 1952 reprint, 10. He there describes the *Institutio* as "just a treatise on the work of the Holy Spirit in making God savingly known to sinful man."

death and resurrection only through union with Him by faith, and that their faith is the creation of the Spirit through the Word, the appointed means of grace. The Puritans followed where Calvin led. With the aid of the light afforded by Scholastic anthropology and assiduous introspection, they expanded Calvin's sketch of the Christian life in enormous detail, but retained his doctrinal framework unchanged. Indeed, they adhered to his method as closely as to his material. Like Calvin, the Puritan expositor was "a practical man, writing to practical men for a practical purpose,"[3] concerned to inculcate, not merely Christian theology, but the Christian religion; like Calvin, therefore, he set out what he had to say concerning the Spirit's work in the order of practice, so that it appeared in the form of treatises on the means of grace and the life of faith. When John Owen published *Pneumatologia* in 1674, he wrote in the Preface: "I know not of any who ever went before me in this design of representing the whole economy of the Holy Spirit, with all his adjuncts, operations and effects"[4]—and this despite the vast output of Puritan "practical divinity" during the preceding century. What Owen meant was that the standard material had never been organized on a theoretical principle, as a *locus* in systematic theology. This was all that he aimed to do in his own book; its contents reveal him completely at one with his Puritan predecessors, as they had been with Calvin. The basic positions on which they all agreed were, that it is the Spirit's work to create faith and thereby to empower men for good works; that He operates through means; that the appointed objective means of grace is the Word, and the prescribed subjective means is to hear the Word in the Scripture and the sermon, to see it in the sacraments, to meditate on it and to pray over it; and that it is therefore man's duty and wisdom to make diligent use of these means to their proper end—the strengthening of faith and the perfecting of gospel obedience.

Alongside the steadily-flowing main stream of Protestant thought on this subject ran the eddying, zigzag rivulets of *enthusiasm*. At their source lay a different doctrine of the Spirit's work. The *enthusiasts* held that, over and above what He may do through the means, the Spirit works in the saints immediately, going beyond Scripture both in revelation of truth and in direct impulses to action. Man's duty, therefore, was to forego religious routine and to wait passively before God until the Spirit spoke. He must not tie himself to the means, for the Spirit was now working above and without means. To be tied to means is legal and carnal; the mark of spiritual religion is immediacy of communion with God. This kind of thought, with its avowed sectarianism, its innate perfectionism and its apocalyptic outlook, is a recurring feature of

---

3. *Calvin and Calvinism*, 71.

4. Owen, *Works*, III:7. Owen had planned to fill this gap in Protestant dogmatics as early as 1653 (X:490 f.; Preface to *Dissertation on the Divine Justice*).

Church history. The Reformation spawned a swarm of such sects. The earliest were the Zwickau Anabaptists. In England, we hear of, among others, the Family of Love, the Muggletonians, Seekers, Ranters, and early Quakers. The Antinomians and their predecessors, the Traskites, though never organized as separate sects, owed some of their own peculiarities to the influence of *enthusiastic* thought, as we shall in part see in the next chapter.

Our present task is not to trace the diverse developments of *enthusiasm* among its various adherents, but merely define the general issue between them as a body and the Calvinistic orthodoxy for which the Puritans and Baxter stood. Theologically, it was the question whether the Spirit reveals truth and creates faith mediately, through the written Word, or immediately, without it. Practically, it was the question of the authority of religious experience. The Puritans held that the norm of Christian life was set out in Scripture, and that Spirit-given experience proclaims itself such by conforming to the pattern there given. "Religious" impressions must be tested, for fallen man easily mistakes the issue of his own corrupt heart for the gift of God, and the Devil is an adept at fostering a counterfeit spirituality in order to distract men from the true. Experiences must therefore be tried by Scripture. Whether it is God's Spirit in the heart or not must be determined by appeal to God's Spirit in the Word. Scripture provides an objective criterion for experience. This was not to deny that Christian experience was the best commentary on Scripture. A man devoid of experimental knowledge of the God of the Bible was not yet a Christian at all; much less could he be an expositor or theologian. His theological talk was no more significant than the babbling of a blind man about a sunset; in the strictest sense, he did not know what he was talking about. There could be no "powerful preaching" without experience, for such preaching was essentially the declaration of "what I smartingly did feel"[5] with a vehemence and passion which only intense piety could beget. To be a powerful preacher, the Puritans insisted, it was necessary to do as did Robert Bolton, who "never taught any godly point, but he first wrought it on his owne heart."[6] Nor, again, could sound academic theology be produced apart from the same discipline. "I hold myself bound in conscience," wrote John Owen, ". . . . not even to imagine that I have attained a proper knowledge of any one article of truth, much less to publish it, unless through the Holy Spirit I have had . . . a taste of it, in its spiritual sense . . . "[7] Experience was therefore indispensable as a means to understanding the truth of God. But this was because experience opened a man's eyes to apprehend the meaning of the objective testimony of Scripture,

5. J. Bunyan, *Grace Abounding*, para. 276.

6. Nicolas Estwick, *A Learned and Godly Sermon Preached . . . at the Funerall of Mr. Robert Bolton*, 1633, 65.

7. *Works*, X:488.

not because it directly mediated new light. In no sense, the orthodox insisted, was it an independent authority. The "enthusiasts," however, treated certain experiences as self-authenticating. Something inherent in them, they claimed, proved their Divine origin. Whatever notions or suggestions these waves of feeling washed into the mind must therefore be of God; and if they were contrary to Scripture, so much the worse for Scripture. Between two such radically opposite points of view, there could only be war; and in this war we find Baxter in the front line. We have already watched him assault the *enthusiasts* for their doctrine of man; in this and the next chapter we shall find him belaboring them for their doctrine of the Holy Spirit.

Baxter stood in the Calvinistic tradition. Like Calvin and his Puritan predecessors, he wrote no systematic work on the doctrine of the Holy Spirit in the believer. The section "De Auxilio Spiritus Sancti" (III:xvi) occupies only ten of the nine hundred pages of *Methodus Theologiae*, and apart from this chapter and three others—the third "Grand Direction" in his *Christian Directory*, I:iii ("How to believe in the Holy Ghost, and live by his grace"), *The Life of Faith* III:iii ("How to live by faith on the Holy Ghost") and *The Catechising of the Families*, XVII ("I believe in the Holy Ghost"), 10, 22 and 4 pages in Orme's reprint respectively[8]—all Baxter's references to the Spirit's work are incidental and fragmentary. Yet in a real sense all his practical writings could be described as Warfield described the *Institutio*: they are all ultimately expositions of the work of the Holy Spirit in bringing salvation to the sinner. We are now to study this process in detail.

In all the activity of the Godhead, the Holy Spirit is "the third perfective principle of operation . . . operating *ad extra*, by communication."[9] It is He who imparts God's image to His works, both in nature and in grace. "Without the Spirit of God, as the perfective principle, nature would not have been nature, Gen. 1:2."[10] It is an error to suppose that "man in innocency had not the Spirit of God . . . for his natural rectitude was the effect of the influx or communication of God's Spirit; and he could have no moral rectitude without it."[11] When man fell, and the Son came into the world to redeem him, the Father gave His Spirit to the Son in full measure (so that "Jesus Christ . . . is the purest, clearest image of the Father"),[12] and it was by the Spirit's power that the man Christ Jesus lived a life of perfect holiness and obtained redemption for a fallen world. After his resurrection, the Son was glorified, but did not thereby cease to be man, nor, therefore, did the Spirit leave him. "The Spirit dwelleth in the human

8. II:188 f., XII:210 f., XIX:88 f.
9. XII:202.
10. p. 203.
11. p. 206.
12. XIII:15.

nature of our Head, and there it can never be lost."[13] From this source, the Head dispenses the Spirit to indwell His members, "not . . . by way of radication, but by way of influence and operation."[14] The effects of His activity in human life are metonymically "called the Spirit, as the sunshine in the room is called the sun."[15]

> God hath made it the office of our Mediator's glorified humanity, to be the cistern that shall first receive the waters of life, and convey them by the pipes of his appointed means to all the offices of his house.[16]

> As Administrator general, the power of giving out the Spirit to mankind is now given to *Him*, even in his humane Nature . . . Though God the Holy Ghost be still proximately the cause of Grace, yet Christ . . . is made by office, the *Mediator and authorized giver of that Spirit and all its Grace*; and so the . . . appointer of the conditions. And Christ is first filled with this Spirit *personally* himself, that he may be a fit Head of vital Influence to all his Members, who by the previous operations of his Spirit are drawn and united to him.[17]

The Spirit is sent into the world to recreate fallen men according to the pattern perfected in Christ's own manhood. Thus, in Aquinas' words, which Baxter never tired of quoting, *gratia non tollit naturam sed perficit*, for grace restores to fallen humanity the image of the Man Who Himself bore and still bears the image of God.

"The three great operations in man, which each of the three persons in the Trinity eminently perform, are *natura, medicina, salus*: the first by the Creator, the second by the Redeemer, the third by the Sanctifier."[18] What *salus* involves is made clear in the following catechetical statement:

> It is the work of the Holy Ghost to sanctify all God's elect; that is, to illuminate their understandings, to convert their wills to God, and to strengthen and quicken them to do their duty, and conquer sin, and save them from the devil, the world, and the flesh . . . Millions perish that God created, and that Christ, in a general sort . . . died for; but those that are sanctified by the Holy Ghost are saved. It is the work of the Holy Ghost to communicate to us the grace of Christ, that the work of creation and redemption may attain their ends.[19]

---

13. V:347.
14. *loc. cit.*
15. XII:401; cf. XVIII:418: "the same Spirit is in heaven, who is in my heart, (as the same sun is in the firmament which is in my house . . .)."
16. V:349.
17. *C.T.*, II:178. Baxter appends eighteen New Testament passages in proof of his position.
18. XII:208.
19. XIX:88 f. (*The Catechising of Families*, XVII).

This statement, we may note, brings out the essential difference between the Calvinism of the Saumur school, the Anglicans at Dort, and Baxter, and that of Perkins, Ames, Owen and the later Reformed tradition. Both accepted unconditional election, human inability and irresistible grace in conversion and perseverance. The latter, however, limited the designed efficacy of Christ's death to those whom God had chosen to bring to faith, thus introducing the particularism of election into their doctrine of atonement, whereas the former extended the scope of the atonement to make it as wide as mankind, and introduced particularism only at the point where the Spirit conveys "differencing special grace,"[20] "distinguishing, separating mercy,"[21] to the elect. As to the nature of the Spirit's work in elect sinners, however, there was virtual unanimity. The difference did not affect this doctrine.

The Spirit had been active in the work of sanctification since the covenant of grace was first published to Adam; else "the godly before Christ's coming in the flesh, would not have been godly, nor in any present capacity of glory."[22] Old Testament saints had enjoyed "that measure of true grace which was necessary to the salvation of believers, before the incarnation and resurrection of Christ, (which was the Spirit of Christ, as the light before sun-rising is the light of the sun), and if they died in that case, they would have been saved . . . "[23] But "this eminent gospel gift of the Holy Ghost, as he is the great Witness and Agent of Christ' was proper only to the final edition of the covenant, and was not given until Christ had come in the flesh, died, risen and ascended in order to give it.[24] Under the Gospel, it is "the great priviledge of believers' to have the Spirit with them as "the great *Agent, Advocate* and *witness* of *Christ in us,* the *divine nature,* and *name* of God and his *mark* upon us: our *witness, earnest, pledge,* and *first-fruits* of life eternal."[25]

The Spirit effects His work by causing man to hear, consider and obey the Word of God, which for the present age is synonymous with the Law of Christ. This Word, communicated and apprehended, is the means through which He acts, and His work consists precisely of the eliciting of a due response to it. "The Spirit cometh not to you, to make you new duty which the Scripture never made your duty, and so to bring an additional law; but to move and help you in that which was your duty before."[26] The objective ordinances and subjective activities which are denominated "means of grace" (preaching, hearing, meditating, praying, and the rest) are such for a twofold reason: first,

---

20. *C.T.*, II:192.
21. XXII:118.
22. XII:203.
23. XII:205.
24. *loc. cit.*; a comment on Jn:7:37 and Acts 19:2.
25. *C.T.*, I:iii, XVI:3, 53.
26. II:198.

because they confront men with God's Word; and, second, because, it is through the Word that the Spirit works faith and new life. The Spirit must not be set against the means, "as if the Spirit did not usually work by the Word."[27] Baxter constantly attacked the Quakers for decrying the written Word, the objective means of grace, in order to exalt the inner light; this, he held, was to 'advance, extol, and plead for the Spirit, against the Spirit" and revealed them to be "enthusiasts, or true fanatics."[28] Similarly, he berated the Antinomian school for their neglect of the regular discipline of meditation and prayer, the subjective means of grace. To their contention that a religion in which one was "tied to the means" was "low and legal,"[29] and that the more excellent way was to cast off all routines of duty and wait passively for the Spirit's quickening breath, Baxter had a trenchant answer: these men were denying their own humanity.

> The Spirit worketh not on man as a dead thing, which hath no principle of activity in itself … but as on a living, free, self-determining agent, which hath duty of its own to perform for the attaining of the end desired. Those therefore that upon the pretence of the Spirit's doing all, and our doing nothing without him, will lie idle and not do their parts with him, and say that they wait for the motions of the Spirit, and that our endeavours will not further the end, do abuse the Spirit, and contradict themselves; seeing the Spirit's work is to stir us up to endeavour, which when we refuse to do, we disobey and strive against the Spirit.[30]

Nor, on the other hand, must the means be set against the Spirit, for means without the Spirit are void.

> There is an admirable, unsearchable concurrence of the Spirit, and his appointed means, and the will of man, in … all the exercises of grace, as there is … of the earth, the sun, the rain, the industry of the gardener, and the seminal virtue of life and specification, in the production of plants … And as wise as it would be to say … it is not the earth but the sun, or not the sun but the rain, or not the rain but the seminal virtue, that causeth plants with flowers and fruits: so wise is it to say, it is not the Spirit but the word and means, or it is not the word and means but the Spirit … They are all con-causes: if the effect be there, they all concur; if the effect were wanting, some of them were

27. III:253.

28. II:189 f.; Baxter elaborates his charge as follows: "They plead the Spirit in themselves against the Spirit in their brethren, yea, and in almost all the church: they plead the authority of the Spirit in them, against the authority of the Spirit in the holy Scriptures; and against particular truths of Scripture … "

29. So William Erbury (cf. *D.N.B.*, *s.v.*) of the religion taught by Bolton, Hooker and John Rogers, in *Testimony*, 1658, 67; quoted by G.F. Nuttall, *op. cit.*, 14, n.1.

30. XII:218; cf. XIII:134: "God will have external objective means and internal subjective means concur because he will work on man agreeably to the nature of man."

wanting . . . Your reason, and conscience, and means would fall short of the effect, if the Spirit put not life into all.[31]

The whole series of means of grace—sermons, sacraments, hearing, reading, meditation, prayer—is employed to no purpose until the Spirit makes them effective to their end. Baxter's conception of "means of grace" appears very clearly from his analysis of the Biblical concept of *grace*. The generic significance of the word, he tells us, is "Mercy contrary to Merit."[32] Specifically, "*Grace* is taken either for the *Favour* of *God*, or for his *Gifts*."[33] In the latter sense, grace is twofold.

> *Objective Grace* is those means which as *Objects* are appointed for *man himself* to *act upon* towards his own Salvation. As a *Christ* to be . . . *accepted*, An *offered glory*, a *certain Promise*, &c. Subjective Grace is that effect which is wrought on mans Soul,"[34]

and consist of a number of separate "graces": repentance, faith, hope, love and so on. Baxter strongly deprecates the tendency to think of "grace" as a mysterious supernatural power or effluence, over and above God's mercy in confronting a man with the Gospel and evoking his acceptance of it. "Do not Imagine that there is certain *vis media* called Grace, which is somewhat Causal between the Creator and the Creature . . . men think that . . . there is some middle force . . . called Grace; whose kind and degree they enquire after."[35] Grace is not the mode or means of Divine action, but its motive and its fruit.

The first part of the Spirit's work is to confront man with the objective means of grace, the gospel; which He effects by the following series of operations:

> The Holy Ghost . . . infallibly inspired the holy apostles and evangelists, first to preach, and then to write the doctrine of Christ . . . The same Spirit in them, sealed this holy doctrine . . . by many miracles and wonderful gifts, by which they did actually convince the unbelieving world, and plant the churches. The same Spirit . . . doth qualify and dispose men for the stated, ordinary ministerial work, (which is to explain and apply the foresaid Scriptures) . . . The same Spirit assisteth the ministers . . . to teach and apply the holy Scriptures according to the necessities of the people . . ."[36]

31. II:193, 198.
32. *Universal Redemption*, 244, 469, *et al.*
33. *C.T.*, II:145.
34. *loc. cit.*
35. Ibid., 195.
36. II:190 f.

The second part of His work consists in internal regeneration and sanctification: new birth, and growth in grace. These must be considered separately.

The reorientation of life which the Word commands and the Spirit effects is so radical and drastic that Scripture calls the man who has passed through it a *new creature*, "in a moral sense (as he is a new man that changeth his mind and manners)."[37] His life becomes the spontaneous outworking of a new disposition, supernaturally implanted.

> The new creature is not as a lifeless engine, (as a clock, or watch, or ship,) where every part must be set in order by the art and hand of man . . . but it is liker to the frame of our own nature, when every part is set in its place and order by the Creator, and hath in itself a living and harmonical principle, which desposeth it to . . . regular action, and is so to be kept in order and daily exercise by ourselves, as yet to be principally ordered and actuated by the Spirit, which is the principal cause.[38]

The Spirit produces the change by enabling him to grasp the truth and significance of the message of the love of God in Christ to sinners,[39] and impelling him to respond to it by hearty repentance and faith in the risen Christ as Savior and Lord. The convert now sets himself to serve Christ, and to win heaven. The proximate cause of this transformation at each stage must be the conscious operation of the man's own mind and will, in submission to the gospel command, but its ultimate cause is the effective operation within him of the Spirit of Christ.

The Arminian controversy had raised in an acute form the question of the precise nature of the Spirit's work in conversion, and contemporary Calvinists discussed the matter in full. All agreed, against Arminianism, that fallen man was spiritually impotent and so unable to convert himself, that converting grace was irresistible, and that it in no way violated or impaired man's natural free will. Here, however, they divided, according to their view of what man's natural free will in fact amounts to, and how God works in producing human action. The great majority took the "intellectualist" position of Aquinas, and

---

37. XIII:237; cf. *C.T.*, I. iii. V. 9, p.19: "the whole state of the *Man, Habitual, Relative* and *Practical* . . . is called in Scripture, a *New Creature*, and the *New Man*, tropically, but not unfitly . . . we use to say in common things, that when an unlearned man is made learned, and a poor man a Prince . . . he is *another man*." The change on mind, will and affections is exhaustively analyzed in the first part of the *Treatise on Conversion* (VII:24 f.).

38. XIII:175.

39. cf. Baxter's "Answer to the Quakers Queries" in *The Quakers Catechism*, 11: "God in Christ is the Sun, Mans Reason is the Eye, The Gospel or Word of God is the external Light flowing to us from the Sun. The Spirit closeth these two together, even the Gospel and our Reason, and by its powerful work in that closure, breedeth a special illumination in the soul which the Word alone could not produce."

held that all acts which are deliberately chosen are, as such, free. "Our Reformed Divines have generally placed Natural Liberty in a Rational Spontaneitie."[40] John Preston's statement is typical: "Reason only is the root and foundation of all Liberty . . . every act of the Will, into which Reason hath influence, is most free."[41] Where man does what he decided to do, there is freedom. But free acts are also constrained acts, necessitated by their object. That which presents itself to the mind as the best of the proposed alternatives is necessarily chosen; for the will automatically closes with the highest seeming good. And behind the concourse of mind and object lies Divine predestination. Man's choices, like all other events, take place ultimately because God willed them, and so took steps to bring them to pass. Within the Thomist party there was a further difference of opinion concerning God's method of evoking the first act of saving faith. Most held that at the Fall man's will contracted a vicious habit of opposition to God, which no mere intellectual enlightenment could break. Whatever his reason may say, fallen man is obstinately determined not to do God's will. "The carnal mind is enmity against God" (Rom. 8:7). Therefore, concurrently with His presentation of the gospel to the mind of the elect sinner, the Spirit effects a *physical renewal* of his will. "God infuseth . . . into the Will, a habit or quality of holinesse, renewing it . . ."[42] As a result, the man becomes aware of inchoate desires for God and His salvation arising spontaneously within his mind, "not so much willings, as wishings and wouldings."[43] Reason, enlightened by the Spirit, takes notice of them and approves; whereupon, "after those initiall inclinations . . . have passed the censure of the understanding . . . then at length doth the Will put forward a compleat and effectuall willingnesse, from which conversion immediately doth follow . . . this Willing is both irresistible and free." It is proximately elicited "in the way of morall perswasion," but is in the last analysis the direct result of the Spirit's prior physical work. This doctrine of "physical regeneration" became part of Reformed orthodoxy.

Cameron and the Saumur school, however, held a different view. They denied that the connection between mind and will had been so disrupted by the Fall that clear, practical knowledge of the way of salvation could no longer move a man to action. If he saw clearly that a life of faith in Christ was the *summum bonum* for him, he would still automatically choose it. The sole reason why so many who hear the gospel fail to respond to it is because they have not yet grasped that what it sets before them is their own highest good. Sin has

40. Theophilus Gale, *Court of the Gentiles*, pt. IV, bk. iii, 11 (1678). For Gale, "an honest self-conceited Non-conformist" (*R.B.*, III:182), cf. *D.N.B.*, s.v.

41. *The Position of John Preston . . . Concerning the Irresistibleness of Converting Grace*, 1654, 10. In his youth, Preston "was drawn on very far in the study of the School-Divines . . . he continued longer in *Aquinas* . . ." (S. Clarke, *Lives of Thirty-Two English Divines*, 79).

42. Preston, *op. cit.*, 5.

43. *Op. cit.*, 6.

darkened their minds. The vicious habit which is every man's legacy from Adam is seated, not in the will, but in the understanding. It is a disinclination, not to do, but to know. To convert men, therefore, the Spirit need do no more than enlighten them as to the full significance for them of the gospel message, which is not a physical but a moral (*ethicum*) work. No physical renewal of the will is necessary; as soon as men realize that life is set before them, they choose it at once. Despite his insistence that what he described was not the (possibly ineffective) *suasio* of the Arminians ("novos semi-Pelagianos"), but *persuasio*, irresistible and certain in its effects, Cameron and his followers were constantly accused of conceding too much to their opponents, and their views met no favor outside Saumur.

Baxter, however, upheld the "voluntarism" of Duns Scotus, and, as we saw, thought of man's will as an inner principle of self-determination, whose freedom consists precisely in the absence of all external constraint. *Voluntas nihil de necessitate vult.* A direct physical operation on the will in regeneration, or for that matter at any other time, would thus be an infringement of its liberty. Saving faith is a free act, and free acts are not necessitated, either by their object or by the Divine influence which sustains all things in existence and without which they could not be. Baxter excluded both kinds of intellectualist from the number of those whom he hoped that his *Catholick Theologie* would reconcile, on the ground that they denied the reality of human freedom altogether:

> I undertake not the Reconciliation of the *Predeterminants*, who hold *That Free-will is nothing but will as related to Reason . . . and that all its acts are as truly necessitated by the efficacious premotion of God, as is the motion of a Clock* . . . (though they will needs call them *free*, because they are *volitions*, as if *willing* and *free-willing* were words of the same signification:) . . . They that think that God cannot make a Creature, whose *Will can determine itself without his predetermination* . . . I am to confute, and not to reconcile . . . There are two sorts that thus subject the *Will* to *absolute caused necessity.* 1 . . .the *Dominicans*, who assert the predetermining premotion of God as necessary to every act natural and free. 2. Those that make the Will as much necessitated by a train of natural *second Causes*, which is *Hobbs* his way, (and, alas, the way of great and excellent healing *Camero*) . . . I now deal with none but those who confess, that God made Man's *Will* at first with a natural *self-determining power*, suited to this earthly state of government . . .[44]

Baxter did not deny that "God hath a *double work* in Illuminating and Converting souls: *One* by *activity* of *exteriour appulsive causes:* The other *within us* on the *faculties* of the soul," but held that "his wayes of co-operation are past

44. *C.T.*, II:4 f.

the reach of man,"⁴⁵ and professed to know nothing at all about them. He was sure, however, that God did not work on the will by physical influences concurrent with, but independent of, the moral influence exercised by the Word in the mind. Irresistible converting grace is no more than effective moral suasion. The Spirit moves man, "not persuading the will . . . immediately by himself, but exciting and so using reason and conscience, as the instruments to persuade the will . . ."⁴⁶ So far, Baxter was in agreement with Cameron, against the orthodox. But he went on to reject all forms of necessitarianism, Cameron's included, as incompatible with free decision on man's part. Necessitation of the will would make man a puppet in God's hands, jumping into thought and action as God pulled the strings; and a puppet is not a moral agent. To suggest, as the intellectualists seemed to him to do, that man in conversion was just such a puppet was to rob God of His glory as *Rector*, drawing man to Himself by moral means, i.e. His laws. "Do not overlook the glory that God designeth to himself in his SAPIENTIAL Kingdom, Government, and operations," was his constant plea.⁴⁷ Christ's kingdom is "a *sapiential frame of Moral Causes*, designed for the *Government* of *man*," in which physical constraint, whether at the level of first or second causes, has no place. Such constraint would destroy its reality. Baxter waxed scornful in his strictures on the orthodox view of God's method in conversion:

> they that slight all this work of God, by the contemptuous name of *Moral Suasion*, and take it to be a *diminutive term* . . . and talk of Gods work of Grace on the soul, as if there were no more in it very honourable, than a *physical Motion*, and God Converted souls but as Boyes whip their Tops, or Women turn their Wheels . . . are *Cartesian blind Theologues*, and overlook the very nature of . . . Theologie . . . which is the *Doctrine* of the *Kingdom of God over man*; . . . they are fitter mechanically to treat of or deal with Stones, Bricks, or Timber, than *men*; being unfit to treat of *humane Government*, much more of *Divine*.⁴⁸

45. *C.T.*, I.iii.IV. 2:16.
46. XXIII:306, n.
47. *C.T.*, II:195.
48. *C.T.*, I.iii.III.36:15. Baxter refers to Descartes' theory of the automatism of brutes. We may note that in the first edition of the *Saints' Rest* (143) Baxter had asserted "the Spirits efficacious changing Physical operation" without qualms; but in the fourth (1653; not the third, as stated in "Confutation of . . . Ludiomaeus Colvinus" in *Apology*, 274), though he left unchanged the discussion of regeneration from which the phrase above quoted is taken, he added an unpaged leaf at the end of it (opposite 160) in which he explained that "Dr. *Twisse* had perswaded me that the work of the Spirit was by efficient Physical infusion . . . Whence I gathered that the word was not properly the Spirits Instrument in converting . . . but a concause in exciting those Habits into Act which by the spirit alone are infused;" but now "I begin to doubt of the soundness" of this view. The whole passage disappeared in the eighth edition (1659). The earliest of Baxter's polemics on the subject is the "Third Kidderminster Disputation, of Physical Predetermination," dated 1654 (Mss., 59:viii,

The importance which Baxter attached to this issue made it desirable to report the conflicting views; but in fact the difference was trivial, and Baxter's polemic served only to obscure it. The metaphysical context of Baxter's thought was the Cartesian world-view, according to which there are two sorts of substances, thinking and non-thinking, and two corresponding sorts of causation, moral and physical. These pairs of categories were mutually exclusive. Baxter could only see the Thomist view through Cartesian spectacles, and so he interpreted the doctrine of a physical renewal of the will as an assertion that at a certain point God stopped treating the soul as a thinking substance and began to treat it in a manner appropriate only to non-thinking substances. It was in vain for the orthodox to protest that this was an illegitimate opposition of two complementary factors, moral suasion by the Spirit through the Word together with the direct implanting of the capacity to receive it and obey it. Baxter was adamant that it must be the one or the other. If the influence was physical, then it could not be rational and moral; if, as he himself asserted, it was rational and moral, then it could not also be physical. But this was not a strictly theological disagreement at all. Both sides subscribed to the Confessional statements that God, the First Cause of all events, "ordereth them to fall out according to the nature of second causes, either necessarily, freely or contingently," and that the Spirit effectually calls men to Christ through the Word, "by his almighty power determining them to that which is good . . . yet so as they come most freely, being made willing by his grace."[49] All they were wrangling about was the correct metaphysical formulation and analysis of these positions. In fact, the issue amounted to no more than whether Cartesian dualism is true. If Baxter's wordy warfare on this subject has any value, it is as protest against the depreciation of manhood by theologians. It certainly does not clarify the mystery of regeneration.

Some grace is given to everyone, but more to some than others. This inequality of privilege depends on the free decision of God in Christ, who owes no man any grace at all, let alone any particular measure of it, and communicates more or less of it at His will. A certain number hear the good news of redemption, some more plainly and powerfully than others; the rest of men do not hear it at all, and enjoy only the rudimentary gospel of a gracious God which is preached by the good things of life. It is not true that every man at every moment has sufficient grace to be saved outright if he responds to it, as the Arminians maintained, but it is no more true, as certain forms of Calvinism asserted, that some men are left completely without hope. The truth,

---

ff. 293-327), which he nearly published as a reply to Gale's strictures on *Catholick Theologie* in *Court of the Gentiles*, IV:iii, but suppressed on hearing of Gale's death (*R.B.*, III:182 f., 185). His fair copy, ready for the press, with a Preface dated May 10, 1679, exists as a quarto Ms., "Miscellanea Baxteriana minora," no. 4).

49. *Westminster Confession*, V:ii, X:i.

Baxter held, lies between these two extremes. Each gracious gift which God's providence bestows is in itself a "*half promise* . . . or a precept to use means with sufficient encouragement,"[50] a token that there are other and greater blessings available for those who will seek them. And none ever seeks God in vain. If some do not find Him, that is their fault. They would have found Him had they responded to the incentives He gave them to seek Him. The effectiveness of external means of grace depends on the recipient's disposition and sin has made it man's natural disposition to spurn and neglect God's gracious overtures. The truth about every ungodly man is that he has received mercies which he has not "improved;" he is, therefore, guilty of ingratitude towards his Divine Benefactor, and guilty too of having quenched the Spirit, who sought through each gift to make him understand its meaning and thereby draw him nearer to God. As God cannot be accused of injustice for giving more knowledge and opportunities to one than to another, so he is in no way blameworthy for the sins and consequent punishment of those who die without Christ. Those who lived in Christian countries might have been converted if they had used the means of grace ready to hand; most of those who did not know the gospel could have learned it had they inquired;[51] and those who could not have done so are still guilty of abusing such means of grace as Nature afforded, and in face of this fact the question whether they would have found the gospel and the Savior had they rightly used these means becomes as irrelevant as it is for man unanswerable. All have in fact neglected the grace they had; none, therefore, may complain if they are given no more, and perish.

There are degrees of grace, both of external means and of internal illumination, and the preparation for "special" internal grace (by which the elect are brought into a state of actual salvation) is "common" grace (such effects of the Spirit's work as do not always lead to conversion, by reason of man's resistance to them). "Universal common" grace, if not thwarted, would lead man up to special grace and salvation. Of common grace, again, there are various degrees. What virtue is found among the heathen results from the Spirit's work.

> All that wisdom and goodness, that is in any without the Christian church, is the work of the Spirit of the Redeemer; as the light which goeth before sun-rising, and after sun-setting, and in a cloudy day, is of the same sun which others see, even to them that see not the sun itself. [52]

50. *C.T.*, II:171.
51. "Had they been . . . diligent . . . in sending to all others . . . where there was a probability of receiving information . . . it's like there is no Nation under Heaven but might have had the Gospel ere now" (*Universal Redemption*, 470 f.).
52. XVIII:289; cf. XII:203: "without somewhat of the Spirit, there would be no moral goodness in any of mankind."

Within the Church, the sphere of proclamation and profession, the Spirit's initial illumination of those who hear the gospel "is a common Work, and thus many are made partakers of the Holy-Ghost, as also by miraculous Gifts, who yet may not fitly be said to be united to Christ."[53] Before a man can come to true repentance and faith in Christ, he must be convinced that the gospel is true. The Spirit's part here is to cause him to see the evidence for it, and rejection of this evidence is "the unpardonable sin against the Holy Ghost."[54] Then he must be humbled for his sins until he hates them and longs to be rid of them. These are both "preparatory works" of common grace. "Our Doctrine…about Preparations," which Baxter, as champion of the Puritan tradition, defended all his life against Antinomianism, is this:

> We hold that Christ is the True Light who lighteth every man that cometh to God; but in various degrees, by various means…Those that Christ converteth savingly, are first in order brought to *understand* the *Meaning* of the *word*, and next to *Believe* the *Truth* of it…what Christ is, and what he hath done and suffered for us, and what need we have of him…And they are moved so seriously to *consider* all this, till it prevail with their wills, first to desire not only their own deliverance from Hell and misery, as all men may do, but also from a state of sin; and then to desire Christ as a Saviour to effect it…they next thankfully *Accept* him by consent, and Trust him and give themselves to him. And all this is Christs own work upon them…So that *coming* to Christ signifieth divers acts, of which one is preparatory to the other.[55]

That "God usually prepareth the soul for Conversion by a common sort of Grace"[56] in this way was a Puritan commonplace, and we have already reviewed the pastoral practice based on it. The man who would be converted must begin at the beginning, and use the means of grace to learn more of gospel truth and his own sin and need. "When men will not … use their common grace, it is just with God to deny them special grace … If you can find something else to do when you should hear the word of God, God will find something else to do when he should give you his saving grace."[57] God "may do what he list with his own, and extraordinarily may in an instant convert the most unprepared malignant obdurate person; yet that is not his usual way."[58] All the time that

---

53. "Confutation of…Ludiomaeus Colvinus" in *Apology*, 254. There is a reference to Heb. 6:4-6.

54. Title of the fourth treatise in *The Unreasonableness of Infidelity* (XX), in which Baxter identifies this sin as the admission of the reality of the miracles of Christ and his apostles coupled with a refusal to attribute them to the Spirit, who in fact witnesses by them to the truth of the gospel.

55. *C.T.*, II:222.

56. p. 170.

57. VII: 253.

58. *C.T., loc. cit.*

Christ is leading men through the slough of despond to the Cross, they continually resist His grace; but He "mercifully boweth the wills of his elect, and, by an insuperable powerful drawing, compels them to come in."[59] The grace which God ultimately gives to the elect "is that, as Austin defineth it, *qua nemo male utitur* [which none misuses]."[60]

The covenanted gift of the Spirit to believers (cf. Acts 2:38, etc.) is quite distinct from the uncovenanted activity whereby He makes them believers.

> That gift of the Spirit…is not only the Spirit of miracles, given in the first times, but some notable (i.e., perceptible) degree of love to our reconciled Father, suitable to the grace and gospel of redemption and reconciliation, and is called the "Spirit of Christ," and the "Spirit of adoption,"[61] which the apostles themselves seem not to have received till Christ's ascension. And this seemeth to be not only different from the gifts of the Spirit common to hypocrites and the unbelievers, but also from the special gift of the Spirit which makes men believers. So that Mr. Tho. Hooker said trulier than I once understood, that vocation is a special grace of the Spirit, distinct from common grace on the one side, and form sanctification on the other side. [62]

Common grace leads a man up to special grace, by which he makes his first act of true faith; "by that act…[the Spirit] doth cause a habit";[63] and the implanting of this habit and of other "graces" with it, is termed sanctification.[64] Baxter's reference to Hooker looks back to the days in which he had rejected "the common Doctrine of the reformed Churches, who" (following the "Golden Chain"[65] of Rom. 8:29-30) "generally make Vocation to be the effecting of faith

---

59. XVII:345; cf. *Collegiat Suffrage*, 76: "such is the spirituall mercy of God towards them (the elect), that though they doe for a while repell and choake the grace of God…God doth urge them againe and againe…till he have thoroughly subdued them to his grace."

60. IX:581.

61. Baxter went out of his way to refute the Antinomian exegesis of Rom. 8:15, Gal. 4:3-6 (as propounded, for instance, by Crisp, *op. cit.*, II:86); cf. IX:54 f.: "by the spirit of adoption is meant…those…workings…which raise in us some childlike affections to God, inclining us in all our wants to run to him in prayer…open our griefs, and cry for redress, and look to him, and depend on him as a child on the father. This spirit of adoption you may have, and yet not be certain of God's special love to you…You much mistake (and those that tell you so) if you think that the spirit of adoption lieth only in the persuasion that you are God's child . . . "

62. V:351; referring to Hooker's *The Soul's Vocation*, 1638.

63. "Confutation of …Ludiomaeus Colvinus" in *Apology*, 274; quoted as Cameron's view, which "his followers still do teach" ("Reply to…Kendall," 132).

64. "Sanctification is taken…in Scripture, either for that change which follows faith (i.e., the implanting of the "new creature"), or else for the whole change of heart and life, whereof faith is but the very entrance or first act, and so (the senses) are distinguished as the Door and the House" ("Confutation . . . " *ut sup.*, 305). The noun is here used in the former narrow sense.

65. *op. cit.*, 282. Perkins' treatise gave the phrase wide currency as a description of these verses; e.g., in *Collegiat Suffrage*, 115, Rom. 8:30 is "that golden chaine of the Apostle."

and repentance...and Remission and Justification to be next, and Sanctification...to be next,"[66] and followed instead his quondam oracle, Pemble, in putting sanctification (which Pemble defined as the infusion of a "generall habit sanctifying all at once")[67] before faith. "The seede of all graces is sown at once,"[68] and faith is its first fruit. "In my youth," Baxter tells us, "the first Controversie that ever I wrote on was a Confutation of Bishop *Downam*...Mr. *Tho. Hooker*, &c. in Defence of *Pemble* herein; but riper thoughts made me burn that Script."[69] "I see no reason to be singular herein," was his final judgment.[70] The question was not one of psychology, but of New Testament exegesis; and his change of mind was due to his realizing that the gift of the Holy Ghost is always there regarded as a part of Christ's new covenant promise to believers. "The Spirit in Scripture is said to be given after our first believing."[71] This change of view made no difference to his practical instruction, for he always followed Downame in holding that "in time the first act of sanctificatiō (which is our regeneratiō) doth concurre both with our justification and effectuall vocation."[72] Priority here is not temporal, but logical. The mistake was simply one of definition and "method": the gift of sanctification, the "*new and soft heart*,"[73] was not, as he had supposed, "the *first special Grace*," which brings the elect to faith, but was one of the gifts which Christ had promised in the new covenant, and bestowed upon believers, as such.

The Spirit in the believer is the dynamic whereby the pattern of life sketched in the last chapter may be progressively realized. "It is his work to make you

---

66. "Confutation . . . " *ut sup.*, 274 Baxter's list of authorities for the standard view (in *C.T.*, I.ii.XVIII.2, 55; II:127) includes Hooker; Downame; Ames; and Robert Rollock (cf. *D.N.B.*, *s.v.*), *Tractatus de Vocatione efficaci* (1597). Rollock was "one of the principal leaders for that method" ("Confutation . . . , *ut sup.*, 247).

67. Pemble, *Vindiciae Gratiae*, 19. Downame attacked the definition as embodying an un-Biblical conception of *grace* borrowed from Scholasticism (*Covenant of Grace*, 1631, 197 f.), and Baxter came to distrust it, thinking it safer to confine oneself to the statement "Christ giveth us his Spirit" in preference to "Christ infuseth Habits." "The one is Gods Language, the other the Schoolmens" (*Saints' Rest*, edd. 4-7, 162).

68. Pemble, *loc. cit.*

69. *C.T.*, II:165. Baxter had strongly advocated Pemble's view, as against divines who "mangle so groundlesly, the Spirit's work upon the soul," in the passage on regeneration in his *Saints' Rest* (ed. 1, 140; later edd., 157) which he first qualified and then suppressed; cf. 334 *sup.*, n. 48.

70. *C.T.*, I.iii.XVIII.2, 56.

71. "Confutation . . . " in *Apology*, 273.

72. *Covenant of Grace*, 197. Baxter admits that Pemble's book, when first he read it "about eighteen or twenty years" earlier (i.e., 1635-7) "perswaded me that Vocation, Conversion, Sanctification, Regeneration and the giving of the Spirit, were all one thing" (additional leaf after *Saint's Rest*, edd. 4-7, 160); and he begins his *Treatise of Conversion* by showing that the first four terms in this list, together with "repentance," are used "in Scripture to express the same work upon the soul" (VII:18 f.).

73. *C.T.*, I.iii.XVIII.2, 55 (cf. Ezk. 36:26).

new and holy."[74] The Christian's own believing pursuit of holiness, itself a witness to His recreative power, is the means through which this sanctifying work is done. The saints are bound in covenant to the third Person in the Trinity no less than to the Father and the Son, and their faith commits them to the following duties towards their Sanctifier:

> 1. Faithfully to endeavour by his power…which he giveth us, to continue our consent to…the…covenant. And, 2. To obey his further motions, for the work of obedience and love. 3. And to use Christ's appointed means with which his Spirit worketh. And, 4. To forbear those wilful sins which grieve the Spirit.[75]

As Christians cooperate with the Spirit in this way, sin will weaken within them, graces will thrive, and they will grow towards maturity. Every facet of Christian character is a part of the fruit of the Spirit. Christlikeness is acheived by His power. As the Christian hears, reads and studies, the Spirit gives him light; as he labors to "improve" light received, the Spirit gives him life; as he lifts his heart to God, the Spirit gives him love. Moreover, his subjective experience testifies to the Spirit's influence no less than his objective transformation. Thus, the Spirit mediates communion with Christ, "turning the sacrament, the word, and Christ himself, *in esse objectivo*, as believed in, into spirit and life to us."[76] He gives foretastes of glory, as we shall see more fully later:[77] "heavenliness is the Spirit's special work."[78] "Indeed," Baxter affirms, "the Spirit here, and heaven hereafter, are the chief of all the promises of God."[79] But the Spirit only works in man as man works with the Spirit. Time and again, therefore, Baxter countered the Antinomian advocacy of "stillness" with appeals such as the following:

> Quench not the Spirit . . . It is as the spring to all your spiritual motions; as the wind to your sails: you can do nothing without it. Therefore reverence and regard its help, and pray for it and obey it, and neglect it not . . .

> Neglect not those means which the Spirit has appointed you to use, for the receiving of its help . . . Pray, and meditate, and hear, and read, and do your best, and expect his blessing . . .[80]

74. XIII:195.
75. XII:217.
76. XVIII:347.
77. Chap. XV.
78. XVIII:287.
79. *loc. cit.*
80. II:196 f. Despite his fully personal conception of the Spirit's person and work, Baxter's pronoun for him is usually "it."

Laziness is not the path of life; there is no blessing for the sluggard. But the saint who strives will find the Spirit helping him. Sometimes His help is more powerful and effective than at other times; and it is the believer's wisdom to make the maximum "improvement" of such occasions, or they may not come his way again:

> Do most when the Spirit helpeth you most…if he extraordinarily help you in prayer, or meditation, improve that help, and break not off so soon as at other times…[81]

> Make one gale of grace advantageous to another. This is a great point of Christian wisdom. The help of the Spirit is not at our command: take it while you have it. Use wind and tide before they cease…he that will not take the Spirit's time, but say, I am not now at leisure, may be left without its help, and taught by sad experience to know, that it is fitter for man to wait on God, then for God to wait on man . . . [82]

Finally, the Spirit leads the believer into assurance of his salvation.

> The same Spirit helpeth believers, in the exercise of grace, to feel it, and discern the sincerity of it in themselves…to conclude that they are justified and reconciled to God, and have right to all the benefits of his covenant. Also, he assisteth them also to rejoice in the discerning of this conclusion.[83]

Baxter held the standard Puritan doctrine of assurance, as outlined earlier.[84] Where his statements differ from those of his predecessors, it is only in accuracy and sobriety. Although, as we saw, he did not think that the doctrine of the final perseverance of the converted was so unambiguously taught in Scripture as to warrant making subscription to it a test of communion,[85] he himself had no doubt that a man who could know himself to have been effectually called might thence safely infer the certainty of his final salvation. As a young man, he tells us, assurance had been his personal and pastoral preoccupation:

"I got all the books that ever I could buy, which laid down evidences and marks of true grace; I liked no sermon so well as that which contained most of these marks; and . . . I preached in this way as much as most."[86] In later years,

---

81. II:197.
82. XII:222.
83. II:191.
84. Chap. VIII, *sup.*
85. Cf. 93 f., *sup.*
86. XXIII:1 (from the new chapter, III:xi, added to the second edition of the *Saints' Rest*, 1651: "A more exact inquiry into the number and use of marks; the nature of sincerity; with other things of great moment in the work of self-examination").

his appetite for introspection decreased;[87] but he always regarded regular "self-judging" as a *sine qua non* of spiritual health, without which "we shall be strangers to ourselves; we can have no well-grounded comfort...neither live reasonably, honestly, safely, nor comfortably, nor suffer and die with solid peace."[88] On the positive side,

> *Assurance* is a most *desirable* thing; it kindleth in us the love of God; it maketh Duty sweet; it maketh *Sufferings easie*, and *Death less terrible*, and *Heaven* more *desired*, and consequently cureth an *earthly Mind*, and leadeth man to a *heavenly Conversation*, and *putteth Life* into all his *Endeavours*.[89]

Every man, therefore, must be urged to seek a well-grounded assurance, and warned against the danger of "false peace." "I thank God I never made any doubt of my salvation," they used to say; "Thou hast the more cause to doubt a great deal, because thou never didst doubt," Baxter replied.[90] "False peace," the child of pride, would ruin the soul; but a Spirit-given assurance was a priceless treasure, the passport to "solid comfort" and heaven on earth.

Such an assurance is neither a feeling nor an experience, but a proposition syllogistically inferred from two premises: first, that Christ in the gospel promises justification, perseverance and eternal life to those who by faith receive Him; secondly, that one has thus personally received Him. The Spirit enables the Christian to discern the truth of both premises. Certainty concerning the second can only be reached through a detailed and prolonged scrutiny of one's daily life. Saving faith is known by its works; the inquirer's problem is to make up his mind whether his works warrant the inference that such faith is present. It is hard to be sure here, for two reasons: partly, because the inveterate partiality of fallen human nature leads every man to view himself through rose-colored spectacles, and partly because saving and common grace differ only in degree, not in kind. Since, as we saw, "the work of grace usually begins in common grace, and so proceeds by degrees till it come to special saving grace,"[91] it is not enough to find some religion in one's life, as opposed to none; for "there is no one act, considered in its mere nature and kind...which a true Christian may

---

87. cf. *R.B.*, I:129 (1645): "I was once wont to meditate on my own *heart*, and to dwell all at home...examining my Sincerity; but now...I see more need...that I should look oft upon Christ, and God, and Heaven."

88. VI:526; for a good illustration of the practice, cf. Margaret Charlton's "self-judging paper" reproduced in Baxter's *Breviate of the Life of Margaret...* (ed. J.T. Wilkinson, as *Richard Baxter and Margaret Charlton*, 71 f., and ed. J. I. Packer, as *A Grief Sanctified*, 2002, 54-56.)

89. *End of Doctrinal Controversies*, 279.

90. XXII:484.

91. IX:92; Baxter continues: "There is a special moral difference, though grounded but in a gradual natural difference...as when the last grain turns the scales," and quotes a statement to this effect from Preston.

perform, but an unsound Christian may perform it also."[92] One's course of life must witness to "the supremacy of God and the Mediator in the soul … above the interest of the flesh" before one may safely conclude oneself a new creature. This is "the one mark by which those must judge of their state that would not be deceived";[93] and the wise man will make allowance for the fact that his judgement is naturally biased in his own favor and be very cautious before he comes to a decision as to whether it is so with him. A hasty and superficial verdict will be certainly disastrous.

> Thousands are deceived about their state, by taking every uneffectual desire and wish, and every striving before they sin, to be a mark of saving grace. Misunderstanding Mr. Perkins, and some others with him, who make a desire of grace itself, and a combat against the flesh to be a sign of renovation by the Spirit; whereas, they mean only, such a desire of grace … as is more powerful than any contrary desires; and such a combating as conquereth … sin … And of this, the saying is very true.[94]

Unsuccessful opposition to temptation, ineffective protests by conscience, remorse without repentance, good resolutions that do not last, crocodile tears such as were shed by the drunkards of Kidderminster, are no safe grounds for assurance. Unambiguous signs of true repentance and habitual subjection to Christ, "heavenliness" of temper and steady victory over sin, must be first forthcoming, and judgment must be reserved until the Spirit enables one to see their presence. Baxter had no doubt that careless and haphazard living made the genuineness of the faith of many Christians impossible of discernment, whether by themselves or by anyone else. "It is only the stronger Christians that attain assurance ordinarily."[95] The carnal Christian robs himself of it. Even those whose sincerity is least questionable fluctuate in grace from day to day, and their assurance, based as it is upon the observation of their own behavior, must fluctuate with it. Perfect assurance cannot be enjoyed by

92. XXIII:16.
93. Ibid., 17 (*Saint's Rest*, III:xi). Baxter had observed, earlier in this chapter, that, in reducing the "many marks" laid down by "the most godly divines" to this one, "I speak against no man more than myself heretofore" (5).
94. XIII:222. Baxter refers to Perkins' *A Graine of Musterd-Seede; or, the Least Measure of Grace…effectuall to salvation*, 1597. The third and fourth of the six theses there argued are: "A constant and earnest desire to be reconciled to God, to beleeve, and to repent…is in acceptation with God, as reconciliation, faith, repentance it selfe;" "To see and feele in our selves the want of any grace pertaining to salvation, and to be grieved therefore, is the grace it selfe: (*Workes*, I:638, 641). Perkins safeguards himself against the misinterpretation of which Baxter complains by his sixth thesis: "the fore-said beginnings of grace are counterfeit, unlesse they increase" (642).
95. IX:94: "he that will attain to a certainty of salvation, must, 1. Have a large measure of grace to be discerned … "

imperfect Christians. To claim a greater degree of assurance than the testimony of one's life warrants is presumption, and the Christian must flee from presumptuous sins. Baxter himself never laid claim to perfect assurance. This was his testimony in 1664: "though I have no such degree of Doubtfulness as is any great trouble to my Soul, or procureth any great disquieting Fears, yet I cannot say that I have such certainty of my own sincerity in Grace, as excludeth *all Doubts and Fears* of the contrary."[96]

Since assurance of salvation depends on the discernment of one's own sincerity, and sincerity of faith is known by the works it begets, the wisest course for one who would have the Spirit lead him into assurance is to seek the Spirit's help in more vigorous Christian living. One of the less desirable but more widespread effects of Puritan preaching had been an unhealthy preoccupation with self-scrutiny to the exclusion and neglect of present duty. Baxter, the avowed enemy of "over-doing" and unbalance at any point in Christian thought or practice, often went out of his way to try and correct this disproportion, and his last word on the subject of assurance is the following "important and importunate request":

> Though it be a duty necessary in its time and place, to examine ourselves concerning our sincerity…yet be sure that the first, and far greater part of your time, and pains, and care, and inquiries, be for the getting and increasing of your grace, than for the discerning it; and to perform your duty rightly, than to discern your right performance. And when you confer with ministers…see that you ask ten times at least, How should I get or increase my faith, my love to Christ, and to his people? for once that you ask, How shall I know that I believe or love? Yet so contrary hath been, and still is, the practice of most Christians among us in this point, that I have heard it twenty times asked, How shall I know that I truly love the brethren? for once that I have heard it demanded, How should I bring my heart to love them better? And the same I may say of love to Christ himself.[97]

After all—as Baxter went to considerable pains to show[98]—a man might be saved without assurance. Many, indeed, were. Some ("almost all the *Papists*, the Arminians, the Lutherans, and as far as I can learn by their Writings, all the ancient Writers for a thousand years after Christ")[99] had been debarred from it by their denial of the certain perseverance of the sanctified. Others, notably

---

96. *R.B.*, I:9; date in margin. There is a similar testimony in *Dying Thoughts* (XVIII:430): "I am not much in doubt of the truth of my love to him [God]…As we are defective in our love, so are we in our certainty of its sincerity. But yet I am not utterly a stranger to myself; I know for what I have lived and laboured . . ."

97. IX:138 f.

98. *Right Method*…Directions XIV-XIX, IX:93 f.

99. *C.T.*, I.iii.258:93.

the "melancholy," proved constitutionally incapable of discerning their sanctification. Others, though regenerate, were so weak and slack and inconstant in their Christian lives that it was impossible to tell whether they were true believers or not. Yet persons in all these categories had undoubtedly been saved. God gives or withholds assurance as He pleases, and for purposes of His own. But no man could be saved without holiness. Assurance, in a sense, was a luxury, whereas holiness was a necessity. And assurance, where given, was given to those who sought first the kingdom of God and His righteousness; and to them alone.

Baxter's account of the work of the Holy Ghost in man's salvation is entirely characteristic of the Puritan tradition. The quarrel we noticed between himself and most of his fellows as to whether the Spirit evoked faith by physical or moral means was a disagreement on metaphysical theory rather than on theological fact; in rejecting a synergistic in favor of a monergistic account of conversion, both were at one. There was not even an appearance of disagreement between them at any other point. They all countered "enthusiasm" by constant reiteration of the truth that the Spirit of grace works in man through means. Man therefore is bound to the means appointed. But they always knew—Baxter, perhaps, more clearly than any—that the Spirit of God is not so bound. He is free, not to do less than God's promises entitle men to expect, but to do more than they dare hope. He may bestow grace in "extraordinary" ways; He may give to one what He denies to another; one may use the means more assiduously than his fellow, and still receive less. Baxter never supposed that when he laid down rules for men he laid them down for God too. Controversy with the "enthusiasts" forced him of define the "method of grace," the prescribed pathway of blessing, with meticulous precision; but, underlying its apparent rigidity, was the knowledge that the Spirit is lord of the "method," and that His operation through the means of grace is often such as to surpass all that man thought possible. Here was the secret of the Lord. To the Calvinistic Puritans, life in the Spirit was as far as possible from legalism and bondage. To be tied to the means was not the drudgery that the "enthusiasts" supposed it to be. The truth was that the Spirit's presence spelt liberty. At the heart of their doctrine of the Holy Spirit in the believer lay solemn exultation at the unmistakable stirrings of the new creature within them and at their own daily discoveries of the unsearchable riches of Christ. This was true of them all, but supremely so of Baxter, whose iron self-discipline bore fruit in a joyful freedom and vigor of spirit that can scarcely be matched in the history of the Christian Church.

Chapter 14

The Errors of Antinomianism

SYNOPSIS

1.   Scope of chapter.
       Baxter's opinion on   origin of Antinomianism
                                  seriousness of its errors
                                  ability of its leaders.

2.   Antinomian account of justification before faith.
       Corollaries: sin need not be forgiven
                      is not punished
                      need not be feared.

3.   Baxter's account of justification by faith.
       Corollaries: believers need to ask pardon for sins
                      are punished for sins
                      must fear and hope:
                              danger of denying this:
                              "Marrow" attacked for denying it.

4.   Antinomian doctrine of the Spirit's work in conversion.
                Faith is knowledge of forgiveness
                        given by a "particular voice of the Spirit"
                              in defiance of the testimony of life
                              suddenly, without previous preparation.
       Antinomian account of difference between old and new covenants;
                      living and dead faith
       Antinomian view of Christian morality:
             love the only "gospel" motive;
             the law not to be taught as a standard set for believers.

5.   Aim of Antinomian teaching: assurance and holiness.
       Effect of Antinomian teaching: presumption and uncertainty.
          "Enthusiasm" of Antinomian position on assurance.

6.   Faith and assurance in Baxter's thought:
                      answer to Antinomian charges of undue complication:
                              keeping men from Christ?
                              heretical doctrine of "preparatory works."

7.   Puritan and Antinomian advice to "afflicted consciences" contrasted:
             Baxter identifies Antinomianism with irreligious formalism:
                      himself with traditional Puritan practice.

8.   Powicke's criticism of Baxter considered:
   Baxter's five arguments against Antinomianism:
   Human nature
   Christian conscience
   Biblical exegesis
   God's holiness
   Christ's work

9.   Conclusion: Baxter's criticisms abundantly warranted.

(Principal Sources: *Aphorisms*; *Apology*; *Confession*; *Right Method* (IX:i f.); *Saint's Rest*, III:vii-xi (XXII:482-XXIII:53); *Catholick Theologie*, II:219-262; *Scripture Gospel Defended*.)

Chapter 14

The Errors of Antinomianism

Antinomians say, we are *Pharisees*...and that *God ever intended to man a pleasant and comfortable life* . . . loosed from the soure life of a Precisian ... But *Antinomians* shall wish to die Puritans...
        —Samuel Rutherford, *A Survey of the Spirituall Antichrist*, II:30.

The contest between the Gospel and Libertinism in the Church, is like the Contest between the Spirit and the flesh within us, and goes much on the same terms.
        —Baxter, 1654

We shall now return to Baxter's lifelong bogey, Antinomianism, and consider his full answer to it. No attempt is here made to give a complete account of the Antinomian school, or to specify differences of detail among its members. We shall confine our attention to such opinions and authors as Baxter singles out for attack. These are, in fact, fully representative of Antinomianism in its most presentable form. We saw earlier that, in Baxter's view, Antinomianism had arisen as a reaction against the "over-doing" of "Tears and Terrors" in a second-rate Puritanism—"many godly *Protestants*, seldom, and unskilfully opening the Mystery of Redemption...preaching almost all for humiliation, and too little of the wonderful Love of God, revealed in *Jesus Christ*."[1] He was probably right here. Reformed piety, which grows out of a vivid sense of sin, easily cools and congeals into a legalistic preoccupation with sins. Assurance comes to be thought presumptuous, faith is reduced to a

---

1. "A defence" in *Scripture Gospel Defended*, 55. The sentence concludes: "till Dr. *Sibbes* and such others, led them into another strein." Cf. "Admonition to Eyre" in *Apology*, Preface: "Blessed be God that...we have such writings as Sibbes, Prestons, Baynes &c. to show them, that Consciences may be Pacified without Antinomianism."

doubtful hope and the sense of sin is cultivated as an end in itself—the pattern of degeneration is familiar enough in Calvinist circles. Some of the less distinguished sermons of Elizabethan and Jacobean Puritans bear the marks of it. And it is certainly true that the Antinomians poured scorn on Puritan orthodoxy for withholding the "comfort" which they themselves sought to give.[2] Their own doctrine, Baxter knew, was not libertine in intention. He gladly testified of the Antinomian leaders "that though they had their Temerities and Blemishes, they were in the main, Men, far from wicked and prophane Lives."[3] But he attacked their positions as bound to prove libertine in effect. This was the whole point and purpose of his onslaught. "Antinomianism comes from gross ignorance, and leads to gross wickedness," he wrote in 1650.[4] It was more than a mistake about the Law; it was a virtual denial of the Gospel, "subverting the very substance of Christian religion...I think it fitter to call them Antigospellers, or Antichristian, or Libertines, than Antinomians."[5] He had little respect for the ability of his opponents, whom he once described as "better to manage a club than an argument."[6] A study of their lives and writings

2. cf. Saltmarsh's complaint, *Free-Grace...*, 37: "many Preachers, like some *Chirurgions* who keep their patients from healing too soone, that they may make the cure the more admired, doe accordingly keep...*soules* with their wounds open..."

3. *Scripture Gospel Defended, loc. cit.*

4. *Works*, XXII:6; cf. "Confutation of ... Ludiomaeus Colvinus" in *Apology*, 248: "Did not I tell you, that an Antinomian Faith will cause Antinomian Piety and practice?"

5. "Admonition to...Eyre," 6; cf. Baxter's comment on Anthony Burgess' *Vindiciae Legis*, published against the Antinomians in 1646: "had he been acquainted with the men as I was, he would have found more need to have vindicated the Gospel against them than the Law" (*J.R.*, first pagination, 22).

6. XXII:492 (*Saints' Rest*); cf. the following review of the principal literature on both sides, from the Preface of the "Admonition to...Eyre": "it was formerly a very rare thing to meet with a man of Learning or considerable Judgement, of that [Antinomian] way: What men had Dr. *Taylor* to deal with? Dr. *Crisp, Eaton, Town*, were the chiefest Champions since, whom Mr. *Burgess*, Mr. *Geree*, Mr. *Bedford* have confuted. At last *Den, Paul Hobson*, Mr. *Saltmarsh* took the chair. The latter strangely cryed up by many ignorant souls, and his weakness laid open by that Excellent, Learned, Reverend Mr. *Gataker*." Thomas Taylor wrote *Regula Vitae, the Rule of the Law under the Gospel*, in 1631, against John Trask, the eccentric apostle of Antinomianism in London (Edward Norice, *The New Gospel, Not the True Gospel. Or, A discovery of the Life and Death, Doctrin, and Doings of Mr. Iohn Trask*, 1638, 4; for details of Trask's life see also E. Pagitt, *Heresiographie*, 6th ed., 1662, 184 f.); Robert Towne answered Taylor in *The Assertion of Grace*, 1644; Stephen Geree attacked Crisp's first fourteen sermons in *The Doctrine of the Antinomians Confuted*, 1644; and Bedford wrote *An Examination of the Chief Points of Antinomianism*, 1647, against Crisp, Towne, and Henry Denne's Sermon, *The Man of Sin Discovered...The Root and Foundation of Antichrist laid open in Doctrine*, 1645. (For Denne, *D.N.B.*, s.v.) Paul Hobson published *Practicall Divinity* and *A Garden Inclosed, and Wisdom Justified*, in 1646. Gataker, learning that he had been quoted with approval among the authorities adduced at the end of *Free-Grace* ("Some truths of *Free-Grace* sparkling in former writers"), attacked the book in *A Mistake, or Misconstruction Removed*, 1646 (reissued in 1652 as *Antinomianism Discovered and Confuted*); Saltmarsh rejoined in *Reasons for Unitie, Peace and Love, With an Answer* (called Shadows flying away) *to...Mr. Gataker*...and Gataker immediately wrote a crushing reply, which Baxter several times recommends, *Shadowes without Substance*,

confirms Baxter's judgment. Crisp, Saltmarsh, Denne, Eaton and their followers, for all their eager sincerity, were temperamentally unstable and intellectually undistinguished.[7] Baxter conducted the controversy with them as we should expect a Puritan pastor to do. For him, the crux was not the theoretical issue concerning justification, but the practical question of the nature of faith, the grounds of assurance and the necessity of good works, and he invariably discussed the former topic in the light of its bearing on the latter.

When, in Chapter X, we examined the Antinomian doctrine of justification, we found that it rested on a crude interpretation of the Redeemer's solidarity with his people: as if the Son of God had become a sinner, and His people had thereby been made innocent. Justification was bestowed on the elect before they believed and could not be forfeited by subsequent sin. God would never see sin in His people; for when He looked on them, He saw only Christ's perfect fulfillment of the law on their behalf. From this position, the Antinomians drew three practical inferences. First: a believer should ignore the guilt of his sins, just as God does. He should neither ask pardon for them, nor allow his joy and assurance to be affected by them. "If a Saint should commit a grosse sin, and upon the committing of it should be startled at it, that would be a great sinne in him."[8] Second: no providential affliction should be interpreted as punishment for sin, or as a call to self-examination and repentance. "The Scripture mentioneth only three causes, why the godly are afflicted in the dayes of the Gospel. 1. To try their faith...2. To conforme and make them like Christ...3. To quicken and increase Faith..."[9] Third: there is

---

1646. All the important orthodox works against Antinomianism, apart from Baxter's own, are included in this list, with the single exception of Samuel Rutherford's *Survey of the Spirituall Antichrist*, 1647. Baxter added a "Postscript" to his "Admonition to...Eyre" specially to recommend this work, "one of the fullest...against the Errors of this Sect, and very usefull to the godly in these seducing times."

7. Some evidence may be quoted. Crisp, "a godly man...But Melancholious" (Rutherford, *Survey*, I:193), swung to Antinomian Calvinism from Arminian legalism; Denne began as "an High Altar man, a bower at the sillables of the name *Jesus*" under Laud (*loc. cit.*) but became a Baptist and Leveller (later recanting; *D.N.B.*); Saltmarsh moved from Conformity to an extreme congregationalism in his pursuit of "new Light," and Crandon reported of him "I have been told by some of his godly acquaintaince, that the man had a natural impotency, or craziness in his brain...his inconsistency with himself...his extreme mutability, and wandering from tropic to tropic, without settledness anywhere, in great measure prove the report to be true" (*Baxter's Aphorisms Exorized and Anthorized*, 1654, 138):Eaton, according to Archbishop Abbot, would in turn "deny, maintaine, confesse, repent" and yet remained incorrigible (G. Huehns, *Antinomianism in England*, 1951, 64).

8. Cradock, *Divine Drops Distilled*, 163; cf. the position of Giles Randall, as ascertained at a Star-Chamber enquiry: "a child of God need not, nay ought not to ask pardon for sin:...it is no lesse than blasphemy for him to do so;" quoted by Gataker, *Gods Eye on His Israel; or Numb. 23:21 cleared from Antinomian abuse*, 1645, "To the...Reader"). Gataker's sermon was occasioned by the Antinomian use of this text to prove that God sees no sin in the justified; an exegesis criticized by Taylor, *Regula Vitae*, 88, and defended by Towne, *Assertion of Grace*, 97 f.

no place in true religion for fear, whether of the temporal consequences of sin or of falling from grace, nor for the hope of reward. Fear and hope are "legal" motives, belonging to an outworn dispensation. It was the covenant of works which said "do this and live"; the covenant of grace says rather "do this from life." "No believer for whom Christ died, should have the least thought in his heart of promoting or advancing himself, or any end of his own by doing what he doth."[10] Hope, in other words, is more a vice than a virtue. Love and gratitude must be the sole incentive to Christian duty. To introduce any other is to revert to the Law.

This is the theoretical basis for the axiom affirmed by Denne: "it is the designe of the Lord Christ, to take away sin out of the consciences of his called people."[11] The gospel tells men to realize that their sins were laid once for all on Christ, and that henceforth sins are completely irrelevant to their relationship with God. They need not ask for sins to be forgiven; they no longer exist to be forgiven. In God's sight, they are simply not there. Men are commanded by the Gospel to believe that this is so, and to serve God out of gratitude for it. This, the Antinomians claimed, is the true meaning of the doctrine of "free justification by Christ alone," the royal road to "comfort" and holiness.

Baxter rejected this account of justification, as we have already seen, and attacked its practical corollaries on a variety of grounds. To the first, he replied that pardon for sin, after as before conversion, was a covenant grant, to be applied for by fulfillment of the statutory conditions on each occasion: "the Renewal of our Faith and Repentance, upon our lapses into discerned wounding sins, is a Condition of the particular pardon of those sins, and our Discharge or Justification from the guilt of them."[12] Yet this necessity is no enemy to assurance of salvation. The law of God still sets the standard and "doth constitute the *Debitum poenae*"; but it cannot threaten actual punishment "because the Promise stops its mouth: So that it gives not any believer any just cause to expect the eventual Execution of it, but only to bewail his sin, and flie to Christ, and beg and receive pardon from him by his Promise."[13] The believer's assurance, therefore, is maintained, not by ignoring his sins on the assumption

9. Towne, *op. cit.*, 112.
10. Crisp, *op. cit.*, 159.
11. H. Denne, *The Man of Sin Discovered . . .* , 9.
12. *Confession*, 56.
13. *Op. cit.*, 129 f. With characteristic honesty, Baxter subjoins the following admission: "But I will add this true Confession of my Heart, however it be taken: Though I have truly spoke my opinion concerning the speed and facility of the pardon of Believers sins; yet I am not able to practice according to this opinion. I find something within me, that will not suffer me so easily or quickly to conclude that I am pardoned: Nay that forceth me to beg pardon daily for all the past sins of my life...and that as earnestly, as if they were newly committed; yea and forceth me to conceive that I do well in so doing: and indeed so carrieth me to it, that I dare not forbear it, nor repent it . . . " (130).

that they are pardoned and forgotten already, but by taking careful note of them and safely securing pardon for each as it occurs. Sins are not pardoned before they are committed, but they may be pardoned immediately afterwards.

To the second corollary, Baxter replied that the punishment of a believer's sins is not wholly remitted on earth. Temporal suffering, like death itself, is a part of it, and is to be recognized as such. Baxter argued this position in his ninth Aphorism, under the impression that it was something of a novelty;[14] but by 1654 he knew better: "I have now I am writing this," he told Crandon, "the Testimonies of (as I remember,) about 20 or 30, that call believers sufferings, punishments, lying by me, which I collected on other occasions: And I think it easie to have as many more . . . I confess many ancient and some later Protestants, do say that believers sufferings are not punishments, but chastisements, taking the word Punishment in a restrained sense for meer Vindictive Punishment . . . But what man that ever read Philosophers, Divines, Lawyers, of the nature of Punishment, can be ignorant that Chastisement is a species of Punishment?"[15] Baxter did not deny that a believer's sufferings were *also* tokens of a Father's love (to "keep me awake, and . . . bid me work while it is day . . . keep me from covetousness, pride and idleness, and tell me where I must place all my hope, and how little the world and all its vanities do signify"),[16] but he insisted that, first and foremost, they were fatherly chastisements which "call me to repentance."[17]

To the third Antinomian contention, Baxter's reply was that in fact the New Testament often appeals to the banned motives of fear and reward, as well as to the motive of thankful love, and that did God not do so His government would be neither wise nor successful; for then he would not be treating man as man. Admittedly, the goal of redemption is to bring man to the place where the motives of fear and hope are no longer necessary to him, but that place is heaven, not earth; and the reason why these motives will be superfluous in heaven is not that the constituents of human nature will there be altered, but that the promised reward will there have ceased to be a prospect and become a permanent possession. To repudiate fear and hope before the prize is won is to deny nature in order to magnify grace. Such unrealistic perfectionism, Baxter well knew, leads to disaster in practice. For the man who does not fear will fall. As long as the Christian is *in via* through this world, sin

14. "The common judgment is, That [believers' sufferings]...are only afflictions of Love, and not punishments. I do not contradict this doctrine through affectation of singularity...but through constraint of Judgement . . . " (*Aphorisms*, 68).

15. "An Unsavoury Volume Anatomized" in *Apology*, 8; cf. 38 f, for a long catena of Scripture texts to prove that believers' afflictions are occasioned by sin.

16. XI:399 f; cf. *Saints' Rest*, III:xii, "The reason of the saints' afflictions here" (XXIII:53 f).

17. cf. *Confession*, 121: "Gods sanctifying the sufferings of the saints, and working out of them a greater good, doth not make them cease to be . . . punishments for our sins."

and Satan seek his downfall; and the means which God uses to safeguard him is his own awareness of danger and his consequent precaution against it. "I still say, therefore, that the doctrine of the Antinomians is the most ready way to apostasy and perdition . . . They cry down the weakness, unbelief and folly of poor Christians, that will apprehend themselves in danger of falling away, and so live in fear . . . I entreat you . . . never to expect such an assurance as shall extinguish all your apprehensions of danger . . . Only he that seeth and apprehendeth it, is likely to avoid it."[18] God-given assurance is the confidence that one's efforts to escape the pitfalls will be successful, not that there are none to be escaped or that no such efforts are needed. Again, the man who does not run will not obtain. The kingdom of heaven must be taken by force. Unless a man makes final salvation his goal and strives for it with all his might, he will miss it. "Search the Scriptures impartially and consider, whether . . . those that seek not, and labour not for it, be not shut out?"[19] Both these motives, fear and hope, are complementary versions of the appeal to self-love; and this appeal must lie at the heart of God's government of man, for self-love is, as we saw, an essential constituent of human nature as such. Dr. Morgan has written: "Baxter could sing with the Jesuit Francis Xavier:

> My God, I love thee—not because
>   I hope for heaven thereby,
> Nor yet because who love thee not
>   Are lost eternally . . .
> Not with the hope of gaining aught;
>   Not seeking a reward;
> But as thyself hast loved me,
>   O ever-loving Lord."[20]

But Baxter could do no such thing; for "to love God, and not our selves, and so to do all without respect to our own good, is no Gospell frame of spirit."[21] While professing the highest admiration for Xavier as a man, he would have objected to his sentiment as Antinomian. He attacked the *Marrow of Modern Divinity* (although "I much value the greatest part of that Book")[22] because it sanctioned the Antinomian account of the difference between the two covenants, of works and of grace: "One saith, Do this and live: the other saith, Live and do this. The one saith, Do this for life; the other saith, Do this from life."[23] The author went on to infer that every appeal to the profit and loss

---

18. IX:124.
19. *Aphorisms*, App., 94.
20. I. Morgan, *op. cit.*, 81 f.
21. *Aphorisms*, App., 82.
22. *op. cit.*, 99.
23. *Marrow* . . . , ed. C.G. M'Crie, 1902, 145; quoted by Baxter, *op. cit.*, 101.

motive was "the voice of the law"[24] and could therefore have no place in the preaching of the new covenant. Such a view, as Baxter pointed out, "would make almost all the New Testament, and the very Sermons of Christ himself to be nothing but the Law of Works"[25]—an inference which Eaton, at least, had actually accepted.[26] But the truth of the matter is, that "the Gospel also saith, Do this for life."

From their basic doctrine of justification before faith, the Antinomians went on to deduce a typically "enthusiastic" account of the Spirit's influence in the application of redemption. It was because Baxter thought that such an inference was inescapable that he so bitterly opposed justification before faith wherever he found it, even in the works of Owen, Eyre, and "Ludiomaeus Colvinus," men who had no Antinomian sympathies at all. We have already glanced at the reasoning involved.[27] If justification precedes faith, faith can only be the subjective apprehension of justification as an accomplished fact. It is, therefore, essentially *knowledge*, the conviction that my sins are pardoned; faith *is* assurance. Faith is not, as the practical Puritans taught, an act of will, "coming to Christ," faith is the subjective certainty that one is in Christ and, therefore, pardoned already. This conviction must derive partly from Scripture (which teaches me that the elect are justified) and partly from the immediate testimony of the Spirit in my conscience (which tells me that I am an elect, and so a justified, child of God). The all absorbing question to the religious public of the mid-seventeenth century was not, what must I do to be saved? so much as, how may I know whether I am elect? Baxter, with all the practical Puritans, insisted that the way to find the answer to the second of these questions was to discover, and act on, the answer to the first. The Antinomians, however, tackled it another way. "The voice of the Spirit to a man's own spirit . . . determines the question," Crisp declared: "even the voice of the Spirit of the Lord speaking particularly in the heart of a person, 'Son, be of good cheer, thy sins are forgiven thee.'"[28] "Would you know that the Lord has laid your iniquities on Christ, you must know it thus: is there a voice . . . within thee, saying particularly to thee in thyself, "Thy sins are forgiven thee?" The gospel as the Antinomians preached it was simply a command to every man to believe himself justified forthwith, and the preaching of this duty, they held, was the means whereby the Spirit creates faith. No man can believe himself justified without Divine aid, for there is never enough evidence in his own life to warrant the supposition

---

24. *Marrow*, 359; quoted, *loc. cit.* This citation (from Part II) shows that Baxter was using the seventh edition of the *Marrow* (1649; first ed., 1645), the earliest to contain the second part.

25. *loc. cit.*

26. Cf. Gataker, *A Mistake . . . Removed*, 10, referring to Eaton's *Honey-Combe*, 84; "Nor do I wonder . . . that Mr. *Eaton* . . . should make *Christ a legal teacher*."

27. cf. Chap. X, *sup.*

28. Crisp, *op. cit.*, II:82, 106.

that he is. Those who had accepted the Puritan doctrine that a believer might through self-examination ascertain his own sincerity must be ruthlessly disillusioned. But when a man finds himself able to fly in the face of the evidence and believe himself justified through Christ, as the gospel calls him to do, that very fact betokens the Spirit's operation and consequently, his election. Eaton is the authority here:

> He that beleeves that Christ has taken away his sinnes is as cleane without sinne as Christ himselfe. And it is no matter that we feele sinne and death still in us, as if Christ had not taken them away . . . that there may be place for faith, wee feele the contrary; for it is the nature of faith to feele nothing; but letting goe reason, shutteth her eyes, and openeth her eares to what is spoken by God.

> Our reason, sense, sight and feeling . . . our strongest enimies . . . strongly perswade us, that wee are not made perfectly holy and righteous . . . it is the very nature, heart and essence of faith to mortifie these enemies, and to tell them, that they are all lying sophisters . . . This is a right and strong faith, when as a man leaveth sense, wisedom, reason, and trusteth wholly to the word of God . . ."[29]

Denne set out a similar evangel in *A conference between a Sick Man and a Minister* (1643), "the sum of that Doctrine, which . . . I have taught." After the minister has thoroughly alarmed the invalid by telling him that the "graces" on which his assurance had been based hitherto do not warrant the conclusion he has drawn from them, the conversation proceeds as follows:

> (S) *You said before, that for assurance I must believe; what must I believe?*
> (M) That God hath forgiven you your sinnes, *and given you eternall life in his son* . . . You must not look at reason . . .
> (S) *God doth not say to me in particular, that my sin is forgiven.*
> (M) If you will beleeve it, he speaketh to you in particular, for he speaketh to every beleever.[30]

The coming of faith, according to the Antinomians, is accompanied by great joy. The Sick Man suddenly believes, and the Minister leaves him rapturous. Until faith is born, however, the seeker must simply wait on God. He cannot make himself ready for it, and should not, therefore, try. Such "preparatory works" as the Puritans prescribed are a waste of time. Attempts at reformation will not commend him to God, and will only distract his

29. Eaton, *op. cit.*, 26, 180 f.
30. Denne, *op. cit.*, 20 f.

attention from Christ to himself. He must not even pray, for God does not hear the prayers of unbelievers. He must "cast his deadly doing down," take his eyes off himself and look to Christ alone, until the conviction that he is Christ's dawns in his soul. He must try to believe until he finds that he does believe. Then, and only then, is he able to "act repentance." "Godly repentance goeth not before, but followeth the knowledge of remission of sins . . . All contrition that proceedeth not from faith, it is no better than sin; but godly repentance is not sin. Therefore it is not before faith . . . Doth any man declare unto you repentance as a means to obtain remission . . . These are the footsteps of the *man of sin*."[31] After faith has come, the believer should never again attempt to base his assurance on marks of sincerity in himself, for, even in the holiest Christian, such marks are never clear enough to carry the weight of the conclusion: "no man under heaven can find that sincerity, in his heart, that may comfort him."[32] As assurance was first gained without reference to works, so it must be sustained. The sole ground for a believer's peace of mind continues to be the Spirit's direct witness in his conscience that he is a child of God.

We have now reached the crucial issue that divided Antinomians from Puritans: the relation between assurance and "works." The Puritans distinguished saving faith (an act of will) from assurance of salvation (an inference), and grounded the latter on observed repentance. The Antinomians identified saving faith with assurance (a conviction, directly implanted in the mind by God) and claimed that repentance flowed from it. They held that when the Puritans taught men to infer their election from their "good works," they were not merely putting assurance out of reach (nobody's works being good enough to warrant the inference), but were revealing themselves to be ignorant of the difference between the old covenant, which said "work," and the new covenant, which says "believe." The difference, they explained, was really this: that under the old covenant assurance of final salvation, had it ever been reached, would have been based on the knowledge that one's works were of sufficient merit to secure it; whereas, under the new covenant, Christ's merit has already secured salvation for his people, and the Spirit assures them of this fact when He evokes their first act of believing. Assurance, whether in its inception or in its maintenance, has under the new covenant nothing to do with a man's own works. It is not a goal to be reached in the course of one's Christian life, but a treasure possessed from the start. Free justification from eternity to eternity, made known to the individual in his first act of faith by God's Spirit, is the sum and substance of the new covenant of grace. Therefore, if a man once assured should afterwards question his standing before God on

31. H. Denne, *The Man of Sin . . .* , 26.
32. Crisp, *op. cit.*, II:72; from the sermon, "Inherent Qualifications are Doubtful Evidences for Heaven."

account of his sins (as the Puritans told him to do), that would show his failure to grasp that he was not now under the law, but under grace. "When you sin against God...you fear you are *hypocrites*...you find *wrath* in your *consciences*: as often as you find *wrath* (that is the work of the Law...) it shows clearly that your persons are not quite freed from the Law . . . "[33] Such timorous mortals have not yet understood that under the new covenant works are simply irrelevant, one way or the other. We may add that "dead faith" to the Antinomian was not, as it was to the Puritan, the faith of "gospel-hypocrites," which fails to prove itself by works, but faith which fails to look to Christ and apprehend the Spirit's testimony to free justification. "If, therefore, the echo to the voice of the Spirit...be...the whole essence of believing; this is certain, where there is...believing, there cannot be a dead faith: the truth is, indeed, that faith that fetches its fruit from a man's righteousness, is dead; for the ground of a lively faith, is goodness wholly without a man's self . . . "[34]

It was from this view of the difference between the two covenants that the Antinomians deduced their theory of Christian morality. The obedience required by the old covenant had been obedience "for life": the law moved men to do what it commanded by promising rewards and threatening punishments. But the new covenant requires only the obedience of faith—obedience, that is "from life," springing out of the reception of the Spirit's testimony that there is nothing to fear and heaven is certain, and animated solely by love and gratitude. Any other motive for action would be "legal," anachronistic and unacceptable to God. The dispensation of law is past, and with it the days of "legal" motives; and the Christian minister's cardinal error is to continue to appeal to them, by preaching as if "the works of the Law" were in some way necessary to salvation. Faith, "comfort" and "gospel-obedience" cannot be promoted, but only impeded, by such means.

The more sober Antinomians, indeed, were willing to concede that the preaching of God's standards, the portrayal of sin and the declaration of sin's penalty was not wholly useless to the Christian, for it kept him near to Christ. "I say, and finde daily," wrote Towne, "that Gods Law taketh hold on the Conscience ... for the least failing ... till justification our continuall refuge, rescue, and deliver the Conscience: let the Law then be still in full force and authoritie, and its very usefull to a Christian; I know none that teach otherwise: thus it driveth to Christ, keepeth the soule close ... "[35] To think of God's wrath against sin makes the believer value his salvation more highly, as he sees where he would have been without it: "and consequently, the more he is stirred up to walk before God in more cheerful and comfortable obedience, and the more

33. Cradock, *op. cit.*, 157.
34. Crisp, *op. cit.*, II:108; cf. Eaton, *The Discovery of the most dangerous Dead Faith* (1644).
35. Towne, *op. cit.*, 145.

thankful he will be."[36] But no Antinomian would allow Christian morality to be taught to believers. To preach "law" and expound "duty" is inevitably to give the impression that salvation is somehow conditional on the performance of the works prescribed, and thus unwarrantably to trouble the believer's conscience and impair his "comfort." "I appeale to your own inward experience," said Towne. "Can you put your Conscience under the *mandatory*, and yet keepe it from the *damnatory* power of the Law?"[37] The right course was to proclaim the new covenant in Christ, to extol "free grace," to dwell on the unconditional promise of justification, which becomes true to everyone who believes it, to call men to bask in the sunshine of God's love—and Christian morality could safely be left to look after itself. The Spirit shed abroad in the hearts of believers would move them to good works far more effectively than ever the threats and cajolements of preachers who mixed up law and grace had done. Or so the Antinomians supposed. Baxter aptly summarizes their view of the two covenants thus: "all that prescribeth duty and hath conditional promises is but a Covenant of works. The Covenant of Grace is only the Spirit's Effectual work: I will, and you shall."[38] The two covenants are irreconcilable and mutually exclusive; they have nothing in common at all. It is not surprising, after this, to hear that "the desperate highest sort of *Antinomians* ... wipe out all the Old Testament with a stroak"[39] and that others were avowed perfectionists. Baxter, however, did not consider such aberrations worthy of serious consideration. They do not appear in the writings of any of the authors we have quoted, nor in the list of "An Hundred of their Errours" in his "Defence of Christ and Free Grace."[40]

The above exposition clearly shows that Antinomianism was far from libertine in intention. Indeed, the way of "working from life" was put forward as the high road to holiness. "When the Spirit of God ... hath set into their soules, by the socket of faith, the candle of Free-Justification, then doe they cast forth the beames of sanctification."[41] "Who can so hate and strive against sinne, even at the first rising or stirring of it, as the beleever?"[42] As, when the saints first sought God, the Spirit wrought faith in them, so now He works their works in them: "Consider...in all the good works that you do, how

---

36. Crisp, *op. cit.*, II:177.

37. Towne, *op. cit.*, 32.

38. *Scripture Gospel Defended*, sig. (A4) verso.

39. *Plain Scripture Proof*, 4; cf. J. Sedgwick, *Antinomianisme Anatomized* (1643) . . . , 29; "there are those who do reject the whole Old Testament"; Gataker takes Saltmarsh to task for setting the two testaments in radical opposition, as if there were no such thing as "free grace" in God's covenant with Israel: "there is no *new way* to Heaven now, but the same that ever was" (*A Mistake...Removed*, 6).

40. In *Scripture Gospel Defended*, 6 f.

41. Eaton, *The Honey-combe* . . . , 166.

42. Towne, *op. cit.*, 131.

wonderful *passive* you are in the doing of them . . . "[43] Indeed, so powerfully would the Spirit work that such safeguards as rules of life, regular routines of prayer and meditation, could safely be cast aside as relics of a bygone age. New covenant saints do not need crutches. Borne along by the Spirit, they will far transcend the attainments of those who toil along the "low and legal" Puritan path. Baxter had to remind the Antinomians that "we are as much and more for Heart-work...than you are."[44] They had no doubt that they could lead troubled consciences into a joyful assurance that would issue in spontaneous sanctity.

But though their intentions were good, their advice was bad. Antinomian soul-surgery, Baxter reports, littered the land with spiritual casualties, hardened hypocrites on the one hand and nervous wrecks on the other. Some were encouraged to presumption:

> [Some] I have known that have wanted assurance, and falling among the Antinomians, were told by them that...it is only the witness of the Spirit without any marks that must give it them...No sooner was this doctrine received, but the receivers had comfort at will...Whence this came, judge you...Sure I am that the sudden looseness of their lives...did certify me that the Spirit of comfort was not their comforter . . . [45]

Some, on the other hand, were driven to despair:

> Some poor souls have languished in doubtings and trouble of mind almost all their days, in expectation of such a kind of witness as the Spirit useth not to give; when in the mean time they have other sufficient means of comfort, and knew not how to improve them; yea, they had the true witness of the Spirit in his inhabitation and holy workings, and did not know it. [46]

"[Antinomian] receipts," Baxter concluded, "are rank poison, gilded with the precious name of Christ and free grace."[47] Not merely had the Antinomians misconceived the meaning of justification by faith and the nature and content of the Christian's assurance; they had erred even more disastrously in setting the Spirit against the means through which He works. In effect, they made each believer's assurance the result of immediate special revelation, a "particular voice" of the Spirit speaking, not merely apart from, but often contrary to the

43. Cradock, *op. cit.*, 172 f. He adds: "It may be some of you understand not what it is to do a thing *without you*, it is too spiritual . . . "

44. *C.T.*, II:258.

45. IX:98 f. Of the few known to Baxter who had claimed to possess the "certain inward word of assurance," "some fell to Debauchery, and some to doubting" ("Defence . . ." in *Scripture Gospel Defended*, 26).

46. IX:54.

47. p. 126.

written Word; which "voice" must not be checked or tested by Scripture, but accepted at its face value. "They are drawn up to the old way of the *Enthusiasts*, telling us, That they are assured by Lights and Revelations . . ."[48] To believe this "voice of the Spirit," in defiance of the judgment which Scripture would pass on one's condition, was "right and strong faith," said the Antinomians; faith comparable with that of Abraham, who "wholly withdrew his minde from the things which he saw and felt, and did as it were forget himselfe."[49] But Baxter knew what to think about "faith" which sets aside Scripture in favor of private revelations, spirits that cannot endure to be tried by the Word. It is little wonder that he thought Antinomianism "rank poison." All its orthodox opponents shared his view of its gravity and danger. [50]

We may now set alongside the Antinomian position concerning the Spirit's work in faith and repentance the relevant part of Baxter's own.

As we saw, faith in Baxter's doctrinal scheme is the condition, not the discovery, of justification, and consists in an act of will, a hearty self-committal to the rule of the Redeemer. Faith can be no more sincere than the repentance which underlies it; a man must be heartily willing to leave sin before he can heartily receive Christ; so the seeker must take steps to get his heart thoroughly alienated from sin and enamoured of Christ before he can be soundly converted. This is the rationale of the "preparatory works" on which the Puritans insisted so much: hearing, reading, meditating, and praying. (Of course he should pray: "an unbeliever may lie under preparing grace, and be on his way in returning to God, though he be not come to saving faith; and in this state he may have many good desires, and such prayers as God will hear.")[51] By the means of these activities, the Spirit brings him to the new birth; after which, he may (in normal circumstances) gain assurance of salvation by self trial, in the manner

48. J. Sedgwick, *op. cit.*, 31. Dr. Huehns (*op. cit.*, 37) thinks that Sedgwick uses the word *Antinomian* "senselessly" when he applies it to "the *Manichees*, the *Marcionites*, the *Montanists*, the *Muscovites*, the *Anabaptists*, the *Socinians* . . ."; but this is the link in his mind, which she has clearly failed to see. All these movements (except Socinianism, which arguably should not be there, but tended to be included in every orthodox execration at that time) exhibited the same tendency to set private revelations above the Scripture, and to innovate in morals as a result.

49. Eaton, *op. cit.*, 176 f; expounding Rom. 4.

50. Cf. (e.g.) T. Bedford, *Examination* . . . Preface: Antinomianism is "one of the most dangerous Doctrines that is broached in these days"; S. Geree, *The Doctrine of the Antinomians . . . Confuted*, sig. (A 2) recto: "a doctrine as dangerous as plausible, and so plausible, that it takes two wayes. First, by the easinesse and pleasantnesse of it, it takes those that be openly profane . . . Secondly, by its seeming so much to magnifie the grace of God and Christ, it takes and taints those, that . . . have begun to deny themselves, out of a sense of their own sinfulnesse, especially if subject to sadnesse and feare or melancholy despaire, &c. as the weaker sex for the most part are, upon whom it works most . . . "

51. IX:49.

already described.[52] Some, however, never attain it, either through uncertainty about the doctrine of the saints' perseverance, or through inability to discern their own sincerity (as is often the case with the melancholy), or through the "exceeding weakness of their natural parts . . . Many honest hearts have such weak heads, that they know not how to perform the work of self-trial; they are not able, rationally, to argue the case . . . if God do not some other way supply to these men the defect of their reason, I see not how they should have clear and settled peace."[53] And even when assurance is attained, it is not invariably accompanied by transports of joy. "That sensible joy is more seldom and extraordinary;"[54] and the wise man will "lay not too much on the high raptures and feelings of comfort which some do possess . . . expect not that they should be long or often."[55]

To the Antinomian charge (true, of course, in point of fact) that Baxter's method was more cumbersome and complicated and less immediately "comfortable" than their own, Baxter had a short, tart answer: "I would not have your doubtings cured by the devil."[56] The longer way round was the safer way home; the shorter route that seemed so inviting petered out in the bog of "carnal security and presumption." The further charge, that the orthodox kept men from Christ, was refuted in fact by Baxter's practice, as indeed it was by the practice of all the "honest old Practical divines"[57] who followed in the steps of Perkins and Sibbes. They all pointed troubled souls directly to Christ, and insisted on "preparations" only in order to make sincere faith possible. "If you would methodically proceed to the attaining of solid comfort," Baxter explained in his *Right Method*,[58] you must first "lay sound apprehensions . . . in your understanding" concerning the love of God, the work of Christ and the nature of faith (Directions III-VIII; I-II are preliminary counsels addressed to the melancholy). Then (IX) "your next work must be . . . actual believing . . . This is not only the method for those that never yet believed, but also for them that have lost the sense of their faith . . . Believe again, that you may know you

---

52. Ch. XIII, *sup.* Baxter adduces twenty arguments in *Right Method* to vindicate against Antinomianism the position that "we may and must raise our assurance and comforts from our own graces and duties" (IX:57 f.), and fourteen more to the same effect in *The Crucifying of the World* (IX:553 f.).

53. XXII:512. A section of the *Right Method* is devoted to showing such that "all a man's comforts depend not so on his assurance, but that he may live a comfortable life without it." (IX:101 f.)

54. XXII:508.

55. IX:130.

56. p. 126.

57. "Admonition to . . . Eyre" in *Apology*, 35.

58. IX:34 f.

59. pp. 46 f.; cf. (e.g.) among other practical Puritans, Joseph Symonds' *Case and Cure of a deserted Soule*, 552 f. (partly quoted in the margin of *Saints Rest*: XXII:506): "Christ is set before

do believe ... "[59] Only after this can you (X) "take notice of your own faith, and thence ... gather assurance of ... your justification, and adoption, and right to glory."[60] When the Antinomians insisted that the call to believe oneself justified without any preliminary repentance or reformation was the only version of the gospel which preserved the authentic note of "free grace," and that to make justification conditional on faith or repentance was to lose it, Baxter replied that this claim was based on a misunderstanding of the sense in which grace is "free." "God's gift of Christ, with all his benefits...is so free as to be without and contrary to our desert; but not so free as to be without any condition...There is no inconsistency for God to be the giver of grace, to cause us to believe and accept of Christ, and yet to make a deed of gift of him...on condition of that faith and acceptance; no more than it is inconsistent to give faith and repentance, and to command them ... He maketh both his command, and his conditional form of promise, to be his chosen means ... of working in us the thing commanded."[61] The further charge leveled over and over again in Antinomian books, that the Puritan demand for "preparatory works" was Arminian or Popish, Baxter brushed aside. The facts refuted it: "there are such a multitude of Treatises, written by the strictest *English Antiarminians* on...preparation to Conversion".[62] Admittedly, "all they that hold all that Doctrine of Preparation for Conversion, which you find in the suffrages of the British Divines in the Synod of *Dort* do not...differ from many of the Lutherans, and Jesuites, nor from many of the Arminians herein":[63] but that was simply because the doctrine was, in fact, true.

Baxter had no doubt that the impulse, and the theology, behind the Antinomian quest for "comfort" at all costs came from the pit, for its outcome in practice was this: men went to the Antinomians troubled about their sins, and all the advice they received was to be troubled about them no longer, for Christ had taken them away. Where the Puritan would have said, put sin out of your life, the Antinomian said, put it out of your mind. Look at the law, consider your guilt, learn to hate sin and fear it, and let it go, said the Puritan; look away from the law and forget your sins and guilt, look away from yourself and stop worrying, said the Antinomian. The way to "comfort", said the orthodox, is to come to Christ, that he may justify you; the way to "comfort", retorted the

---

you, stirre up your selves to take hold of him ... Christ will not shut the door upon you when you come ... You sit poring and searching for pillars of hope within you ... but the ready way to make the business clear, is by going to Christ; stand not so much upon this *quaere*, Whether you have believed in truth or no, but put all out of doubt by a present faith ... "

60. IX:52 f.
61. XII:324.
62. *C.T.*, II:101.
63. *Op. cit.*, II:171.

Antinomian, is to believe here and now that Christ has already justified you, so that nothing more remains for you to do. The law must still be preached to believers as a standard, to show them what God requires, the Puritans insisted; the law is not to be preached at all, for God now requires of men nothing beyond belief, the Antinomians replied. A Christian, said the Puritans, must be taught to prove his faith by his works, to fear lest he should fail to do so, and to labor for heaven with all his might. Good works are not the condition of present justification, but they are necessary to final salvation. A Christian, answered the Antinomian, must not permit himself to act from any other motives than joy and thanks that salvation is already and inalienably his. The Spirit in him will in fact lead him into all good works, but such works are in themselves as irrelevant to final salvation as they are to justification. In short, Antinomianism made repentance unnecessary for assurance, and good works unnecessary for heaven. Its leaders proclaimed the paradox that sanctity would spontaneously appear in the lives of those who knew they did not need it; but Baxter, knowing human nature, did not believe them. He consistently treated Antinomianism as an exotic and streamlined version of the happy-go-lucky religion of the pagan Englishman which the Puritan pastors had fought for so long, a religion equally notable for its liberal offers of "comfort" to those who were not entitled to it. With reference to the disputed doctrine of "preparatory works" ("the great necessary doctrine for the breaking of hard hearts, and confuting the presumptions of the prophane"), he commented:

> It is worth the observation of every heart honest Christian, how prophanness and Antinomianism, do run hand in hand, and speak with one tongue, and put our Divines to one and the same labour. So that in this point of preparation for Christ, and many others, we must confute the same conceits of both.[64]

When Crandon seconded the Antinomian onslaught against Puritan preachers, Baxter rose to their defense as follows:

> I solemnly profess, that in all my daies, since I understood any thing of these matters, the thing that all the carnal and scandalous and formall preachers about us were blamed, and censured for, by all the godly of my acquaintance (till the Warres) was their too liberal giving out pardon and free grace and hope of salvation to the ungodly, and making the gate wider and the way broader than Christ had made it, and preaching comfort so generally, that all the wicked might take it to themselves: and that the generality of Godly, Conscionable Ministers went the contrary way, searching, differencing, driving to through (*sic* sc. through to) humiliation, and broakenness of heart, and Reformation of Life, and were very cautelous in all their offers of pardon, lest

---

64. "Admonition to . . . Eyre" in *Apology*, 36.

the prophane should snatch it . . . and that this was the only preaching that godly people then loved . . . and that wicked men hated, and for which they reproached the Preachers as Puritans and Precisians, and were use to say, that they would make men mad. This Testimony I leave against Mr. *Crandons* reproach of the *English* Ministry.[65]

The safe way was still along the old paths, and the only way to counter Antinomianism was to recall men to them. The following admonition to the Christian public may fitly conclude this exposition:

Highly value, and diligently reade . . . practical, searching Authours . . . be thankfull for them as the greatest blessing of this age, wherein it excelleth other ages, as this Land doth other Nations. I would not advise Countrey people of Vulgar capacities to trouble their heads with much Controversie, no not against the Antinomists themselves. But as a better preservative I would every family that hath a care of spiritual things, would but keep in their houses, hands and hearts, four or five of our old solid successful practical Divines, and I should not fear the prevalency of Antinomianism: Especially get . . .[66]

The usual book list follows.

Was Baxter fair to Antinomianism? Powicke thinks not. He holds that Baxter, the assiduous exponent of faith and obedience as the duty required by the new covenant, failed to see what to the Antinomians was clear, that in Christ God "has abolished the soul's merely legal relation to himself and called it to a filial relation of reverence, trust and love out of which the stream of a Christ-like life will flow as from a perennial fount." He concludes: "If Baxter had been more of a mystic and possessed a deeper sympathy with Paul's mystic experience of life in Christ, he would have been a far wiser critic of so-called Antinomians...As it was, the predominantly intellectual caste (*sic*) of his spirituality made him "hard-grained" towards such as these—to his own serious loss."[67] But this seems unfair to Baxter, and misses the point of his criticisms. Baxter knew perfectly well that faith inaugurates a relationship no longer "merely legal," but filial and intimate, between man and God, and that the mainspring of the Christian life is thankful love. He never denied that the Christian works "from life." He was less rhapsodic and more analytical than his opponents in speaking of such things, but that does not mean that he overlooked them or thought the Antinomians wrong in asserting them. He attacked them because they went on to deny that a Christian must also work "for life." This, he held, was blasphemous, and ruinous to souls. "I have Five

65. "An unsavoury volume . . . anatomized" in *Apology*, 11.
66. *Op. cit.*, 10.
67. Powicke, *Life*, 241 f.

Arguments against these Men," he wrote: "1. The Essential Nature of Man. 2. The Nature of God, and his Government. 3. The Office and Work of Christ, and Grace. 4. The whole Bible. 5. The consent of...Christians."[68]

The first of these arguments has already been examined in detail. Baxter claimed that aimless action was contrary to human nature; that if men were told that working would gain them nothing, then they would not work, and could not be expected to. Man was in fact made to be moved by the appeal to self-love, the profit and loss motive. No other motive is so powerful, for no other instinct is so deep-rooted. Appeal to self-love caused man's fall, and appeal to self-love must restore him. Man, as man, is a self-regarding creature, and man, as fallen, is a sin-loving, flesh-pleasing creature, and his love of sin can only be cured by enlisting his self-love against it. But this was precisely what the Antinomians on principle refused to do. "They make all duties a matter of courtesie,"[69] and therefore optional; they denied them to be means to man's goals, and therefore necessary. Antinomianism, therefore, could never effectively wean men from their sins, and its principles, Baxter was sure, "if practiced...will certainly damne."[70] The fifth argument was an appeal to the fact that the Church has always condemned as heretical the doctrine that holiness is not necessary to salvation. The Antinomian teachers "contradict the experiences of the souls of Believers; and the very nature of the New-man is against them...A sound-hearted Christian . . . hath something within him that potently strives against Libertinism . . . "[71] It was always so; true Christians have never been able to stomach the doctrine of the irrelevance of sin. The fourth argument rested on detailed exegesis. As we have seen, Baxter undertook to refute the Antinomian version of the two covenants, and to show the true nature of faith, repentance, justification and obedience. He claimed to prove from Scripture that Christian assurance is a confidence of persevering in faith and good works, not an expectation of arrival which does not depend on making the journey; that "legal" motives are perfectly proper in the preaching of the gospel; and that "600 Texts...speak of the necessity of an inherent and active Righteousness"[72] as a condition of final salvation. We have examined these positions already.

The second and third arguments have not yet appeared in this chapter, but for Baxter they were the most decisive of all in settling him against Antinomianism. They determined his perspective and gave him his sense of direction throughout the controversy. The two arguments reduce to the following axiom: *God is holy; therefore the end of his saving activity towards*

68. "A Defence" in *Scripture Gospel Defended*; "To the Reader".
69. Rutherford, *op. cit.*, II:29 (second pagination).
70. *Aphorisms*, App., 94.
71. "Admonitions to ... Eyre," Preface.
72. "A Defence . . . ," *ut sup.*

men is to make them holy too. Christ redeemed and justifies them, and the Spirit sanctifies them, that they might bear God's image in holiness. The grace of a righteous God is given in order to make righteous men. This was what the Antinomians had forgotten. "But Christ did not die or merit to change God's nature, and make him more indifferent in his love to the holy and the unholy . . . "[73] Baxter stated his mind most fully on this subject in the Preface to his *Confession of his Faith*:

> Two things are requisite to make man Amiable in the eyes of God...One is his suitableness to the Holiness of Gods Nature: The other respecteth his Governing Justice...Were we Holy, he would love us as a Holy God: and were we Innocent, he would encourage us as a Righteous and Bountiful Governour...We must *Be* Good, before we can *Live* as the Good. In both these respects man was Amiable in the eyes of his Maker, till sin depraved him, and deprived him of Both. To *Both* these must the Saviour again Restore him; and this is the work that he came into the World to do...Christ came not to possess God with any false opinion of us...He came not to perswade his Father to judge *us* to be *Well*, because *He* is *Well*...If Christ only were Righteous, Christ only would be reputed and judged Righteous, and Christ only would be Happy...We must bear his own Image, and be Holy as he is Holy, before he can Approve us, or Love us in Complacency . . . He Regenerateth us, That he may Pardon us; and pardoneth us, that he may further sanctifie us . . .

And Baxter considered it an insult to Divine wisdom and holiness to suppose that

> Through the imputation of Christs Righteousness, God judgeth the most swinish impenitent wretch, (so he be elect) to be righteous in his sight, and the object of his complacency. As if a man should fall in love with a Toad, upon a false supposition that it is a Lark . . .

God takes pleasure only in His own holy image; and the goal of redeeming love is the restoration of that image in man. This passage alone, Orme comments, "demolishes the whole system of Antinomianism.[74]

And surely Baxter's criticisms must command general agreement. For, whatever we may think of his theology in detail, there can be no doubt that his is the Biblical presentation of God's nature and purpose in grace, and that sanctification is in Scripture a *sine qua non* of final salvation, and that sin in believers is there represented as a much more serious thing than the Antinomians could, or did, allow. Indeed, their sublime supernaturalism was

73. *Works*, XII:353.
74. *Works*, I:459.

only possible because their doctrine of sin, and their sense of sin, were so deficient. This myopia they shared with most of the perfectionist and "enthusiastic" movements in the Church's history. Again, it is simple matter of fact that the holiest men in the Church's history (among whom must be numbered Baxter himself) have been men who have worked "for life" as much as "from life" and have retained a deep sense of their own shortcomings to their dying day. Outstanding sanctity has not come in the same way from the ranks of those who assert the irrelevance of sin. And it is undeniable also that the Antinomian conception of faith itself is viciously intellectualistic. Powicke is much too kind to it when he calls it Pauline. It would be more accurate to call it Gnostic. For it is a matter of knowing without doing; of ascertaining, as distinct from apprehending; of receiving a truth, rather than of receiving a Savior. It begins and ends in the mind. In the Puritan, and the New Testament, sense of the phrase, the Antinomian never "comes to Christ" at all. That would be doing something, and the age of "doing" for salvation is past. Passivity is the way of life; activity is legal and Popish. Man's part is simply to believe himself a justified child of God, whatever conscience may say. We need not wonder that union and communion with Christ are Puritan rather than Antinomian themes. Antinomianism requires faith *about* Christ, but does not insist that this must become faith *in* Christ. It is not, therefore, surprising that Baxter fought Antinomianism to the last ditch. It is to his credit that he did. No conscientious pastor and evangelist in his position could have done anything else.

Chapter 15

"Heart-Work and Heaven-Work"

SYNOPSIS

1. Introduction: aim of chapter, to focus the hope of glory.

2. The Spirit makes possible a "taste" and "sight" of heaven and
   implants desire for it

3. Two methods of reaching a positive conception of heaven:
   (i) Analysis of the idea of perfection (*Dying Thoughts*):
   perfection of each faculty—mind, will, active power—
   in perfect fellowship with God.
   (ii) Imaginative development of Scripture imagery (*Saints'
   Everlasting Rest*):
   purpose of Scripture imagery;
   Baxter's picture of heaven;
   joy promoted by memory of the past:
   knowledge of hell;
   fellowship with the rest of the Church.

4. Practical importance of clear conceptions of heaven for the Christian:
   the end determines the means:
   Baxter's experience.

5. Directions for heavenly meditation:
   fixing a time
   consideration (mind and affections)
   soliloquy (address to will)
   prayer

6. Helps to heavenly meditation:
   need of self-discipline;
   hard work;
   advantage of reading the books of creation and providence;
   special help of the Spirit.

7. Effects of heavenly meditation.

8. Heavenly meditation a catholic practice:
   Baxter's acknowledged mastery among Puritans.

9. Conclusion: the desire for heaven central in sanctification:
   the marks of the Christian.

(Principal Sources: *The Saints' Everlasting Rest* (XXII-XXIII); *The Duty of Heavenly Meditation Reviewed*; *Dying Thoughts* (XVIII:239 f.).)

Chapter 15

"Heart-Work and Heaven-Work"

Hoc tamen habeamus constitutum, neminem bene in Christi schola profecisse, nisi qui et mortis et ultimae resurrectionis diem cum gaudio expectet. [So let us consider this settled: that no one has got far in the school of Christ who does not joyfully look ahead to the day of death and final resurrection.]

—Calvin, *Institutio* III.ix.5.

He talked in the pulpit with great freedom about another world, like one that had been there, and was come as a sort of express from thence, to make a report concerning it.

—Calamy, *Own Life*, I:220 f.

We have studied mankind, created and fallen; we have seen what the Son of God did for the redemption of the race; we have surveyed the life which the gospel requires of the redeemed; we have seen how the Holy Spirit draws men into a state of salvation, and how through the means provided God gives what He commands; and we are now to complete our review of Baxter's soteriology by seeing what he has to tell us about the Christian hope and the Christian's life of hope. Here we take our leave of "Clergie Mens Contentions, and Church-distracting Controversies"[1] and move into the calmer waters of aspiration and practice, where, as Baxter well knew, all true believers are at one.

To Baxter, the practical significance of the doctrine that the Spirit indwells God's elect could be summed up by saying that the Spirit both enables and

---

1. *Catholick Theologie*, "Preface."

impels believers to foretaste heaven on earth. Faith, as we saw, expresses itself in obedience to the Redeemer's law; we are now to see that it also expresses itself in hope. The believer looks and longs for the day of full redemption, the more so by reason of the anticipations of it that the Spirit imparts. It is His work to turn "notional" and "organical" knowledge of it into a degree of "real" knowledge. Through His influence, knowledge by description becomes knowledge by acquaintance. He gives, in the Biblical phrase, a "sight" and a "taste" of the things objectively revealed in the written Word;[2] and heaven's joys are among them. Theological study may lead a man to orthodoxy, but only the Spirit can bring him to knowledge.

> Reason is fain first to make use of notions, words, or signs; and to know terms, propositions and arguments, . . . is its first employment . . . but it is the illumination of God that must give us an effective acquaintance with the things spiritual and invisible, which these notions signify, and to which our organical knowledge is but a means.[3]

So Baxter, polymath, philosopher, and divine, found himself constrained again and again to pray:

> Alas! my Lord, it is not all the learning in the world; no, not of theology, which consisteth in the knowledge of words and methods, which I can take for the satisfactory, heavenly light. To know what Thou hast written in the sacred book, is not enough to make me know my glorified Saviour, my Father and my home....O let me not have only dreaming knowledge of words and signs, but quickening light, to show the things which these words do signify, to my mind and heart.[4]

Sound words can be learned from men, but light and heat must be given by God. The most learned need to pray for illumination. It is, in fact, the Spirit himself within them who moves them to do so, and to do so effectively. "When we set ourselves to pray, it is both a sign that the Spirit exciteth, and a certain proof that he will...afford us his assistance."[5] And so it proves. By Divine blessing upon their own diligent meditation ("close" is the Puritan word), they taste the powers of the world to come,

---

2. Cf., for passages which illustrate the Puritan fondness for these metaphors, G.F. Nuttall, *The Holy Spirit*, 39 f.

3. XVIII:297.

4. p. 383; cf. 258: "When I can prove the truth of the word of God, and the life to come, with the most convincing, undeniable reasons, I feel need to cry and pray daily to God, to increase my faith."

5. XII:223.

There is in a Christian a kind of spiritual taste whereby he knows these things, besides his mere discursive reasoning power...Oh that you would be persuaded to try this course, to be much in feeding on the hidden manna, and to be frequently tasting the delights of heaven. It is true, it is a great way off from our sense, but faith can reach as far as that ...[6]

One part of the Spirit-given new nature is a spontaneous impulse to "heavenliness." A believer delights to seek things above, and it is his wisdom to resist the contrary earthbound lusting of the flesh and follow where the Spirit leads. "We fall in with the heavenly Spirit in his own way, when we set ourselves to be most heavenly. Heavenly thoughts are the work which he would set you on; and the love of God is the thing which he works you to thereby...In such thoughts we are most likely to meet with the Spirit, with whose nature and design they are so agreeable."[7] That the life which springs from believing contemplation of the world to come is to Baxter "the Divine life" has already appeared. Our present task is to inquire how much he thought that a Christian may discover about his future home and what use he should make of this knowledge.

Baxter employed two complementary methods in order to form some notion of what was in store for him. The first was to analyze the idea of perfection. This is the method followed in the long soliloquy published as *Mr. Baxter's Dying Thoughts upon Philippians 1.23*.[8] Heaven is there conceived as a state in which every faculty is made faultless and wholly occupied in knowing and enjoying God. "What is heaven to me but God? God, who is light, and life, and love, communicating himself to blessed spirits, perfecting them in the reception, possession and exercise of life, light and love, for ever...God...is heaven and all to me."[9] "It is the presence of God that maketh heaven to be heaven."[10] Heaven thus begins on earth; "the knowledge and love of God in Christ is the beginning or foretaste of heaven."[11] Full enjoyment, however, is yet future: "we ask for perfection, and we shall have it, but not here."[12] How and where we shall enter heaven, how the soul will exist without the body in the intermediate state and how soul and body will unite again at the general

---

6. XXIII:235.

7. XII:222.

8. "One of the most beautiful of his books" in Powicke's opinion (*Under the Cross*, 97); though he is mistaken in thinking it was written in 1683, the year of its publication. That it was actually composed in 1676 is proved by the statement in a letter to Sir Matthew Hale, dated May 5 of that year: "I am writing my own funerall sermon on Phil. 1.23." The letter was published in *John Rylands Library Bulletin*, XXIV:i, 1940, 173 f.

9. XVIII:426.

10. XXII:122.

11. XII:576.

12. XVIII:369.

resurrection, are matters completely opaque to us ("a hundred of these questions are better left...Had all these been needful to us, they had been revealed"),[13] but both reason and revelation assure us that immortality and retribution after this life are certainties. In heaven, Baxter's omnivorous appetite for knowledge is to be satiated at last. Understanding will be perfect. He will know everything, and know it thoroughly, by direct intuition, as God knows it. "All sciences are there perfect, without our ambiguous terms, or imperfect axioms, and rules of art . . . "[14] "I shall quickly, in heaven, be a perfect philosopher."[15] To arouse his own eagerness, he sets before himself the celestial curriculum:

> I. I shall know God better. II. I shall know the universe better. III. I shall know Christ better. IV. I shall know the church, his body, better, with the holy angels. V. I shall better know the methods and perfection of the Scripture...VI. I shall know the methods and sense of disposing providence better. VII. I shall know the divine benefits, which are the fruits of love, better. VIII. I shall know myself better. IX. I shall better know every fellow-creature...X. And I shall better know all that evil, sin, Satan and misery, from which I am delivered.[16]

All that is obscure now will be gloriously plain then. Moreover, in heaven Baxter expects his will to be perfected. It will be free from external distraction, "a body of cross interests and inclinations . . . a world of inferior good, which is the bait . . . for the flesh . . . God's mercies will not be made there the tempter's instruments." Inner conflicts will be over: "there will be nothing in me that is cross to itself; no more war or striving in me; not a law in my mind, and a law in my members, that are contrary to each other...all will be at unity and peace within."[17] Frustration will be a thing of the past: "I shall have all whatsoever I would have, and shall be and do whatsoever I would be and do."[18] Unimpeded, undistracted, the whole man will be joyfully devoted to the joyous activity of loving God. "Perfect, joyful complacency in God is the heaven which I desire and hope for":[19] "seeing and loving will be the heavenly life."[20] Moreover, in heaven the soul's capacity for action will be perfected too: "there are good works in heaven, and far more and better than on earth."[21] Heaven is the place of perfect praise and perfect service. A man's reach will not there exceed his

13. p. 259.
14. p. 367.
15. p. 359.
16. p. 356f.
17. p. 368.
18. p. 369.
19. p. 371.
20. p. 389.
21. *loc. cit.*

grasp; aspiration will be equaled by achievement. There is peace and pleasure for evermore. Much about it is of necessity obscure to the saints on earth; the soul's "thoughts about its future state must be analogical and general, and partly strange";[22] but Christians may rest in the sure confidence that death ushers in a change for the better. "In heaven we shall have not less, but…more excellent sense and affections of love and joy, as well as more excellent intellection and volition; but such as we cannot now clearly conceive of."[23]

The idea of heaven gained by the use of this first method may, however, be amplified by the use of a second: the elaboration of "analogical collections…from the present operations and pleasures of the soul in flesh, to help our conception of its future pleasures."[24] This approach supplements the other. Baxter developed it in his first and greatest book, the *Saints' Everlasting Rest: or, A Treatise of the Blessed State of the Saints in their Enjoyment of God in Glory*. "The heavenly Christian…ever excelleth the rest of men," Baxter there wrote, "but when he is nearest heaven he excelleth himself."[25] The book, for all its bulk and unevenness, is a standing witness to the truth of his own dictum. His imagination was never so vivid and fertile, nor his style so urgent and compelling, nor his appeal so powerful and urgent, as in the eddying torrent of vision, argument and entreaty which fills the eight hundred quarto pages of the *Saints' Rest*. It is a work of amazing vitality and freshness, the more so when one recalls the circumstances in which it was written. In the course of it, Baxter gives a vivid and detailed statement of the Rationale of this "analogical" method in a passage which we may quote at length:

> It is very considerable, how the Holy Ghost doth condescend in the phrase of Scripture, in bringing things down to the reach of sense; how he sets forth the excellences of spiritual things in words that are borrowed from the objects of sense; how he describeth the glory of the new Jerusalem in expressions that might take even with flesh itself…doubtless if such expressions had not been best, and to us necessary, the Holy Ghost would not have so frequently used them: he that will speak to man's understanding, must speak in man's language, and speak that which he is capable to conceive…
>
> …But what is my scope in all this?…that we make use of these phrases of the Spirit to quicken our apprehensions and affections…and use these low notions as a glass, in which we must see the things themselves, though the representation be exceeding imperfect, till we come to an immediate perfect sight.[26]

22. p. 337.
23. p. 394.
24. *loc. cit.*
25. XXIII:225.
26. XXIII:375 f.

The purpose of the Biblical imagery is to make thoughts of heaven concrete and attractive, and the Christian's wisdom is to let his imagination feed on it accordingly. So, in the first part of the *Saint's Rest*, Baxter elaborates a graphic description of the rest which remains for the people of God, the state in which sin and sorrow are past and God and his Christ are seen, loved and enjoyed. He pictures Christ's return, the general resurrection, the final judgement and the entry of God's people into the full glory of their inheritance. He imagines the wondering ecstasy with which the redeemed will recall their earthly pilgrimage. "To stand in heaven, and look back on earth...how must it needs transport the soul and make it cry out...Is this the end of believing? Is this the end of the Spirit's workings? Have the gales of grace blown me into such a harbour?

Is it hither that Christ hath enticed my soul?...Is my mourning, my sad humblings, my heavy walking, groanings, complainings, come to this?...So will the memory of the saints for ever promote their joys."[27] He even envisages the sight of the well-merited misery of the damned as increasing their admiration of their God and their thankfulness for the mercy of election. They themselves had deserved hell as much as anyone, yet a gracious God had brought them to heaven. "Distinguishing, separating mercy affecteth more than any mercy";[28] and the sight of those in hell will quicken their sense of it. "The Scripture seems to affirm, that as the damned souls shall, from hell, see the saints' happiness, to increase their own torments, so shall the blessed, from heaven, behold the wicked's misery to the increase of their own joy."[29] He goes on to imagine the delights of fellowship with the universal Church, with Jewish saints and Christian saints, Fathers, Reformers and Puritans, in a passage so striking that it deserves quotation at length:

> It cannot choose but be comfortable to me to think of that day, when I shall join with Moses in his song, with David in his psalms of praise, and with all the redeemed in the song of the Lamb for ever; when we shall see Enoch walking with God, Noah enjoying the end of his singularity, Job of his patience, Hezekiah of his uprightness...Will it be nothing conducible to our comforts

27. XXII:60 f
28. p. 118.
29. p. 119. The texts to which Baxter refers are Rev. 16:5-6, 18:20, 19:7-8. The idea is as old as Tertullian, and is formally stated by Aquinas, *Summa Theol.* III. Suppl. Q. 94, 1: "In order that the saints may enjoy their beatitude more thoroughly, a perfect sight of the punishments of the damned is granted to them." If it be allowed that retributive justice is a glorious Divine attribute, the notion is not obviously sub-Christian. That God's justice is in fact glorious was asserted by Baxter, as it is by all Reformed theologians. Cf. p. 84: "That the...damned live, is to be ascribed to him; that they live in misery, is long of themselves...They shall...live, whether they will or no, for God's glory, though they live not to their own comfort, because they would not."

to live eternally with Peter, Paul, Austin, Chrysostom, Jerome, Wickliffe, Luther, Zuinglius, Calvin, Beza, Bullinger, Zanchius, Paraeus, Piscator, Camero; with Hooper, Bradford, Latimer, Glover, Saunders, Philpot; with Reighnolds (i.e. Rainold(e)s), Whitaker, Cartwright, Brightman, Bayne, Bradshaw, Bolton, Ball, Hildersham, Pemble, Twisse, Ames, Preston, Sibbs?[30]

Baxter often refers to the communion of saints as a principal ingredient in heaven's joy. His bitter experience, as pastor and statesman, of the pride and partiality which set Christians at each other's throats and shattered Christ's Church to fragments made him long for the perfect peace and love of heaven. The triumph in the English Church of sectarianism over catholic principles was to him the greatest tragedy of his life. As his hopes for Church peace on earth grew fainter, we find him dwelling more and more upon the truly catholic churchmanship of the new Jerusalem. Bates records that his greatest comfort as he lay dying was to meditate on the description of Mount Zion in Heb. 12, a passage which, he said, "deserved a thousand thousand thoughts...O how comfortable is that promise: Eye hath not seen, nor ear heard, neither hath it entered into the heart of man to conceive, the things God hath laid up for those who love him."[31] But, as we see, God reveals them to His people by His Spirit; and the Spirit enables them, as they think on these things, in a measure to realize their eschatology experimentally, and to foretaste heaven while yet on earth.

The importance of knowing what lies at the end of the Christian pilgrimage seemed to Baxter incalculable. Man is a rational creature. His activity, as rational, consists of choosing means to ends. The more strongly he desires an end, the more carefully will he use the means to it. "The *Love* of the end is it that is the *poise* or spring, which setteth every Wheel a going . . ."[32] But an unknown end

30. p. 122. The list of Reformation martyrs reflects Baxter's reading of Foxe, as do several references to martyrs' deaths elsewhere in the *Saints' Rest* (cf. 75, 159, XXIII:393). To look forward to meeting the heroes of faith in heaven, and to follow their example on earth, is an essential part of the duty of holding communion with the saints as Baxter understood it; cf. *Directory*, III:x, "Directions about our communion with holy souls departed, now with Christ;" and *Life of Faith*, III:xxvi, "How by faith to be followers of the saints...and to hold communion with the heavenly society." The following passage illustrates the use of such thoughts: "it will greatly satisfy the soul against the suspicions and fears of unbelief, when faith seeth all the glorified saints, that are actually saved by Christ already...Methinks I hear Enoch, Joshua, Abraham, Peter, Paul, John, Cyprian, Macarius, Augustine, Melancthon, Calvin, Zanchius, Rogers, Bradford, Hooper, Jewel, Grindal, Usher, Hildersham, Ames, Dod, Baines, Bolton, Gataker, with thousands such, as men standing on the further side of the river, and calling to us that must come after them, Fear not the depths, or storms, or streams; trust boldly that vessel, and that faithful pilot; we trusted him, and none of us have miscarried, but all of us are here landed safe...Who would not boldly follow such a multitude of excellent persons, who have sped so well?" (XII:554).
31. *Funeral Sermon*, 127, quoting I Cor. 2:9.
32. *R.B.*, I:129.

cannot be desired. "It is a known, and not merely an unknown God and happiness, that the soul doth joyfully desire."[33] And a man who neither knows nor cares where he is going is unlikely to travel very fast. Baxter was thoroughly persuaded of the truth of his basic principle in this matter:

> Though I have heard many pious men say, "Let us study how to come to heaven, and let others study how great the joys are; yet have I found, by reason and experience, as well as Scripture, that it is not our comfort only, but our stability, our liveliness in all our duties...the vigour of our love, thankfulness and all our graces, yea, the very being of our religion, and Christianity itself, that dependeth on the believing, serious thoughts of our rest. The end directeth to, and in the means.[34]

> It is the heavenly Christian that is the lively Christian. It is strangeness to heaven that makes us so dull; it is the end that quickens to all the means; and the more frequently and clearly this end is beheld, the more vigorous will all our motion be...We run so slowly, and strive so lazily, because we so little mind the prize.[35]

The Christian, therefore, should animate himself daily to love and obedience by means of "heavenly meditation," "the delightfulest task to the spirit, and the most tedious to the flesh, that ever men on earth were employed in."[36] The importance of this practice is made plain by the twelve "moving considerations" which make up the chapter, "Motives to a Heavenly Life" in part IV of the *Saint's Rest*. The chapter concludes as follows:

> Reader, stop here, while thou answerest my question: Are these considerations weighty, or not? Are these arguments convincing, or not? Have I proved it thy duty, and a flat necessity, to keep thy heart on things above, or have I not? Say yea or nay, man! If thou say nay, I am confident thou contradictest thine own conscience, and speakest against the light that is in thee, and thy reason tells thee thou speakest falsely . . . [37]

Baxter was tireless in his insistence that there is no healthy Christianity without "heaven-work." "Meditation is the life of most other duties; and the view of heaven is the life of meditation."[38] When in 1670 Giles Firmin criticized the

33. XVIII:295.
34. XXII:20.
35. XXIII:237.
36. p. 175; from the "Introduction" to Part IV of the *Saints' Rest*, "A Directory for the getting and keeping of the Heart in Heaven.
37. p. 263.
38. p. 323.

emphasis on meditation in the *Saints' Rest*, as encouraging unbalance and melancholy,[39] Baxter at once wrote a tract defending his position. In it he once again recorded his own testimony to the value of the practice in a passage of striking interest and power:

> I find that whatever else I think of, of Christ, of Scripture, of Promises, of Threatenings, of sin, of Grace, &c. if I leave out *Heaven* and make it not the chief point of my Meditation, I leave out the sence and Life of all. Thence must I fetch my Light, or I must be Dead, and my *Motives* or I must be Dull, or not sincere ... My Hearing, Reading, and Studies grow to Common things, if Heaven be not the principal part; My life groweth toward a common and a carnal life, when I begin to leave out Heaven: Death groweth terrible to my thoughts, and Eternity strange and dreadful to me, if I live not in such frequent and serious thoughts of the Heavenly Glory, as may render it familiar and grateful to my soul...And I find my self unfit to Live or to Die, and that my soul is void of the true Consolation...when I grow a stranger to Heavenly Thoughts, and consequently to Heavenly Affections: And that as nothing will serve turn instead of Heaven to be my Happiness, so nothing will serve turn instead of Heaven to make up the end of my Religion, and forme my Heart and Life to Holiness. And therefore by experience I counsel all Christians that are able to perform it, especially Ministers, and Learned men, to be much in the serious fore-thoughts of Heaven ...[40]

Baxter gives detailed directions for meditation. First, a time must be set apart for it, as indeed for all duties as far as possible. Over against the haphazardness of zealots and "enthusiasts" who would do nothing till they felt themselves "moved by the Spirit," Baxter, the devotee of "method," strongly advocated an Evangelical rule of life. "Stick not at their scruple, who question the stating of times as superstitious...a Christian should have a set time for every ordinary duty, or else when he should practice it, it is ten to one but he will put it by. Stated time is a hedge to duty ...If we considered of the ordinary works of the day, and suited out a fit season and proportion of time to every

---

39. In *The Real Christian*. For Firmin, cf. *D.N.B.*, *C.R.* s.v. It is only fair to Baxter to point out that in his second practical book, the *Right Method...* (1653), he himself had plainly stated that "studying and serious meditating be not duties for the deeply melancholy" (IX:24) and given the following explicit warning: "whereas in my Book of Rest, I so much press a course of heavenly meditation, I do intend it only for sound heads, and not for the melancholy, that have weak heads and are unable to bear it. That may be their sin which to others is a very great duty...they will but disable themselves..."(IX:191 f.). They should instead spend extra time in "conference with judicious Christians" and praise and thanks.

40. *The Duty of Heavenly Meditation Reviewed* (finished, Oct. 1, 1670; printed, 1671), 31 f. In his "Premonition" to the second edition of *Self-Denial*, Baxter tells us that the last part of the *Saint's Rest* was, with *Self-Denial* and *Life of Faith*, most frequently read of all his writings "for the use of my own soul, in its daily work" (XI:iv); and notes how "we...press that on others which we find most necessary to ourselves."

work, and fixed this in our memory and resolution…and never break it but upon unexpected extraordinary cause…we should be better skilled, both in redeeming time and performing duty."[41] Each man must discover what time for meditation suits him best. (Baxter's own best time, he tells us, was in "the evening, from sun-setting to twilight; and sometimes in the night, when it is warm and clear.")[42] The time must not be too short; for "as I cannot get me heat with walking, no nor running neither, . . . unless I *continue* some considerable time, no more can I in Prayer and Meditation."[43] Baxter advises, therefore, "set apart one hour or half hour every day"[44] for this venture.

The aim of the "set and solemn acting of all the powers of the soul upon this most perfect object, rest, by meditation"[45] is "to use your understandings for the warming of your affections, and to fire your hearts by the help of your heads"; to turn light into heart. "He is the best Christian who hath the readiest passage from the brain to the heat."[46] The method is one of consideration followed by soliloquy. The first stage consists in bringing the relevant truths before the mind as clearly and fully as possible and awakening ("acting") the various affections—love, desire, hope, courage and joy—as is appropriate. When the object of contemplation has thus become an object of love, desire and delight, then is the time to enter upon the second stage, "pleading the case with our own souls . . . Soliloquy is a preaching to oneself."[47] The aim here is to move oneself to resolute Christian practice. Soliloquy thus corresponds to the "improvement," the "uses" of doctrine, in a Puritan sermon. If heaven is so desirable, the Christian must say to himself, should I not be working much harder and running much faster in order to make sure of reaching it? The following graphic passage sufficiently indicates what Baxter has in mind.

> In thy meditations upon all these incentives…preach them over earnestly to thy heart, and expostulate and plead with it by way of soliloquy, till thou feel

---

41. XXIII:318 f.

42. 324; Baxter notes that evening meditation was practiced by Isaac (Gen. 24:63) and Bishop Hall. To the end of his life, Sylvester tells us, he "set some time apart every day for that weighty work" (*Elisha's Cry . . .* , 15).

43. *Duty of Heavenly Meditation Reviewed*, 19.

44. XXIII:406; cf. *Duty . . .* , 16 f.: "to them that have Ability and opportunity, at least a quarter or 1/2 an hour, if not more, is best to Edification…I prove it from the Aptitude of the Means to its end."

45. XXIII:310.

46. pp. 338, 340. Baxter quotes with approval Bernard's dictum (*Cant.*, serm. 46): "contemplationis accessus duo sunt, unus in intellectu, alter in affectu; unus in lumine, alter in fervore; unus in acquisitione, alter in devotione" (314). [There are two entrances into contemplation, one in understanding, the other in desiring; one in light, the other in heat; one in gaining (knowledge), the other in devotion (to God).]

47. p. 369.

the fire begin to burn...Dispute it out with thy conscience... There is much
more moving force in this earnest talking to ourselves, than in bare cogitation,
that breaks not out into mental words. Imitate the most powerful preaching
that ever thou wast acquainted with...There is more in this than most
Christians are aware of, or use to practice. It is a great part of a Christian's
skill and duty, to be a good preacher to himself...Two or three sermons a
week from others, is a fair proportion; but two or three sermons a day from
thyself, is ordinarily too little ... [48]

Finally, believers should pass on "from this speaking to ourselves, to speak to
God" in prayer; which is "the highest step that we can advance to in the work."[49]
Earnest desire and hearty resolution, poured out in prayer, can never lack God's
blessing. Such prayers take heaven by storm.

Many collateral activities bear on the success of these endeavors. Physical
discipline and self-control are preconditions of it. "God useth to give his
heavenly cordials upon an empty stomach ... fasting from the world, doth best
prepare you for this heavenly feast ... command a total fast in your affections;
and try then whether you be not fitter to ascend, and whether God will not
reveal himself more clearly than before."[50] Attachment to the Creator
presupposes detachment from the creatures. And success demands hard work.
"Reader, heaven is above thee, the way is upward. Dost thou think, who art a
feeble, short-winded sinner, to travel daily this steep ascent without a great
deal of labour and resolution?"[51] "You shall find your own hearts your greatest
hinderer...they will hold off, that you will hardly get them to the work ... they
will betray you by their idleness...they will interrupt the work by ... turning
aside to every object...they will spoil the work by cutting it short."[52] The
Christian must prepare to do battle with wandering thoughts and inveterate inner
reluctance whenever he seeks to set his affections on things above. The habit of
meditation will, however be greatly promoted by hearing sermons about heaven
("happy the people that have a heavenly minister!"),[53] by talking to other
Christians about heaven, and by assiduously reading the books of creation
and providence.

48. II:392; in *Saint's Rest* IV:x, Baxter gives similar advice ("mark the most affecting, heart-
melting minister...set him as a pattern before thee for thy imitation; and the same way that he
takes with the hearts of his people, do thou take with thy own heart"), and appends a model
outline soliloquy, divided into a "doctrine" and six "uses."
49. XXIII:373.
50. IX:549.
51. XXIII:283.
52. p. 399.
53. p. 249.

Make an advantage of every object thou seest, and of every passage of divine providence, and of every thing that befalls in thy labour and calling, to mind thy soul of its approaching rest. As all providences and creatures are means to our rest, so do they point us to that as their end. Every creature hath the name of God, and our final rest, written upon it...O learn to open the creatures, and to open the several passages of providence, to read of God and glory there...we might have a fuller taste of Christ and heaven in every bit of bread that we eat, and in every draught of beer we drink, than most men have in the use of the sacrament."[54]

And there will be times when the Spirit's help will be given in an unusual way. "Dost thou not feel sometimes a strong impulsion to retire from the world, and draw near to God? O . . . take the offer, and hoist up sail while thou mayst have this blessed gale. When this wind blows strongest, thou goest fastest . . ."[55]

How the diligent practice of heavenly meditation enables the Christian to resist the blandishments of the world and the flesh and to overcome the fear of death, how it spurs him on to a life of tireless service under the most trying circumstances and begets "obedient patience" in face of pain, isolation and ill-treatment, how it clears the head and purifies the heart, driving out narrow judgments and mean motives, are topics about which Baxter had much to say; but we cannot here follow him further. Perhaps his own life is as clear and full an exposition of these matters as anything he wrote.

Baxter insisted that his teaching on meditation, strange though it might seem to some of his Puritan readers, was nothing new in the catholic church of Christ. Soliloquy, he points out, is frequently exemplified in Scripture ("how doth David plead with his soul against its dejections, and argue it into a holy confidence and comfort!)"[56]; moreover, "the like you may see in the meditations of holy men of latter times, as Austin, Bernard, &c: so that this is no new path which I persuade you to tread, but that which the saints have ever used . . ."

54. p. 300.
55. p. 307.
56. p. 368; adducing Ps 42:5, 11, 43:5, 103:1 f, 104:1 f., 146:1 f., 116:7.
57. XXII:18.
58. In part IV, Cyprian is quoted 24 times, Augustine 22 and Gerson 7. Bernard appears only 3 times; so that Ladell is quite inaccurate and misleading when he writes "it is significant that he refers the reader almost entirely to the works of St. Augustine and St. Bernard" (*Richard Baxter*, 1925, 135). Cyprian is highly praised: "Cypr. de Mortalitate (and others of his) is excellent (XXIII:192 n.); "read Cyprian's excellent contemplation of the world's vanity and wickedness, from his prospect in the mount, Epist. i. ad Donat." (262 n.). So is Gerson: "the nine considerations of Gerson are excellent" (217 n.); "Read this (an excerpt), you libertines, and learn better the way of devotion from a Papist: (285 n.). The only authors quoted with comparable frequency are the moralists, Seneca and Clement of Alexandria, whose dissuasives against self-indulgence and fear of death are frequently cited.

Among the authoritative exponents of meditation whom he quotes in the margin of the second edition of the *Saint's Rest* ("for the sweetness of the matter...as also to free myself from the charge of singularity"),[57] those most often cited and most highly recommended are Cyprian, Augustine and Gerson.[58] Heavenly meditation had, indeed, been inculcated by Calvin[59] as a central activity in the Christian life, and by other Puritan authors before Baxter's time,[60] but the *Saint's Rest* was the first Puritan attempt to treat the subject on a large scale. And, indeed, it was the last; for it was recognized at once that the work which Baxter had done did not need doing again. His mastery was never questioned. From many testimonies we may quote one: that of John Eliot, who wrote to Baxter on August 6, 1656, to say how much he had been helped in illness by the *Saint's Rest*, particularly by "that blessed poynt and patterne of holy meditation," and to urge him to "spend the rest of your life in writing practical meditations. The world is full of polemical books, and doctrinal...it is a rare gift, especially to follow a meditation to the bottom, and bring it to an issue, and to put it forth for a patterne;" and this is a field "wherein so few have laboured."[61] The immediate and sustained popularity of the *Saint's Rest*, unrivalled in its day by that of any religious book of its size, showed that this was no isolated opinion.

We have now followed Baxter to the heart and height of Christian practice. This is life in the Spirit, a life which at once anticipates and promotes the believer's restoration to the perfection for which men were made. We saw earlier what Christ requires of his subjects; we now see how righteousness is fulfilled through the Spirit. Duty, fixed by Christ's law, is done by the Spirit's power. The Spirit leads a man's mind and heart up to heaven, and thus sets in motion the activities by which sin is progressively destroyed and love made perfect. Desires are only rooted out as other desires are grafted in to replace them. Sinful affections cannot be driven out except by holy affections. Only when heaven possesses a man's heart can the world be effectively excluded from it, and he himself set free from the corrupting influence of selfish motive for whole-hearted service of God and his fellows. But nothing can occupy a man's heart to which he never gives a thought. The Spirit's part, therefore, is to set Christians thinking of heaven, apprehending it, desiring it, and so living for it. It is the object that calls forth desire: the Spirit presents the object to the mind,

---

59. *Inst.*, III.ix, "De Meditatione Futurae Vitae."

60. Cf. (e.g.) R. Bolton, *Some Generall Directions for a Comfortable Walking with God*, 1625, 65 (tenth of the "Generall preparatives"): "Let thy soule full often soare aloft upon the wings of faith...and bathe it selfe before hand with many a sweet meditation in that everlasting blisse above ..." Bolton also published *Meditations on the Life to Come*, 1628.

61. Mss. 59, iii. f. 7. Baxter replied (f.9) that he liked the idea, but "my worke is all cutt out to my hands by Providence and necessity." The letters were published by Powicke, *Some unpublished correspondence of the Reverend Richard Baxter ...* (1931), cf. 19, 21.

and the resulting desire leads to action forthwith. He moves them to pray for light in order that He may give it, and He gives it in order that they may then be moved to pray for strength to live by it. This prayer, too, He evokes in order that He may answer it. Thus the Spirit of God carries on the work of sanctification, by evoking man's cooperation and seconding his endeavors. The power which actually roots out sins and implants graces in their stead is His, just as the power which time and again raised Baxter's body from a death-bed and would, he knew, raise it incorruptible at the last day was His; but the means through which He exercises His power is rational human activity. He works on and in man, but on man as man, not as on a stone. Man is active, not passive, when the Spirit moves him. The Spirit shows him that his holiness, God's end for him, is also his happiness, his own natural end for himself, and thus sets him seeking and using the means to it. He awakens interest and desire, and so evokes action. By this means God's end is gained, through man's working to gain his own. God works in him, therefore he works himself; and so the process of his restoration goes on.

Tension and trust, therefore, mark the Spirit-filled man of God—the bracing, ennobling tension of a sustained and victorious warfare against sin, and the unwavering trust of a sober but well-grounded hope of perfect purity and the vision of God. His life is one of intense activity and intense peace. Humble and submissive before his God, and therefore bold and inflexible before his fellows, fearing his Maker so much that he fears men not at all, he rides post-haste along the road to the city of God, undistracted by anything on the way because preoccupied with thoughts of the joy that awaits him. His life is a whole, organized, "methodized"; one thing he does, and one only; each particular activity has its rationale as a means to this single goal. He looks straight forward; and as the bride awaits her wedding day, as the invalid anticipates recovery, so he hopes and waits for the day when he will leave the wilderness of this world for a better country above. This was the doctrine that Baxter taught and adorned; this is the clue to an understanding of his thought and his life; and here, perhaps, at this point of aspiration, is the fittest place to take our leave of him.

> Come, Lord, when Grace hath made me meet,
>   Thy blessed Face to see:
> For if thy work on earth be sweet,
>   What will thy Glory be?
>
> Then I shall end my sad complaints,
>   And weary sinful daies;
> And joyn with the triumphant Saints,
>   That sing Jehovah's Praise.

My Knowledge of that Life is small,
 The Eye of Faith is dim:
But it's enough that Christ knows all;
 And I shall be with him.[62]

62. *Poetical Fragments*, 62

Conclusion

SYNOPSIS

1.   Aim: to suggest an evaluation of Baxter's theology.

2.   Revision of received judgments of Baxter.
                a. Not vague nor inconsistent:
                        a clear, methodical, systematic, organized thinker.
                b. Baxter's theological affinities:
                        Calvinistic fundamentals;
                        Arminian view of God's penal law
                                hence of redemption and justification.

        "Hypothetical universalism" before Baxter:
                aimed to magnify God's love;
                inconsistent on God's love;
                        nature and extent of atonement.
        Baxter improved the system by his "political method."
        Baxter's affinity with Usher's group.

3.   Baxter sought to be "catholic" in his doctrine of man's salvation.
        Assessment of his claim:
                a. Catholic elements common to Reformed thought generally;
                        Trinitarian structure of thought;
                        God's glory the goal of all.
                b. Catholic doctrine of man as God's rational creature.
                        Three corollaries:
                        rationalism
                        concern for method and political method
                        opposition to "immediacy" and doctrines of "physical
                                influence."
        On Baxter's method: trichotomy artificial;
                                political method naïve;
        due to defective application of catholic principles;
        based on over-simplified view of the universe.
        Catholicity of Baxter's stress on kingdom of God
                                unity of knowledge
        On Baxter's opposition to "immediacy": overdone;
                due to over-simplified view of nature of reason;
                yet a timely and catholic reaction to the sects of his day.

        c. Baxter's doctrine of justification:
                Eschatological—present and future;

Conciliatory—reconciling Protestants and Papists;
Reactionary—political union substituted for mystical union in
dogmatic construction.

    d. Catholicity of Baxter's practical theology:
        Unique grasp of eschatological character of Christian life.

4.   Baxter's theology still valuable.

Conclusion

Paradoxical as it may seem, I hold that it is the extreme unification of Bonaventure's doctrine which has made it look incomplete and unsystematized; it is easier to deny that the details form part of a system, than to grasp the system in its entirety and think out each detail in the function of the whole.

—E. Gilson, *The Philosophy of St. Bonaventure*, 480 f.

As *for me*, the Author *knoweth not what to call me, unless it be a* Baxterian, *as intending to be a* Haeresiarcha.

—Baxter, 1680.

He formed no party but kept a position of his own which was so central as at the time to seem eccentric.

—G. F. Nuttall, *The Holy Spirit . . .* , 169.

Baxter's doctrine of man, created, fallen, redeemed and restored, is now before us. We have traced its ramifications and dug into its sources in some detail. We have tried to reconstruct his point of view, to read the books that shaped his thought, and to watch his mind at work polishing, refining and "methodizing" the ideas they gave him. All this was necessary if we were to "place" him accurately amid the eddying cross-currents of Puritan theological debate. Our review of the practical side of his teaching has been far less complete as a treatment of the material available, but we have said as much as seemed necessary to complete the exposition of our subject. We have aimed to give a sympathetic presentation of our material, and so have largely eschewed critical judgments. This seemed wise, partly because in an age that is such a stranger to classical Reformed theology such judgments would be hazardous and probably premature, and partly because Baxter's ideas are well worth thinking about in their own right, and the writer would only have distracted his readers from so doing by interpolating his own opinions into the text. Both Orme and Powicke fell into this trap, and both largely failed as a result to do justice to Baxter's merits as a theologian. The time has now come, however, if not to attempt a definitive evaluation of Baxterianism ourselves, at least to suggest the lines along which it should be attempted.

First, however, we must correct some of the received opinions concerning it, a selection of which we collected in the Introduction. And we may begin by dismissing as completely baseless the idea that Baxter's theology is vague and inconsistent. Nothing could be further from the truth. Certainly, Baxter used certain words in unfamiliar senses and with unfamiliar precision, but he was lavish with definitions and perfectly clear and orderly in expressing himself. As he repeatedly told his critics (to their great annoyance), there was not the least excuse for misunderstanding him; their failure to grasp his meaning simply betokened minds that were either lazy and careless, too workshy to take the trouble of mastering his vocabulary, or else incapable of precise thought; and in either case they would have been wiser had they said nothing and not made such a display of their ineptitude. He would have spoken in the same way to some of his professed admirers in modern times. Complaints about his "refined and intangible distinctions" tell us more about the critics than about the author thus taken to task. In actual fact, Baxter was probably as exact and consistent a thinker as any in the Church's history. Certainly, he excelled them all in his virtuosity as a "methodist." He claimed to have used the key of "method" to unlock doors and open up recesses in theology where it had never been tried before. For instance, he had "methodized" the Divine attributes and relations, which the rest of theologians "use to name over...like as they put their money or chess-men into a bag, without any method at all."[1] And he had arranged Christian theology in a scheme which he considered the apotheosis of "method":

> the method of the whole doctrine of Christianity set together, is the most admirable and perfect in the world; beginning with God in unity of essence, proceeding to his trinity of essential active principles, and of persons, and so to his trinity of works, creation, redemption and regeneration, and of relations of God and man accordingly;[2] and to the second trinity of relations, as he is our Owner, Ruler and chief Good; and hence it brancheth itself into a

---

1. XII:390; cf. the protest in *C.T.*, I. i. 12, 2 f: "We would not give a Prince his Titles so confusedly, nor draw his Picture monstrously, with the arms where the feet should be, and the feet where the arms, or the back before, and the face behind, unless we exposed him purposely to scorn..."

2. As set out in the Baptismal Covenant.

> multitude of benefits flowing from all these relations of God to man, and a
> multitude of answerable duties flowing from our correlations to God, and all
> in perfect method, twisted and inoculated into each other, making a kind of
> circulation between mercies and duties, as in man's body there is of the arterial
> and venal blood and spirits, till in the issue, as all mercy came from God, and
> duty subordinately from man, so mercy and duty do terminate in the
> everlasting pleasure of God ultimately, and man subordinately, in that mutual
> love which is here begun, and there is perfected.[3]

We have now examined this "method" in detail, and can recognize the justice
of Baxter's claim for it. It is simple, suggestive and sublime. Even the modern
reader, who no longer treats *ordo* as the test of truth, feels its fascination. It is a
work of art in the modern sense of the phrase even more than in Baxter's. And,
once its outlines are grasped, everything in Baxterianism falls into place; the
puzzles solve themselves, and the disconcerting distinctions are seen to flow
naturally and inevitably from the system's heart. A more exact and integrated
body of thought it would be hard to find.

Again, we have now settled the question of Baxter's theological affinities,
and may here sum up what we have found. The foundation of his thought
about man's redemption was unquestionably Calvinistic. He could subscribe
the Westminster standards, and took his stand on the pronouncements of the
Synod of Dort. He believed wholeheartedly in total depravity, unconditional
election, effectual calling by monergistic regeneration, and the final
perseverance of the saints. But he introduced certain Arminian elements into
the superstructure by his adoption of Grotius' "political method," which led
him to a fundamental disagreement with the orthodox Calvinist doctrine of
God. Socinianism had forced Calvinists to make explicit the presupposition of
their soteriology—that God's penal law and punitive justice are inexorable
and immutable expressions of the Divine holiness, so that exact retribution
for sin is the unchanging law of the universe. Baxter, however, found the
rationale of God's laws and punishments, not in His nature, but in His rectoral
relation to man. God has decreed to glorify himself by a display of wise and
good government; He has purposed to compass His ends for men by this means;
and the making and executing of penal law is a necessary ingredient in good
government. But there is no reason why He should not modify or repeal the
penal sanctions of His law, if the principles of good government would not be
thereby violated. This was not to suggest that He ever could or would change
its precept, nor to deny that sin is unclean and loathsome in His sight, so that
in so far as man identifies himself with it he cuts himself off from God. But it
was to assert explicitly that the necessity of punishing sin was external to God,

---

3. XXI:212.

and not, therefore, unconditional. Orthodox Calvinists believed that God would deny Himself did he not punish sin as it deserved, and went on to assert that He only forgave sins to those who had committed them on the ground of their punishment in a Substitute of His own appointing. This was the position Owen sought to safeguard when he argued against Grotius and Baxter that Christ paid the exact penalty of the broken law. Only Penal suffering, the Calvinists claimed, could satisfy for sin. But Baxter here aligned himself with the Arminians and Socinians, denying that God required in all circumstances an exact penal equivalent for each particular sin. This was the element of truth in Owen's persistent insinuations that Baxter taught "an almost pure Socinian Justification and Exposition of the Covenant of Grace." On this foundation the other Arminian bricks in his dogmatic structure were laid. He denied that Christ's death was a case of penal substitution, affirming that its whole effect was to procure a new law of grace for the world, and he insisted that faith is imputed for what under the new law it is —"evangelical righteousness"—and so is the proper ground of justification.

In his Arminian analysis of the work of Christ, Baxter went beyond the earlier Calvinistic advocates of universal redemption, the followers of Cameron and Amyraldus in France and of Usher and Davenant in England. These theologians had been content to invoke the "redemption" metaphors, *payment* and *purchase*, and to assert simply that Christ actually satisfied for all men's sins and that the salvation he won, though available to the world, is actually conveyed only to the elect, whom God brings to faith. Their motive in maintaining the universal reference of the atonement was twofold: to do justice to the Biblical evidence as they understood it, and to secure a basis for evangelism. But analysis revealed that their view, which at first sight seems to magnify God's love by proclaiming its universality, actually discredits it. Orthodox Calvinism was consistent in teaching that God's love is powerful and effective; that whom He loves He saves through the work of His Son and Spirit; that, therefore, those who are not saved were never the objects of his love at all. Arminianism was consistent in teaching that God's love is a universal benevolence, equal to all but effective to none but those who cooperate with grace, and that it rests, not with God, but with man himself whether he will thus cooperate or not. But "hypothetical universalism" was thoroughly inconsistent in teaching that God loves all and yet saves only the elect. If God loves all, why did he not elect all? How can he be said to love the non-elect, whom He might have chosen to save but in fact deliberately passed over? How does Christ's death commend the love of God to those whom He has no intention of bringing to faith, so that they might profit by it? Plainly, on this view, the love of God means different things to different people: to one it means an effective saving activity, to another it means an ineffective inclination to bless which is thwarted by God's own decision. The second is in any case scarcely comprehensible, and to call it love when that word has already been used to denominate the first is an abuse of language. Neither reason nor Scripture warrants such a distinction.

Again, the mediating view was self-contradictory concerning the nature of the atonement. Orthodox Calvinism was consistent in describing redemption as the rendering of full satisfaction to God's law in man's stead, and thence inferring that it was limited in its designed scope to the elect. This is clear, for God's acceptance of satisfaction must automatically have terminated the liability to punishment of those for whom it was made. Having received satisfaction for them, God is now bound in justice to discharge them. But only the elect, whom He brings to faith, escape His wrath; therefore only they were redeemed. Arminianism was also consistent in describing redemption as the removal of an obstacle to forgiveness, and thence inferring that its designed scope was universal. God's acceptance of satisfaction, on this view, terminated man's liability to punishment by securing a change in the law which condemned him. The amended law of God now held out a free pardon to all who believe. Redemption thus conferred an actual right to salvation on none, but made salvation possible for all on the further condition of faith. But "hypothetical universalism" was not consistent. It sought to combine a Calvinist view of the nature of the atonement with an Arminian view of its scope. But if redemption was universal in its designed extent, and yet consisted in the offering of satisfaction to God's law, so that Christ actually satisfied for the sins of the reprobate, then it was impossible to avoid the conclusion that God has been both unwise, because Christ's death for them was pointless, and unjust, because He was bound to save those for whom He had accepted satisfaction without requiring further conditions on their part. He ought in justice to have given them faith, as He does in the case of the elect, rather than condemned them for the lack of it. On the premises of Reformed theology, therefore, "hypothetical universalism" as argued prior to Baxter was intolerable. Its advocates, seeking to set up a half-way house between Calvinist orthodoxy and Arminian heresy, had actually fallen between the two stools.

But Baxter stabilized and improved their view. He escaped the second inconsistency by accepting a thoroughly Arminian construction of the atonement and evaded the first by denying the propriety of inquiries about the relation between God's general love to the world and His special love to the elect. There are certain questions, he held, that creatures may not ask, and this is one of them. God's general love and desire for the salvation of all, which the gospel proclaims, is an expression of rectoral benevolence; but His special love is a part of the secret purpose of the Proprietor of the universe for the disposal of His possessions; and men may not pry into the connection between God's plans in these two distinct relations. Subjects may be sure that their ruler has intentions of his own of which his laws give no hint; but they may be equally sure that such matters are none of their business. Their part is to obey the laws made for their government; for, whatever else their ruler may have in mind, he will certainly reward them if they do and punish them if they do not. This may not be a wholly satisfactory analogy for thinking of God's "double will," but it is at least an intelligible one, and by introducing it Baxter made the best of "hypothetical universalism" that can ever be made of it. It is less than just to speak of him as one of Amyraldus' camp-followers. He was not. It was his "political method," his determination to make God's rectoral relationship regulative in his dogmatic construction, which led him independently to this view. And if orthodox Calvinists were to attack "Baxterianism" to any purpose, it could only be on the grounds that its "political method" was inappropriate and its doctrine of God's law and justice unscriptural. But this issue was never raised in his lifetime.

As regards the details of his system, Baxter stood alone. But in his general attitude and standpoint he was typical of the little group of Puritan Churchmen headed by Usher, of which Davenant, Hall and Gataker were the most notable members. They were all shy scholars, men of a Cranmerish spirit, and their culture was deeper, their thought more rationalistic, their Calvinism more conciliatory, their doctrine more deeply tinged by Patristic study and their churchmanship more catholic and comprehensive, than was the case with any of the militant partisan Presbyterians and Independents. They were men of a different stamp. In London in 1654, when Baxter was still in his thirties and Usher over seventy, the old Archbishop had welcomed him as a man after his own heart, and Baxter had discovered that Usher "owned my Judgement" in nearly everything. His respect for Usher was unbounded, and his deepest affinities were with the group which Usher led. He may truly be described as their last representative, preserving their views intact in an untheological and sectarian age that could scarcely comprehend them. We do not understand him, either as a theologian or as an ecclesiastical statesman, till we recognize this fact.

Baxter styled himself a "meer Catholick," and catholicity was his constant concern, in doctrine no less than in churchmanship. He saw, as no other man of his day saw, that the theologian's task is to elucidate the Church's faith, to which Scripture bears a normative witness; and he would not speak till he was sure that it was the historic faith to which he was giving expression. This was why he steeped himself in the Church's literary heritage, and why he was so contemptuous of "ignorant' and "unstudied" divines, whose every word betrayed an entire lack of acquaintance with historical theology. It was not enough to be able to rattle off texts; heretics could do that; no man was fit to teach till he had studied the Church's faith in its historical expression. Here we see the motive behind his frequent parade of authorities, and also the reason for his suspicion and distaste of claims to "new light." The idea that God might reveal in the seventeenth century truths of which the Church had hitherto known nothing seemed to him monstrous. This, too, was the reason why he was so bitter against the "over-orthodox": not because he differed from them as to the substance of the faith (he did not), but because they talked and behaved as if an elaborate Calvinistic theology was necessary to salvation, and thus consigned whole generations of the Church to hell. And while it is true that Baxter was a scholar, a traditionalist, an intellectual aristocrat, by temperament, it was only because he was convinced that it was his duty to be so that he gave rein to these traits in his theological activity. Again, it was his devotion to the ideal of catholicity that made him wary of extremes and inclined him always to take the middle road. He knew that truth usually lay there; and his belief that he held catholic truth was strengthened when he observed that his position was half-way between Calvinism and Arminianism, between legalism and Antinomianism, between a Jewish justification, by one's works entirely, and a libertine justification which had no effect on one's works at all, between the Spirit-intoxicated exuberance of sectarian "enthusiasm" and the moribund formalism of a great part of Christendom. The quest for catholicity was dominant in all his thinking, and it is as a catholic theologian that he would have asked to be judged. We may, therefore, fitly conclude our study by briefly considering his claim to teach a "catholic theology" of the redemption and restoration of man.

In general, as has become clear, Baxter's theology has the "catholic" shape—the balanced Trinitarian form of the Creed and Baptismal covenant. To restore these proportions after centuries of lop-sidedness was one of the services rendered to Christian thought by Calvin in his *Institutes*. Again, Baxter saw God's glory as the final cause of all things. To this the theocentric teleology which pervaded and ruled his thinking bears eloquent witness. This was another "catholic" insight stressed by Calvin and central in Calvinism. This, however, is not the place to prove the catholicity of Reformed theology as such. We shall take it for granted, and go on to consider the distinctive elements in Baxter's version of it.

The key to his thought about redemption was his doctrine of man. As a Puritan, a Renaissance man and a seventeenth-century Englishman, he found in anthropology an absorbing and controlling interest. And here, at the centre, his catholicity is not open to question. He stressed man's natural dignity as a rational creature, made in the image of God to know and love his Maker, conscious, purposive and free. He saw only too clearly the contrast between what man was made to be and what he has become, and thus was able to portray with catholic breadth and depth sin's idiocy, unloveliness, guilt and pollution. The startling "modernity" of his anatomy of sin is itself a testimony to its catholicity. Baxter on sin would be up-to-date in any age. From his anthropology sprang most of the distinctive features of his thought. In the first place, it was the source of his rationalism. This was a catholic, Augustinian rationalism, *fides quaerens intellectum*, far different from the unbelieving, individualistic rationalism of the age following his death. It expressed confidence about man rather than skepticism about his Maker. Its twin axioms—that nothing is intelligible at all except in relation to God, and that nothing is wholly incomprehensible to the pious mind—are simple expressions of Baxter's basic conviction that man was made to know God in and through His works. They are in fact the foundations of the catholic idea of a Christian culture that Augustine formulated in *The City of God*. In the second place, Baxter's anthropology explains his preoccupation with method; for apart from method understanding seemed to him unattainable, and understanding is part of man's creaturely vocation. It explains also why he hit on a "political method" in particular: God, he held, treats man as man, and therefore rules him by the only appropriate means—moral government. In the third place, it accounts for his adamant opposition to the immediacy of the "enthusiasts" and the "physical work" of regeneration taught by orthodox Calvinists: in each case, he maintained, it was being suggested that God moves man by non-moral means, and this was to dishonor the Creator by affirming that He dishonored His own image in the creature.

There is something less than catholic about the way Baxter developed his method and his polemic against "enthusiasm." For the first, the marvelous industry which he showed in trichotomizing cannot but impress the modern reader as largely wasted effort. "It is more calculated to amuse as a curious speculation," Orme wrote primly, "than to answer any important practical purpose."[4] "Hypothetical...conjectural...phantastic...of no use either to practical religion or to theological science," was Jenkyn's verdict.[5] Again, his assumption that seventeenth-century political ideas were the key to Biblical theology appears today absurdly naïve. Yet it is important to see that the defects of his method arise, not from a wrong principle so much as from right principles inadequately applied. That it is the Christian's duty to relate all he knows to God and seek its meaning in God is a catholic truth, even if the Ramist way of doing it, by systematic subdivision, does not work. That a fruitful dialectic may and must go on between God's special revelation in the Church's gospel and his general revelation in the world's culture is a catholic truth, even if treating the categories of contemporary political discussion as a mould into which the gospel must be poured is the wrong way to initiate it. The truth is that Baxter was tackling this program under the handicap of an over-simplified view of the nature of the world. This over-simplification was part of his inheritance. Like the majority of eclectics, he was no original thinker. The raw

---

4. *Works*, I:471.
5. Essay prefixed to *Works of the Puritan Divines: Baxter*, 1846, li.

material with which his mind worked was derived from books, and all his originality appears in his power to develop, polish and "methodize" the ideas of others. In the realm of presuppositions, we find that he was wholly at the mercy of the past; he accepted traditional outlooks without question, and continued to defend old paths of thought at a time when most thinkers had abandoned them. His maintenance of the pre-scientific world-view of mediaeval physics and Ramist methodology was a case in point. So was his naïve fusion of Biblical theology with political theory, which was only possible at all on the unhistorical, pre-scientific principles of Mediaeval exegesis. Baxter did not realize that, because of its drastic over-simplifications, the old culture was threadbare, outworn, and in its death-throes all the time that he labored to rejuvenate it. His solution of the problems of philosophical theology was defective, simply because he never recognized how complicated those problems are. The intellectual apparatus with which he worked was not good enough for implementing the catholic ideal in Christian philosophy. And yet, despite these criticisms, it must be recognized that Baxter's method was here loyal to catholic truth in ways that transcended the outlook of his age and have only recently become clear.

In the first place, modern exegesis has recognized what Baxter, the honest Bible-reader, saw three hundred years ago: that the Kingdom of God and the world-wide Lordship of Christ are central Biblical themes, which Protestant theology, before and since Baxter's day, has unduly neglected.[6] We can not accept all the details of Baxter's exposition of them, but equally we can not deny him credit for insisting that a genuinely catholic theology must be one whose structure permits justice to be done to them. Again: the Church today is discovering to its cost how true it is that the natural and historical sciences need theology to set their perspective and interpret their findings, and how foolish has been the *laissez-faire* attitude that has permitted these disciplines to develop the delusion of their own autonomy. We now see that scientific technique is a tool, at the service of an idea; and unless theology furnishes the right idea, science will inevitably be pressed into the service of the wrong one. And here too we must give Baxter full credit for clearly seeing and proclaiming this truth in the days when modern science was being born. It would have been well had some of its progenitors listened to him. Now at last, at the end of two centuries during which the gap between Christian and scientific thought was allowed to widen till it became an almost impassable gulf which has not yet been satisfactorily bridged, we can judge the truth and wisdom of Baxter's insistence that knowledge is a unity under God, and secular studies should

---

6. "Protestantism stands in a theological tradition in which the priestly and prophetic ministries of Christ have been strongly worked out but in which the kingly office has been obscured," W. A. Visser 't Hooft, *The Kingship of Christ*, 1948, 13.

never be allowed to isolate themselves from theology. In both these instances, time has shown that the right road for the catholic Church was that along which Baxter pointed.

Something similar may be said of Baxter's opposition to "immediacy" in Christian experience. At first sight, he seems to go too far. Church history supports Dr. Nuttall's judgement that here he "over-did."[7] There is abundant evidence that God sometimes reveals Himself and His will in "extraordinary" ways, through intuition apart from ratiocination and by impressions that are sudden and discontinuous with the previous flow of thought. Such things are not common but they are certainly not always illusory. The truth is that here again Baxter's intellectual heritage failed him. He learned from his books and accepted without question an over-simplified view of reason. According to Ramus and the Scholastics, "thought" as such was a bare logical structure, a concatenation of propositions. Imagery was adventitious decoration, which could and should be stripped off when one sought the meaning of utterances. Thinking meant ratiocination and nothing else. The age of Locke and Berkeley had not yet come, and the place of imagery and intuition in thought had not yet been recognized. Holding as he did the received view, Baxter was completely mystified by (for instance) thinkers like Jacob Boehme and Peter Sterry, for he could not detach their thought from the imagery in which it was expressed. Nor, again, could he see sense in the mental processes of the Quakers, who depreciated logic and cultivated intuition in such an exaggerated and, indeed, really dangerous way. These facts show up the limitations of his doctrine of reason. His error was to make ratiocination the sole mark of rationality. He might have seen his mistake by reflecting on some of the recorded experiences of prophets and apostles, which on his view, must be dismissed as sub-human; but Baxter, as we noted earlier, was never a man to criticize his presuppositions. And yet, having said this much, we must give Baxter credit for a thoroughly catholic attitude to the "enthusiasts" of his day. Christian experience shows that ratiocination is the normal medium of communion with God; intuitions are rare, and when they come, ratiocination is their usual context; and the possibilities of self-deception are limitless as soon as one allows oneself to hope and hunt for them. The Bible nowhere promises them, or encourages Christians to expect them; instead, it directs Believers to disciplined, ratiocinative meditation and prayer. And when the sects ran wild in a delirious pursuit of "immediacy," decrying doctrine and discipline, execrating theology and theologians, leaving the old paths to chase "new light," the only course open to a catholic teacher was to protest with all his might and do battle for the historic faith and the appointed means of grace. This Baxter did; and his catholic instinct was not here astray. Whatever may be said about the possibilities of intuitive

7. *The Holy Spirit . . .* , 170f.

apprehension of God in principle, there seems no doubt that the groups he opposed were self-deluded in fact.

Baxter's doctrine of justification by faith must next be briefly considered. We may first notice two characteristic points which Baxter himself urged in its favor. The first was, that it preserves the eschatological framework of Pauline justification, as an event that is in one sense present and in another future, and is not complete till the last day. Here again Baxter, the honest Bible-reader, had noticed something which other Reformed theologians had been inclined to overlook. The second point was, that it was a mediating doctrine, on the premises of which, Baxter claimed, it was possible to bring together, not only wrangling Protestants, but Papists too; as in his *Catholick Theologie* and elsewhere he tried to show. One may suspect that Baxter was too ready to treat "conciliatory" and "catholic" as convertible terms; but it is interesting to find that he was not the first to claim that there was virtually no difference between the Reformed doctrine, rightly stated, and the Roman. In one of those intriguing snatches of gossip which punctuate his books, he tells us that "I heard as eminent Divines as most I know…in a publick meeting say, that Bishop *Usher* and Mr. *Gataker* affirmed that the Papists did not fundamentally differ from us in the Doctrine of Justification."[8] His oracles had reached the same conclusion before him. How far, however, they could have endorsed the details of his statement of the doctrine is not clear. It is the least catholic, because the most reactionary, part of Baxter's theology. The key to catholic soteriology is and always was the *unio mystica* between Christ and His people which God's Spirit creates through man's faith. Orthodox Reformed theology amplified and developed this idea by drawing out its Biblical foundation, the election of the Church and the covenant of redemption, and by reconstructing soteriology in the light of it. The doctrine of the penal substitution of Christ for the elect was one result of this process, and justification by His righteousness imputed was another. The disputed doctrine of justification before faith sprang from the same root. Antinomian abuse of this principle made Baxter shy away from it in his own dogmatic construction. He did not deny that the mystical union was a fact, but he denied strenuously that it was a theological category. He substituted for it the idea of political union between Christ and the Church, and reinterpreted the received doctrines of atonement and justification accordingly, as we have seen. But this "method," though enabling him to stress Christ's Lordship in a thoroughly catholic manner, must be put down as an eccentricity of his own, and the fact that it commended itself to nobody in his own day or since is itself sufficient refutation of its claim to be a part of catholic truth.

Baxter's title to catholicity is strongest of all when we consider his practical theology. Few, if any, have been able to match the profundity and thoroughness

---

8. *Of Justification*, 94.

of his teaching on the Christian life. In one respect, at least, he caught the spirit of the New Testament in a way that is still unique among Protestant devotional writers: he grasped the eschatological character of Christian religion. All the Puritan pastors knew and taught that the flesh lusts against the Spirit in a regenerate man, and will continue to do as long as he is on earth. But Baxter went further. He saw the objective reference of this inner conflict. He knew that since Christ's coming the two ages, that which is and that which is to come, had been overlapping. The second was already present, as hidden manna for the saints. And he realized that the deepest truth about the flesh and the Spirit is that they belong to different worlds. The flesh is the sum of earthbound, selfish, Godless desire, obstinately anchored below. The Spirit, the new creature within, has an affinity with heaven; it expresses itself in affection set above. To walk in the Spirit, therefore, involves a life of positive, practical "heavenliness," fed by meditation and having its fruit in disinterested good works. All one's life must be organized as a hierarchy of means to the one great end—winning Christ, and heaven. All one's hopes must be centered on the world to come. The Christian must race through this world as a stranger and pilgrim, his eyes fixed on the goal, his heart set where his treasure is. None of his fellow-Puritans grasped so profoundly the practical implications of the truth that man is redeemed and restored for life, not in this world, but in the world to come. None of them entered so deeply into the "other-worldliness" of the New Testament. Strong as is Baxter's claim to recognition as teaching a catholic theology of man's redemption and restoration, his claim to teach a catholic piety is stronger still, and is not likely to be contested.

With the magnificent confidence that is only found among the truly humble, Baxter was out of doubt that in days to come, when men were wiser, they would turn back to his theology and receive it as the catholic faith. His hope was never fulfilled; nor could it be, in the way that he hoped. "Baxterianism" was too deeply rooted in the seventeenth-century thought-world to survive its decay, and Baxter's own contribution to catholic truth was more uneven than supposed, for, with all his breadth of mind, he was much more a man of his age than he realized. And yet, if we strip his ideas of their seventeenth-century dress, he has as much to teach us as any man of his day. He was a gifted theologian, more stimulating in his mistakes than many lesser men in their orthodoxy; and he was a great Christian. Throughout a sect-ridden, blindly partisan age, his watchword was Augustine's apophthegm: "contra rationem nemo sobrius: Contra Scripturam nemo Christianus: contra ecclesiam nemo catholicus." It is hoped that the present study has contributed to a better understanding of this lonely but unwavering protagonist of rational, catholic Christianity.

Appendix I

Some Bibliographical Notes

Several of Baxter's books have an interesting and complicated history. In the following notes (which make no claim to bibliographical completeness) we shall elucidate the origin and fortunes of some of those most relevant to our study.

(i) *Universal Redemption of Mankind, by the Lord Jesus Christ.*
A treatise on this subject was almost the first work Baxter projected, and the last to be published. At the end of the *Aphorisms* (for the history of which, see p. 204 f. *sup.*) appears the following "Postscript":

> Whereas there is in this Book an intimation of something which I have written of *Universall Redemption,*[1] understand, that I am writing indeed a few pages on that subject onely by way of Explication, and an Essay for the Reconciling of the great differences in the Church thereabouts; But being hindered by continuall sickness, and also observing how many lately are set a work on the same subject[2] ... I shall a while forebear, to see if something may come forth, which may ... save me the labour: Which if it come not to pass, you shall shortly have it, if God will enable me.

On p. 164 of the "Appendix" Baxter refers to the treatise again:

---

1. *Aphorisms*, 7, 64, 92, 197.
2. Baxter notes John Stalham (cf. *D.N.B.*, s.v.), *Vindiciae Redemptionis*, 1647; Obadiah Howe, *The Universalist Examined and Convicted*, 1648; Thomas Whitfield, *A Refutation . . . of Thomas More . . .* , 1646; John Owen, *Sanguis Jesu Salus Electorum*: or, *the Death of Death in the Death of Christ*, 1648. They were all in whole or part polemics against *The Universality of Gods Free Grace in Christ to Mankind*, 1646, by Thomas Mo(o)re, "a Weaver of *Wisbitch* and *Lyn*, of excellent Parts: (*R.B.*, I:50).

But these things…I am handling in a fitter place, (in a small tract of *Universall Redemption*.) But the last week I have read *Amiraldus* against *Spanhemius* exercitations,[3] who hath opened my very heart, almost in my own words…I am now unresolved, whether to hold my hand or to proceed.

In a letter to Tombes, written in early September, 1649,[4] Baxter says that he has "one Treatise in the Press, whereof part is unfinished, and another or two at least under hand." The former was the *Saints' Rest*;[5] one of the latter must be *Universal Redemption*, which is promised in the *Saints' Rest*, and the second may have been the abortive attack on Downame referred to earlier.[6] In the "Postscript" to *Plain Scripture Proof* (345 f.; dated November 12, 1650), in which Baxter appeals for "animadversions" on his *Aphorisms* as a preliminary to a second edition, he declared it his intention "to contract and annex what I had prepared of Universal Redemption (because I will not provoke the angry world with any more contentious Volumns, if I can chuse)." But the second edition of the *Aphorisms* never appeared. When, late in 1653, he sat down to write his *Confession*, he stated in the first chapter that he had not merely suppressed "that book which did offend them, but also laid by those Papers of Universal Redemption which I had written, lest I be further offensive."[7]

In 1664 or 1665,[8] Baxter listed among his unpublished papers "a Disputation for some *Universality of Redemption*, which hath lain by me near Twenty years unfinished"; it was laid aside, Baxter tells us, after the appearance of Amyraldus' book noted above, Davenant's *Dissertationes Duae, prima de morte Christi, altera de praedestinatione et reprobatione* (1650), and John Daille's *Apologia…adversus Friderici Spanhemii Exercitationes de Gratia Universali* (1655), "which contained the same Testimonies of concordant Writers which I had prepared to produce." That this was the treatise published by Joseph Read in 1694 is proved, not merely by Sylvester's marginal note to this effect, but by the closing paragraph (480): "When I had got thus far, *Dalleus's* Defence of Universal Redemption … came out … I not only stopt my work but cast away

---

3. *Specimen Animadversionum in Exercitationes de Gratia Universali*, 1648. Spanheim's book appeared in 1646.

4. In the fourth edition of *Plain Scripture Proof*, 1656, 404 ff., Baxter printed correspondence between Tombes and himself from September, 1649, to January of the next year. The passage in the text (406) comes from an undated reply to Tombes' letter of Sept. 3, which Tombes answered on Sept. 10.

5. The "Dedication of the Whole" is dated Jan. 15, 1649/50.

6. cf. 339, *sup.*

7. *Op. cit.*, 2; cf. the remark in the epistle "To the Poor in Spirit" prefixed to *Right Method…* (dated, May 7, 1653) to the effect that the works "I have most laboured in, must lie buried in the dust" (IX:xvii).

8. *R.B.*, I:123 ("written for the most part in 1664," "Breviate of the Contents…Part I").

a multitude of Testimonies which I had collected."[9] Read reveals ("To the Reader") that Baxter had toyed with the idea of publishing the book later in the fifties: "the Ministers ... who ... heard these Disputations at their Monthly Meeting, were generally desirous to have them printed"; and the first task he was given when he became Baxter's assistant in 1657 was "to transcribe these Papers ... for the Press." Read supposed that the work was then first composed when delivered as lectures[10] to the ministers ("about the 40th year of his Age"), but the evidence in the text shows that this was not so. When Baxter withheld it again we do not know. That he still intended its publication appears from the reason he gives why the topic is not discussed in *Catholick Thologie* ("Because I must give you a special Disputation or Tractate on that subject")[11] and in *M.T.* ("Quoniam Tractatum peculiarem de hac controversia iamdudum scripsi (etsi nondum typis impressum)).[12] Only on July 17th, 1691, however, did he give the manuscript sheets to Read, "signifying his willingness to have them Printed." The work bears no internal marks of anything more than verbal revision; all that was certainly added was two cross-references to *M.T.* (33, 502). No hint is given as to why Read then delayed its publication for three more years ("To the Reader" is dated June 18, 1694); perhaps he was waiting for the Crispian controversy (see below, 413 f.) to die down.

(ii) *Rich. Baxters Apology; Rich. Baxter's Confession of his Faith; Of Justification.* When Baxter appealed for animadversions on his *Aphorisms*, the result somewhat exceeded his expectations. In a letter to Peter Ince, dated Nov. 21, 1653, he stated that he had "suppressed yᵉ offensive booke against yᵉ importunity of neere 40 letters...it hath cost me three or four years labor mainly, to write private replies to yᵉ animadversions of many bretheren."[13] He had solicited these comments for his own instruction, and had no thought of publishing the debates. But in 1653 Thomas Blake brought out *Vindicae Foederis*, which included an attack on the *Aphorisms*, and before Baxter's reply was finished George Kendall's Θεοκρατία appeared, containing a further assault. "After this, I was informed of divers others that were ready to write against my Doctrine, and some that had written, and were ready to publish it, and divers others that were desirous to send me their Animadversions"; and he decided that, to save himself the trouble of "endless private Replies,"[14] he would publish an answer

9. There is a similar note on 376: "here *Amyraldus* and *Dallaeus* coming forth stopt me."
10. The book is cast into the form of an extended academic disputation (480), and is followed by a typical "determination" prepared for the monthly meeting, "Of Special Redemption" (481-502).
11. *Op. cit.*, I:ii, 54.
12. *Op. cit.*, second pagination, 55.
13. Mss. 59, I.f.11. For Ince, Rector of Donhead St Mary, Wilts, cf. *C.R.*, s.v.
14. "Preface Apologetical" prefixed to the answer to Blake in *Apology*.

to Kendall, and prefix to it what he had at first designed as a "private Reply" to Blake. On August 1, he completed "The Reduction of a Digressor or Rich. Baxter's Reply to Mr George Kendall . . . " and wrote a "Preface Apologetical" to go before "Rich. Baxters Account Given to . . . Mr T.Blake of the Reasons of his Diisent . . ." Just then, however, a Latin tract by Louis du Moulin, *De Fidei Partibus in Justificatione* (1653), fell into his hands. It was written under the pseudonym Ludiomaeus Colvinus, and affirmed Twisse's doctrine of justification before faith. Baxter therefore determined to confute it, and to append the confutation to the first two parts of his book. He had in fact written this third part before he discovered who the author really was. Next, as soon as this was done, he saw *Vindiciae Justificationis Gratuitae*, a new book by William Eyre of Salisbury, vigorously asserting justification before faith. It originated as a reply to *Justification by Faith* (1652), a printed sermon by Benjamin Woodbridge, Twisse's successor at Newbury. There had already been some acrimonious verbal exchanges between these two,[15] and Eyre's book was none too temperate in expression. It also included ("To the Christian Reader") some hostile remarks about Baxter, who had recommended Woodbridge's sermon in the Epistle before his *Right Method*. Once more Baxter felt called to take up his pen, and finished his reply before the date of the first Postscript, Nov. 26, 1653. Meanwhile, he had learned, from Eyre's prefatory Epistle and other sources, that John Crandon, Rector of Fawley, Hampshire, was preparing a large-scale attack on the *Aphorisms*, abusive and wrong-headed, designed to prove that Baxter was a Papist. Baxter referred to the book in a third Postscript to "Rich. Baxter's Admonition to Mr William Eyre...concerning his Miscarriages," in a way that suggests that he had already seen the main part of it, as we know that he did at some point before its publication.[16] To forestall its appearance, he brought out his reply to Eyre separately in January, 1654. On March 8, he wrote two Epistles Dedicatory in preparation for the appearance of the complete *Apology*. He was already engaged in his next book, promised in the third Postscript mentioned above, "a plain and full Confession of my Faith, and especially in the Point in question: How much is it that I ascribe to man or any of his actions in the work of Justification? He had reached what later became page 85 in the published work when, some time in the Spring of that year, Crandon's colossus, *Mr Baxters Aphorisms Exorized and Anthorized*, appeared, and he found prefixed to it a commendatory Epistle from the licenser, the

---

15. Cf. Eyre, *op. cit.*, chap. I, "An Account of the Origin of the Debate."

16. "I had beforehand got all save the beginning and end, out of the Press, and wrote so much of an Answer as I thought it worthy, before the Publication of it" (*R.B.*, I:110 f.). This probably refers to the two pages of the third Postscript, though Dr. G. F. Nuttall, "Richard Baxter's *Apology* (1654): its occasion and composition" (*J.E.H.*, IV.i, p. 74), thinks it implies something more elaborate. But Baxter is positive that he never intended to answer it until he saw Caryl's Epistle ("To the Reader" before "An Unsavoury Volume...Anatomized" in *Apology*).

celebrated Joseph Caryl. This made him retract his original decision to ignore it. He wrote a reply to Caryl's strictures on his own theology; then he went on to specify "Reasons Which forced me to dissent from the judgement of Mr *Caryll* concerning the substance of the book which he commendeth;" and thus, "while I set down things as they came to hand...I presently made a medley work."[17] On review, he decided that his dissection of Crandon's book was too bulky and not sufficiently germane to the main theme for his *Confession*, so he sent it to the printer as a fifth part of his *Apology*. His final touch to this book was a further promise of more to come. In a Postscript dated May 23, 1654, which he added, together with some Errata, at the end of the answer to Kendall, he noted that Kendall had returned to the assault in *Sancti Sanciti*, 1654, this time on the subject of the saints' perseverance, and declared his intention of writing a further reply; which, however, Archbishop Usher persuaded him to forego.[18] The *Apology* appeared in June, 1654,[19] and the *Confession* the following year. Together with his reply to Caryl's epistle, Baxter included in the latter an answer to the tract *Of the Death of Christ*[20] which Owen published in 1650 as a defense of his strictures on Grotius' theory of the atonement, to which Baxter had taken exception in the Appendix to the *Aphorisms*.

The volume *Of Justification* (1658) contains four disputations and two sets of letters. The first part is a reply to Blake's comments (in the Postscript to *The Covenant Sealed*, 1655) on Baxter's criticism in the *Apology* of his doctrine of faith. It was finished, Baxter tells us in his Preface "sixteen months ago," and is dated Nov., 1656. Baxter asserts, against Blake, that justifying faith respects Christ as King and Teacher, as well as resting on His shed blood. In the second part, he argues, against attacks on his own position made by Anthony Burgess in *The True Doctrine of Justification Asserted* (1654), and again in his lectures on John 17 (1656), that faith is the condition, rather than the instrument, of a man's justification. He appends three short letters of comment on the *Aphorisms* that he had extorted from Burgess during the winter of 1649/50, together with his own replies. The third part is a vindication of his doctrine of the need of a twofold righteousness for justification against John Warner, of Christchurch, Hampshire (*C.R.*, s.v.), who had attacked it in his *Diatriba Fidei Justificantis* (1657). A concluding epistle to Warner is dated Dec. 25, 1657. Then follows (225 f.) correspondence between Baxter and Tombes about the *Aphorisms*,

17. *Apology, loc. cit.*

18. cf. *R.B.*, I:110: "meeting me at *London*" (while Baxter was serving on the Fundamentals Committee, 1654), "he (Kendall) was...earnest to take up the Controversy, engaging Mr. *Vines* to persuade me that Bishop *Usher* might determine it...I quickly yielded to Bishop *Ushers* Arbitriment, who owned my Judgement about Universal Redemption, Perseverance, &c. but desired us to write against each other no more."

19. The story of the *Apology* is told more fully in Dr. Nuttall's article referred to above (483, note 1). There are articles on Caryl, Du Moulin and Woodbridge in *D.N.B.*, and on Eyre in *C.R.*

20. *Works*, X.

dating from the first half of 1651. Tombes seems to have been among the first to respond to Baxter's appeal for animadversions. Baxter published them now because, in the third part of *Antipaedobaptism* (1657), Tombes had printed, without his knowledge, selections from their correspondence about the status of children in the church, and he feared that these further exchanges might appear in the same way; so he published them himself. The last part of the book consists of what appears to be one of the Determinations prepared for the monthly meeting. It decides the question, whether the "faith" which Paul opposes to works and requires for justification to the exclusion of works, is a single, momentary physical act, in the negative.

(iii) *A Treatise of Justifying Righteousness.*

The *Aphorisms* extorted one more volume in their defense from their tireless author. Thomas Tully[21] in *Justificatio Paulina sine Operibus* (1674), an attack on Bull's *Harmonia Evangelica* (1670), belabored the *Aphorisms* with much heat but not a great deal of light as to their actual drift. "In Vindication of the Truth and my self,"[22] Baxter then published, first, *Two Disputations of Original Sin* (1675) written for the Minister's Meeting some twenty years before, and, second, *A Treatise of Justifying Righteousness* (1676), in two parts. The first was a tractate "Of the Imputation of Christ's Righteousness to Believers: In what sense sound Protestants hold it; And, Of the false devised sense, by which Libertines subvert the Gospel," to which was added "An Answer to Dr. Tullies Angry Letter," i.e. the printed *Letter to Mr. Richard Baxter, occasioned by several Injurious Reflections of his, on a Treatise entitled: Justificatio Paulina* which Baxter's remarks in the Preface to the Disputations had called forth. The Preface to the tract on Imputation is dated July 20, 1672. Baxter there tells us that it was originally composed to dispel prejudice against himself and his doctrine. Perhaps the Declaration of Indulgence in March of that year, holding out as it did possibilities of a wider pulpit ministry, had made him think it desirable to write it, so as to clear his name as far as possible with the Nonconformist public. However, for some reason he laid it aside at the time and published it only now. The second part of the book consists of his discussion of Christopher Cartwright's animadversions on the *Aphorisms* (dated May 26-June 16, 1652), followed by Cartwright's rejoinder, "Exceptions against a Writing of Mr. R. Baxters, in Answer to his Animadversions . . . " (an elaborate piece of work which Cartwright had wished to publish, but had been unable to because Baxter had temporarily lost his manuscript),[23] and Baxter's concluding summary of

---

21. cf. *D.N.B.*, s.v.

22. *R.B.*, III:172.

23. *Op. cit.*, "To the Reader": "my Friend, Mr. *Sound*, who interceded between us for Communication of Papers, made me think, that Mr. Cartwright was not willing, that so large Pains…should be so buried: But I could not return him his *Exceptions* as he desired, because they were lost." For Cartwright, cf. *D.N.B.*, s.v.

the points at issue, "The Substance of Mr. Cartwright's Exceptions Considered." More than once Baxter expressed in print his appreciation of these exchanges with Cartwright.[24]

(iv) *The Scripture Gospel Defended.*
Baxter thought that he had killed Antinomianism. "I must here record my thanks to God for the success of my Controversial Writings against the Antinomians," he wrote in 1664-5; "now they little appear, and make no noise among us at all, nor have done these many years."[25] However, after 1660 a theological rift appeared within Nonconformity, the Independents as a body retreating to a higher and higher Calvinism while the so-called "Presbyterians" generally inclined to something approaching Baxter's position. "Many of the Independents inclining to half Antinomianism, suggested suspicions against Dr. *Manton*, Dr. *Bates*, Mr. *Howe* and my self...as if we were half Arminians," Baxter recorded in 1677.[26] There had already been ominous hints of trouble to come. His sermons preached at the Pinner's Hall lecture between November, 1672 and January, 1673 had raised an outcry:

> when I had preached there but four sermons, I found the Independents so quarrelsome with what I said, that all the City did ring of their . . . false Accusations. It was cryed abroad among all the Party, that I preached up *Arminianism*, and Free-Will...and O! what an odious Crime was this.[27]

Then, in 1690, Tobias Crisp's sermons were reprinted by his son Samuel, with a prefatory Epistle in which Baxter was attacked for asserting at the Pinner's Hall Lecture, that "A mans first believing is by external Arguments, not by the Operation of the Spirit."[29] To make matters worse, twelve Nonconformist

---

24. cf. *R.B.*, I:107, *C.T.*, Preface.
25. *R.B.*, I:111.
26. *R.B.*, III:182.
27. p. 103.
28. Crisp gives the date of the sermon in question: Jan. 17, 1673 ("To the Christian Reader"). In fact, Crisp had certainly misunderstood Baxter, who would never oppose "internal" and "external" means as he was here accused of doing.
29. "To the Reader" before "A Defence . . . " in *Scripture Gospel Defended*. The twelve were: George Griffith(s), George Cokayn, Isaac Chauncey, John Howe, Vincent Alsop, Richard Bures, Hanserd Knollys, Nathaniel and Increase Mather, Thomas Powell, John Turner and John Gammon. There are notices in *C.R.* of all except Knollys (for whom cf. *D.N.B.*) and Gammon, who was pastor of a church in Whitechapel and is only known as the author of *Christ a Christian's Life* (1691). Of the twelve, Cokayn had contributed an Epistle to the third volume of Crisp's sermons (1646) which was reprinted in the new edition, and Chauncey, Nathaniel Mather and Griffiths later wrote in its defense. Increase Mather objected to the teaching of *Scripture Gospel defended*, as appears from *Magnalia Christi Americana* (1702), III:36. The four or five to whom Baxter refers would include Howe; Alsop, who resigned his Pinner's Hall lectureship as a protest against Dr.

ministers, including Howe, had subscribed a prefixed attestation concerning the authenticity of the eight new sermons in the volume. Baxter insisted that this could not be construed as other than an endorsement of their doctrine, and was extremely annoyed, for he was "past doubt, that Four or Five of them are against it." Howe dissuaded Baxter from printing a wrathful pamphlet against the practice of soliciting attestations by promising to prefix to John Flavel's book, *A Blow at the Root*, then going to press, "a sort of an Apology,"[30] explaining that the twelve had never intended to certify more than that the sermons were genuine. This was done; seven of the twelve signed it.[31] Meanwhile, Baxter printed *The Scripture Gospel Defended, and Christ, Grace, and Free Justification Vindicated Against the Libertines* . . . (1691). It consisted of two short books: "A Breviate of the Doctrine of Justification," written in 1677,[32] and "A Defence of Christ and Free Grace," which contains "an Hundred of their (Antinomian) Errors Described." "To the Reader" before "A Defence . . ." and the "Postcript" to "A Breviate" (73) are dated Jan. 15 and 20, 1690/1, respectively. This small volume touched off a controversy that raged for the remaining few months of Baxter's life and split Dissent from top to bottom during the next two or three years. Such was the legacy of the man who "medled much with Controversies ... to end them."

Williams' expulsion in 1694 and with him founded the Salter's Hall lecture; Turner, "a man of great Sincerity...and profitable Labours and Industry," at whose church, in New Street near Fetter Lane, Baxter preached a weekly lecture, when not prevented by ill-health, from Jan. 24, 1672/3, till 1675 (*R.B.* III:95, 103, 142, 151, 155); and Bures, Turner's successor in 1692 as minister of a church in Leather Lane, Hatton Garden: "a very valuable Man, of the old Puritan stamp" (Calamy).

30. Calamy, *Life of Howe*, 182; cf. *Own Life*, I:322-5.

31. Howe, Alsop, the Mathers, Turner, Bures and Powell.

32. Cf. Powicke, *Under the Cross*, 175 f.

Appendix II

Corrections in the *Aphorisms*

When Baxter wrote the *Aphorisms,* he tells us in the Preface to *Catholick Theologie,* "being young, and unexercised in writing, and my thoughts yet undigested, I put into it many uncautelous words (as young Writers use to do)." The fact that in 1651 he suspended it has sometimes been interpreted as a sign that he came to repudiate a great deal of it. It is of interest, therefore, to note the passages which he later corrected. The following list is mainly compiled from Baxter's elaborate discussion of Cartwright's animadversions, to which he added a few further marginal notes when he published it in *J.R.* in 1676; a few additional items are supplied by the *Apology, Confession,* and the disputations *Of Justification.*

Misprints:

(1) p. 165, central section of Thesis XXXV (from "1. both…" to "…specially") should be bracketed (Cartwright, 156):
   p. 327, "spiritual" should be "special" (Cartwright, 291).

(2) p. 15: Baxter retracted the view that Adam would have continued on earth in Paradise had he not fallen, and withdrew his claim that it was held by "most Divines" (Cartwright,19; see 135 and note 4, *sup.*)

(3) p. 45, 51: Baxter revoked his assertions that the personal imputation of Christ's active and passive obedience was held by "most of our ordinary Divines," and "the vulgar sort of unstudied Divines;" the former, because he doubted whether this was the majority view (*J.R.,* "Of Imputation," 174), and the latter, because it was a piece of gratuitous rudeness (Answer to Blake, in *Apology,* 50). In his "Admonition to…Eyre," he revoked an

unnecessary sneer at George Walker's controversial performances (cf. 280, note 3, *sup.*).

(4)   p. 68, 70: in the statements: the "common judgement" is that "Christ has taken away the whole curse" and Christians' sufferings "are only afflictions of love, and not punishments," and: "the very nature of affliction is to be a loving punishment," "affliction" is a slip for "chastisement" (Cartwright, 45; "An Unsavoury Volume…Anatomized" in *Apology*, 33). Baxter also came to doubt whether the common judgement of Reformed divines was as he had said (*Apology, ut sup.*, 23), and to regret his use of "curse" for "punishment," as suggesting personal vindictiveness on God's part.

(5)   p. 83: Baxter revoked his assertion in Thesis XI that the Covenant of Works was still in force, promising life for obedience and threatening disobedient sinners with death; Lawson convinced him that it was not in force at all, and that all the promises and threats which God now addresses to man are those of the Covenant of Grace (Cartwright, 58; see 216 and note 11, *sup.*).

(6)   p. 129: Thesis XXIV asserts that faith, as such, fulfils the law of grace perfectly and so "is in its kind a perfect Righteousness; and so far we may admit the doctrine of personall Perfection." Baxter defended this usage to Cartwright, but added in the margin in 1675 a propos of their "strife about the word (Perfect)": "I repent that I used the word, because most may mistake it, and it may do harm." Such a usage gained nothing and could only mislead.

(7)   p. 134 f.: Thesis XXV claimed that it was improper to speak, as Protestants commonly did, of Christ's justifying, first, individuals and, second, their acts, because (a) to speak of the justifying of acts was not Scriptural; (b) justification presupposes accusation, and it is persons, not their acts, which are accused. He dismissed these arguments later as sophistical, on the grounds that a Christian's faith (which comprises a series of acts) will be specifically accused by Satan at the judgment of being hypocritical, and will there need to be specifically justified (Cartwright, 137, 141).

(8)   p. 225: Thesis LVII, asserting that man was justified by the act, not the habit, of faith (because the covenant does not say "(he that is disposed to beleeve shall be saved) But (he that believeth)"), was recanted (Cartwright, 171; "Reply to …Kendall" in *Apology*, 125). John Wallis' animadversions persuaded Baxter that it is both the habit and the act, together, which justify (*Of Justification*, 86).

(9) p. 250: Thesis LXVII, which asserts that Christ, not the promises and benefits of the new covenant, is "the proper Object of justifying faith," was revoked as embodying a false antithesis (Cartwright, 188).

(10) p. 286: Thesis LXXII asserts that affiance (trust) is the result of receiving Christ as Lord and Savior, and is thus "but a fruit of the principal justifying Act of Faith." For proof, Baxter simply refers to Downame's confutation of Pemble in *The Covenant of Grace*. He acknowledged to Cartwright (204, 209) that this was not clear: he had used affiance to mean "*quieting* trust" only, but in a larger sense, as an act of will as well as a state of feeling, affiance was not a fruit, but an essential part of faith. In the margin he adds a further clarification: "I should have said, that there is first Affiance on the Speakers Veracity in the Assent of Faith; and then a quieting Affiance in the Consent, when it is strong; and a practical Affiance, in venturing . . . and hoping for the reward." Trichotomy was needed to make it clear.

Of these acknowledged faults, no. 4 is a verbal slip, nos. 7, 8, 9, and 10 are cases of imprecise expression and incomplete analysis, and only nos. 2 and 5 betoken a change of view. We must not, therefore, misunderstand Baxter's suspension of the *Aphorisms*. What displeased him about the book was its evident immaturity, its defects in "method" and the "incautelous words" it contained. "I think the main doctrine of it sound" (*C.T.*, Preface, *ut sup.*).

Select Bibliography

(i)   Bibliographical sources.
Grossart, A. B. "Annotated list of the writings of Richard Baxter," appended to
R. Baxter, What we must do to be Saved, 1868.
Matthews, A. G. The Works of Richard Baxter: an Annotated List, 1933.
Waterhouse, G. Literary relations of England and Germany in the Seventeenth
Century, 1934.

(ii)   Works of Reference.
Calamy Revised, ed. A. G. Matthews, 1934.
Dictionary of National Biography, ed. Sir J. Stephen and Sir S. Lee.
The New Schaff-Herzog Encycolpaedia of Religious Knowledge, ed. S. M. Jackson,
1908-12.

(iii)   Works of Richard Baxter
Practical works: 4 vols., 1707, 1858; 23 vols., of which the first is a "Life," ed. W.
Orme, 1830; cited from Orme, in whose edition the more important of Baxter's
practical writings appear as follows. The dates given are those of publication.
Vols.   II-VI: A Christian Directory, 1673.
        VII: A Treatise of Conversion, 1657; A Call to the Unconverted,
                1658; Now or Never, 1662.
        VIII: Directions and Persuasions to a Sound Conversion, 1658;
                Directions for Weak, Distempered Christians and The
                Character of a Sound, Confirmed Christian, 1669; God's Goodness
                    Vindicated, 1671.
        IX: The Right Method for a Settled Peace of Conscience, 1653;
                The Crucifying of the World by the Cross of Christ, 1658.
        X: A Saint or a Brute, 1662; The One thing Necessary, 1684;
                Cain and Abel Malignity, 1689.
        XI: A Treatise of Self-Denial, 1660; Obedient Patience, 1683.

XII: *The Life of Faith* (1660-1670)

XIII: *The Divine Life,* 1664; The *Divine Appointment of the Lord's Day, Proved,* 1671; etc.

XIV: *The Reformed Pastor,* 1656; *Confirmation and Restauration, the necessary means of Reformation and Reconciliation,* 1658.

XV: *Knowledge and Love Compared,* 1689; *Compassionate Counsel to all Young Men,* 1681; *The Reformed Liturgy,* 1661; etc.

XVI: *Catholic Unity,* 1660; *The true Catholic and Catholic Church Described,* 1660; etc.

XVII: *The Vain Religion of the Formal Hypocrite,* 1660; Sermons (including two published together as *True Christianity; or, Christ's Absolute Dominion,* 1655).

XVIII: Sermons; *Dying Thoughts,* 1683; etc.

XIX: *The Poor Man's Family Book,* 1674; *The Catechising of Families,* 1683.

XX-XXI: *The Unreasonableness of Infidelity,* 1655; *The Reasons of the Christian Religion,* 1667; *More Reasons for the Christian Religion,* 1672.

XXII-XXIII: *The Saints' Everlasting Rest,* 1650.

Other Works (in order of publication);

(i) Primary sources:

Aphorismes of Justification, 1649 (cited as *Aphorisms*).

Plain Scripture Proof of Infant Church-membership and Baptism, 1651.

Rich. Baxter's Apology, 1654 (Apology).

Rich. Baxter's Confession of his Faith, 1655 (*Confession*).

Richard Baxters account of his present thoughts concerning...Persevernance, 1657.

Of Justification, 1658.

Two disputations of Original Sin, 1675.

Richard Baxter's Catholick Theologie, 1675 (*C.T.*)

More Proofs of Infants Church-membership, 1675.

Rich. Baxter's Review of the State of Christian Infants, 1676.

A Treatise of Justifying Righteousness, 1676 (*J.R.*).

Methodus Theologiae Christianae, 1681 (*M.T.*).

An End of Doctrinal Controversies, 1691.

Universal Redemption of Mankind by the Lord Jesus Christ, 1694.

(ii) Other publications cited in the text:

The Humble Petition of Many Thousands...of the County of Worcester, 1652.

The Worcestershire Petition to the Parliament for the Ministry of England defended, 1653.

Christian Concord; or, the Agreement of the Associated Pastors and Churches of Worcestershire, 1653.

Humble Advice . . . to . . . Parliament, 1655.

The Quakers Catechism, 1655.

The Agreement of divers ministers . . . of Worcester . . . for Catechising, 1656

Certain Disputations of Right to the Sacraments, 1658.

One Sheet against the Quakers, 1657.

The Judgment and Advice of the...Associated Ministers of Worcestershire...In reply to John Durey's proposals . . . , 1658.

The Grotian Religion Discovered, 1658.

Five Disputations of Church-government and Worship, 1659.

A Holy Commonwealth, 1659.

The Cure of Church-Divisions, 1670.

A Defence of the Principles of Love, 1671.

The Duty of Heavenly Meditation Reviewed, 1671.

How far Holinesse is the Design of Christianity, 1671.

The Difference between the power of Magistrates and Church-pastors, 1671.

The Judgment of Nonconformists, of the interest of Reason, in matters of Religion, 1671.

Church-history of the government of Bishops and their Councils abbreviated, 1680.

A Breviate of the Life of Margaret, 1681 (cited from J.T. Wilkinson's reprint, *Richard Baxter and Margaret Charlton*, 1928).

Poetical Fragments, 1681.

An Apology for the Nonconformists' Ministry, 1681

A Treatise of Episcopacy, 1681.

A Second True Defence of the Meer Nonconformists, 1681.

A Third Defence of the Cause of Peace, 1681.

The True History of Councils enlarged and defended, 1682.

Of the Immortality of Mans Soul, 1682.

Catholic Communion Defended, 1684.

Against the Revolt to a Foreign Jurisdiction, 1691.

Richard Baxter's Penitent Confession, 1691.

The Certainty of the Worlds of Spirits, 1691.

The Protestant Religion truly Stated and Justified, 1692.

The Poor Husbandman's Advocate against Rich Racking Landlords, 1926 (ed. F. J. Powicke: in *Rylands Library Bulletin*, Jan. 1926, and separately, as *The Reverend Richard Baxter's Last Treatise*).

The Prostestant Religion Truly Stated and Justified, 1692.

Reliquiae Baxterianae, ed. M. Sylvester, 1696 (R.B.).

Dr. Williams' Library Mss. 59 (I-VI, Letters; VII-XII, unpublished treatises); *Miscellanea Baxteriana Minora* (4to).

(iv) *Select works on Baxter.*
Bates, W. *A Funeral-Sermon for...Mr. Richard Baxter*, 1692.
Gordon, A. "Richard Baxter as a founder of Liberal Nonconformity" in *Heads of English Unitarian History*, 1895, 56 f.
Ladell, A. R. *Richard Baxter*, 1925.
Martin, H. *Puritanism and Richard Baxter*, 1946.
Morgan, I. *The Nonconformity of Richard Baxter*, 1946.
Nuttall, G. F. *Richard Baxter and Philip Doddridge*, 1951.
Orme, W. "The Life and Times of Richard Baxter: with a Critical Examination of his Writings" (vol. I of his edition of the *Practical Works*), 1830.
Powicke, F. J. *A Life of the Reverend Richard Baxter*, 1924 (*Life*); *The Reverend Richard Baxter Under the Cross*, 1927 (*Under the Cross*).

(v)   *Select sixteenth and seventeenth-century works:*
(a)   The Antinomian Controversy
        1. Antinomians:
        Crisp, T. *Christ Alone Exalted* (1832 ed.).
        Denne, G. A.   *A Conference between a Sick Man and a Minister*, 1643.
        _____. *The Man of Sin Discovered*, 1645.
        Eaton, J. *The Honey-Combe of Free Justification*, 1642.
        Towne, R. *The Assertion of Grace*, 1644.
        Saltmarsh, J. *Free-grace*, 6th ed., 1649.
        2. Orthodox:
        Bedford, T. *An Examination of the Chief Points of Antinomianism*, 1647.
        Gataker, T. *Gods Eye on His Israel*, 1645.
        _____. *A Mistake, Or Misconstruction Removed*, 1646.
        _____. *Shadowes without Substance*, 1646.
        Geree, S. *The Doctrine of the Antinomians Confuted*, 1644.
        Rutherford, S. *A Survey of the Spirituall Antichrist*, 1647.
        Sedgwick, J. *Antinomianisme Anatomized*, 1643.
        Taylor, T. *Regula Vitae, the rule of the Law under the Gospel*, 1631.

(b.)   Others:
        Ames(ius), W. *The Marrow of Sacred Divinity*, 1642.
        _____. *Conscience with the Power and Cases thereof*, 1643.
        Ball, J. *The Covenant of Grace*, 1645.
        Bolton, R. *Instructions for a Right Comforting of Afflicted Consciences*, 1631.
        _____. *Some Generall Directions for a Comfortable Walking with God*, 1625.

Bradshaw, J. *A Treatise of Justification*, 1615.

Calvin, J. *Institutio Religionis Christianae*, 5th ed., 1559.

Cameron, J. *Ioannis Cameronis…*ΤΑ ΣΩΖΟΜΕΝΑ, 1642.

Culverwell, E. A Treatise of Faith, 7th ed., 1633.

Davenant, J. *A Dissertation of the Death of Christ*, appended to *Colossians*, tr. J. Allport, 1832.

Dort, Synod of: *Canones Synodi Dordrechtanae*, 1619.

_____. *The Collegiat Suffrage of the Divines of Great Britaine*, 1629.

Downame, G. *A Treatise of Justification*, 1633.

_____. *The Covenant of Grace*, 1631.

F., E. *The Marrow of Moderne Divinity*, 1645-9, ed. C. G. M'Crie, 1902.

Goodwin, J. *Imputatio Fidei*, 1642.

Goodwin, T. *Works*, ed. J. C. Miller, 1861.

Grotius, H. *Defensio fidei catholicae de satisfactione Christi*, 1617.

Hooker, T. *The Souls Preparation for Christ*, 1632.

Lawson, G. *Theopolitica*, 1659.

Owen, J. *Works*, ed. W. Goold, 1850-55.

Pemble, W. *Vindiciae Gratiae*, ed. 3, in *Workes*, 1635.

Perkins, W. *Workes*, 3 vols., 1609-17.

Preston, J. *The New Covenant*, 1629.

_____. *The Position of John Preston concerning the Irresistiblenesse of Converting Grace*, 1654.

Rogers, J. *The Doctrine of Faith*, 1627.

Sibbes, R. *Works*, ed. A. B. Grosart, 1862.

Theses Salmurienses (Syntagma Thesium Theologicarum in Academia Salmuriensi…disputatarum), 3 vols., 1641-51.

Ursinus, Z. *Corpus Doctrinae Christianae*, ed. D. Paraeus, 1598.

Westminster Confession and Catechisms, 1643-47.

Wotton, A. *De Reconciliatione*, 1624.

(vi)   *Select modern works.*

Brett, G. S. *History of Psychology*, 1912-21.

Haller, W. *The Rise of Puritanism*, 1938.

Heppe, H. *Reformed Dogmatics*, 1950.

Huehns, G. *Antinomianism in England*, 1951.

Hodge, C. *Systematic Theology*, 1873-4.

Miller, P. *The New England Mind: The Seventeenth Century*, 1939.

_____. "The Marrow of Puritan Divinity" in *Publications of the Colonial Society of Massachusetts*, XXXII:247 f.

Nuttall, G. F. *The Holy Spirit in Puritan Faith and Experience*, 1946.

Stoughton, J. *History of Religion in England*, 4th ed., 1901.

Warfield, B. B. *Calvin and Calvinism*, 1931.

_____. *The Plan of Salvation*, 1952 ed.

Willey, B. *The Seventeenth Century Background*, 1934.

Wood, T. *English Casuistical Divinity during the Seventeenth Century*, 1952.

Index Nominum

Printed in the United States
72260LV00004B/88